Reading STREET

Program Authors

Peter Afflerbach

Camille Blachowicz

Candy Dawson Boyd

Elena Izquierdo

Connie Juel

Edward Kame'enui

Donald Leu

Jeanne Paratore

Sam Sebesta

Deborah Simmons

Alfred Tatum

Sharon Vaughn

Susan Watts Taffe

Karen Kring Wixson

PEARSON

Glenview, Illinois • Boston, Massachusetts
Chandler, Arizona • Upper Saddle River, New Jersey

We dedicate Reading Street to
Peter Jovanovich.

His wisdom, courage,
and passion for education
are an inspiration to us all.

ISBN-13: 978-0-328-47026-6
ISBN-10:   0-328-47026-0

Copyright ©2011 by Pearson Education, Inc., or its affiliates.

All Rights Reserved. Printed in the United States of America. This publication is protected by copyright, and permission should be obtained from the publisher prior to any prohibited reproduction, storage in a retrieval system, or transmission in any form or by any means, electronic, mechanical, photocopying, recording, or likewise. For information regarding permission, write to Pearson Curriculum Group, Rights & Permissions, One Lake Street, Upper Saddle River, New Jersey 07458.

Pearson, Scott Foresman, and Pearson Scott Foresman are trademarks, in the U.S. and/or other countries, of Pearson Education, Inc., or its affiliates.

1 2 3 4 5 6 7 8 9 10   17 16 15 14 13 12 11 10 09

Any Path, Any Pace

"Welcome to
Reading Street!
Bienvenidos too."

PEARSON

Find Your Place on Reading Street!

Who said so?

The Leading Researchers,

Program Authors

Peter Afflerbach, Ph.D.
Professor
Department of Curriculum
and Instruction
University of Maryland
at College Park

Camille L. Z. Blachowicz, Ph.D.
Professor of Education
National-Louis University

Candy Dawson Boyd, Ph.D.
Professor
School of Education
Saint Mary's College of California

Elena Izquierdo, Ph.D.
Associate Professor
University of Texas at El Paso

Connie Juel, Ph.D.
Professor of Education
School of Education
Stanford University

Edward J. Kame'enui, Ph.D.
*Dean-Knight Professor of
Education and Director*
Institute for the Development of
Educational Achievement and
the Center on Teaching and Learning
College of Education
University of Oregon

Donald J. Leu, Ph.D.
*John and Maria Neag Endowed
Chair in Literacy and Technology
Director, The New Literacies
Research Lab*
University of Connecticut

Jeanne R. Paratore, Ed.D.
Associate Professor of Education
Department of Literacy and
Language Development
Boston University

P. David Pearson, Ph.D.
Professor and Dean
Graduate School of Education
University of California, Berkeley

Sam L. Sebesta, Ed.D.
Professor Emeritus
College of Education
University of Washington, Seattle

Deborah Simmons, Ph.D.
Professor
College of Education and
Human Development
Texas A&M University

Alfred W. Tatum, Ph.D.
*Associate Professor and Director
of the UIC Reading Clinic*
University of Illinois at Chicago

Sharon Vaughn, Ph.D.
*H. E. Hartfelder/Southland
Corporation Regents Professor
Director, Meadows Center for
Preventing Educational Risk*
University of Texas

Susan Watts Taffe, Ph.D.
Associate Professor in Literacy
Division of Teacher Education
University of Cincinnati

Karen Kring Wixson, Ph.D.
Professor of Education
University of Michigan

Consulting Authors

Jeff Anderson, M.Ed.
Author and Consultant
San Antonio, Texas

Jim Cummins, Ph.D.
Professor
Department of Curriculum,
Teaching and Learning
University of Toronto

Lily Wong Fillmore, Ph.D.
Professor Emerita
Graduate School of Education
University of California, Berkeley

Georgia Earnest García, Ph.D.
Professor
Language and Literacy Division
Department of Curriculum
and Instruction
University of Illinois at
Urbana-Champaign

George A. González, Ph.D.
Professor (Retired)
School of Education
University of Texas-Pan American,
Edinburg

Valerie Ooka Pang, Ph.D.
Professor
School of Teacher Education
San Diego State University

Sally M. Reis, Ph.D.
*Board of Trustees Distinguished
Professor*
Department of Educational
Psychology
University of Connecticut

Jon Scieszka, M.F.A.
*Children's Book Author
Founder of GUYS READ
Named First National Ambassador
for Young People's Literature 2008*

Grant Wiggins, Ed.D.
Educational Consultant
Authentic Education
Concept Development

Lee Wright, M.Ed.
Pearland, Texas

Practitioners, and Authors.

Consultant

Sharroky Hollie, Ph.D.
Assistant Professor
California State University
Dominguez Hills

Teacher Reviewers

Dr. Bettyann Brugger
Educational Support Coordinator–Reading Office
Milwaukee Public Schools
Milwaukee, WI

Kathleen Burke
K–12 Reading Coordinator
Peoria Public Schools, Peoria, IL

Darci Burns, M.S.Ed.
University of Oregon

Bridget Cantrell
District Intervention Specialist
Blackburn Elementary School
Independence, Missouri

Tahira DuPree Chase, M.A., M.S.Ed.
Administrator of Elementary English Language Arts
Mount Vernon City School District
Mount Vernon, NY

Michele Conner
Director, Elementary Education
Aiken County School District
Aiken, SC

Georgia Coulombe
K–6 Regional Trainer/Literacy Specialist
Regional Center for Training and Learning (RCTL), Reno, NV

Kelly Dalmas
Third Grade Teacher
Avery's Creek Elementary, Arden, NC

Seely Dillard
First Grade Teacher
Laurel Hill Primary School
Mt. Pleasant, South Carolina

Jodi Dodds-Kinner
Director of Elementary Reading
Chicago Public Schools, Chicago, IL

Dr. Ann Wild Evenson
District Instructional Coach
Osseo Area Schools, Maple Grove, MN

Stephanie Fascitelli
Principal
Apache Elementary, Albuquerque Public Schools, Albuquerque, NM

Alice Franklin
Elementary Coordinator, Language Arts & Reading
Spokane Public Schools, Spokane, WA

Laureen Fromberg
Assistant Principal
PS 100 Queens, NY

Kimberly Gibson
First Grade Teacher
Edgar B. Davis Community School
Brockton, Massachusetts

Kristen Gray
Lead Teacher
A.T. Allen Elementary School
Concord, NC

Mary Ellen Hazen
State Pre-K Teacher
Rockford Public Schools #205
Rockford, Illinois

Patrick M. Johnson
Elementary Instructional Director
Seattle Public Schools, Seattle, WA

Theresa Jaramillo Jones
Principal
Highland Elementary School
Las Cruces, NM

Sophie Kowzun
Program Supervisor, Reading/Language Arts, PreK-5
Montgomery County Public Schools
Rockville, MD

David W. Matthews
Sixth Grade Teacher
Easton Area Middle School
Easton, Pennsylvania

Ana Nuncio
Editor and Independent Publisher
Salem, MA

Joseph Peila
Principal
Chappell Elementary School
Chicago, Illinois

Ivana Reimer
Literacy Coordinator
PS 100 Queens, NY

Sally Riley
Curriculum Coordinator
Rochester Public Schools
Rochester, NH

Dyan M. Smiley
English Language Arts Program Director, Grades K-5
Boston Public Schools, Literacy Department, Boston, Massachusetts

Michael J. Swiatowiec
Lead Literacy Teacher
Graham Elementary School
Chicago, Illinois

Dr. Helen Taylor
Director of Reading/English Education
Portsmouth City Public Schools
Portsmouth, VA

Carol Thompson
Teaching and Learning Coach
Independence School District
Independence, MO

Erinn Zeitlin
Kindergarten Teacher
Carderock Springs Elementary School
Bethesda, Maryland

Any Path, Any Pace

v

UNIT 4

One of a Kind

In this Teacher's Edition Unit 4, Volume 2

WEEK 4 · America's Champion Swimmer: Gertrude Ederle

Women Athletes Online Directories

WEEK 5 · Fly, Eagle, Fly!

Purple Coyote Trickster Tale

WEEK 6 · Interactive Review

What does it mean to be unique?

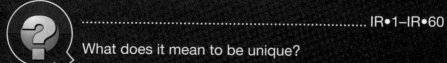

In the **First Stop** on Reading Street

- Dear Third Grade Teacher

- Research into Practice on Reading Street

- Guide to Reading Street

- Assessment on Reading Street

- Customize Writing on Reading Street

- Differentiated Instruction on Reading Street

- ELL on Reading Street

- Customize Literacy on Reading Street

- Digital Products on Reading Street

- Teacher Resources for Grade 3

- Index

 GO Digital!

See It!

- Big Question Video

- Concept Talk Video

- Interactive Sound-Spelling Cards

- Envision It! Animations

Hear It!

- eSelections

- eReaders

- Grammar Jammer

- Leveled Reader Database

Do It!

- Vocabulary Activities

- Online Journal

- Story Sort

- 21st Century Skills Activities

- Online Assessment

- Letter Tile Drag and Drop

UNIT 1

Living and Learning

Volume 1

WEEK 1 • When Charles McButton Lost Power
Narrative Poem..20a–55q
How a Kite Changed the World Narrative Nonfiction
Differentiated Instruction SI OL A ELL ....DI•1–DI•25

WEEK 2 • What About Me? Fable 56a–89q
How the Desert Tortoise Got Its Shell Porquoi Tale
Differentiated Instruction SI OL A ELL ....DI•26–DI•50

WEEK 3 • Kumak's Fish Tall Tale................................90a–121q
How to Catch a Fish Newspaper Article
Differentiated Instruction SI OL A ELL ....DI•51–DI•75

Volume 2

WEEK 4 • Supermarket Expository Text 122a–159q
Money from Long Ago Picture Encyclopedia
Differentiated Instruction SI OL A ELL ....DI•76–DI•100

WEEK 5 • My Rows and Piles of Coins
Realistic Fiction 160a–193q
Learning About Money Web Sites
Differentiated Instruction SI OL A ELL ....DI•101–DI•125

WEEK 6 • Interactive Review ....IR•1–IR•60
Which skills help us make our way in the world?
Unit 1 Reading Poetry 194–197a

Customize Writing .... CW•1–CW•20
Customize Literacy.. CL•1–CL•47
Let Learn Amazing Words .... OV•1–OV•3

UNIT 2

Smart Solutions

Volume 1

Volume 2

UNIT 3

People and Nature

Volume 1

Volume 2

UNIT 4

One of a Kind

Volume 1

Volume 2

UNIT 5

Cultures

Volume 1

Volume 2

UNIT 6

Freedom

Volume 1

Volume 2

Skills Overview

Key

T Tested Skill

🎯 Target Skill

	WEEK **1** **The Man Who Invented Basketball** Biograhy pp. 28–41 **My Turn at Bat: The Story of My Life** Autobiography pp. 46–51	WEEK **2** **Hottest, Coldest, Highest, Deepest** Expository Text pp. 62–75 **Paul Bunyan and the Great Lakes** Legend pp. 80–83
Question of the Week	How do talents make someone unique?	What makes nature's record holders unique?
Amazing Words	*potential, mock, idle, audition, thrill, ecstatic, necessary, result, rise, succeed, verge*	*plunged, competitors, evergreens, lumber, valuable, champ, sprinter, acrobat, weaken, ranger*
Phonics	Irregular Plurals	Vowels: r-Controlled /er/ spelled *ir, er, ur, ear, or,* and *ar, or, ore, oar*
Literary Terms	Point of View	Author's Craft
Story Structure/ Text Features	Time Line/ Map	Bold Print/ Key Words
Comprehension	**T** 🎯 **Skill** Generalize 🎯 **Strategy** Summarize Review **Skill** Graphic Sources	**T** 🎯 **Skill** Graphic Sources 🎯 **Strategy** Important Ideas Review **Skill** Main Idea and Details
Vocabulary	**T** 🎯 **Skill** Unfamiliar Words	**T** 🎯 **Skill** Unknown Words
Fluency	Accuracy	Appropriate Phrasing/ Punctuation Cues
Writing	Persuasive Text Trait: Conventions	Imaginative Story Trait: Conventions
Conventions	Singular and Plural Nouns	Subject and Object Pronouns
Spelling	Irregular Plurals	Vowels R-Controlled
Speaking/Listening	Presentation	Media Literacy: Weather Forecast
Research Skills	Dictionary	Bar Graphs

Get Ready to Read

Read and Comprehend

Language Arts

The Big Question

What does it mean to be unique?

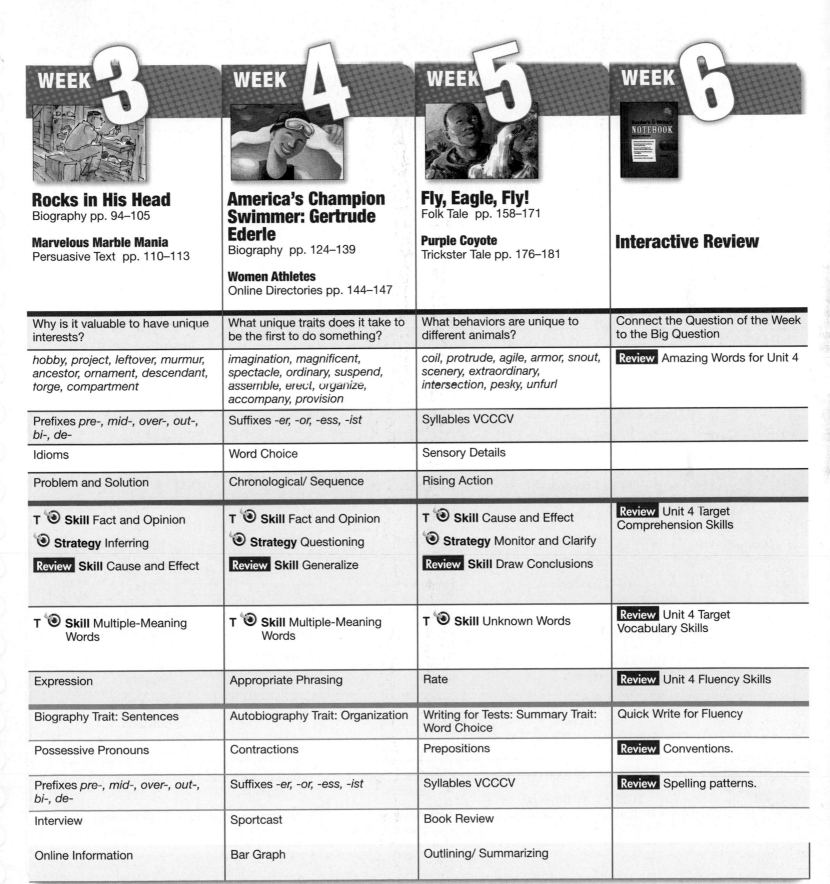

WEEK 3	WEEK 4	WEEK 5	WEEK 6
Rocks in His Head Biography pp. 94–105 **Marvelous Marble Mania** Persuasive Text pp. 110–113	**America's Champion Swimmer: Gertrude Ederle** Biography pp. 124–139 **Women Athletes** Online Directories pp. 144–147	**Fly, Eagle, Fly!** Folk Tale pp. 158–171 **Purple Coyote** Trickster Tale pp. 176–181	**Interactive Review**
Why is it valuable to have unique interests?	What unique traits does it take to be the first to do something?	What behaviors are unique to different animals?	Connect the Question of the Week to the Big Question
hobby, project, leftover, murmur, ancestor, ornament, descendant, forge, compartment	*imagination, magnificent, spectacle, ordinary, suspend, assemble, erect, organize, accompany, provision*	*coil, protrude, agile, armor, snout, scenery, extraordinary, intersection, pesky, unfurl*	**Review** Amazing Words for Unit 4
Prefixes *pre-, mid-, over-, out-, bi-, de-*	Suffixes *-er, -or, -ess, -ist*	Syllables VCCCV	
Idioms	Word Choice	Sensory Details	
Problem and Solution	Chronological/ Sequence	Rising Action	
T ⊙ **Skill** Fact and Opinion ⊙ **Strategy** Inferring **Review** **Skill** Cause and Effect	T ⊙ **Skill** Fact and Opinion ⊙ **Strategy** Questioning **Review** **Skill** Generalize	T ⊙ **Skill** Cause and Effect ⊙ **Strategy** Monitor and Clarify **Review** **Skill** Draw Conclusions	**Review** Unit 4 Target Comprehension Skills
T ⊙ **Skill** Multiple-Meaning Words	T ⊙ **Skill** Multiple-Meaning Words	T ⊙ **Skill** Unknown Words	**Review** Unit 4 Target Vocabulary Skills
Expression	Appropriate Phrasing	Rate	**Review** Unit 4 Fluency Skills
Biography Trait: Sentences	Autobiography Trait: Organization	Writing for Tests: Summary Trait: Word Choice	Quick Write for Fluency
Possessive Pronouns	Contractions	Prepositions	**Review** Conventions.
Prefixes *pre-, mid-, over-, out-, bi-, de-*	Suffixes *-er, -or, -ess, -ist*	Syllables VCCCV	**Review** Spelling patterns.
Interview	Sportcast	Book Review	
Online Information	Bar Graph	Outlining/ Summarizing	

UNIT 4

Monitor Progess

SUCCESS PREDICTOR	WEEK 1	WEEK 2	WEEK 3	WEEK 4
Word Reading — **Phonics**	Irregular Plurals	Vowels: r- Controlled	Prefixes *pre-, mid-, over-, out-, bi-, de-*	Suffixes *-er, -or, -ess, -ist*
WCPM — **Fluency**	Accuracy 95–105 WCPM	Appropriate Phrasing/ Punctuation Cues 95–105 WCPM	Expression 95–105 WCPM	Appropriate Phrasing 95–105 WCPM
Vocabulary — **Lesson Vocabulary**	**T** disease **T** guard **T** freeze **T** terrible **T** study **T** popular **T** sports **T** basketball	**T** outrun **T** tides **T** deserts **T** waterfalls **T** peak **T** average **T** depth **T** erupted	**T** stamps **T** spare **T** chores **T** attic **T** labeled **T** customer **T** board	**T** drowned **T** strokes **T** medals **T** current **T** continued **T** stirred **T** celebrate
Vocabulary — **Oral Vocabulary/ Concept Development** (assessed informally)	potential mock idle audition thrill ecstatic necessary result rise succeed verge	plunged competitors evergreens lumber valuable champ sprinter acrobat weaken ranger	hobby project leftover murmur ancestor ornament descendant forge compartment	imagination magnificent spectacle ordinary suspend assemble erect organize accompany provision
Retelling — **Text Comprehension**	**T** 🔄 **Skill** Generalize **T** 🔄 **Strategy** Summarize	**T** 🔄 **Skill** Graphic Sources **T** 🔄 **Strategy** Important Ideas	**T** 🔄 **Skill** Fact and Opinion **T** 🔄 **Strategy** Inferring	**T** 🔄 **Skill** Fact and Opinion **T** 🔄 **Strategy** Questioning

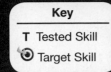

Key

T Tested Skill

🎯 Target Skill

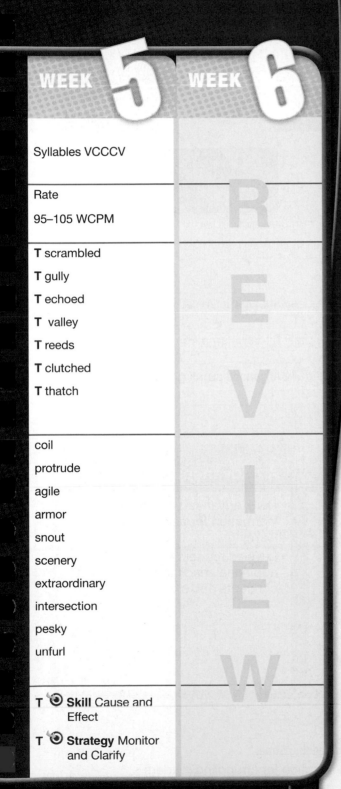

WEEK 5	WEEK 6
Syllables VCCCV	R E V I E W
Rate 95–105 WCPM	
T scrambled **T** gully **T** echoed **T** valley **T** reeds **T** clutched **T** thatch	
coil protrude agile armor snout scenery extraordinary intersection pesky unfurl	
T 🎯 **Skill** Cause and Effect **T** 🎯 **Strategy** Monitor and Clarify	

Online Classroom

Manage Data

- Assign the Unit 4 Benchmark Test for students to take online.

- Online Assessment records results and generates reports by school, grade, classroom, or student.

- Use reports to disaggregate and aggregate Unit 4 skills and standards data to monitor progress.

- Based on class lists created to support the categories important for AYP (gender, ethnicity, migrant education, English proficiency, disabilities, economic status), reports let you track adequate yearly progress every six weeks.

Group

- Use results from Unit 4 Benchmark Tests taken online through Online Assessment to measure whether students have mastered the English-Language Arts Content Standards taught in this unit.

- Reports in Online Assessment suggest whether students need Extra Support or Intervention.

Individualized Instruction

- Tests are correlated to Unit 4 tested skills and standards so that prescriptions for individual teaching and learning plans can be created.

- Individualized prescriptions target instruction and accelerate student progress toward learning outcome goals.

- Prescriptions include remediation activities and resources to reteach Unit 4 skills and standards.

UNIT 4

Assessment and Grouping
for Data-Driven Instruction

4-Step Plan for Assessment
1 Diagnose and Differentiate
2 Monitor Progress
3 Assess and Regroup
4 Summative Assessment

STEP 1 Diagnose and Differentiate

Baseline Group Test

Diagnose

To make initial grouping decisions, use the Baseline Group Test, the TPRI, or another initial placement test. Depending on student's ability levels, you may have more than one of each group.

Differentiate

If... student performance is **then...** use the regular instruction and the daily Strategic Intervention small group lessons.

If... student performance is **then...** use the regular instruction and the daily On-Level small group lessons.

If... student performance is **then...** use the regular instruction and the daily Advanced small group lessons.

Small Group Time

SI Strategic Intervention

- Daily small group lessons provide more intensive instruction, more scaffolding, more practice, and more opportunities to respond.
- Reteach lessons in the *First Stop on Reading Street* provide more instruction with target skills.
- Leveled readers build background and practice target skills and vocabulary.

OL On-Level

- Explicit instructional routines teach core skills and strategies.
- Daily On-Level lessons provide more practice and more opportunities to respond.
- Independent activities provide practice for core skills and extension and enrichment options.
- Leveled readers provide additional reading and practice core skills and vocabulary.

A Advanced

- Daily Advanced lessons provide instruction for accelerated learning.
- Leveled readers provide additional reading tied to lesson concepts and skills.

Additional Differentiated Learning Options

Reading Street Intervention Kit
- Focused intervention lessons on the five critical areas of reading: phonemic awareness, phonics, vocabulary, comprehension, and fluency.

My Sidewalks on Reading Street
- Intensive intervention for struggling readers

Use these tools during lesson teaching to **monitor student progress.**

- **Skill and Strategy** instruction during reading

- **Don't Wait Until Friday** boxes to check retelling, fluency and oral vocabulary.

- **Weekly Assessment** on Day 5 checks comprehension and fluency.

- **Reader's and Writer's Notebook** pages at point of use

- **Weekly Tests** assess target skills for the week

- **Fresh Reads** for Fluency and Comprehension

Weekly Tests

Fresh Reads for Fluency and Comprehension

STEP 3 **Assess and Regroup**

Use these tools during lesson teaching to **assess and regroup.**

- **Weekly Assessments** Record results of weekly assessments in retelling, comprehension, and fluency to track student progress.

- **Unit Benchmark Assessment** Administer this assessment to check mastery of unit skills.

- **Regroup** We recommend the first regrouping to be at the end of Unit 2. Use weekly assessment information and Unit Benchmark Assessment performance to inform regrouping decisions. Then regroup at the end of each subsequent unit.

Unit Assessment Charts in First Stop

Group					
Baseline Group Test →	**Regroup** Units 1 and 2 →	**Regroup** Unit 3 →	**Regroup** Unit 4 →	**Regroup** Unit 5 →	**End of Year**
Weeks 1-6	Weeks 7-12	Weeks 13-18	Weeks 19-24	Week 25-30	Weeks 31-36

Outside assessments, such as DRA and DIBELS, may recommend regrouping at other times during the year.

STEP 4 **Summative Assessment**

Use these tools after lesson teaching to **assess students.**

- **Unit Benchmark Assessments** Use to measure a student's mastery of each unit's skills.

- **End-of-Year Benchmark Assessment** Use to measure a student's mastery of program skills covered in all six units.

Unit and End-of-Year Benchmark Assessments

Concept Launch

Understanding By Design

Grant Wiggins, Ed. D.
Reading Street Author

"Big ideas are the building material of understandings. They can be thought of as the meaningful patterns that enable one to connect the dots of otherwise fragmented knowledge."

One of a Kind

THE BIG **What does it mean to be unique?**

Let's Think About Reading!

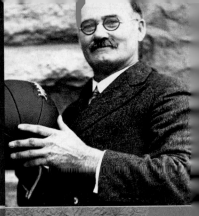

The Man Who Invented Basketball: James Naismith and His Amazing Game BIOGRAPHY

 connect to Social Studies

 How do talents make someone unique?

Paired Selection
My Turn at Bat: The Story of My Life AUTOBIOGRAPHY

Hottest, Coldest, Highest, Deepest EXPOSITORY TEXT

 connect to Science

What makes nature's record holders unique?

Paired Selection
Paul Bunyan and the Great Lakes LEGEND

 connect to Science

Rocks in His Head BIOGRAPHY

Why is it valuable to have unique interests?

Paired Selection
Marvelous Marble Mania PERSUASIVE TEXT

 connect to Social Studies

America's Champion Swimmer: Gertrude Ederle BIOGRAPHY

What unique traits does it take to be the first to do something?

Paired Selection
Women Athletes ONLINE DIRECTORIES

 connect to Science

Fly, Eagle, Fly! FOLK TALE

What behaviors are unique to different animals?

Paired Selection
Purple Coyote TRICKSTER TALE

Theme Launch • xxi

UNIT 4

Small Group Time
Flexible Pacing Plans

Key

SI Strategic Intervention
OL On Level
A Advanced
ELL ELL

A **OL** **SI**

5 Day Plan

DAY 1	• Reinforce the Concept
	• Read Leveled Readers
	  Concept Literacy
	  Below Level

DAY 2	• ◎ Comprehension Skill • ◎ Comprehension and Strategy • Read Main Selection
DAY 3	• ◎ Vocabulary Skill • Read Main Selection
DAY 4	• Practice Retelling • Read Paired Selection

DAY 5	• Reread for Fluency
	• Reread Leveled Readers
	  Concept Literacy
	  Below Level

4 Day Plan

DAY 1	• Reinforce the Concept
	• Read Leveled Readers
	  Concept Literacy
	  Below Level
	• ◎ Comprehension Skill
	• ◎ Comprehension and
	  Strategy
	• Read Main Selection

DAY 2	• ◎ Vocabulary Skill • Read Main Selection
DAY 3	• Practice Retelling • Read Paired Selection

DAY 4	• Reread for Fluency
	• Reread Leveled Readers
	  Concept Literacy
	  Below Level

3 Day Plan

DAY 1	• Reinforce the Concept
	• Read Leveled Readers
	  Concept Literacy
	  Below Level
	• ◎ Comprehension Skill
	• ◎ Comprehension and
	  Strategy
	• Read Main Selection

DAY 2	• Practice Retelling • Read Paired Selection

DAY 3	• Reread for Fluency
	• Reread Leveled Readers
	  Concept Literacy
	  Below Level

ELL

5 Day Plan

DAY 1	• Concepts • Listening (Read Aloud) • Phonemic Awareness/ Phonics
DAY 2	• Concepts • Vocabulary • Phonemic Awareness/ Phonics • Spelling
DAY 3	• Concepts • Vocabulary • Comprehension
DAY 4	• Concepts • Vocabulary • Read ELL/ELD Readers
DAY 5	• Concepts • Vocabulary • Conventions • Editing and Revising

4 Day Plan

DAY 1	• Concepts • Listening (Read Aloud) • Phonemic Awareness/ Phonics
DAY 2	• Concepts • Vocabulary • Comprehension
DAY 3	• Concepts • Vocabulary • Read ELL/ELD Readers
DAY 4	• Concepts • Vocabulary • Conventions

3 Day Plan

DAY 1	• Concepts • Listening (Read Aloud) • Phonemic Awareness/ Phonics
DAY 2	• Concepts • Vocabulary • Comprehension
DAY 3	• Concepts • Vocabulary • Read ELL/ELD Readers

This Week's ELL Overview

ELL Handbook

- Maximize Literacy and Cognitive Engagement
- Research Into Practice
- Full Weekly Support for Every Selection

America's Champion Swimmer: Gertrude Ederle
- Multi-Lingual Summaries in Five Languages
- Selection-Specific Vocabulary Word Cards
- Frontloading/Reteaching for Comprehension Skill Lessons
- ELD and ELL Reader Study Guides

- Transfer Activities
- Professional Development

Daily Leveled ELL Notes

ELL notes appear throughout this week's instruction and ELL Support is on the DI pages of your Teacher's Edition. The following is a sample of an ELL note from this week.

English Language Learners

Beginning Write several words with suffixes from the Decodable Practice Reader on the board, such as *teacher, artist, actress,* and *editors.* Point to each word as you say it aloud. Then underline the letters that spell the suffix. Have students repeat the words with you. Repeat the procedure for suffixes using words such as *conductors, driver, inventor,* and *chemist.*

Intermediate After reading, have students find pairs of words with the same suffix. For example: *teacher* and *driver; artist* and *chemist; editor* and *conductor.*

Advanced After reading, have students choose words with different suffixes and use them orally in sentences about jobs.

Advanced High After reading the story, have students choose 4 or 5 words with suffixes and write a sentence for each word.

ELL by Strand

The ELL lessons on this week's Support for English Language Learners pages are organized by strand. They offer additional scaffolding for the core curriculum. Leveled support notes on these pages address the different proficiency levels in your class. See pages DI•91–DI•100.

ELL Guy
Dr. Jim Cummins

The Three Pillars of ELL Instruction

ELL Strands	Activate Prior Knowledge	Access Content	Extend Language
Vocabulary pp. DI•92–DI•93	Preteach	Reteach	Leveled Writing Activities
Reading Comprehension p. DI•97	Frontloading	Sheltered Reading	Summarizing
Phonics, Spelling, and Word Analysis p. DI•95	Preteach	Teach/Model	Practice
Listening Comprehension p. DI•94	Prepare for the Read Aloud	First Listening	Second Listening
Conventions and Writing p. DI•99	Preteach	Teach/Model	Leveled Practice Activities
Concept Development p. DI•91	Activate Prior Knowledge	Develop Concept	Daily Activities

This Week's Practice Stations Overview

Six Weekly Practice Stations with Leveled Activities can be found at the beginning of each week of instruction. For this week's Practice Stations, see pp. 116h–116i.

Small Group Teacher-led

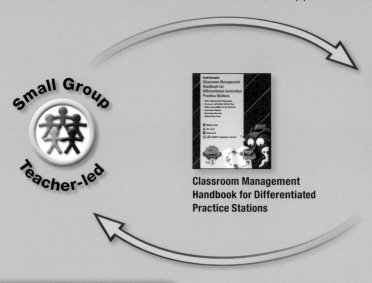

Classroom Management Handbook for Differentiated Practice Stations

Practice Stations

Daily Leveled Center Activities

 Below   Advanced

 On-Level   E L L

Practice Stations Flip Charts

	Word Wise	**Word Work**	**Words to Know**	**Let's Write!**	**Read For Meaning**	**Get Fluent**
Objectives	• Spell words with prefixes *pre-, mid-, over-, out-, bi-,* and *de-*.	• Identify and pronounce words with prefixes *pre-, mid-, over-, out-, bi-,* and *de-*.	• Identify the meanings of multiple-meaning words.	• Write a biography about someone you know.	• Identify fact and opinion in expository text.	• Read aloud with expression.
Materials	• *Word Wise* Flip Chart Activity 19 • Teacher-made word cards • dictionary • pencils • paper	• *Word Work* Flip Chart Activity 19 • Teacher-made word cards • paper • pencil	• *Words to Know* Flip Chart Activity 19 • Teacher-made word cards • dictionary • pencil • paper	• *Let's Write!* Flip Chart Activity 19 • paper • pencils	• *Read for Meaning* Flip Chart Activity 19 • Leveled Readers • paper • pencils	• *Get Fluent* Flip Chart Activity 19 • Leveled Readers

This Week on Reading Street!

Question of the Week

What unique traits does it take to be the first to do something?

One of a Kind

Week 4

Daily Plan

Don't Wait Until Friday

Whole Group

- ◉ Fact and Opinion
- ◉ Multiple Meaning Words
- • Fluency/Phrasing
- • Writing/Conventions
- • Research and Inquiry

MONITOR PROGRESS — Success Predictor

Day 1 Check Oral Vocabulary	Day 2 Check Word Reading	Day 3 Check Retelling	Day 4 Check Fluency	Day 5 Check Oral Vocabulary

Small Group

Teacher-Led

- • Reading Support
- • Skill Support
- • FLuency Practice

Practice Stations

Independent Activities

Customize Literacy More support for a balanced literacy appoach, see pp. CL•1–CL•45.

Customize Writing More support for a customized writing approach, see pp. CW•11–CW•20.

Whole Group

- • Writing: Autobiography
- • Conventions: Contractions
- • Spelling: Suffixes -er, -or, -ess, -ist

Assessment

- • Weekly Tests
- • Day 5 Assessment
- • Fresh Reads

You Are Here! Unit 4 Week 4

This Week's Reading Selections

Main Selection
Genre: **Biography**

Paired Selection
21st Century Skills

Decodable Readers

Leveled Readers

ELL and ELD Readers

Resources on Reading Street!

	Build Concepts	**Phonics**	**Comprehension**
Whole Group	 Let's Talk About pp. 116–117	 Student Edition pp. 118–119 Decodable Readers Sound–Spelling Cards	 Envision It! Skills/ Strategies  Comprehension Skills Lesson pp. 120–121
Go Digital	• Concept Talk Video	• Interactive Sound-Spelling Cards • Decodable eBooks	• Envision It! Animations • eSelections
Small Group and Independent Practice	 America's Champion Swimmer: Gertrude Ederle pp. 124–125 ELL and ELD Readers Leveled Readers Decodable Readers	 Decodable Readers Practice Stations Flip Chart	America's Champion Swimmer: Gertrude Ederle pp. 124–125 ELL and ELD Readers Leveled Readers Envision It! Skills/ Strategies RWN Cover Practice Stations Flip Chart
Go Digital	• eReaders • eSelections • Decodable eBooks	• Letter Tile Drag and Drop • Decodable eBooks	• Envision It! Animations • eSelections • eReaders
Customize Literacy	• Leveled Readers • Decodable Readers	• Decodable Readers	• Envision It! Skills and Strategies • Handbook • Leveled Readers
Go Digital	• Concept Talk Video • Decodable eBooks • eReaders	• Decodable eBooks	• Envision It! Animations • eReaders • Decodable eBooks

Question of the Week
What unique traits does it take to be the first to do something?

Vocabulary

Envision It! Word Cards

Vocabulary Skills Lesson pp. 122–123

- Envision It! Word Cards
- Vocabulary Activities

Fluency

Let's Learn It! pp. 148–149

Decodable and Leveled Readers

- eSelection
- Decodable eBooks
- eReaders

Conventions and Writing

Let's Write It! pp. 142–143

Decodable Readers

- Grammar Jammer
- Online Journal

Envision It! Word Cards

America's Champion Swimmer: Gertrude Ederle pp. 124–125

Practice Stations Flip Chart

Words!

RWN Cover

- Envision It! Word Cards
- Vocabulary Activities
- eSelection

- Envision It! Word Cards

- Vocabulary Activities

America's Champion Swimmer: Gertrude Ederle pp. 124–125

Practice Stations Flip Chart

Leveled Readers

ELL and ELD Readers

- eSelection
- eReaders

- Leveled Readers
- Decodable Readers

- eReaders
- Decodable eBooks

RWN Cover

America's Champion Swimmer: Gertrude Ederle pp. 124–125

Practice Stations Flip Chart

- Grammar Jammer
- Online Journal

- Reader's and Writer's Notebook

- Grammar Jammer
- Online Journal

You Are Here!
Unit 4
Week 4

My 5-Day Planner for Reading Street!

MONITOR PROGRESS — Don't Wait Until Friday

	Check Oral Vocabulary **Day 1** pages 116j–121f	Word Reading **Day 2** pages 122a–131e

Get Ready to Read	**Concept Talk,** 116j
	Oral Vocabulary, 117a
	  ordinary, imagination, assemble, magnficent
	Listening Comprehension, Read Aloud, 117b
	Phonics/Word Analysis, 118a–119b
	READ Decodable Practice Reader, 119a–119b
		Concept Talk, 122a
		Oral Vocabulary, 122b
		  organize, erect
		Phonics/Word Analysis, 122c
		  Suffixes -er, -or, -ess, -ist
		Literary Terms, 122d
		  Word Choice
		Text Structure, 122d
		  Chronological/Sequence

Read and Comprehend	**Comprehension Skill,**
	  ◉ Fact and Opinion, 120a
	Comprehension Strategy,
	  ◉ Questioning, 120a
	READ Comprehension, 120–121
	Model Fluency, Appropriate Phrasing, 120–121
	Introduce Lesson Vocabulary, 121a
	  drowned, strokes, medals, current, continued,
	  stirred, celebrate
		Vocabulary Skill,
		  ◉ Multiple Meaning Words, 122e
		Vocabulary Strategy, 122–122e Context Clues
		Lesson Vocabulary, 122–123 drowned, strokes,
		  medals, current, continued, stirred, celebrate
		READ Vocabulary, 122–123
		Model Fluency, Appropriate Phrasing, 122–123
		READ Main Selection, *America's Champion Swimmer:*
		  Gertrude Ederle, 124–131a

Language Arts	**Research and Inquiry,** Identify Questions, 121b
	Spelling, Suffixes -er, -or, -ess, -ist, 121c
	Conventions, Contractions, 121d
	Handwriting, Letter Spacing and Joining of Strokes,
	  121d
	Writing, Autobiography, 121e–121f
		Research and Inquiry, Navigate/Search, 131b
		Conventions, Contractions, 131c
		Spelling, Suffixes -er, -or, -ess, -ist, 131c
		Writing, Autobiography: Organization/Paragraphs,
		  131d

You Are Here!
Unit 4
Week 4

Question of the Week
What unique traits does it take to be the first to do smehting?

Check Retelling	Check Fluency	Check Oral Vocabulary
Day 3 pages 132a–143c	**Day 4** pages 144a–149e	**Day 5** pages 149f–149q

Concept Talk, 132a
Oral Vocabulary, 132b
   suspend, accompany
Phonics/Word Analysis, 132c–132d
Decodable Story, 132d
Comprehension Check, 132e
Check Retelling, 132f
	Concept Talk, 144a
	Oral Vocabulary, 144b
	   provision, spectacle
	Phonics/Word Analysis,
	   144c–144f
	Decodable Story, 144f
	21ˢᵗ Century Skill: Online
	   Directories, 144g
		Concept Wrap Up, 115f
		Check Oral Vocabulary, 149g
		   ordinary, imagination, assemble,
		   magnficent, organize, erect,
		   suspend, accompany, provision,
		   spectacle
		Amazing Ideas, 149g
		Review ◉ Fact and Opinion, 149h
		Review ◉ Contractions, 149h
		Review **Phonics/Word Analysis** 149i
		Review **Literary Terms** 149i

READ Main Selection,
   America's Champion Swimmer:
   Gertrude Ederle, 132–139a
Retelling, 140–141
Think Critically, 141a
Model Fluency,
   Appropriate Phrasing, 141b
Research and Study Skills, 141c
	READ Paired Selection,
	   "Women Athletes", 144–147a
	Let's Learn It!, 148–149a
	   Fluency: Approriate Phrasing
	   Vocabulary: Multiple Meaning
	   Words
	   Listening and Speaking:
	   Sportscast
		Fluency Assessment,
		   Appropriate Phrasing, 149j–149k
		Comprehension Assessment,
		   ◉ Fact and Opinion, 149l

Research and Inquiry,
   Analyze, 141d
Conventions, Contractions, 141e
Spelling, Suffixes -er, -or, -ess, -ist,
   141e
Let's Write It!, Autobiography,
   142–143a
Writer's Craft, Headings and
   Subheads, 143b–143c
	Research and Inquiry,
	   Synthesize, 141d
	Conventions,
	   Contractions, 141e
	Spelling, Suffixes -er, -or, -ess,
	   -ist, 149c
	Writing, Autobiography,
	   149d-149e
		Research and Inquiry,
		   Communicate, 149n
		Conventions,
		   Contractions, 149o
		Spelling Test, Suffixes -er, -or, -ess,
		   -ist, 149o
		Writer's Craft, Contractions, 149p
		Quick Write for Fluency, 149q

Week 4

Grouping Options for Differentiated Instruction
Turn the page for the small group time lesson plan.

Planning Small Group Time on Reading Street!

SMALL GROUP TIME RESOURCES

Look for this Small Group Time box each day to help meet the individual needs of all your children. Differentiated Instruction lessons appear on the DI pages at the end of each week.

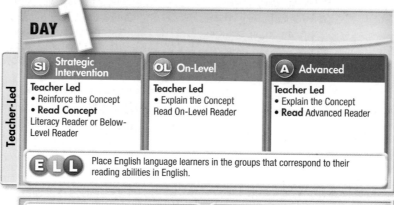

DAY 1

SI Strategic Intervention	**OL** On-Level	**A** Advanced
Teacher Led • Reinforce the Concept • **Read Concept** Literacy Reader or Below-Level Reader	**Teacher Led** • Explain the Concept Read On-Level Reader	**Teacher Led** • Explain the Concept • **Read** Advanced Reader

Teacher-Led

ELL Place English language learners in the groups that correspond to their reading abilities in English.

Practice Stations
• Read for Meaning
• Get Fluent
• Word Work

Independent Activities
• Concept Talk Video
• *Reader's and Writer's Notebook*
• Inquiry and Research

ELL

Helen Wills Moody:
America's Tennis Champion
by Martina Williams

ELL Reader

Helen Wills Moody:
America's Tennis Champion
by Martina Williams

ELD Reader

ELL Poster

You Are Here!
Unit 4
Week 4

Day 1

SI Strategic Intervention	**Reinforce the Concept,** DI•76–DI•77 **Read Decodable Reader, and Concept Literacy Reader** or **Below-Level Reader**
OL On-Level	**Expand the Concept,** DI•82 **Read On-Level Reader**
A Advanced	**Extend the Concept,** DI•87 **Read Advanced Reader**
ELL English Language Learners	• Concepts and Oral Vocabulary • Listening (Read Aloud) DI•91–DI•100

Reading Street
Intervention Kit

Reading Street
Practice Stations Kit

 Question of the Week
What unique traits does it take to be the first to do something?

 **SI** Strategic Intervention

Women Who Were First!
By Sharon Franklin

Concept Literacy Reader

 OL On-Level

Great Women in U.S. History
Biography
by Megan Litwin
illustrated by Aleksey Ivanov

On-Level

A Advanced

Changing Times: Women in the Early Twentieth Century
by Kristin Cashore

Advanced
Reader

Decodable Practice Readers
Units 4-6
• Practice phonics skills
• Blending practice
• Reread for fluency

Decodable
Readers

Below-Level

AMERICA'S CHAMPION SWIMMER: Gertrude Ederle
by David A. Adler
Illustrated by Terry Widener

America's Champion Swimmer: Gertrude Ederle,
pp. 124–125

Women Athletes
"Women Athletes" pp. 144–145

Small Group Weekly Plan

Day 2	Day 3	Day 4	Day 5
Reinforce Comprehension, DI•78 **Read Main Selection,** p. 124	**Reinforce Vocabulary,** DI•79 **Read Main Selection,** p. 124	**Reinforce Comprehension,** Practice Retelling, DI•80 **Read Paired Selection,** p. 144	**Practice Fluency,** DI•81 **Reread Decodable Reader,** and **Concept Literacy Reader** or **Below-Level Reader**
Expand Comprehension, DI•83 **Read Main Selection,** p. 124	**Expand Vocabulary,** DI•84 **Read Main Selection,** p. 124	**Reinforce Comprehension,** Practice Retelling, DI•85 **Read Paired Selection,** p. 144	**Practice Fluency,** DI•86 **Reread On-Level Reader**
Extend Comprehension, DI•88 **Read Main Selection,** p. 124	**Extend Vocabulary,** DI•89 **Read Main Selection,** p. 124	**Extend Comprehension,** Practice Retelling, DI•90 **Read Paired Selection,** p. 144	**Practice Fluency,** DI•90 **Reread Advanced Reader**

• **Concepts**
• **Vocabulary**
• **Phonics and Spelling**
  DI•91–DI•100
	• **Concepts**
	• **Vocabulary**
	• **Comprehension**
	  DI•91–DI•100
		• **Concepts**
		• **Vocabulary**
		Read ELL Reader
		  DI•91–DI•100
			• **Concepts**
			• **Vocabulary**
			  DI•91–DI•100

Practice Stations for Everyone on Reading Street!

Word Wise
Prefixes *pre-*, *mid-*, *over-*, *out-*, *bi-*, and *de-*

Objectives
• Spell words with prefixes *pre-*, *mid-*, *over-*, *out-*, *bi-*, and *de-*.

Materials
• *Word Work* Flip Chart Activity 19
• Teacher-made word cards
• dictionary   • pencils   • paper

Differentiated Activities

⚫ Choose word cards until you have one each with *pre-*, *mid-*, *over-*, *out-*, *bi-*, and *de-*. Write the words in a list. Write sentences using words. Circle the prefix in each word.

▲ Choose word cards until you have two with each prefix: *pre-*, *mid-*, *over-*, *out-*, *bi-*, and *de-*. Write the words. Write sentences using them. Circle the prefix in each word.

⬛ Choose word cards until you have two with each prefix: *pre-*, *mid-*, *over-*, *out-*, *bi-*, and *de-*. List the words and write sentences using them. Add other words with these prefixes to your list.

Technology
• Online Dictionary

Word Work
Prefixes *pre-*, *mid-*, *over-*, *out-*, *bi-*, and *de-*

Objectives
• Identify and pronounce words with prefixes *pre-*, *mid-*, *over-*, *out-*, *bi-*, and *de-*.

Materials
• *Word Work* Flip Chart Activity 19
• Teacher-made word cards
• paper   • pencil

Differentiated Activities

⚫ Choose ten word cards. Write the words in a list. Say each word. Think of other words you know with these prefixes. Group the words by prefix. Add them to your list.

▲ Choose twelve word cards, and write the words. Say each word. Make a six-column chart with the prefixes as headings. Add other words with these prefixes to your chart.

⬛ Choose fifteen word cards, and make a six-column chart with the prefixes as headings. Write the words in the correct column. Add other words with these prefixes to your chart. Circle the prefixes.

Technology
• Modeled Pronunciation Audio CD

Words to Know
Multiple-meaning words

Objectives
• Identify the meanings of multiple-meaning words.

Materials
• *Words to Know* Flip Chart Activity 19
• Teacher-made word cards
• dictionary   • pencil   • paper

Differentiated Activities

⚫ Choose three word cards. Write the words. Use a dictionary to find two meanings for each word. Write two sentences for each word to show its different meanings.

▲ Choose four word cards, and write the words. Use a dictionary to find two meanings for each word. Write two sentences for each word to show its multiple meanings.

⬛ Choose six word cards, and write the words. Use a dictionary to find each word's multiple meanings. Write at least two sentences for each word to show their multiple meanings.

Technology
• Online Dictionary

You Are Here! Unit 4 Week 4

Use this week's materials from the Reading Street Practice Stations Kit to organize this week's stations.

Let's Write!
Biography

Objectives
• Write a biography about someone you know.

Materials
• *Let's Write!* Flip Chart Activity 19
• paper   • pencils

Differentiated Activities

⬤ Think of someone you know and admire. Write a biography that tells about this person's life. Include interesting facts and details about this person that your readers will want to know.

▲ Write a biography that tells about the life of someone you know and admire. Include facts about this person that will be interesting to your readers. Make sure you use complete sentences.

◼ Write a biography about a person you know and admire. Include facts about this person that will interest your readers. Combine short, choppy sentences so your writing is easier to read.

Technology
• Online Graphic Organizers

Read for Meaning
Fact and opinion

Objectives
• Identify fact and opinion in expository text.

Materials
• *Read for Meaning* Flip Chart Activity 19
• Leveled Readers
• paper   • pencils

Differentiated Activities

⬤ Choose and read one of the books your teacher provides. Think about the information and ideas the author includes. Write one sentence that tells a fact from the selection. Write one sentence that tells an opinion.

▲ Choose and read one of the books your teacher provides, and think about the facts and opinions the author includes. Write two sentences that give facts from the selection. Write two sentences that give opinions.

◼ As you read the book you chose, distinguish between statements of fact and statements of opinion. Write a paragraph telling about some of the facts and opinions the author provides in the selection.

Technology
• Leveled Reader Database

Get Fluent
Practice fluent reading.

Objectives
• Read aloud with expression.

Materials
• *Get Fluent* Flip Chart Activity 19
• Leveled Readers

Differentiated Activities

⬤ Work with a partner. Choose a leveled reader. Take turns reading a page from the book. Use the words and punctuation to help you read with correct expression. Provide feedback to your partner.

▲ Work with a partner. Choose a leveled reader. Take turns reading a page from the book. Use the words and punctuation to help you read with correct expression. Provide feedback to your partner.

◼ Work with a partner. Choose a leveled reader. Take turns reading a page from the book. Use the words and punctuation to help you read with correct expression. Provide feedback to your partner.

Technology
• Leveled Reader Database
• Reading Street Readers CD-ROM

Week 4

Objectives
- Introduce the weekly concept.
- Develop oral vocabulary.

Today at a Glance

Oral Vocabulary
ordinary, imagination, assemble, magnificent

Word Analysis
Suffixes *-er, -or, -ess, -ist*

Comprehension
◉ Fact and opinion
◎ Questioning

Fluency
Appropriate phrasing

Lesson Vocabulary
Tested vocabulary

Research and Inquiry
Identify questions

Spelling
Suffixes *-er, -or, -ess, -ist*

Conventions
Contractions

Handwriting
Cursive letters *r, s*

Writing
Autobiography

Concept Talk

Question of the Week
What unique traits does it take to be the first to do something?

Introduce the concept

To further explore the unit concept of One of a Kind, this week students will read, write, and talk about what unique traits it takes to be the first to do something. Write the Question of the Week on the board.

ROUTINE | **Activate Prior Knowledge** | **Team Talk**

1. **Think** Have students think about someone who was the first to do something and the traits the person has.
2. **Pair** Have pairs of students discuss the Question of the Week.
3. **Share** Call on a few students to share their ideas with the group. Guide the discussion and encourage elaboration with prompts such as:
   - Why would someone want to be the first person to achieve something?
   - How would you describe someone who works hard to achieve a goal?

Routines Flip Chart

Anchored Talk

Develop oral vocabulary

Have students turn to pp. 116–117 in their Student Editions. Look at each of the photos. Then, use the prompts to guide discussion and create the *Unique traits for being first* concept map. Remind students to ask and answer questions with appropriate detail.

- Why is a picture of George Washington on this page? (He was the first president.) What traits do you think George Washington had? How was he different from an *ordinary* man? (He was a good leader and a hard worker.) Let's add *Leadership* and *Hard worker* to our concept map.
- Neil Armstrong was the first person to stand on the moon. What *magnificent spectacle* do you think he saw? (Possible responses: He saw the surface of the moon all around him; he saw space.)

Objectives
• Listen closely when someone speaks, ask questions and comment about the topic. • Take part in discussions and offer ideas that build on the ideas of others.

Oral Vocabulary

Let's Talk About

Being First

• Ask questions about bravery, imagination, and determination.

• Pose and answer questions about what it takes to be first at something.

• Discuss historical firsts.

READING STREET ONLINE
CONCEPT TALK VIDEO
www.ReadingStreet.com

You've learned **176** Amazing Words so far this year!

Student Edition pp. 116–117

Amazing Words

You've learned **1 7 6** words so far.

You'll learn **0 1 0** words this week.

ordinary	erect
imagination	suspend
assemble	accompany
magnificent	provision
organize	spectacle

Writing on Demand

Writing Fluency
Ask students to respond to the photos on pp. 116–117 by writing as well as they can and as much as they can about the unique traits it takes to be the first to do something.

• What traits should astronauts have? (Possible responses: bravery, determination, imagination) Let's add *Bravery, Determination,* and *Imagination* to the concept map.

```
        ┌────────────────┐
        │  Unique traits │
        │ for being first│
        └────────────────┘
   ┌─────────┬────────┬──────────┬──────────────┬─────────────┐
┌──────────┐┌──────────┐┌─────────┐┌─────────────┐┌────────────┐
│Leadership││Hard worker││ Bravery ││Determination││ Imagination│
│  skills  ││          ││         ││             ││            │
└──────────┘└──────────┘└─────────┘└─────────────┘└────────────┘
```

Connect to reading
Tell students that this week they will be reading about females who were the first to achieve something. Throughout the week, encourage students to add concept-related words to this week's concept map. Encourage students to ask relevant questions about things they don't understand.

ELL Preteach Concepts Use the Day 1 instruction on ELL Poster 19 to assess and build background knowledge, develop concepts, and build oral vocabulary.

ELL

English Language Learners
ELL support Additional ELL support and modified instruction is provided in the *ELL Handbook* and in the ELL Support lessons on pp. DI•91–DI•100.

Listening comprehension
English learners will benefit from additional visual support to understand the key terms in the concept map. Use the pictures on pp. 116–117 to scaffold understanding.

Frontload for Read Aloud Use the modified Read Aloud on p. DI•94 of the ELL Support lessons to prepare students to listen to "A First in Space: Ellen Ochoa" on p. 117b.

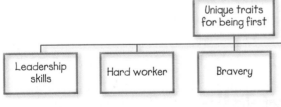

ELL Poster 19

Objectives
- Develop listening comprehension.
- Develop oral vocabulary.

Check Oral Vocabulary
SUCCESS PREDICTOR

Oral Vocabulary
Amazing Words

Introduce Amazing Words

"A First in Space: Ellen Ochoa" on p. 117b is about the first Hispanic American female in space. Tell students to listen for this week's Amazing Words—*ordinary, imagination, assemble,* and *magnificent*—as you read.

Model fluency

As you read "A First in Space: Ellen Ochoa," model appropriate phrasing by grouping words in a meaningful way and paying attention to punctuation cues.

Teach Amazing Words

Amazing Words Oral Vocabulary Routine

> ordinary
> imagination
> assemble
> magnificent

1 Introduce Write the word *imagination* on the board. Have students say the word aloud with you. In "A First in Space: Ellen Ochoa," we learn that Ochoa had a vivid *imagination* as a child. Does the author include any context clues for this word? Supply a student-friendly definition.

2 Demonstrate Have students answer questions to demonstrate understanding. How is daydreaming a way of using your *imagination*? How do you know if someone has a good *imagination*?

3 Apply Ask students to give a personal example of *imagination*.

See p. OV•1 to teach *ordinary, assemble,* and *magnificent.*

Routines Flip Chart

Apply Amazing Words

To build oral language, lead the class in a discussion about the Amazing Words' meanings. Remind students to ask and answer questions with appropriate detail, and to build on the ideas of others.

Don't Wait Until Friday

MONITOR PROGRESS **Check Oral Vocabulary**

During discussion, listen for students' use of Amazing Words.

If... students are unable to use the Amazing Words to discuss the concept,

then... use Oral Vocabulary Routine Card in the Routines Flip Chart to demonstrate words in different contexts.

Day 1	Day 2	Day 3	Day 4	Day 5	
Check Oral Vocabulary	Check Word Reading	Check Retelling	Check Fluency	Check Oral Vocabulary	Success Predictor

Read Aloud

A First in Space: Ellen Ochoa

When Dr. Ellen Ochoa was growing up, few women dreamed of going into space. Ellen was different, though. She was no ordinary woman!

The first American woman did not go into space until 1983. In 1993 Ellen Ochoa reached a goal that was truly a first. She became the first Hispanic-American woman in space.

Ellen Ochoa was born on May 10, 1958, in Los Angeles. Her interest in exploring space started at a young age. Her vivid imagination helped her dream of the day when she could go into space. Ellen also had a great desire to learn. She studied hard in school. Math and science were her favorite subjects.

Ellen's combined love of math and science grew. It helped her decide what to study in college. She majored in physics at San Diego State University, where she graduated in 1980. Physics is a special branch of science that deals with changes in matter. But one degree wasn't enough for Ellen. She received a master of science degree in 1981 and a doctorate in electrical engineering in 1985. Both of these degrees were from Stanford University.

Along with her keen interest in science and her brilliant mind, Ellen had an intense curiosity about everything she came in contact with. This led her to invent a tool that helped find flaws in the production of a variety of small manufacturing parts.

She later helped assemble other tools that would become helpful in the science field.

Although remaining an inventor could have led to a magnificent career, Ellen wanted more. She saw a way to combine her scientific knowledge with her long-time interest in space exploration. In 1990 she was selected by NASA (National Aeronautics and Space Administration) to join the astronaut program. She became an astronaut in 1991.

After a few years of serving in several positions at NASA, the big day finally came. Ellen's childhood dream became a reality! In April 1993 she went into space on the Space Shuttle *Discovery*. Ellen became the first Hispanic-American woman in space.

During the nine-day mission on the *Discovery*, Ellen and the rest of the crew performed many tasks. The *Discovery* mission was the first of several space flights for Ellen. Her roles on the other space flights varied. Since her first flight, she has logged hundreds of hours in space.

Throughout the years, Ellen has received a number of awards, including a Distinguished Service Medal. One of Ellen's highest achievements was to help develop the International Space Station.

To this day, Ellen Ochoa still plays a major role in space exploration.

Oral Vocabulary

Success Predictor

Word Analysis
⊙ Suffixes

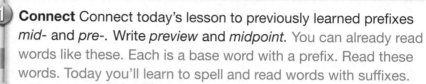

ROUTINE Word Parts Strategy

① **Connect** Connect today's lesson to previously learned prefixes *mid-* and *pre-*. Write *preview* and *midpoint*. You can already read words like these. Each is a base word with a prefix. Read these words. Today you'll learn to spell and read words with suffixes.

② **Model** Write *painter*. *Painter* is a two-syllable word formed from the base word *paint* and the ending, or suffix, *-er*. Point out each word part, read the parts, and then read the word. Often suffixes like *-er* change how a base word is used. For example, *painter* names a person who paints. Write *visitor, player, collector, princess,* and *harpist*. Model how to read each word by covering the suffix, reading the base word *(visit, play, collect, prince, harp)*, reading the suffix, and reading the whole word. Discuss how the suffix changes the meanings of the base words.

③ **Guide Practice** Continue the process in step 2. This time have students read the words with you. Identify the suffix in each word and tell how it changes the meaning of the base word. Point out the spelling changes.

artist	swimmer	seller	editor	actress	builder
hostess	sailor	tourist	countess	writer	farmer

④ **Review** What do you know about reading words with suffixes? When you recognize a suffix, cover the suffix, read the base word first, read the suffix, and then read the whole word.

Routines Flip Chart

Model   Have students turn to p. 118 in their Student Editions. Each word on this page has a suffix. The first word has the suffix *-er*. I cover the suffix and read the base word *teach*. Adding the suffix *-er* gives me *teacher*.

Guide practice   For each word in Words I Can Blend, ask students to identify the base word and the suffix and then read the whole word.

If... students have difficulty reading a word,
then... model reading the parts and then the whole word, and then ask students to read it with you.

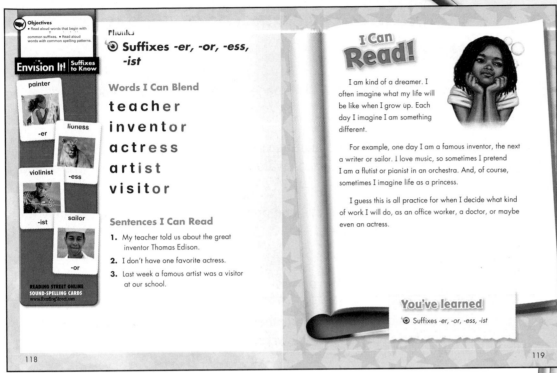

Objectives
• Read aloud words that begin with common suffixes. • Read aloud words with common spelling patterns.

Phonics

Suffixes -er, -or, -ess, -ist

Words I Can Blend

teacher

inventor

actress

artist

visitor

Envision It! | Suffixes to Know

painter
-er
lioness
violinist
-ess
-ist
sailor
-or

READING STREET ONLINE
SOUND-SPELLING CARDS
www.ReadingStreet.com

Sentences I Can Read

1. My teacher told us about the great inventor Thomas Edison.
2. I don't have one favorite actress.
3. Last week a famous artist was a visitor at our school.

118

I Can Read!

I am kind of a dreamer. I often imagine what my life will be like when I grow up. Each day I imagine I am something different.

For example, one day I am a famous inventor, the next a writer or sailor. I love music, so sometimes I pretend I am a flutist or pianist in an orchestra. And, of course, sometimes I imagine life as a princess.

I guess this is all practice for when I decide what kind of work I will do, as an office worker, a doctor, or maybe even an actress.

You've learned

Suffixes -er, -or, -ess, -ist

119

Student Edition pp. 118–119

Decode and Read

Read words independent of context

After students can successfully combine the word parts to read the words on p. 118 in their Student Editions, point to words in random order and ask students to read them naturally.

Read words in context

Have students read each of the sentences on p. 118. Have them identify words in the sentences that have suffixes.

Team Talk Pair students and have them take turns reading each of the sentences aloud.

Chorally read the I Can Read! passage on p. 119 with the students. Then have them read the passage aloud to themselves.

On their own

For additional practice, use the *Reader's and Writer's Notebook* p. 280.

Reader's and Writer's Notebook, p. 280

Differentiated Instruction

SI **Strategic Intervention**

Read words with suffixes If students have difficulty reading base words, then use the Bending Strategy Routine on the Routines to practice blending decodable base words. Flip Chart. Tell students that adding the suffixes -er, -or, -ess, and -ist does not change the pronunciation of the base word.

Vocabulary Support

You may wish to explain the meaning of these words.

actress a female who acts

hostess a woman who receives another person as her guest

countess the wife of a count or an earl

flutist a person who plays the flute

pianist a person who plays the piano

English Language Learners

Pronunciation Assist students with the articulation of suffixes. Focus on mouth positions when saying words such as *teacher* and *hostess*.

Contrastive Analysis Chart See also the Contrastive Analysis Chart in the *First Stop* book.

Language transfer In Spanish, *-er* is pronounced like *air*, such as *better* and *faster* as be-tair and fas-tair. Pronounce these words and have students pronounce them after you.

Objectives

- Apply knowledge of suffixes to decode unknown multisyllabic words when reading.
- Decode and read words in context and independent of context.
- Practice fluency with oral rereading.

Decodable Practice Reader 19A
Suffixes

Read words independent of context

Have students turn to the first page. Have students read each word.

Read high-frequency words

Have students read the high-frequency words *are, people, do, a, what, said, you, the, of, two, wants, watched, their, should, they, to, would,* and *your* on the first page.

Preview Decodable Practice Reader

Have students read the title and preview the story. Tell them that they will read words with suffixes.

Read words in context

Pair students for reading and listen as they read. One student begins. Students read the entire story, switching readers after each page. Partners reread the story. This time the other student begins. Make sure students are monitoring their accuracy when they decode words.

Decodable Practice Reader 19A

Corrective feedback

If... students have difficulty reading a word,
then... refer them to the Sound-Spelling Cards to
identify the word parts. Have them read the word parts
individually and then together to say the word.

- What is the new word?
- Is the new word a word you know?
- Does it make sense in the story?

Check decoding and comprehension

Have students retell the story to include characters, setting, and
events. Then have students find words in the story that have
suffixes. Students should supply *teacher, artist, actress, editors,
conductors, driver, writer, inventor, firefighter,* and *chemist.*

Reread for Fluency

Have students reread Decodable Practice Reader 19A to develop
automaticity decoding words with suffixes.

ROUTINE **Oral Rereading**

① **Read** Have students read the entire book orally.

② **Reread** To achieve optimal fluency, students should reread the text
three or four times.

③ **Corrective Feedback** Listen as students read. Provide corrective
feedback regarding their fluency and decoding.

Routines Flip Chart

**English Language Learners
Leveled Support: Suffixes**

Beginning Write several words
with suffixes from the Decodable
Practice Reader on the board,
such as *teacher, artist, actress,*
and *editors.* Point to each word
as you say it aloud. Then underline the letters that spell the suffix.
Have students repeat the words
with you. Repeat the procedure
for suffixes using words such as
conductors, driver, inventor, and
chemist.

Intermediate After reading,
have students find pairs of
words with the same suffix. For
example: *teacher* and *driver;
artist* and *chemist; editor* and
conductor.

Advanced/Advanced High
After reading the story, have
students choose 4 or 5 words
with suffixes and write a sentence
for each word.

Objectives

- Identify facts and opinions to aid comprehension.
- Use the questioning strategy to aid comprehension.
- Read grade-level text with appropriate phrasing.

Skills Trace

⊙ **Fact and Opinion**

Introduce U4W3D1; U4W4D1; U6W1D1

Practice U4W3D2; U4W3D3; U4W3D4; U4W4D2; U4W4D3; U4W4D4; U6W1D2; U6W1D3; U6W1D4

Reteach/Review U4W3D5; U1W4D3; U6W3D3; D3; U4W4D5; D3; D3; U6W1D5

Assess/Test
Weekly Tests U4W3; U4W4; U6W1
Benchmark Tests U4

Skill ↔ Strategy
🔁 Fact and Opinion
🔁 Questioning

Introduce fact and opinion

A statement of fact can be proved true or false. How can I prove that something is true? (look in a reference book, ask an expert, or use my own knowledge and experience) An opinion cannot be proved true or false. How can I identify a statement of opinion when reading? (look for clue words of a judgment or belief) Have students turn to p. EI•7 in the Student Edition to review fact and opinion. Then read "Swim!" with students.

Student Edition p. EI•7

Model the skill

Think Aloud Today we're going to read about swimming. Have students follow along as you read the second paragraph of "Swim!" I see the word *best* in the first sentence. This is a clue word that indicates an opinion or judgment. I cannot prove this statement true or false. The other sentences are facts. I can check in a reference book to verify that these statements are true.

Guide practice

Have students finish reading "Swim!" on their own. After they read, have them use a graphic organizer like the one on p. 120 and identify statements of fact and opinion from the passage.

Strategy check

Questioning Remind students that asking questions helps a reader focus on the rereading and monitor their comprehension. Model asking a question about the second paragraph and reading to find the answer.

Model the strategy

Think Aloud When I read the third paragraph, I asked myself why people do not get hurt when swimming. I reread the second paragraph and thought about my own knowledge. There is little or no impact when you are swimming. You cannot twist an ankle or break an arm in the water. Have students review the strategy of questioning on p. EI•23 of the Student Edition.

Student Edition p. EI•23

On their own

Use p. 250 in the *Reader's and Writer's Notebook* for additional practice with fact and opinion.

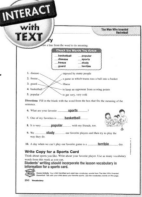

Reader's and Writer's Notebook

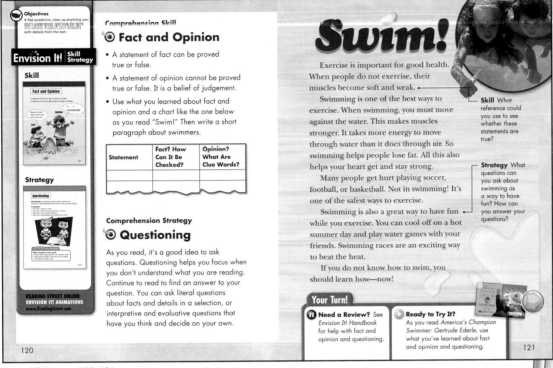

Student Edition pp. 120–121

Model Fluency
Appropriate Phrasing

Model fluent reading

Have students listen as you read paragraph 2 of "Swim!" with appropriate phrasing. Explain that you will group phrases together then pause, using punctuation to help you.

ROUTINE Choral Reading

1. **Select a passage** Use paragraph 2 of "Swim!"
2. **Model** Have students listen as you read with appropriate phrasing.
3. **Guide practice** Have students read along with you.
4. **On their own** For optimal fluency, students should reread three or four times with appropriate phrasing.

Routines Flip Chart

English Language Learners

Fact and opinion Provide oral practice by having students state facts and opinions about this week's weather. Then write these sentences on the board and read them aloud. Have students identify whether each sentence is a fact or an opinion, then support their answers.

- Everyone likes to swim.
- Swimming is fun.
- Swimming makes your muscles stronger.

Objectives
- Activate prior knowledge of words.
- Identify questions for research.

Vocabulary
Tested Vocabulary

Lesson vocabulary

Have students complete sentences by filling in the blanks with lesson words.

Activate prior knowledge

Display the lesson words and discuss what students already know about these words. Then write incomplete sentences on the board, such as those below. Have students identify the lesson word that completes each sentence and makes sense in context. Students may need to check the glossary.

- In our family, we _____ each other's accomplishments. (celebrate)
- The cat _____ sleeping after Sammy moved it off his lap. (continued)
- The ocean _____ was particularly strong yesterday. (current)
- Sadly, the woman _____ in the river. (drowned)
- The gymnast earned three gold _____ at the competition. (medals)
- Dad _____ the soup to mix the ingredients. (stirred)
- Jamal knows all the basic swimming _____. (strokes)

Related words

Ask how *celebration* and *celebrate* are related in meaning.

At the end of the week, students can review these fill-in-the-blank sentences or create their own with a partner.

Use the Strategy for Words with Meaningful Parts Routine to help students read multisyllabic words.

Preteach Academic Vocabulary

 Academic Vocabulary Write the following words on the board:

heading	word choice
contraction	apostrophe
notes	subheading

Have students share what they know about this week's Academic Vocabulary. Use the students' responses to assess their prior knowledge. Preteach the Academic Vocabulary by providing a student friendly description, explanation, or example that clarifies the meaning of each term. Then ask students to restate the meaning of the Academic Vocabulary term in their own words.

Research and Inquiry
Identify Questions

Teach Discuss the Question of the Week: *What unique traits does it take to be the first to do something?* Tell students they will research female athletes and their unique traits. They will present their findings as a biography on Day 5.

Model I'll start by brainstorming a list of questions about female athletes and their traits. First, I'll think about female athletes, though I will only write about one. I watched Misty May Treanor in the Olympic Games. I also like to watch Maria Sharapova play tennis. Some possible questions could be *What were their childhoods like? When did they begin the sport?* and *How much time do they dedicate to playing and practicing the sport?*

Guide practice After students have brainstormed inquiry questions, explain that tomorrow they will conduct an online research of their questions. Help students identify keywords that will guide their search.

On their own Have students work individually, in pairs, or in small groups to write an inquiry question.

INTERNET GUY
Don Leu

21st Century Skills

Weekly Inquiry Project
Day 1 Identify Questions
Day 2 Navigate/Search
Day 3 Analyze
Day 4 Synthesize
Day 5 Communicate

Academic Vocabulary

notes notes are short sentences, phrases, or words written down to remind one of what was read or heard.

Small Group Time

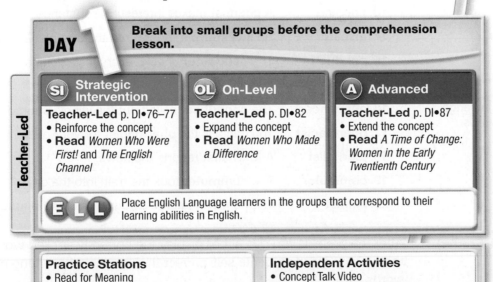

DAY 1 Break into small groups before the comprehension lesson.

Teacher-Led

(SI) Strategic Intervention
Teacher-Led p. DI•76–77
• Reinforce the concept
• **Read** *Women Who Were First!* and *The English Channel*

(OL) On-Level
Teacher-Led p. DI•82
• Expand the concept
• **Read** *Women Who Made a Difference*

(A) Advanced
Teacher-Led p. DI•87
• Extend the concept
• **Read** *A Time of Change: Women in the Early Twentieth Century*

ELL Place English Language learners in the groups that correspond to their learning abilities in English.

Practice Stations
• Read for Meaning
• Get Fluent
• Word Work

Independent Activities
• Concept Talk Video
• *Reader's and Writer's Notebook*
• Inquiry and Research

ELL

English Language Learners Multilingual vocabulary
Students can apply knowledge of their home languages to acquire new English vocabulary by using the Multilingual Vocabulary Lists (*ELL Handbook*, pp. 433–444).

Objectives
- Spell words with suffixes -er, -or, -ess, and -ist.
- Use and understand contractions.
- Write cursive lowercase letters r and s in words.

Spelling Pretest
Suffixes -er, -or, -ess, -ist

Introduce   This week we will spell words with the suffixes -er, -or, -ess, and -ist. Explain that each spelling word is formed by combining a root word with a suffix.

Pretest   Use these sentences to administer the spelling pretest. Say each word, read the sentence, and repeat the word.

1. **dentist**	The **dentist** cleaned my teeth.
2. **editor**	The **editor** chose this week's news stories.
3. **artist**	The **artist** was well-known.
4. **hostess**	It takes skill to be a good **hostess.**
5. **actress**	This **actress** performed on stage and in film.
6. **swimmer**	Gertrude Ederle was a champion **swimmer.**
7. **seller**	Are you the **seller** of this bike?
8. **tutor**	Sue's older sister works as a math **tutor.**
9. **tourist**	I would like to be a **tourist** in the city.
10. **organist**	Do you know the **organist?**
11. **lioness**	A female lion is a **lioness.**
12. **shipper**	The **shipper** packed our dishes carefully.
13. **chemist**	A **chemist** makes interesting substances.
14. **investor**	An **investor** put money into the company.
15. **conductor**	The **conductor** checks everyone's tickets.

Challenge words

16. **announcer**	The **announcer** called out the winning number.
17. **pharmacist**	You can ask the **pharmacist** for your prescription.
18. **journalist**	A **journalist** reports the news.
19. **commuter**	The **commuter** took the train into the city.
20. **pianist**	The concert featured a young, talented **pianist.**

Self-correct   After the pretest, you can either display the correctly spelled words or spell them orally. Have students self-correct their pretests by writing misspelled words.

On their own   For additional practice, use the *Let's Practice It! DVD.*

Let's Practice It!!
TR DVD•247

Conventions
Contractions

Teach Display Grammar Transparency 19, and read aloud the explanation and examples in the box. Point out the contractions *we've* and *won't*.

Model Model writing the correct form of the contraction including placement of the apostrophe, and the two words from which the contraction is formed to complete items 1 and 2. Show how the contraction is formed from the original two words.

Grammar Transparency 19

Guide practice Guide students to complete items 3 and 4. Remind them to identify the words from which the contraction is formed. Record the correct responses on the transparency.

Daily Fix-It Use Daily Fix-It numbers 1 and 2 in the right margin.

Connect to oral language Have students read sentences 5–7 on the transparency and write the contraction to correctly complete each sentence.

Handwriting
Cursive letters *r* and *s*

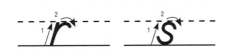

Model letter formation Display the cursive lowercase letters *r* and *s*. Follow the stroke instruction pictured to model letter formation.

Model letter spacing and joining of strokes Explain that writing legibly means letters are spaced correctly. Point out that the strokes forming *r* and *s* should be joined properly. Model writing this sentence smoothly: *Vanessa tries to write to her sister.* Make sure the letters are spaced properly and that strokes are joined correctly.

Guide practice Have students write these sentences. *Is your brother inside his bedroom? Her bassoon sounds rather sharp.* Circulate around the room, guiding students.

Academic Vocabulary

A **contraction** is formed by joining two separate words and using a punctuation mark called an **apostrophe** (') to indicate missing letters.

Daily Fix-It

1. Isnt Brian the best swimer on the team? (*Isn't; swimmer*)
2. He gos to the pool for a work out every morning. (*goes; workout*)

English Language Learners Conventions Have students work in pairs to practice using contractions correctly. The first partner says a sentence using two separate words, and the second repeats the sentence using the proper contraction. Then partners switch roles. Ask students to practice the following: *I will/I'll; had not/hadn't; could have/could've.*

Objectives
- Use context to distinguish between multiple-meaning words.
- Read grade-level text with appropriate phrasing.

Vocabulary Strategy for
⊙ Multiple-Meaning Words

Student Edition p. W•11

Teach multiple-meaning words

Envision It!

Tell students that a multiple-meaning word is a word which has several definitions given within the dictionary listing for the word, but all are somewhat related and have the same root. Explain that using context can help students decide which meaning the author intended. Refer students to *Words!* on p. W•11 in the Student Edition for additional practice.

Write on the board: *It is important to remember safety rules when we swim.*

Model the strategy

Think About It

I read the word *rules.* I know *rules* can have more than one meaning. I think about the context of the sentence. In this sentence, *rules* means "what to do and not do."

Guide practice

Write this sentence on the board: *The river's strong current carried the bottle and its message far away.* Have students determine the meaning of *current* using context clues. For additional support, use *Envision It! Pictured Vocabulary Cards* or *Tested Vocabulary Cards.*

On their own

Read "Learn to Swim" on p. 123. Have students use context clues to write a definition for *step.* For additional practice use *Reader's and Writer's Notebook*, p. 283.

Reader's and Writer's Notebook, p. 283

Review
Key features

Review the key features of an autobiography with students. You may want to post the key features in the classroom so that students can refer to the features while working on their autobiographies.

Key Features of an Autobiography

- tells the story of a person's own life
- may cover a person's whole life or only part of it
- written in first person

ROUTINE **Quick Write for Fluency** **Team Talk**

1. **Talk** Have students discuss the key features of autobiographies in pairs.
2. **Write** Each student writes a few sentences defining an autobiography.
3. **Share** Partners read their sentences to one another.

Routines Flip Chart

Wrap Up Your Day

✔ **Build Concepts** Have students discuss what unique traits it takes to do something.

✔ **Oral Vocabulary** Have students use the Amazing Words they learned in context sentences.

✔ **Homework** Send home this week's Family Times newsletter in the *Let's Practice It! DVD* • 248–249.

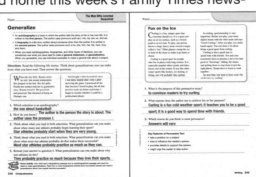

Let's practice It!
TR DVD•248–249

E L L

English Language Learners
Leveled support: Read like a writer

Beginning Have students read the first two paragraphs of "My Autobiography" aloud. Have them practice with a partner until they can read the paragraphs without hesitation.

Intermediate Ask students to circle any unfamiliar words in "My Autobiography." Have them guess the meaning of the words from context and then confirm their guesses in a dictionary.

Advanced/Advanced High Have students suppose that they are going to interview the author of "My Autobiography." Ask them to prepare three questions that they would like to ask the author.

Preview DAY 2

Tell students that tomorrow they will read about a famous female swimmer.

Objectives
- Expand the weekly concept.
- Develop oral vocabulary.

Today at a Glance

Oral Vocabulary
organize, erect

Word Analysis
Suffixes *(-er, -or, -ess, -ist)*

Literary Terms
Word choice

Text Structure
Chronological sequence

Lesson Vocabulary
⊙ Multiple-meaning words

Reading
"Learn to Swim"
America's Champion Swimmer: Gertrude Ederle

Fluency
Appropriate phrasing

Research and Inquiry
Navigate/Search

Spelling
Suffixes *(-er, -or, -ess, -ist)*

Conventions
Contractions

Writing
Autobiography

Concept Talk

Question of the Week

What unique traits does it take to be the first to do something?

Expand the concept
Remind students of the weekly concept question. Tell students that today they will begin reading *America's Champion Swimmer: Gertrude Ederle.* As they read, encourage students to think about unique traits Trudy has.

Anchored Talk

Develop oral language
Use the photos on pp. 116–117 and the Read Aloud, "A First in Space: Ellen Ochoa," to talk about the Amazing Words: *ordinary, imagination, assemble,* and *magnificent.* Add the words to the concept map to develop students' knowledge of the topic. Discuss the following questions. Remind students to ask relevant questions and answer with appropriate detail. Encourage students to build on other's ideas when they answer.

- Why might it be good to have a *magnificent imagination*?
- Would you rather read the biography of an *ordinary* person or someone who achieved greatness? Why?
- Why is it important to follow directions when you *assemble* something?

Oral Vocabulary
Amazing Words

ordinary	erect
imagination	suspend
assemble	accompany
magnificent	provision
organize	spectacle

Teach Amazing Words

Amazing Words — Oral Vocabulary Routine

1 **Introduce** Write the Amazing Word *organize* on the board. Have students say it aloud with you. Relate *organize* to the photographs on pp. 116–117 and "A First in Space: Ellen Ochoa." Why would an astronaut need to *organize* his or her training? Why would it take many people to *organize* an astronaut's mission in space? Have students determine the definition of the word. (To *organize* is to arrange things in a certain order.)

2 **Demonstrate** Have students answer questions with appropriate detail to demonstrate understanding. How do you *organize* your day? How do you *organize* supplies when you work on a school project?

3 **Apply** Have students apply their understanding. What are some synonyms and antonyms for the word *organize*?

See p. OV•1 to teach *erect*.

Routines Flip Chart

Apply Amazing Words

As students read "Learn to Swim" on p. 123, have them think about how they could *organize* their day to incorporate swimming lessons. Have them talk about statues they might *erect* at a swimming pool to decorate it or to honor good swimmers.

Connect to reading

Explain that today students will read about Gertrude Ederle, a woman who was the first to do something. As they read, they should think about how the Question of the Week and the Amazing Words *organize* and *erect* might apply to her.

Differentiated Instruction

 Strategic Intervention
Have students explain how they organize their time during the day.

A **Advanced**
Tell students to think what would happen if your community was going to erect a statue of a local hero. Have them write a paragraph identifying the person and describing the statue.

Connect to Social Studies

Explain that the events in the selection took place in the early 1900s. Use this opportunity to discuss the terms *year, decade,* and *century.*

ELL **Reinforce Vocabulary** Use the Day 2 instruction on ELL Poster 19 to teach lesson vocabulary and the lesson concept.

ELL Poster 19

Word Analysis
Suffixes

Review | Review the suffixes *-er, -or, -ess,* and *-ist,* pointing out that suffixes are added to the end of base words.

Read words independent of context | Display these words. Have the class decode the words. Then point to the words in random order and ask students to read them quickly.

speaker	visitor	waitress	tourist
actress	realist	inventor	golfer

Corrective feedback | Model reading the base word and then the suffix, and then ask students to read the word with you.

Read words in context | Display these sentences. Have the class read the sentences.

Team Talk Have pairs take turns reading the sentences naturally.

> The **countess** bowed before the **princess.**
> The **artist** painted a picture of the **sailor.**
> The **pitcher** threw the ball to the **catcher.**

Don't Wait Until Friday

MONITOR PROGRESS Words with Suffixes

Write the following words and have the class read them. Notice which words students miss during the group reading. Call on individuals to read some of the words.

printer	cleaner	tutor	leader	**Spiral Review**
duchess	shipper	thinker	checker ←	Row 2 reviews words with digraphs sh, th, ch.
seller	resell	reader	reread ←	Row 3 contrasts words with prefixes and suffixes.

If... students cannot read words with suffixes at this point,

then... use the Small Group Time Strategic Intervention lesson, pp. DI•80, to reteach suffixes. Continue to monitor students' progress using other instructional opportunities during the week. See the Skills Trace on p. 118a.

Day 1	Day 2	Day 3	Day 4	Day 5	
Check Oral Vocabulary	Check Word Reading	Check Retelling	Check Fluency	Check Oral Vocabulary	Success Predictor

Literary Terms
Word Choice

Teach word choice

Tell students that writers use specific words and phrases to communicate clearly. No matter what type of writing an author is doing, word choice is important to communicate meaning.

Model word choice

Think Aloud Let's look at "Swim!" and analyze the author's word choice. Let's look for words that describe. In the first paragraph, the author says your muscles can become "soft and weak" without exercise. *Soft* and *weak* are examples of descriptive words the author chose. Do you think these are good descriptive words? Why or why not? (**Possible response:** Yes, they describe muscles.)

Guide practice

Read the fourth paragraph of "Swim!" and analyze the author's word choice. Point out the descriptive phrases "Hot summer day" and "water games."

On their own

Have students analyze the author's word choice in "Learn to Swim."

Text Structure
Chronological/Sequence

Teach chronological sequence

Today we will begin reading a biography. A biography often uses a chronological text structure. The events are in sequential order. This means the author tells about events in the person's life in the order in which they occurred.

Model the strategy

Think Aloud I see on the first page of *Gertrude Ederle* that the author tells me she was born in 1906. As I continue reading, I learn about her childhood. Thinking about the chronological order helps me understand the selection.

Guide practice

As students read the selection, discuss the text structure with them, noting how it follows a chronological sequence. Point out how dates can help students follow the order of events.

On their own

As they read the selection, students can make a time line to help them follow the chronological order.

Academic Vocabulary

word choice how an author avoids using the same words over and over and chooses interesting, vivid, and specific words to make his or her meaning clear and keep the attention of his or her audience

Objectives
- Use context to distinguish between multiple-meaning words.
- Read grade-level text with appropriate phrasing.

Vocabulary Strategy for ↻ Multiple-Meaning Words

Teach multiple-meaning words

Envision It!

Tell students that a multiple-meaning word is a word which has several definitions given within the dictionary listing for the word, but all are somewhat related and have the same root. Explain that using context can help students decide which meaning the author intended. Refer students to *Words!* on p. W•11 in the Student Edition for additional practice.

Student Edition p. W•11

Write on the board: *It is important to remember safety rules when we swim.*

Model the strategy

Think About It

I read the word *rules.* I know *rules* can have more than one meaning. I think about the context of the sentence. In this sentence, *rules* means "what to do and not do."

Guide practice

Write this sentence on the board: *The river's strong current carried the bottle and its message far away.* Have students determine the meaning of *current* using context clues. For additional support, use *Envision It! Pictured Vocabulary Cards* or *Tested Vocabulary Cards*.

On their own

Read "Learn to Swim" on p. 123. Have students use context clues to write a definition for *step.* For additional practice use *Reader's and Writer's Notebook*, p. 283.

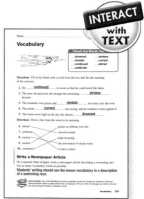

Reader's and Writer's Notebook, p. 283

Objectives
- Use context clues to figure out
- words that have more than one meaning.

Envision It! Words to Know

medals

celebrate

current

continued
drowned
stirred
strokes

READING STREET ONLINE
VOCABULARY ACTIVITIES
www.ReadingStreet.com

Vocabulary Strategy for

Multiple-Meaning Words

Context Clues You may read a word that doesn't make sense in a sentence. The word may have another meaning. For example, *safe* can mean "free from harm" or "a metal box for storing money and valuables."

1. Try the meaning of the word that you know. Does it make sense in the sentence?

2. If not, perhaps the word has another meaning. Read on and look at the words around it to figure out another meaning

3. Try the new meaning in the sentence. Does it make sense?

Read "Learn to Swim" on page 123. Look for words that can have more than one meaning. Use nearby words to figure out a new meaning.

Words to Write Reread "Learn to Swim." Think about another sport or activity you know. Write an article about it, including the rules for safety. Use words from the Words to Know list in your article.

LEARN TO SWIM

Some people swim for exercise, some swim in races, and some swim for fun. But no matter the reason, everyone should learn how to swim. People have **drowned** because they couldn't swim.

The first step is to learn to float, bob, and tread water. Then learn to swim the basic **strokes**—front crawl, backstroke, breaststroke, and sidestroke. These are different ways of moving through the water quickly.

Take your time when you're learning to swim. You're not trying to win **medals** in the Olympics. You do want to coordinate your arms, legs, and breathing.

Even after you know how to swim, never swim where there is no lifeguard. Ocean tides can pull you under, a river's **current** can sweep you away, and weather can cause problems too. One swimmer **continued** to swim after it started to rain. High winds **stirred** up the water. Luckily, a boater helped the swimmer back to shore.

So, **celebrate** the beginning of your life-long swimming adventure. Everyone into the pool!

Your Turn!

Need a Review? For additional help with context clues and multiple-meaning words, see *Words!*

Ready to Try It? Read *America's Champion Swimmer: Gertrude Ederle,* pp. 124–139.

122 | 123

Student Edition pp. 122–123

Reread for Fluency
Appropriate Phrasing

Model fluent reading

Read the first paragraph of "Learn to Swim" aloud, modeling using appropriate phrasing. Tell students that you are using commas and end punctuation to help you know when to pause after reading a phrase.

ROUTINE **Choral Reading**

1 **Select a Passage** Use the first paragraph of "Learn to Swim."

2 **Model** Have students listen as you read with appropriate phrasing.

3 **Guide practice** Have students read along with you.

4 **On their own** For optimal fluency, students should reread three or four times with appropriate phrasing.

Routines Flip Chart

Lesson Vocabulary

celebrate to do something special in honor of a special person or day

continued kept up; kept on going

current a flow or stream of water

drowned died or caused to die under water or other liquid because of lack of air to breathe

medals pieces of metal, like coins, that are given as prizes or rewards

stirred mixed something by moving it around with a spoon or stick

strokes single, complete movements made over and over again

Differentiated Instruction

SI Strategic Intervention
Multiple-meaning words Have students verify the meaning of *current* in a dictionary.

 ELL

English Language Learners
Build Academic Vocabulary
Use the lesson vocabulary pictured on p. 122 to teach the meanings of *medals, continued,* and *current.* Call on students to point to a picture and use its corresponding word in a sentence.

Objectives
- Understand the elements of biography.
- Use text features to preview and predict.
- Set a purpose for reading.

AMERICA'S CHAMPION SWIMMER:

Gertrude Ederle

by David A. Adler
illustrated by Terry Widener

Genre A biography gives facts about a real person's life. Why do you think the author wrote a biography about Gertrude Ederle?

124

Question of the Week
What unique traits does it take to be the first to do something?

125

Student Edition pp. 124–125

Build Background

Discuss accomplishments

Team Talk Have students turn to a partner and discuss the Question of the Week and these questions about accomplishments. Encourage students to answer the questions with appropriate detail.

- What are some accomplishments someone might want to achieve?
- Why might people celebrate someone else's accomplishments?
- What effect might the success of a female athlete have on other females?

Connect to selection

Have students discuss their answers with the class. Possible responses: Someone might set a goal to learn to swim and then do it. If someone achieves a goal, people might celebrate the achievement and others might gain the confidence needed to achieve something on their own. One female's success might open the door for other female athletes.

Prereading Strategies

Genre

A **biography** is a form of literary nonfiction that tells about a real person's life. It is written by another person in 3rd person point of view, using pronouns such as *she*, *he*, and *they*. A biography may cover a person's whole life or only part of it or a single incident. It is different from an autobiography, in which the author uses 1st person point of view and tells about his or her own life, using pronouns such as *I* and *my*.

Preview and predict

Have students read the title of the selection and the names of the author and illustrator. Have them use key words in the title and the illustrations to predict what they think the selection will be about. Then have them tell how this selection will be different than an autobiography.

Set purpose

Have students set their own purposes for reading this selection. To help students set a purpose, ask them to think about the achievements of Gertrude Ederle.

Strategy Response Log

Have students use p. 25 in the *Reader's and Writer's Notebook* to review and use the strategy of questioning.

Small Group Time

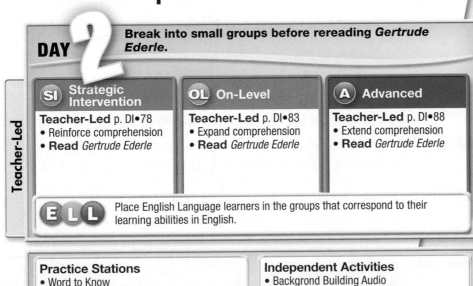

DAY 2

Break into small groups before rereading *Gertrude Ederle.*

Teacher-Led

SI Strategic Intervention	**OL** On-Level	**A** Advanced
Teacher-Led p. DI•78 • Reinforce comprehension • **Read** *Gertrude Ederle*	**Teacher-Led** p. DI•83 • Expand comprehension • **Read** *Gertrude Ederle*	**Teacher-Led** p. DI•88 • Extend comprehension • **Read** *Gertrude Ederle*

ELL Place English Language learners in the groups that correspond to their learning abilities in English.

Practice Stations
• Word to Know
• Get Fluent
• Word Wise

Independent Activities
• Backgrond Building Audio
• *Reader's and Writer's Notebook*
• Research and Inquiry

Differentiated Instruction

 Strategic Intervention

Author's craft Work with students to set a purpose for reading, or if time permits, have students work with partners to set purposes.

 Advanced

Have students learn about the lives of women in the early 1900s. Students should share their findings with the class.

 Multidraft Reading

To assist struggling readers and to deepen reading for all, apply multidraft reading protocols. For each reading, have students set the purpose indicated.

• **First reading** — Literal comprehension: discuss Guide Comprehension questions to monitor and clarify understanding.

• **Second reading** — Application of skills: answer higher-order thinking skills questions to develop deeper understanding of text and make connections to the real world.

ELL

English Language Learners
Build background To build background, review the selection summary in English (*ELL Handbook* p. 139). Use the Retelling Cards to provide visual support for the summary.

Objectives
- Identify facts and opinions to improve comprehension.

In 1906 women were kept out of many clubs and restaurants. In most states they were not allowed to vote. Many people felt a woman's place was in the home.

But Gertrude Ederle's place was in the water.

Gertrude Ederle was born on October 23, 1906. She was the third of six children and was raised in New York City, where she lived in an apartment next to her father's butcher shop. Her family called her Gertie. Most everyone else called her Trudy.

Trudy spent her early years playing on the sidewalks of New York. It wasn't until she was seven that she had her first adventure in the water. While visiting her grandmother in Germany, Trudy fell into a pond and nearly drowned.

After that near disaster, Trudy's father was determined to teach her to swim. For her first lesson, he tied one end of a rope to Trudy's waist and held on to the other end. He put Trudy into a river and told her to paddle like a dog.

Trudy mastered the dog paddle. She joined her older sister Margaret and the other children in the water and copied their strokes. Soon Trudy swam better than any of them.

Student Edition pp. 126–127

Guide Comprehension
Skills and Strategies

Teach fact and opinion

Fact and Opinion Write the following sentences on the board and have students determine which of the statements is a fact and which is an opinion: *Gertrude Ederle was born on October 23, 1906.* (Fact) *Trudy swam better than any of her friends.* (Opinion)

If... students are unable to distinguish between statements of fact and statements of opinion,

then... model guiding students in identifying facts and opinions.

Model the skill

How could I check or verify whether the first sentence is a fact? (look in an encyclopedia or look it up on the Internet) So, the first sentence can be proved true or false. What phrase in the second sentence tells me that this might be an opinion? (better than any) A statement of opinion is someone's judgment, belief, or way of thinking about something. It cannot be proved true or false.

On their own

Have students reread pp. 126–127 to find more statements of fact about Gertrude Ederle. Ask students what conclusions they can draw based on those facts. Have them support their assertions with evidence in the text. For additional practice see the *Let's Practice It! DVD-ROM.*

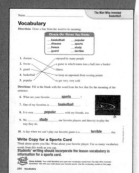

Extend Thinking
Think Critically

⊙ Fact and Opinion • Analysis Find one statement of fact from page 126 and give one statement of opinion. How do you know it is a fact? Why is it an opinion? Possible response: *Gertrude Ederle was born on October 23, 1906* is a fact. It can be proven true or false. *It wasn't fair that women could not vote in 1906* is an opinion. That is the way I feel about something. It cannot be proven true or false.

Higher-order thinking skills

Genre • Evaluation Should you expect this selection to have mostly facts or mostly opinions? Why? Possible response: It will have facts. Biographies are literary nonfiction that tell facts about the events of a person's life. The author may include his opinions as well.

Author's Purpose • Analysis Why do you think the author tells readers that Trudy "nearly drowned"? Possible response: He might have used the words "nearly drowned" to help readers understand that Trudy did not know how to swim at all. It helps readers understand the severity of the situation. It also helps readers understand how significant it is that Trudy later became an accomplished swimmer.

Differentiated Instruction

 **Strategic Intervention**

To aid comprehension, help students locate New York, New Jersey, Paris, Germany, and the English Channel on a world map. Explain that these locations are important in the biography. Have students refer to the map as they read.

ELL

English Language Learners
Activate prior knowledge
Create a word web with "Swimming" in the center hub. Work with students to add words that tell what they know about swimming. We're going to read about how Gertrude Ederle learned to swim. What do you know about swimming? What can happen if you do not know how to swim? What do you do when you swim?

From that summer on, it was hard to keep Trudy out of the water. She *loved* to swim. At the age of thirteen she became a member of the New York Women's Swimming Association and took lessons there.

At fifteen Trudy won her first big race.

The next year, she attempted to be the first woman to swim the more than seventeen miles from lower Manhattan to Sandy Hook, New Jersey. When Trudy slowed down, her sister Margaret yelled, "Get going, lazybones!" And Trudy did. She finished in just over seven hours. And she beat the men's record.

People were beginning to notice Gertrude Ederle. Newspapers described her as courageous, determined, modest, and poised. They called her the most perfect swimmer. Trudy's mother said she was "just a plain home girl."

In 1924 this "plain home girl" was good enough to make the U.S. Olympic team. Trudy won three medals at the games in Paris. Her team won more points than all the other countries' swimming teams combined.

By 1925 Trudy had set twenty-nine U.S. and world records. She was determined to take on the ultimate challenge: the English Channel. Many had tried to swim the more-than-twenty-mile-wide body of cold, rough water that separates England from France. But only five men—and no women—had ever made it all the way across.

Student Edition pp. 128–129

Guide Comprehension
Skills and Strategies

Teach generalize

Review **Generalize** Ask students what generalization they can make about the English Channel after reading p. 129. (Many people fail when trying to swim across the English Channel.

If... students have difficulty making a generalization,
then... model how to recognize generalizations.

Model the skill

What clue word on page 129 helps you recognize a generalization about the English Channel? (many) I can make my own generalization by reading more information in the text. I can generalize that many people fail when trying to swim across the English Channel. What are some details that support my generalization? (The English Channel was the "ultimate challenge." The water is cold and rough. Only five men and no women had ever made it across.)

On their own

Have students make or identify other generalizations from the selection. For additional practice with generalizing, use the *Let's Practice It!* DVD.

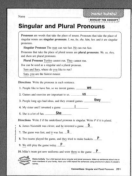

Let's Practice It!
TR DVD•251

Extend Thinking

Higher-order
thinking
skills

Review **Generalize • Evaluation** What are two details that support the generalization that Gertrude Ederle was courageous? Possible response: She attempted and succeeded at being the first woman to swim from lower Manhattan to Sandy Hook, New Jersey. She decided to swim the English Channel even though only five men and no women had ever done it successfully.

Point of View • Synthesis What point of view does the author use in the biography? Possible response: third person How would the point of view be different if the selection was an auto-biography? Why? Possible response: The point of view would be first person if the selection were an autobiography because Gertrude Ederle would be telling her own story. She would use words such as *I* and *we.*

Make Inferences • Synthesis Why did Trudy's sister, Margaret, yell and call her "lazybones" while Trudy swam? Possible response: Margaret probably knew Trudy well. She knew yelling at her and calling her names would motivate Trudy. It may have worked since Trudy beat the men's record for the swim.

Differentiated Instruction

 Strategic Intervention

Vocabulary The first paragraph on p. 129 uses the words *courageous, determined, modest,* and *poised* to describe Trudy. Help students understand the meaning of each word by providing synonyms and examples for each trait.

 Advanced

Fact and Opinion Have students learn more about swimming the English Channel and write down these facts. Then have students write an opinion sentence based on each of the statements they have written.

English Language Learners
Vocabulary Focus students' attention on the term *lazybones* in the last paragraph on p. 128. *Lazybones* is people use when someone is being lazy, not moving quickly, or sleeping a lot. Ask students to describe a time when they felt like a "lazy-bones."

Questioning Read aloud the last paragraph on p. 129. What questions could you ask about this paragraph? Have students share their questions and how they might find the answers.

Objectives

- Use context to distinguish among multiple-meaning words.

Many people were sure Trudy couldn't do it. A newspaper editorial declared that Trudy wouldn't make it and that women must admit they would "remain forever the weaker sex."

It didn't matter to Trudy what people said or wrote. She was going to swim the Channel.

Early in the morning on August 18, 1925, Trudy stepped into the water at Cape Gris-Nez, France, the starting point for the swim. For almost nine hours she fought the strong current. Then, when Trudy had less than seven miles to go, her trainer thought she had swallowed too much water and pulled her, crying, from the sea.

Trudy did not give up her dream. She found a new trainer, and a year later, on Friday, August 6, 1926, she was ready to try again.

Trudy wore a red bathing cap and a two-piece bathing suit and goggles that she and her sister Margaret had designed. To protect her from the icy cold water, Margaret coated Trudy with lanolin and heavy grease. The greasing took a long time—too long for Trudy. "For heaven's sake," she complained. "Let's get started."

130   131

Student Edition pp. 130–131

Guide Comprehension
Skills and Comprehension

Teach multiple-meaning words

⊙ Multiple-Meaning Words Write the following sentence from the selection on the board. *For almost nine hours she fought the strong current.* Have students read the sentence and use context to determine the meaning of the word *current.*

If... students are unable to determine the meaning of the word *current,*
then... model using context to figure out the correct meaning.

Model the skill

I see the word *current.* When I read this word, I think of the meaning "up-to-date," as in current address or current events. Does this meaning make sense in this sentence? (no) It must have a different meaning here. I look at the words around it. What words help me understand the meaning? (Trudy is swimming in water. She is fighting a strong current.) What does *current* mean in this sentence? (the flow of water)

On their own

Have students use context to determine the correct meaning of the word *matter* in the second paragraph on p. 130 (something that is being considered). For additional practice use *Reader's and Writer's Notebook* p. 287.

Reader's and Writer's Notebook, p. 287

Extend Thinking

Higher-order thinking skills

 Multiple-Meaning Words • Analysis What two meanings can you think of for the word *channel?* (a band of frequency on a TV or radio; a wide passage of water) Use context clues to tell the meaning of the word *channel* on page 130, paragraph 2. (When I look for context clues within the sentence, I see the word *swim.* This tells me that the meaning of *channel* in the sentence is a wide passage of water.)

Draw Conclusions • Evaluation What conclusion can you draw from the fact that Trudy found a new trainer after her first trainer pulled her from the sea? What in the text supports your idea? (She was not going to give up. The text says that on Friday, August 6, 1926, she was ready to try again.)

Prior Knowledge • Evaluation • Text to Self Trudy was not able to finish the swim. What effect did this have on her determination to succeed? (It drove her to try again. It did not discourage her.) How might you have responded in a similar situation? (I would have tried again, too.)

Check Predictions Have students look back at the predictions they made earlier and discuss whether they were accurate. Then have students preview the rest of the selection and either adjust their predictions accordingly or make new predictions.

If you want to teach this selection in two sessions, stop here.

Differentiated Instruction

 Strategic Intervention

Fact and opinion Arrange students in small groups, providing a topic for each, such as swimming and coaching. Have students write statements of fact and opinion about their topic. Groups can share their statements. Other groups can decide which statements are fact and which are opinions.

A **Advanced**

Critical thinking Have students discuss Trudy's character traits. Ask them to consider how these traits have helped her achieve success so far in the selection.

English Language Learners
Sentence structure Some sentences on pp. 130–131 have complex sentence structures and may be difficult for students to comprehend. For these sentences, read them aloud with students and paraphrase the content.

Objectives
- Find pertinent information from online sources.
- Spell words sing the suffixes -er, -or, -ess, and -ist.
- Use and understand contractions correctly

Research and Inquiry
Navigate/Search

Teach

Have students generate a plan for gathering relevant information for their biography. Students should search the Internet using their inquiry questions and keywords from Day 1. Explain that students should search for and collect information from multiple sources of oral and written information, including interviews. For example, students might download and listen to an audio file of an interview with their chosen female athlete.

Model

Think Aloud I first searched for Misty May-Treanor. I found her own Web site. I glanced at the site, and I plan on using it for one source. I know I want to include information from an interview, so I searched *interview Misty May-Treanor.* I found several interviews. One of them is an audio file. I will download it and listen to the interview.

Guide practice

Have students continue their review of Web sites they identified. Remind students to differentiate among facts and opinions as they read about their chosen athlete. Tell students to take simple notes about their findings as they conduct their research.

On their own

Have students write down Web addresses, authors, and the dates the Web sites were last updated to create a Works Cited page.

Conventions
Contractions

Teach

Write *we* and *are* on the board. Ask students to name the contraction formed by putting these words together. (we're) Do the same for *did* and *not,* and *should* and *have.*

Guide practice

Have students review something they have written to see if they can replace any words with contractions. Write the contractions named by students.

Daily Fix-It

Use Daily Fix-It numbers 3 and 4 in the right margin.

Connect to oral language

Have students look for and read aloud contractions found in *America's Champion Swimmer.* Ask them to identify the two words from which each contraction is formed. (*wasn't,* p. 127; *couldn't, wouldn't, didn't,* p. 130; *Let's,* p. 131; *it's, didn't,* p. 132; *couldn't,* p. 134)

On their own

For additional practice, use *Reader's and Writer's Notebook* p. 284.

Reader's and Writer's Notebook p. 284

Spelling
Suffixes *-er, -or, -ess, -ist*

Teach

Remind students that their spelling words for this week have the suffixes *-er, -or, -ess,* and *-ist.* Remind students that the suffixes *-er, -or,* and *-ist* often mean someone who is or does something. The suffix *-ess* means "a female who does something." Also remind students that the base may be a word part, a word root, or a word that has had a spelling change, such as doubling the *m* in swimmer.

Reader's and Writer's Notebook p. 285

Guide practice

Have students write each spelling word and underline the suffix.

On their own

For additional practice, use *Reader's and Writer's Notebook* p. 285.

Daily Fix-It

3. The swimmer jump into the pool with a spelash. (*jumps* or *jumped; splash*)
4. A tuter will helped her with some strokes. (*tutor; help*)

ELL

English Language Learners
Conventions To provide students with practice on contractions, use the modified grammar lessons in the *ELL Handbook* and Grammar Jammer online at: www.TexasReadingStreet.com

Writing—Autobiography
Writing Trait: Organization

Introduce the prompt

Remind students that they will be writing an autobiography this week. Review the key features of an autobiography. Remind students that they should think about these features as they plan their writing. Then explain that they will begin the writing process for an autobiography today. Read aloud the writing prompt.

> **Writing Prompt**
>
> Think about your own life and experiences. Now write an autobiography.

Select main topics

 Think Aloud To help choose the main topics for your autobiography, let's think about some of the most important experiences in your life.

Display a story sequence chart, and use it to model planning your writing. I will begin my autobiography by including information about when I was born. I can include details about the time and place. Write information about birth date and birthplace in the first box of the chart. Ask students what other events in someone's life might be good to include in an autobiography. Fill in the chart with their examples. Discuss the details of the examples to generate ideas for an outline and first draft.

Gather information

Remind students that they can do research by looking at journals or talking to family members to help them think of more ideas for their autobiography. Remind them to keep this chart as the students will refer back to it tomorrow as they draft.

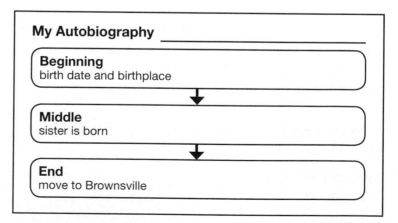

Circulate around the room as students use the chart to choose the main events for their autobiography. Talk briefly with students who are having trouble completing the chart. Ask struggling students to consider what experiences in their life have been most important.

MINI-LESSON

Developing Main Ideas

■ The main topics of your autobiography will be the central ideas of your paragraphs. You can develop these ideas by using a K-W-L chart. I might want to remember more information about my best friend. **On the board, make a K-W-L chart.** In the K column, I write down what I know: *Cassandra was my best friend, and she lived next door.* Fill in the K column of the chart on the board.

■ Now I think about what I want to know to fill in details. I want to know how Cassandra and I first met. So I put that in the W column. **Fill in the W column of the chart.** When I find out, either by remembering or by looking in my journal, I put the information in the L column.

Have students fill out their own K-W-L charts using the form on p. 286 of their *Reader's and Writer's Notebook.* Explain that they will use these charts to add specific details to the paragraphs of their autobiographies.

ROUTINE — Quick Write for Fluency — Team Talk

① **Talk** Students discuss their chosen main events in pairs.

② **Write** Each student writes a paragraph summarizing his or her main events.

③ **Share** Partners read their paragraphs to one another.

Routines Flip Chart

Wrap Up Your Day

✔ Build Concepts What did you learn about Gertrude Ederle?

✔ Fact and Opinion What facts and opinions did the author include in this part of the story?

✔ Questioning What questions might you ask about things you don't understand?

Differentiated Instruction

 Advanced

Reading an autobiography
Have students read a chapter of an autobiography by a well-known figure. Then have them briefly present to the class the events described in the chapter.

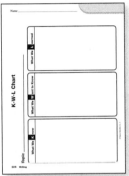

Reader's and Writer's Notebook p. 286

Teacher Tip

Encourage students to ask themselves questions in order to generate ideas for their autobiographies.

 **Preview DAY 3**

Tell students that tomorrow they will read about how Gertrude Ederle makes history.

Objectives
• Expand the weekly concept.
• Develop oral vocabulary.

Today at a Glance

Oral Vocabulary
suspend, accompany

Word Analysis
Suffixes *-er, -or, -ess, -ist*

Comprehension Check/Retelling
Discuss questions

Reading
America's Champion Swimmer: Gertrude Ederle

Thinking Critically
Retelling

Fluency
Appropriate phrasing

Research and Study Skills
Bar graphs

Research and Inquiry
Analyze

Spelling
Suffixes *-er, -or, -ess, -ist*

Conventions
Contractions

Writing
Autobiography

Concept Talk

Question of the Week

❓ What unique traits does it take to be the first to do something?

Expand the concept

Remind students of the Question of the Week. Discuss how the question relates to Gertrude Ederle. Tell students that today they will read about her second attempt to swim the English Channel. Encourage students to think about how Trudy and her sister organize the event.

Anchored Talk

Develop oral vocabulary

Use illustrations and topic sentences to review pp. 126–131 of *Gertrude Ederle*. Discuss the Amazing Words *organize* and *erect*. Add these and other concept-related words to the concept map. Use the following questions to develop students' understanding of the concept. Remind students to ask and answer questions with appropriate detail and to give suggestions based on the ideas of others.

• Trudy *organized* her time and training. Why is it important to *organize* your time when working to achieve a goal?

• To stand *erect* means to stand tall, as if proud. Why would you stand *erect* if you are working to achieve a goal?

Oral Vocabulary
Amazing Words

Amazing Words

ordinary	erect
imagination	suspend
assemble	accompany
magnificent	provision
organize	spectacle

 Amazing Words Oral Vocabulary Routine

Teach Amazing Words

1. **Introduce** Write the word *suspend* on the board. Have students say it with you. Yesterday we read that Trudy had to *suspend* her attempt to swim the English Channel. Have students determine a definition of *suspend*. (To *suspend* is to stop something for a period of time.)

2. **Demonstrate** Have students work in student-led groups to answer questions to demonstrate understanding. Why did Trudy have to *suspend* her attempt to swim the English Channel? (Her trainer thought she had swallowed too much water, so he pulled her from the water.)

3. **Apply** Have students apply their understanding. Have you ever had to *suspend* an activity you were working on? Why? For how long?

See p. OV•1 to teach *accompany*.

Routines Flip Chart

Apply Amazing Words

As students read pp. 132–139 of *Gertrude Ederle,* have them consider how the Amazing Words *suspend* and *accompany* apply to Trudy's accomplishment.

Connect to reading

Explain that today students will read about Trudy's second attempt to swim the English Channel. As they read, students should think about how the Question of the Week, and the Amazing Words *suspend* and *accompany,* apply to her journey.

ELL Expand vocabulary Use the Day 3 instruction on ELL Poster 19 to help students expand vocabulary.

ELL Poster 19

Objectives

- Decode and read words with suffixes.
- Apply knowledge of sound-spellings to decode unknown words when reading.
- Decode and read words in context and independent of context.

Word Analysis
Sort Words

Model word sorting

Write *-er, -or, -ess,* and *-ist* as heads in a four-column chart. Now we are going to sort words. We'll put words with the suffix *-er* in the first column. Words with the suffix *-or* will go in the second column. Words with the suffix *-ess* will go in the third column, and words with the suffix *-ist* will go in the fourth column. I will start. Write *countess* and model how to read it, using the Word Parts Strategy Routine on p. 118a. *Countess* is made up of the word *count* and the suffix *-ess,* so I'll write *countess* in the third column. Model reading *dentist* and *inventor* in the same way.

Guide practice

Use the practice words from the activities on 118a for the word sort. Point to a word. Have students read the word, identify its parts, and tell where it should be written on the chart.

For corrective feedback, model reading the base word and then the suffix.

-er	-or	-ess	-ist
swimmer	inventor	countess	dentist
writer	collector	actress	artist
farmer	sailor	hostess	tourist

Fluent Word Reading

Model

Write *rancher.* I know that *-er* is a suffix. I know the base word *ranch.* I can put the parts together to read *rancher.*

Guide practice

Write the words below. Look for the word parts you know. When I point to the word, we'll read it together. Allow one second per word part previewing time for the first reading.

dancer	editor	duchess	guitarist	visitor	settler

On their own

Have students read the list above three or four times, until they can read one word per second.

Blend and Read

Read words independent of context
Have students turn to p. 45 in *Decodable Practice Reader 3.2* and find the first list of words. Each word in this list has a suffix. Let's decode and read these words. Be sure that students identify the base word and suffix in each word.

Next, have students read the high-frequency words.

Preview Decodable Practice Passage
Have students read the title and preview the story. Tell them that they will read words with suffixes.

Read words in context
Chorally read the story along with the students. Have students identify words in the story that have suffixes. Make sure that students are monitoring their accuracy when they decode words.

Team Talk Pair students and have them take turns reading the story aloud to each other. Monitor students as they read to check for proper pronunciation and appropriate pacing.

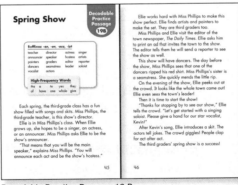

Decodable Practice Passage 19 B

Differentiated Instruction

 Advanced

Suffixes Challenge more advanced students to read words containing both a prefix and a suffix. They should isolate the prefix, then the suffix, and then identify the base word. Next they should blend the syllables in sequence to read the whole word.

Comprehension Check

Have students discuss each question with a partner. Ask several pairs to share their responses.

☑ **Genre • Analysis**

What part of Trudy's life does the biography focus on? How can you tell the selection is a biography and not an autobiography? **Possible response:** The author focuses on Trudy's swimming career, but he also tells about her childhood. The author uses words like *she* and *her* rather than *I* and *me.*

☑ **Fact and opinion • Evaluation**

What conclusion can you draw about Trudy's father from facts presented in the text? How can you support your conclusion? **Possible response:** I can conclude that Trudy's father was a wise man. I know this because of the fact that after Trudy's near disaster, he taught her to swim.

☑ **Questioning • Synthesis**

Why is asking questions a useful strategy when you don't understand something you read? **Possible response:** When I ask questions, I realize what I don't understand. Then I can try to find the answers.

☑ **Multiple-meaning words**

Trudy's mother calls her a "plain home girl." How do you know which meaning of *plain* the author intends? **Possible response:** The author uses *plain* to mean simple and ordinary. I know because of the context. Everyone calls Trudy the "most perfect swimmer," but her mother calls her "plain."

☑ **Connect text to self**

What is a goal you would like to achieve? What can you learn from Trudy? **Possible response:** I would like to run a mile in under seven minutes. Trudy shows me the importance of practice and drive. She kept trying.

Strategy Response Log

INTERACT with TEXT

Have students write questions about Trudy's swimming career in *America's Champion Swimmer: Gertrude Ederle* on p. 25 in the *Reader's and Writer's Notebook.*

Check Retelling

Have students retell *America's Champion Swimmer: Gertrude Ederle,* summarizing information in the text in a logical order.

If... students leave out important details,
then... have students look back through the illustrations in the selection.

Small Group Time

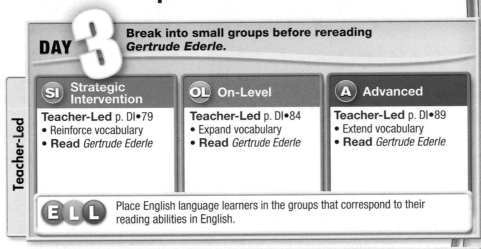

DAY 3

Break into small groups before rereading *Gertrude Ederle.*

Teacher-Led

SI Strategic Intervention

Teacher-Led p. DI•79
• Reinforce vocabulary
• **Read** *Gertrude Ederle*

OL On-Level

Teacher-Led p. DI•84
• Expand vocabulary
• **Read** *Gertrude Ederle*

A Advanced

Teacher-Led p. DI•89
• Extend vocabulary
• **Read** *Gertrude Ederle*

ELL Place English language learners in the groups that correspond to their reading abilities in English.

Practice Stations
• Let's Write
• Get Fluent
• Word Work

Independent Activities
• AudioText: *Gertrude Ederle*
• *Reader's and Writers Notebook*
• Research and Inquiry

English Language Learners
Check retelling To support retelling, review the multilingual summary for *America's Champion Swimmer: Gertrude Ederle* with the appropriate Retelling Cards to scaffold understanding.

Finally, at a little past seven in the morning, she stepped into the water. "Gee, but it's cold," Trudy said.

Trudy's father, her sister Margaret, her trainer, and a few other swimmers were on board a tugboat named *Alsace*. The boat would accompany Trudy to make sure she didn't get lost in the fog and was safe from jellyfish, sharks, and the Channel's powerful currents. There was a second boat, too, with reporters and photographers on board.

As the *Alsace* bobbed up and down in the choppy water, Margaret wrote in chalk on the side of the boat, "This way, Ole Kid." She drew an arrow that pointed to England.

To entertain Trudy, Margaret and some of the others sang American songs, including "The Star-Spangled Banner" and "East Side, West Side." Trudy said the songs kept her "brain and spirit good."

At first the sea was calm.

Trudy swam so fast that her trainer was afraid she would tire herself out. He ordered her to slow down.

Trudy refused.

At about ten-thirty in the morning, Trudy had her first meal. She floated on her back and ate chicken and drank beef broth. A while later, she ate chocolate and chewed on sugar cubes. Then she swam on.

132

133

Student Edition pp. 132–133

Guide Comprehension
Skills and Strategies

Teach questioning

Questioning Tell students that sometimes they might wonder about things as they read. Then they should ask questions to help improve their comprehension. Students might ask questions to anticipate content, clarify confusion, or reflect on what they have learned. Have students read the last sentence of the second paragraph on page 132. Ask what question they might ask.

If... students are unable to ask a good question about important text information,
then... use the model to help them formulate a meaningful question.

Model the strategy

I wonder why reporters and photographers would follow Trudy. Why might the author have told me this information? (The information helps me understand how important the swim was. No woman in history had accomplished Trudy's goal of swimming the English Channel.)

On their own

Have students read pp. 132–133 and ask and answer literal, interpretive, and evaluative questions to seek clarification. Have students support their answers with evidence from the text and make corrections and adjustments as needed.

Extend Thinking
Think Critically

Higher-order thinking skills

 Questioning • Synthesis What other questions might you ask about these pages? See if a partner can help you answer each question. Possible responses: Who sailed on the boat the Alsace? Why was it important for Trudy's family to accompany her? Did having her family there make a difference to Trudy?

Fact and Opinion • Evaluation What is one fact and one opinion from pages 132–133? Fact — Trudy's father, sister, and trainer were on a tugboat. Opinion — The water was cold.

Cause and Effect • Analysis Did Margaret's singing have the effect on Trudy that she hoped for? How do you know? Yes, Trudy kept swimming and said the singing kept her "brain and spirit good."

Differentiated Instruction

A Advanced

Have students find out about *Alsace.* Have them discuss the significance of the ship's name.

Connect to Science

Fog is a cloud touching the ground. It usually forms overnight when the air cools to a temperature near the dew point, and the water vapor in the air condenses into water droplets.

English Language Learners
Questioning Read aloud the second paragraph on p. 132. Model using the questioning strategy to deepen comprehension. There were parts of the paragraph I did not understand. I will ask my questions then reread to find the answer. How many boats were there? There were two. Who was on each boat? Trudy's father, sister, trainer, and other swimmers were on the first boat. Reporters and photographers were on the second boat. What other questions can I ask about the paragraph?

At about one-thirty in the afternoon, it started to rain. A strong wind stirred the water. For a while, Trudy would swim forward a few feet only to be pulled back twice as far.

By six o'clock the tide was stronger. The waves were twenty feet high. The rough water made the people aboard the *Alsace* and the news boat seasick.

Trudy's trainer was sure she couldn't finish the swim. He told her to give up.

"No, no," Trudy yelled over the sound of the waves. She kept swimming.

In the next few hours, the rain and wind became stronger and the sea rougher. At times the rough water pulled the boats away, out of Trudy's sight. She was scared. It was eerie being out there all alone.

Now Trudy began to have trouble kicking in the water. When the *Alsace* came close again, Trudy said her left leg had become stiff. Her trainer was frightened for her. He yelled, "You must come out."

"What for?" Trudy shouted, and kept swimming.

Trudy continued to fight the tide and the constant stinging spray of water in her face. She knew she would either swim the Channel or drown.

As Trudy neared Kingsdown, on the coast of England, she saw thousands of people gathered to greet her. They lit flares to guide her to shore.

At about nine-forty at night, after more than fourteen hours in the water, Trudy's feet touched land. Hundreds of people, fully dressed, waded into the water to greet her. When she reached the shore, her father hugged Trudy and wrapped her in a warm robe.

"I knew if it could be done, it had to be done, and I did it," Trudy said after she got ashore. "All the women of the world will celebrate."

Student Edition pp. 134–135

Guide Comprehension
Skills and Strategies

Teach fact and opinion

◉ **Fact and Opinion** After students have read pp. 134–135, have them list two facts from the pages. Ask them how they would confirm that the facts are true. (Possible responses: The waves were twenty feet high at six o'clock. Thousands of people waited on the shore to greet Trudy.)

If... students have difficulty identifying two facts,
then... model using text clues to identify facts in expository texts.

Model the skill

Does the author include any dates or numbers on these pages? (yes) I see that by six o'clock the waves were twenty feet high. I could check an Internet site to verify this fact. The author also says thousands of people waited to greet Trudy. I could also verify this information by looking in a book or on the Internet.

On their own

Ask students to draw conclusions about the facts they identified and support their assertions with textual information. Then have students reread the two pages and look for two opinions.

Extend Thinking
Think Critically

Higher-order thinking skills

 Fact and Opinion • Evaluation What was Trudy's opinion of her accomplishment? She had succeeded and all women would be proud. What detail from the selection supports the opinion? Trudy said, "All the women of the world will celebrate."

Summarize • Analysis How do you form a summary? Summarize the important points on pages 129–130 in the order they happened. Possible responses: I know that a summary is a way to present the most important information. I can look for topic sentences and important dates as I read. I can make sure I understand what I read, and then put the main ideas together into a summary; Trudy's first attempt to cross the English Channel was on August 18, 1925. She did not make it. She tried again on August 6, 1926 and was successful.

Review **Generalize • Synthesis** What is one generalization you can make about the English Channel? It is a cold, rough body of water that can change very quickly.

Differentiated Instruction

 Strategic Intervention

Advanced questioning Have students work in pairs to reread pp. 134–135, identifying when comprehension breaks down. Have them record questions and reread to find the answer.

Connect to Science

Swimming in a strong current can propel or slow a swimmer. A current has an effect on a swimmer's motion much like a force such as a pull or push.

ELL

English Language Learners
Vocabulary Some vocabulary in the selection may be difficult for students to understand. Explain unfamiliar words and phrases such as *stirred the water, seasick, eerie,* and *stinging spray.*

Trudy swam the Channel in just fourteen hours and thirty-one minutes. She beat the men's record by almost two hours. In newspapers across the world, Trudy's swim was called history-making. Reporters declared that the myth that women are the weaker sex was "shattered and shattered forever."

Trudy sailed home aboard the SS *Berengaria*. After six days at sea, the ship entered New York Harbor.

Two airplanes circled and tipped their wings to greet Trudy. People on boats of all kinds rang their bells and tooted their horns to salute her. Foghorns sounded.

136

Trudy climbed into an open car for a parade up lower Broadway. An estimated two million people, many of them women, stood and cheered. They threw scraps of newspaper, ticker tape, pages torn from telephone books, and rolls of toilet paper.

When her car arrived at the New York city hall, Mayor Jimmy Walker praised Trudy for her courage, grace, and athletic prowess. "American women," he said, "have ever added to the glory of our nation."

Student Edition pp. 136–137

Guide Comprehension
Skills and Strategies

Teach multiple-meaning words

Multiple-Meaning Words Ask students to use context clues to determine the meaning of the word *beat* in the first paragraph on p. 136. (to do better than others in a competition)

If... students are unable to discern the correct meaning,
then... model using context clues to determine meaning.

Model the skill

I know the word *beat* has two meanings. How can I tell which meaning the author intends? (Use context clues.) What words in the sentence and surrounding sentences help me know which meaning the author intends? (The first sentence gives Trudy's time for swimming the Channel. If she beat men's records, I know the author means she had the best record.

On their own

Have students use context clues to determine the meaning of the word *called* in the first paragraph on p. 136. Have students monitor and adjust their comprehension as they figure out the meaning of the word.

Extend Thinking
Think Critically

Higher-order thinking skills

 Multiple-Meaning Words • Analysis The word *record* has multiple meanings. It can be pronounced different ways, too, according to the meaning. Which meaning and pronunciation does the author intend in the first paragraph on page 136? **The author intends for the word *record* to mean "the best done so far," such as the fastest time for completing something. The pronunciation is REHK uhrd.**

Inferring • Synthesis What did Trudy's record-breaking swim prove to people about women athletes? **Possible responses: Women could physically keep up with men. Women could be successful athletes.**

Word Choice • Analysis What effect do the words *rang* and *tooted* have in the last paragraph on page 136? **They help the reader experience the celebration.**

Monitor and Clarify • Analysis Re-read to learn the answer to these questions: Where did Trudy begin the swim? **(France)** Where did she end? **(England)** Where was Trudy's celebration parade? **(New York)** Have students make adjustments and corrections when their understanding breaks down.

SI **Strategic Intervention**

Visualize After students read the first paragraph on p. 137, discuss how visualization can help them understand the events. Students may not be familiar with ticker tape. Explain that ticker tape refers to small pieces of paper, sometimes called confetti.

ELL

English Language Learners
Point out the italicized *Berengaria* on p. 136. Explain that ship titles are written in italics.

President Calvin Coolidge sent a message that was read at the ceremony. He called Trudy "America's Best Girl." And she was. Gertrude Ederle had become a beacon of strength to girls and women everywhere.

138   139

Student Edition pp. 138–139

Guide Comprehension
Skills and Strategies

Teach questioning

⊙ **Questioning** Remind students that they ask questions to help them monitor comprehension and understand what they have read.

If... students have difficulty asking a question,
then... model generating a question about important text information.

Model the strategy

After I finish reading, I ask myself questions to help me understand things I'm not sure of. The text tells me that President Calvin Coolidge sent a message that was read at the ceremony. I wonder why he did that. Possible response: The President wanted Trudy and everyone else to know that he thought this was a very important event.

On their own

Have students ask and answer interpretive and evaluative questions to monitor comprehension and seek clarification. Tell students to support their answers with evidence from the text and make corrections and adjustments as needed.

Extend Thinking
Think Critically

Higher-order thinking skills

 Questioning • Analysis What is an example of a literal question you can ask about the selection? What are some details in the text that support the answer to the question? Possible responses: In what year did Trudy successfully swim the English Channel? (1926) Where was Trudy from? (New York City)

Review **Generalize • Synthesis** Trudy's sister was at more than one race. Based on this, what generalization can you make about her? Possible response: She supports her sister's decision to be a swimmer. She is proud of Trudy. She can help in ways that others cannot.

Comprehension Check

Spiral review

Cause and Effect • Analysis What event caused Trudy to learn to swim? She fell in the water and almost drowned, so her father gave her a swimming lesson.

Important Ideas • Synthesis What are some important facts and details in the selection? Possible response: Trudy Ederle lived in a time when women were not seen as equal to men. She almost drowned but then learned to swim. She beat records and swam in the Olympics. On her second attempt, she swam the English Channel, breaking the previous record. She became a role model for everyone, especially female athletes.

Check Predictions Have students return to the predictions they made earlier and confirm whether they were accurate.

Differentiated Instruction

 Strategic Intervention

Questioning Have students work in pairs to reread pp. 132–139, asking literal, interpretive, and evaluative questions to deepen understanding.

A **Advanced**

Fact and opinion Remind students that when reading a biography, it is important to differentiate between facts and the author's opinion of the person. Have students make a list of important ideas from the selection, separating the author's opinions and factual information.

English Language Learners
Metaphor Point out the phrase "beacon of strength" on p. 139. Guide students in using context to understand the meaning of the metaphor.

Objectives

- Identify facts and opinions to aid comprehension.
- Use the questioning strategy to aid comprehension.

Check Retelling

SUCCESS PREDICTOR

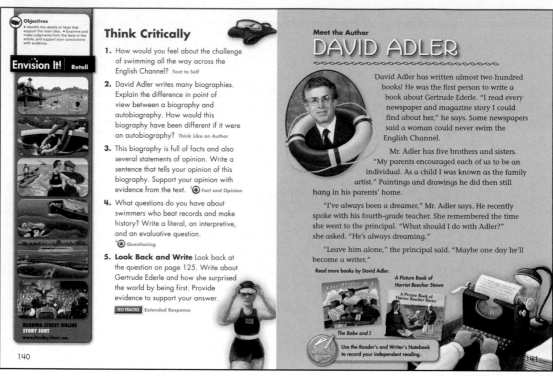

Objectives

- Identify the details or facts that support the main idea. • Examine and make judgments from the facts in the article, and support your conclusions with evidence.

Envision It! Retell

Think Critically

1. How would you feel about the challenge of swimming all the way across the English Channel? **Text to Self**

2. David Adler writes many biographies. Explain the difference in point of view between a biography and autobiography. How would this biography have been different if it were an autobiography? **Think Like an Author**

3. This biography is full of facts and also several statements of opinion. Write a sentence that tells your opinion of this biography. Support your opinion with evidence from the text. **Fact and Opinion**

4. What questions do you have about swimmers who beat records and make history? Write a literal, an interpretive, and an evaluative question. **Questioning**

5. **Look Back and Write** Look back at the question on page 125. Write about Gertrude Ederle and how she surprised the world by being first. Provide evidence to support your answer.

TEST PRACTICE Extended Response

READING STREET ONLINE
STORY SORT
www.ReadingStreet.com

140

Meet the Author
DAVID ADLER

David Adler has written almost two hundred books! He was the first person to write a book about Gertrude Ederle. "I read every newspaper and magazine story I could find about her," he says. Some newspapers said a woman could never swim the English Channel.

Mr. Adler has five brothers and sisters. "My parents encouraged each of us to be an individual. As a child I was known as the family artist." Paintings and drawings he did then still hang in his parents' home.

"I've always been a dreamer," Mr. Adler says. He recently spoke with his fourth-grade teacher. She remembered the time she went to the principal. "What should I do with Adler?" she asked. "He's always dreaming."

"Leave him alone," the principal said. "Maybe one day he'll become a writer."

Read more books by David Adler

The Babe and I

A Picture Book of Harriet Beecher Stowe

Use the Reader's and Writer's Notebook to record your independent reading.

141

Student Edition pp. 140–141

Retelling

Envision It! Have students work in pairs to retell the selection, using the Envision It! Retelling Cards as prompts. Remind students that they should accurately describe the main topic and important ideas and use key vocabulary as they retell. Monitor students' retellings.

Scoring rubric

Top-Score Response A top-score response makes connections beyond the text, describes the main topic and important ideas using accurate information, evaluates facts and opinions, and draws conclusions from the text. For a complete rubric see the *First Stop* book.

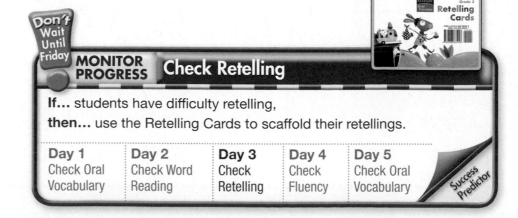

Grade 3
Retelling Cards

Don't Wait Until Friday

MONITOR PROGRESS Check Retelling

If... students have difficulty retelling,

then... use the Retelling Cards to scaffold their retellings.

Day 1	**Day 2**	**Day 3**	**Day 4**	**Day 5**
Check Oral Vocabulary	Check Word Reading	Check Retelling	Check Fluency	Check Oral Vocabulary

Success Predictor

Think Critically

Text to self

1. I like to swim, but I would be scared to swim that far.

Think like an author

2. A biography uses the third-person point of view. An autobiography uses the first-person point of view. If this selection had been written as an autobiography, Trudy would tell her own story.

 Fact and opinion

3. This biography is inspiring to people of all ages and abilities. The text supports my opinion because it is about different ages and stages of Trudy's life.

Questioning

4. Have any swimmers beat Trudy's records? What kind of people are swimmers who try to beat records? Would these swimmers make good role models or heroes?

 Writing on Demand

5. **Look Back and Write** To build writing fluency, assign a 10–15 minute time limit.

Suggest that students use a prewriting strategy, such as brainstorming or using a graphic organizer, to organize their ideas. Remind them to establish a topic sentence and support it with facts, details, or explanations. As students finish, encourage them to reread their responses, revise for organization and support, and proofread for errors in grammar and conventions.

Scoring rubric

> **Top-Score Response** A top-score response uses evidence from the text to tell about how Gertrude Ederle surprised the world by being first.
>
> **A top-score response should include:**
>
> • The English Channel is more than twenty miles wide and is cold and rough.
>
> • Only five men and no women had ever swum all the way across the English Channel.
>
> • Trudy failed on her first attempt to swim the English Channel, but she surprised the world when she succeeded on her second try.

Differentiated Instruction

SI **Strategic Intervention**
Have students work in pairs to find evidence in the text of how Trudy surprised the world.

Meet the Author

Have students read about author David Adler on p. 141. Ask them how he shares his research findings in *America's Champion Swimmer: Gertrude Ederle.*

Independent Reading

After students enter their independent reading information into their Reading Logs, have them paraphrase a portion of the text they have just read. Remind students that when we paraphrase, we express the meaning of a passage, using other words and maintaining logical order.

 ELL

English Language Learners
Retelling Use the Retelling Cards to discuss the selection with students. Give students each a card and then have them organize themselves in the correct sequence and use the cards to retell the selection.

Check Retelling

Success Predictor

Objectives
- Read grade-level text with appropriate phrasing.
- Reread for fluency.
- Explain information displayed graphically.

Model Fluency
Appropriate Phrasing

Model fluent reading

Have students turn to p. 132 of *America's Champion Swimmer: Gertrude Ederle.* Have students follow along as you read this page. Tell them to listen for pauses between phrases. Explain that you will look at the punctuation in the sentences to help you decide when to pause.

Guide practice

Have students follow along as you read the page again. Ask questions to be sure students comprehend the text. Then have them reread the page as a group without you until they read with appropriate phrasing and with no mistakes. Ask questions to be sure students comprehend the text. Continue in the same way on p. 133.

Reread for Fluency

Corrective feedback

If... students are having difficulty reading with the right phrasing, **then...** prompt:

- Are there commas to tell me that a group of words belong together?
- Are there groups of words that should be read together?
- Try to read groups of words, not word-by-word.

ROUTINE **Choral Reading**

1. **Select a passage** For *America's Champion Swimmer: Gertrude Ederle,* use p. 134.
2. **Model** Have students listen as you read p. 134 with appropriate phrasing.
3. **Guide practice** Have students read along with you.
4. **On their own** For optimal fluency, students should reread three or four times with appropriate phrasing.

Routines Flip Chart

Research and Study Skills
Bar Graphs

Teach

Review with students that bar graphs are useful for comparing data. Ask students what kind of texts use graphs. Students may mention textbooks, newspapers, magazines, or almanacs. Show a graph from a content area text and use it to explain the following information:

- A bar graph shows data, or information, in visual form. The title and labels tell what information the graph shows and compares.
- A bar graph uses bars that go up and down (vertical) or bars that go across (horizontal) to compare amounts, groups, or things over a period of time.

Provide small groups of students with examples of bar graphs. Have each group show its bar graph to the class and explain what it shows.

Guide practice

Discuss these questions:

How do you know what information a bar graph shows? (The title and labels tell you what the bar graph is about.)

How do you read a bar graph? (Once you know what information the graph shows, you read each label at the bottom and follow each up the left side of the graph.)

After groups describe their bar graphs, ask specific questions about the data.

On their own

Have students review the instructions and complete p. 288 of the *Reader's and Writer's Notebook*.

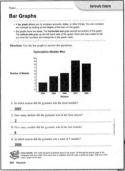

Reader's and Writer's
Notebook p. 288

Objectives

- Analyze data for usefulness
- Understand and correctly use contractions.
- Spell frequently misspelled words correctly.

Research and Inquiry
Analyze

Teach

Tell students that today they will analyze their findings and may need to change the focus of their original inquiry question.

Model

 Now that I've done research, I need to analyze what I've found. I have gathered a lot of facts about Misty May-Treanor, but I need to find additional information. I've also collected a lot of opinions from different authors. I need to make sure I distinguish among the facts and opinions. I now need to narrow my focus. What part of Treanor's life do I want to focus on? I think I will include basic facts about her childhood and focus the biography on her volleyball playing.

Guide practice

Have students analyze their findings. They may need to refocus or narrow their inquiry question. Remind students that sorting their findings into categories can help them see where they lack information.

On their own

Provide categories for students' research, such as *childhood, training,* and *achievements.* Have students organize their notes into the provided categories.

Conventions
Contractions

Review

Remind students that this week they learned about contractions.

- A contraction is a word made by putting two words together.
- When two words are joined in a contraction, an apostrophe shows where letters have been left out.

Daily Fix-It

Use Daily Fix-It numbers 5 and 6 in the right margin.

Connect to oral language

Have the class complete these sentence frames by replacing the underlined words with either the correct contraction or the word parts.

> **I will not swim today.**
>
> **I can't wait to race.**

On their own

For additional support, use the *Let's Practice It! DVD.*

Let's Practice It!
TR DVD•252

Spelling
Suffixes *-er, -or, -ess, -ist*

Frequently misspelled words

The words *who, once,* and *one* are words that students often misspell. These words are difficult because the sound /w/ can be spelled in different ways. Think carefully before you write these words. Have students practice writing these words by writing sentences using each one.

On their own

For additional support, use *Reader's and Writer's Notebook* p. 289.

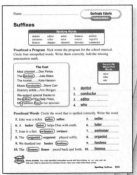

Reader's and Writer's
Notebook p. 289

Daily Fix-It

5. Didnt you learn the backstroke. (*Didn't; backstroke?*)

6. He do the backstroke in races but the crawl is faster. (*does; races,*)

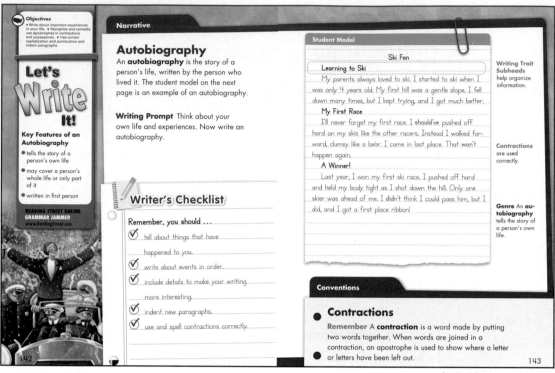

Student Edition pp. 142–143

Let's Write It!
Autobiography

Teach

Use pp. 142–143 in the Student Edition. Direct students to read the key features of autobiography that appear on p. 142. Remind students that they can refer to the information in the Writer's Checklist as they write their own autobiographies.

Read the student model on p. 143. Point out the paragraph organization as well as the first person point of view in the model.

Connect to conventions

Remind students that contractions are formed from two words, using an apostrophe to show where letters are omitted. Point out the correct use of contractions in the model.

Writing—Autobiography
Writing Trait: Organization

Display rubric

Display Scoring Rubric 15 from the *Teacher Resource DVD* and go over the criteria for each trait under each score. Then, using the model in the Student Edition, choose students to explain why the model should score a 4 for one of the traits. If a student offers that the model should score below 4 for a particular trait, the student should offer support for that response. Remind students that this is the rubric that will be used to evaluate the autobiography they write.

Differentiated Instruction

SI Strategic Intervention

Monitor comprehension Ask students to pay attention to any places where they become confused as they read the student model. Then suggest that they reread to help clarify their understanding.

Scoring Rubric: Autobiography

	④	③	②	①
Focus/Ideas	Clear, focused autobiography with many supporting details	Most ideas in autobiography clear and supported	Some ideas in autobiography clear or off-topic	Autobiography with no clarity or development
Organization	Organized logically into paragraphs; follows a clear sequence	Organized logically, with generally strong paragraphs; sequence is fairly clear	Attempt to organize into paragraphs, but not clearly; weak sequence	No apparent organizational pattern in use of paragraphs or sequence
Tone	Engaging; shows writer's feeling about subject	Evident voice connecting with reader	Weak voice	Flat writing with no identifiable voice
Word Choice	Vivid, precise word choice	Accurate word choice	Limited or repetitive word choice	Incorrect or very limited word choice
Sentences	Varied sentences in logical progression	Not as varied; order mostly logical	Too many similar sentences	Many fragments and run-ons
Conventions	Excellent control and accuracy; contractions used correctly	Good control, few errors; contractions mostly used correctly	Weak control; contractions used incorrectly	Serious errors that obscure meaning

Story sequence chart

Have students get out the story sequence chart that they completed yesterday. If their charts are not complete, have them reflect on their own experiences and take notes in order to finish their charts.

Write

You will be using your story sequence chart as you write the paragraphs for the first draft of your autobiography. When you are drafting, don't worry if your autobiography does not sound exactly the way you want it. You will have a chance to revise it tomorrow.

English Language Learners
Professional development
Teachers need "to plan instructional activities that give students opportunities to use the new forms and modes of expression to which they are being exposed." —L. Wong Fillmore and Catherine E. Snow

Objectives
- Write a first draft of an autobiography.
- Organize draft effectively into paragraphs.

Writing, continued
Writing Trait: Organization

MINI-LESSON

Using Paragraphs Effectively

■ **Introduce** Explain that prose writing is organized into paragraphs. Each paragraph should develop one main idea with supporting details. Also point out that writers indent paragraphs to show the transition from one to the next. Display the Drafting Tips to students. Remind them that the focus of drafting is to get their ideas down in an organized way. Then display Writing Transparency 19A.

My First Pet

I wanted pet for a long time. My parents said that I could have one. They asked me what kind of pet I wanted. I am quiet and like to sit by the window. So, I thought Id ask for a cat. My sister is alergic to cat hair. So I asked for a rabbit instead.

At the Pet Store

We went to the pet store to pick out my rabbit. In the cage at the store, there were a bunch of rabbits. They were cute. I picked one out.

The man took it out of the cage and handed it to me. Its fur was nice. He told me how to feed it and take care of it.

Fluffy's New Home

On the way home, my mom asked me what my rabbit's name was. I said its name was Fluffy. Now Fluffy lives with my family and me. I feed Fluffy carrots and rabbit food, and change her water every day. I'm so glad to finally have a pet of my own!

Unit 4. America's Champion Swimmer: Gertrude Ederle   Writing Model **19A**

Writing Transparency 19A

Drafting Tips

✔ Use the sequence of events as they happened to organize your draft.

✔ Write your autobiography in the first person, using the pronoun *I*.

✔ Don't worry about grammar or mechanics while drafting. You can fix any mechanical errors at the proofreading stage.

 Think Aloud I'm going to write the first paragraph of my autobiography, *My First Pet*. I want to get my ideas on paper in an organized way. I won't worry about revising or proofreading, since those steps come later in my writing process. I want to make sure that my paragraphs are each organized around a single main idea.

Have students use the drafting tips to guide them in developing their drafts. Remind them to organize each of their paragraphs around a single main idea.

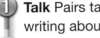 **Quick Write for Fluency** **Team Talk**

1. **Talk** Pairs talk about the important events in their lives that they are writing about.

2. **Write** Each student writes a paragraph about an important event in his or her life, using contractions.

3. **Share** Partners check each other's paragraphs for correct use of contractions.

Routines Flip Chart

Wrap Up Your Day

✔ **Build Concepts** Have students discuss the challenges Gertrude Ederle faced as she swam the English Channel.

✔ **Fact and Opinion** How could you tell that this story really happened?

✔ **Questioning** How did asking questions help you understand the selection?

Differentiated Instruction

 Advanced

Paragraphs Have students read a short magazine article, focusing on the way it uses paragraphs. Ask them to underline the topic sentence of each paragraph.

Academic Vocabulary

A **subhead** labels a section of a piece of writing.

Preview DAY 4

Tell students that tomorrow they will read about a famous Olympian.

Objectives
- Expand the weekly concept.
- Develop oral vocabulary.

Today at a Glance

Oral Vocabulary
provision, spectacle

Word Analysis
Suffixes *-er, -or, -ess, -ist*

21 Century Skills
Online directories

Reading
"Women Athletes"

Let's Learn It!
Fluency: Appropriate phrasing

Vocabulary: Multiple-meaning words

Listening and speaking: Sportscast

Research and Inquiry
Synthesize

Spelling
Suffixes *-er, -or, -ess, -ist*

Conventions
Contractions

Writing
Autobiography

Concept Talk

Question of the Week

❓ What unique traits does it take to be the first to do something?

Expand the concept

Remind students that this week they have read about female firsts. Tell students that today they will read about women athletes while learning how to use an online directory.

Anchored Talk

Develop oral language

Use the illustrations and topic sentences to review pp. 132–139 of *America's Champion Swimmer: Gertrude Ederle.* Discuss the Amazing Words *suspend* and *accompany.* Add these and other concept-related words to the concept map. Use the following questions to develop students' understanding of the concept. Remind students to ask and answer questions with appropriate detail and to build on other students' answers.

- Have you ever had to *suspend* something you were working on? Why might an athlete *suspend* other activities while training?

- Many people accompanied Trudy as she swam the English Channel. When do you need someone to *accompany* you? Why does a coach *accompany* an athlete?

𝓢𝓽𝓻𝓪𝓽𝓮𝓰𝔂 𝓡𝓮𝓼𝓹𝓸𝓷𝓼𝓮 𝓛𝓸𝓰

Have students complete p. 25 in the *Reader's and Writer's Notebook.* Then have students work with a partner to answer their questions.

Oral Vocabulary
Amazing Words

Amazing Words

ordinary	erect
imagination	suspend
assemble	accompany
magnificent	provision
organize	spectacle

Amazing Words — Oral Vocabulary Routine

Teach Amazing Words

1. **Introduce** Write the concept word *provision* on the board. Have students say it aloud with you. During Trudy's second attempt to swim the English Channel, Margaret brought *provisions* for Trudy. Have students determine a definition of *provision*. (A *provision* is something provided to meet a need.)

2. **Demonstrate** Have students answer questions to demonstrate understanding. What *provisions* would you need if you were going on a trip in the desert? (water, food)

3. **Apply** Have students apply their understanding. List *provisions* you might need in different situations, such as *provisions* for an astronaut in space or a mountain climber.

See p. OV•1 to teach *spectacle*.

Routines Flip Chart 00

Apply Amazing Words

As students read "Women Athletes" on pp. 144–147, have them think about *provisions* athletes need and why athletic events are *spectacles.* Encourage students to ask relevant questions about things they don't understand.

Connect to reading

Help students establish a purpose for reading. As they read today's selection about female athletes, have them think about how the Question of the Week and the Amazing Words *provision* and *spectacle* apply to these women.

ELL Produce Oral Language Use the Day 4 instruction on ELL Poster 19 to extend and enrich language.

ELL Poster 19

Objectives

• Identify and read words with prefixes *pre-*, *mid-*, *over-*, *out-*, *bi-*, and *de-*.

• Read words fluently independent of context.

Word Analysis
Prefixes

Review prefixes

To review prefixes *pre-*, *mid-*, *over-*, *out-*, *bi-*, and *de-*, write these words: *preview, midnight, overpriced, outbid, bicycle, deactivate.* We studied words like these last week. What do you know about decoding words with prefixes? (Identify the base word and the prefix. Then combine the two parts to read the word.) Have students read the words. Then review what each prefix means: *pre-*, before; *mid-*, middle; *over-*, too much; *out-*, surpassing; *bi-*, two; *de-*, not, opposite. Use the base word and prefix to figure out what each word means.

Review

(*preview*–"view before," *midnight*–"middle of the night," *overpriced*–"priced too much,"–"*outbid*–"bid higher," *bicycle*–"cycle with two wheels," *deactivate*–"to not activate")

If... students are unable to identify the prefix and figure out what each word means,

then... refer them to Sound-Spelling Cards 150, 151, 156, 159, 160, and 161.

Guide practice

Draw a six-column chart. When I say a word, listen for the prefix. Hold up the number of fingers to tell me which prefix you hear and the column to place the word in: *overdue, outbid, decode, pre-owned, midsummer, bifocal, defuse, prepaid, midstream, overbite, bimonthly, outclass, prerecord, overdid, midweek, outdo, dehumidify, biannual, overjoyed, outdated, prequel, derail, midwest, biped.* Write each word in the appropriate column. Then have students read the words. Ask volunteers to underline the prefix in each word and tell the word's meaning.

1 pre	2 mid	3 over	4 out	5 bi	6 de
pre-owned	midsummer	overdue	outbid	bifocal	decode
prepaid	midstream	overbite	outclass	bimonthly	defuse
prerecord	midweek	overdid	outdo	biannual	dehumidify
prequel	midwest	overjoyed	outdated	biped	derail

On their own

For additional practice, use the *Let's Practice It!* DVD.

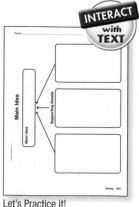

Let's Practice it!
TR DVD • 253

Decodable eBooks

Whole Group

Fluent Word Reading
Spiral Review

Read words independent of context

Display these words. Tell students that they can already decode some words on this list. Explain that they should know other words because they appear often in reading.

Have students read the list three or four times until they can read at the rate of two to three seconds per word.

Word Reading

feet	early	their	scarves	the
disturb	men's	world	workout	watched
have	worm	children	certain	shirts
earth	elves	of	mice	dirty

Corrective feedback

If... students have difficulty reading whole words,
then... have them use sound-by-sound blending for decodable words or chunking for words that have word parts, or have them say and spell high-frequency words.

If... students cannot read fluently at a rate of two to three seconds per word,
then... have pairs practice the list until they can read it fluently.

Differentiated Instruction

SI Strategic Intervention

Prefixes To assist students having difficulty with prefixes, focus on only one prefix at a time. Write words with the prefix *pre-* on separate cards. Have students identify the prefix and the base word and then combine the parts to read the word. Discuss what the prefix means and how it changes the meaning of the word. Repeat using words with the prefixes *mid-, over-, out-, bi-,* and *de-.*

Spiral Review

These activities review

• previously taught high-frequency words *their, watched, have, of, the.*

• irregular plurals; *r*-controlled vowels spelled *ear, or, er, ir, ur.*

ELL

English Language Learners
Fluent word reading Have students listen to a more fluent reader say the words. Then have them repeat the words.

Objectives

- Read words fluently in context.
- Apply knowledge of sound-spellings to decode unknown words when reading.
- Practice fluency with oral rereading.

Read words in context

Display these sentences. Call on individuals to read a sentence. Then randomly point to review words and have students read them. To help you monitor word reading, high-frequency words are underlined and decodable words are italicized.

Sentence Reading

It is too *early* to *disturb* <u>the</u> *children*.
After the *workout*, the *men's feet* were *dirty*.
I'm *certain* there are millions of *mice* in our *world*.
The *elves* <u>have</u> bright red *scarves* to match *their shirts*.
We *watched* the *worm* tunnel into a mound <u>of</u> *earth*.

Corrective feedback

If... students are unable to read an underlined high-frequency word,

then... read the word for them and spell it, having them echo you.

If... students have difficulty reading an italicized decodable word,

then... guide them in using sound-by-sound blending or chunking.

Reread for Fluency

Have students reread the sentences to develop automaticity decoding words.

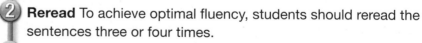

ROUTINE **Oral Rereading**

1. **Read** Have students read all the sentences orally.

2. **Reread** To achieve optimal fluency, students should reread the sentences three or four times.

3. **Corrective Feedback** Listen as students read. Provide corrective feedback regarding their fluency and decoding.

Routines Flip Chart

Decode and Read

Read words independent of context

Have students turn to p. 47 in *Decodable Practice Reader 3.2* and find the first list of words. Each word in this list has a suffix. Let's decode and read these words. Be sure that students identify the base word and suffix in each word.

Next, have students read the high-frequency words.

Preview Decodable Practice Passage

Have students read the title and preview the story. Tell them that they will read words with suffixes.

Read words in context

Chorally read the story along with the students. Have students identify words in the story that have suffixes. Make sure that students are monitoring their accuracy when they decode words.

Team Talk Pair students and have them take turns reading the story aloud to each other. Monitor students as they read to check for proper pronunciation and appropriate pacing.

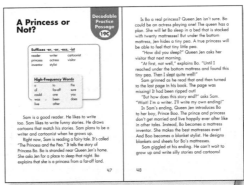

Decodable Practice Passage 19C

Differentiated Instruction

 Advanced

Decodable Words Have students write their own sentences using some of the decodable words found in the sentences on p. 144e.

21st Century Skills
Online Directories

Introduce online directories

Explain to students that technology is all around us. Tell them that online directories are one type of technology we use today. Ask students to share what they already know about online directories, such as what they are and how they work.

Discuss the skill

Discuss with students how the Internet has changed the way we find information. For example, ask: How can you use the Internet to learn about a famous female athlete? (type her name in a search engine) Explain: Before the Internet, available information was more limited. You could read only what was available in the library. Review steps to locate information on the Internet. Then explain that an online directory can help us locate information. An online directory groups Web sites by topics.

On the board, draw a sequence organizer like the one below. Ask the following questions to help students complete the organizer:

• How can you find an online directory? Possible response: search the Internet

• How can an online directory help you find information? Possible response: You type in a keyword and click on links to find Web sites with relevant information.

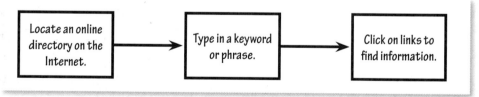

Locate an online directory on the Internet. → Type in a keyword or phrase. → Click on links to find information.

Guide practice

Have students work in pairs to list the benefits of using an online directory when searching for information on the Internet. Ask them to share their lists with the class.

Connect to reading

Tell students that they will now read about using an online directory to locate information about women athletes. Have the class think about times when using an online directory would be helpful.

Small Group Time

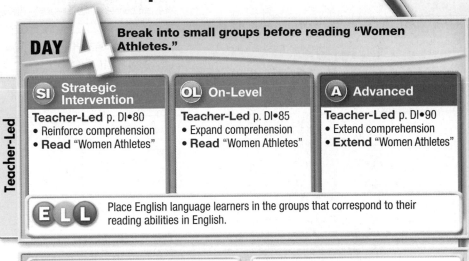

DAY 4 Break into small groups before reading "Women Athletes."

Teacher-Led

(SI) Strategic Intervention
Teacher-Led p. DI•80
- Reinforce comprehension
- **Read** "Women Athletes"

(OL) On-Level
Teacher-Led p. DI•85
- Expand comprehension
- **Read** "Women Athletes"

(A) Advanced
Teacher-Led p. DI•90
- Extend comprehension
- **Extend** "Women Athletes"

ELL Place English language learners in the groups that correspond to their reading abilities in English.

Practice Stations
- Read for Meaning
- Get Fluent
- Words to Know

Independent Activities
- AudioText: "Women Athletes"
- *Reader's and Writer's Notebook*
- Inquiry and Research

Student Edition pp. 144–145

Guide Comprehension
Skills and Strategies

Teach online directories

21st Century Skills: Online Directories Have students preview "Women Athletes" on pp. 144–147. Have them look at the online directory and the steps the user took to reach the article about Wilma Rudolph. Discuss how the design of an online directory makes it easy to navigate. Have students find the list of topics and the list of categories on p. 145. Then ask: Why did the user click on Olympics on the first screen?

If... students are unable to explain why the user clicked on Olympics, **then...** use the model to guide students in using online directories.

Model the skill

Think Aloud An online directory gives different topics. The user is searching for women athletes, so she clicked on Olympics, assuming there would be a link for women athletes within that topic.

On their own

Have students work in pairs to use an online directory to find information about female athletes who have set world records.

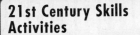
Extend Thinking
Think Critically

Higher-order thinking skills

Draw Conclusions • Evaluation In an online directory, what happens with each click of the mouse? Will there be more or fewer Web sites with each click? Explain your answer. Possible responses: With each click, the results get narrower and more specific. There will be fewer Web sites with each click because as you narrow your search, fewer Web sites will be relevant.

 Questioning • Synthesis What questions should you ask yourself when deciding which link to click on? Possible responses: What information do I want to find? What kinds of Web sites am I likely to find within each link?

Differentiated Instruction

SI Strategic Intervention

Online directories Guide students in navigating the online directory in the Student Edition. Discuss each link and why only certain ones are relevant to the search.

A Advanced

Online directories Have students select another topic from the online directory and list possible Web sites it would contain.

English Language Learners
Evaluating Web sites Remind students that they should evaluate written information for its relevance. Direct students to look at the online directory on p. 145. Ask: Which link would you click if you wanted to find out the score of an important football game? (Sports) When might you click on the link for Health, Technology? (Possible response: when you want to find information about staying healthy or using a computer)

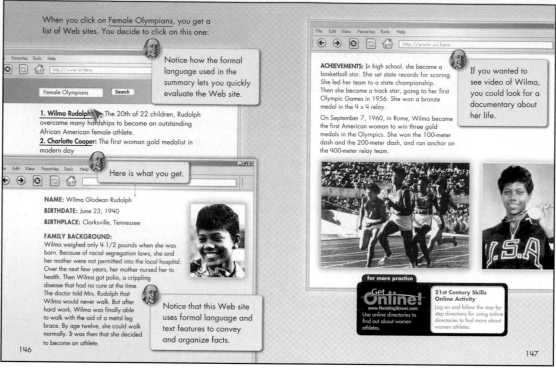

When you click on Female Olympians, you get a list of Web sites. You decide to click on this one:

Notice how the formal language used in the summary lets you quickly evaluate the Web site.

Favorites Tools Help

http://www.url.here

Female Olympians   Search

1. Wilma Rudolph: The 20th of 22 children, Rudolph overcame many hardships to become an outstanding African American female athlete.
2. Charlotte Cooper: The first woman gold medalist in modern day

File Edit View Favorites Tools Help

http://www.url.here

ACHIEVEMENTS: In high school, she became a basketball star. She set state records for scoring. She led her team to a state championship. Then she became a track star, going to her first Olympic Games in 1956. She won a bronze medal in the 4 x 4 relay.

On September 7, 1960, in Rome, Wilma became the first American woman to win three gold medals in the Olympics. She won the 100-meter dash and the 200-meter dash, and ran anchor on the 400-meter relay team.

If you wanted to see video of Wilma, you could look for a documentary about her life.

Edit View Favorites Tools Help

Here is what you get.

NAME: Wilma Glodean Rudolph
BIRTHDATE: June 23, 1940
BIRTHPLACE: Clarksville, Tennessee

FAMILY BACKGROUND:
Wilma weighed only 4 1/2 pounds when she was born. Because of racial segregation laws, she and her mother were not permitted into the local hospital. Over the next few years, her mother nursed her to health. Then Wilma got polio, a crippling disease that had no cure at the time. The doctor told Mrs. Rudolph that Wilma would never walk. But after hard work, Wilma was finally able to walk with the aid of a metal leg brace. By age twelve, she could walk normally. It was then that she decided to become an athlete.

Notice that this Web site uses formal language and text features to convey and organize facts.

for more practice
Get **Online!**
www.ReadingStreet.com
Use online directories to find out about women athletes.

21st Century Skills Online Activity
Log on and follow the step-by-step directions for using online directories to find more about women athletes.

146   147

Student Edition pp. 146–147

Guide Comprehension
Skills and Strategies

Teach online directories

21st Century Skills: Online Directories Remind students that an online directory provides a list to Web sites about a topic. Clicking on a Web site will take you directly to it. Then ask: What other female athlete could the reader have read about?

If... students are unable to identify the other Web site,
then... use the model to guide students in reading the online directory.

Model the skill

Think Aloud When the user clicked on Female Olympians, she got a list of Web sites. I can see Wilma Rudolph. This is the first Web site. The second one I see is Charlotte Cooper. If the user clicked on her name, the online directory would take the user to a Web site about Charlotte Cooper.

On their own

Have students practice using online directories to gain information about other female athletes.

Extend Thinking
Think Critically

Higher-order thinking skills

 Fact and Opinion • Evaluation Does the Web site about Wilma Rudolph provide facts, or opinions? Would you expect most Web sites in this category to give facts, or opinions? Why? **Possible responses:** The Web site presents facts about Rudolph. Most Web sites might include facts, but the authors would likely include opinions as well.

Review **Generalize • Synthesis** What generalization can you make about using an online directory? **Possible response:** Most online directories help you locate information in just a few clicks.

21st Century Skills
Online Directory

For more practice

Show students how to locate the Web site by clicking on the appropriate links. Be sure that they follow the step-by-step directions for using an online directory. Discuss with students how an online directory can help them locate information quickly. Ask students to compare and contrast the language and conventions of an online directory to the language and conventions of a search engine or Web-based news article. Make sure students understand how communication changes when moving from one genre of media to another.

Differentiated Instruction

 Strategic Intervention

Online directories Help students navigate an online directory and a search engine. Show them how they are alike and how they are different.

A **Advanced**

Online directories Have students use an online directory to locate information about Charlotte Cooper.

English Language Learners
Reading a Web site Discuss the Web site shown on pp. 146–147 with students. Discuss each heading and the information it contains. For example, ask: What information would you find in the section called Family Background? (information about Rudolph's childhood)

Objectives

- Read with fluency.
- Distinguish between multiple-meaning words and homographs.
- Deliver a sportscast.

Check Fluency WCPM

SUCCESS PREDICTOR

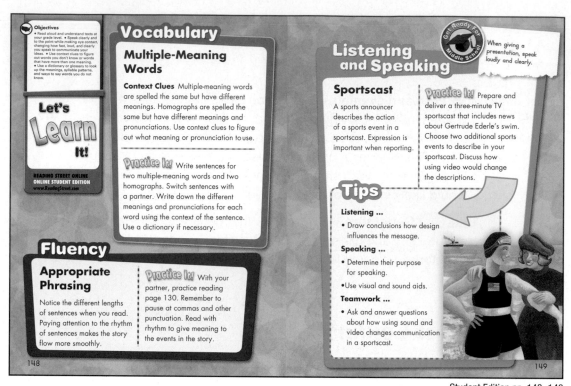

Objectives
Read aloud and understand texts at your grade level. • Speak clearly and to the point while making eye contact, changing how fast, loud, and direct you speak to communicate your ideas. • Use context clues to figure out words you don't know or words that have more than one meaning. • Use a dictionary or glossary to look up the meanings, syllable patterns, and ways to say words you do not know.

Let's Learn It!

READING STREET ONLINE
ONLINE STUDENT EDITION
www.ReadingStreet.com

Vocabulary

Multiple-Meaning Words

Context Clues Multiple-meaning words are spelled the same but have different meanings. Homographs are spelled the same but have different meanings and pronunciations. Use context clues to figure out what meaning or pronunciation to use.

Practice It! Write sentences for two multiple-meaning words and two homographs. Switch sentences with a partner. Write down the different meanings and pronunciations for each word using the context of the sentence. Use a dictionary if necessary.

Fluency

Appropriate Phrasing

Notice the different lengths of sentences when you read. Paying attention to the rhythm of sentences makes the story flow more smoothly.

Practice It! With your partner, practice reading page 130. Remember to pause at commas and other punctuation. Read with rhythm to give meaning to the events in the story.

Listening and Speaking

When giving a presentation, speak loudly and clearly.

Sportscast

A sports announcer describes the action of a sports event in a sportscast. Expression is important when reporting.

Practice It! Prepare and deliver a three-minute TV sportscast that includes news about Gertrude Ederle's swim. Choose two additional sports events to describe in your sportscast. Discuss how using video would change the descriptions.

Tips

Listening ...
- Draw conclusions how design influences the message.

Speaking ...
- Determine their purpose for speaking.
- Use visual and sound aids.

Teamwork ...
- Ask and answer questions about how using sound and video changes communication in a sportscast.

148 / 149

Student Edition pp. 148–149

Fluency
Appropriate Phrasing

Guide practice

Use the Student Edition activity as an assessment tool. Make sure the reading passage is at least 200 words in length. As students read aloud with partners, walk around to make sure their phrasing is appropriate and that they use punctuation as a guide.

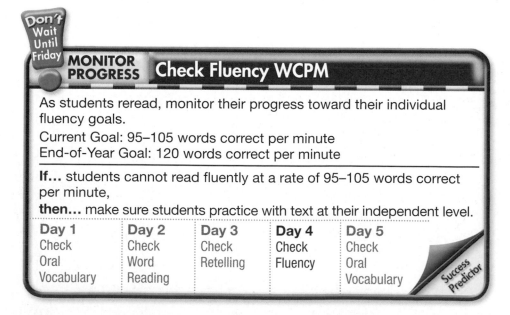

Don't Wait Until Friday

MONITOR PROGRESS — Check Fluency WCPM

As students reread, monitor their progress toward their individual fluency goals.

Current Goal: 95–105 words correct per minute
End-of-Year Goal: 120 words correct per minute

If... students cannot read fluently at a rate of 95–105 words correct per minute,
then... make sure students practice with text at their independent level.

Day 1	Day 2	Day 3	Day 4	Day 5
Check Oral Vocabulary	Check Word Reading	Check Retelling	Check Fluency	Check Oral Vocabulary

Success Predictor

Vocabulary
Multiple-Meaning Words

Teach multiple-meaning words

Context Clues Write the following sentences on the board: *Please close the door. The post office is close to the school.* Have students name the word that appears in each sentence. Point out the different pronunciations. Explain that words that are spelled the same but have two different sounds and meanings are called homographs.

Guide practice

Have students identify the homographs in the following sentences: *The usher will lead you to your seat. Timmy broke the lead on his pencil.*

On their own

Ask students to list and write the meanings of homographs and multiple-meaning words. Have students use a dictionary to copy down the different pronunciations.

Delivering a Sportscast

Remind students that they should be aware of their posture and body language when delivering their sportscast. Additionally, students should use notes or other memory aids to help them deliver their sportscast.

Listening and Speaking
Sportscast

Teach

Tell students that sportscasters often write down what they are going to say. Students should record facts about Gertrude Ederle's historic swim. They should also make notes about the two or more sports they want to talk about.

Guide practice

As students are preparing their sportscast, walk around the room, making sure students are considering the length of their sportscast. Remind students to listen attentively, speak coherently with appropriate rate, volume, enunciation, and conventions of language, and make eye contact with one another.

On their own

Have students practice their sportscast with a partner.

English Language Learners
Practice pronunciation Assist pairs of students by modeling the correct pronunciation of the homographs in the lesson.

Success Predictor

Objectives

- Use a word processing program to prepare a biography.
- Review contractions.
- Correctly spell words with suffixes *-er, -or, -ess,* and *-ist.*

Research and Inquiry
Synthesize

Teach Have students synthesize their research findings and results. Review how to choose relevant information from a number of sources and organize it logically. Students should organize their notes into provided categories about their athlete, such as *childhood, training,* and *achievements.* Suggest that students use a chart to sort their information into categories.

Guide practice Have students use a word processing program to prepare for their presentations on Day 5. Remind them to use a large enough font so that they can read it while standing in front of the class.

On their own Have students continue organizing and combining their research findings as they plan the presentations of their biographies.

Conventions
Contractions

Test practice   Remind students that grammar skills, such as contractions, are often assessed on important tests.

- Contractions are formed by combining two words.
- An apostrophe is used to show where letters have been omitted.

Daily Fix-It   Use Daily Fix-It numbers 7 and 8 in the right margin.

On their own   For additional practice, use *Reader's and Writer's Notebook* p. 290.

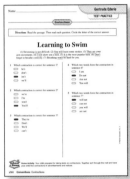

Reader's and Writer's
Notebook p. 290

Spelling
Suffixes *-er, -or, -ess, -ist*

Practice spelling strategy   Supply pairs of students with index cards on which the spelling words have been written. Have one student read a word while the other writes it. Then have students switch roles. Have them use the cards to check their spelling and correct any misspelled words.

On their own   For additional practice, use the *Let's Practice It! DVD*.

Let's Practice It!
TR DVD•254

Daily Fix-It

7. Hurry, or you'll miss you're swiming lesson. (*your; swimming*)

8. Julia and her left really erly. (*she; early*)

Objectives
- Revise draft of an autobiography.
- Apply revising strategy, adding.
- Use vivid, specific details to develop paragraphs.

Writing—Autobiography
Revising Strategy

MINI-LESSON

Revising Strategy: Adding

■ Yesterday we wrote autobiographies about our own lives and experiences. Today we will revise our drafts. The goal is to make your writing clearer, more interesting, and more informative.

■ Display Writing Transparency 19B. Remind students that revising does not include corrections of grammar and mechanics. Tell them that this will be done during the lesson as they proofread their work. Then introduce the revising strategy of adding.

■ When you revise, ask yourself, *What can I add to my draft to make my writing clearer, more interesting, and more vivid?* The revising strategy of adding is the one in which more information is added to help bring your writing to life. Let's look at the first paragraph. This paragraph includes some details, but they are not very specific. Since this is an autobiography, I want to make sure the reader understands the author's personality. I'll need to add some more vivid details here.

Writing Transparency 19B

Revising Tips

✔ Use sensory language and comparisons to make your descriptions more vivid.

✔ Add information to support the central idea and make your writing more detailed.

Tell students that as they revise, they should not only look for places where they might add information to make their descriptions clearer and more vivid, but they should also make sure that each paragraph has a single, clearly stated main idea.

Peer conferencing

Peer Revision Have students work in groups of three on peer revision. Each member of the group should write two questions on the draft of each of the other group members. Ask students to focus on asking questions that will help to make the details in the draft clearer and more vivid.

Have students revise their drafts using their group members' questions from Peer Revision as well as the key features of autobiography to guide them. Be sure that students are using the revising strategy of adding.

Circulate around the room to monitor students and conference with them as they revise. Remind students correcting errors that they will have time to edit tomorrow. They should be working on content and organization today.

Write Guy
Jeff Anderson

Teaching Trait-by-Trait: Focus

In a writing conference, choose one aspect of a student's draft, not many things. This will help the student more than trying to think about multiple writing traits at once. Maybe there is one skill at this student's growing edge of knowledge that I can help him improve. I'd hate to see that lost in a swarm of my other comments.

ROUTINE **Quick Write for Fluency** **Team Talk**

1. **Talk** Pairs discuss what they read about Gertrude Ederle in *America's Champion Swimmer.*

2. **Write** Each student writes a paragraph telling what he or she learned.

3. **Share** Partners read each other's paragraphs and check for paragraph structure and vivid details.

Routines Flip Chart

English Language Learners
Writing: Support revision
Suggest that students read their drafts aloud. Have them identify any places in their draft where they become confused while reading. Then have them revise those places to make their drafts clearer.

Wrap Up Your Day

✔ **Build Concepts** What did you learn about Wilma Rudolph?

✔ **Oral Vocabulary** Monitor students' use of oral vocabulary as they respond: When people assemble for an Olympic event, do they expect something ordinary or something magnificent?

✔ **Text Features** Ask students how graphics helped them understand the selection.

Preview DAY 5

Remind students to think about Wilma Rudolph's unique traits.

Objectives
• Review the weekly concept.
• Review oral vocabulary.

Today at a Glance

Oral Vocabulary

Word Analysis
Suffixes -er, -or, -ess, -ist

Comprehension
◉ Fact and opinion

Lesson Vocabulary
◉ Multiple-meaning words

Assessment
Fluency
Comprehension

Research and Inquiry
Communication

Spelling
Suffixes -er, -or, -ess, -ist

Conventions
Contractions

Writing
Autobiography

Check Oral Vocabulary
SUCCESS PREDICTOR

Concept Wrap Up

Question of the Week

? **What unique traits does it take to be the first to do something?**

Review the concept
Have students look back at the reading selections to find examples that demonstrate being first.

Review Amazing Words
Display and review this week's concept map. Remind students that this week they have learned ten amazing words related to being first. Have students use the Amazing Words and the concept map to answer the question *What unique traits does it take to be the first to do something?*

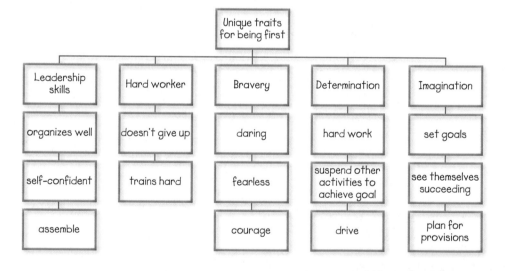

ELL **Check Concepts and Language** Use the Day 5 instruction on ELL Poster 19 to monitor students' understanding of the lesson concept.

ELL Poster 19

Amazing Ideas

Connect to the Big Question

Have pairs of students discuss how the Question of the Week connects to the Big Question: *What does it mean to be unique?* Tell students to use the concept map and what they have learned from this week's Anchored Talks and reading selections to form an Amazing Idea—a realization or "big idea" about being unique. Remind partners to give suggestions that build on each other's ideas. Then ask each pair to share their Amazing Idea with the class.

Amazing Ideas might include these key concepts:

- Someone who is unique does not follow the crowd or try to be like everyone else.
- Being unique is not always easy.
- If you are unique, people like you for who you are.

Write about it

Have students write a few sentences about their Amazing Idea beginning with "This week I learned…"

Amazing Words

ordinary	erect
imagination	suspend
assemble	accompany
magnificent	provision
organize	spectacle

Don't Wait Until Friday

MONITOR PROGRESS | **Check Oral Vocabulary**

Have individuals use this week's Amazing Words to describe a unique person. Monitor students' ability to use the Amazing Words and note which words you need to reteach.

If... students have difficulty using the Amazing Words,
then... reteach using the Oral Vocabulary Routine, pages 117a, 122b, 132b, 144b, OV•2.

Day 1	Day 2	Day 3	Day 4	Day 5
Check Oral Vocabulary	Check Word Reading	Check Retelling	Check Fluency	Check Oral Vocabulary

Success Predictor

ELL

English Language Learners
Concept map Work with students to add new words to the concept map.

Oral Vocabulary **Success Predictor**

Objectives
- Review fact and opinion.
- Review multiple-meaning words.
- Review suffixes *(-er, -or, -ess, -ist).*
- Review word choice.

Comprehension Review
Fact and Opinion

Student Edition p. EI•7

Teach fact and opinion

Review the definitions of statements of fact and statements of opinion on p. 120. Remind students that statements of fact can be correct or incorrect and that statements of opinion can be well supported or poorly supported. For additional support have students review p. EI•7 on fact and opinion.

Guide practice

Have partners identify the facts and opinions and evaluate whether they are well supported or not.
Have student pairs find an example of a statement of opinion in *America's Champion Swimmer: Gertrude Ederle.* Then have pairs tell whether their statement of opinion is well supported and whether their statement of fact is correct.

On their own

For additional practice with fact and opinion, use the *Let's Practice It! DVD.*

Let's Practice It!
TR DVD•255

Vocabulary Review
Multiple-Meaning Words

Teach multiple-meaning words

Remind students to use context to help them distinguish among multiple-meaning words.

Guide practice

Write the following sentence on the board and review how to use context to determine the meaning of the word *end. Cami counted fifty strokes as she swam from one end of the pool to the other.*

On their own

Have students write two sentences for the word *current.* The word should have a different meaning in each sentence. Partners can trade sentences and identify the context clues that help them determine each word's meaning.

Word Analysis Review
Suffixes

Suffixes

Write the following sentences on the board. Have students read each one, first quietly to themselves and then aloud as you track the print.

1. **The violinist watched the conductor.**

2. **The visitor asked the waitress for a special menu.**

3. **The actor and actress were performers in a play.**

4. **The cyclist pedaled after the leader of the group.**

5. **The explorer presented his discoveries to the princess.**

Team Talk Have students discuss with a partner which words have suffixes, and ask them to identify the suffixes. Then call on individuals to share with the class.

Literary Terms Review
Word Choice

Teach

Have students reread pp. 132–133 of *Gertrude Ederle.* Remind students that authors use specific words to communicate meaning.

Guide practice

Point out exact words and phrases on p. 132, such as *powerful currents* and *choppy water.* Discuss how these words help readers form a picture of the setting and events in their mind. Ask students to think about how readers' comprehension might be different without these words and phrases. Have students point out other examples of exact words.

On their own

Have students make a two-column chart with the headings *word choice* and *effect.* Ask them to use the chart to analyze the author's word choice on p. 133.

Objectives
• Read grade-level text with fluency.

Assessment

Check words correct per minute

Fluency Make two copies of the fluency passage on page 149k. As the student reads the text aloud, mark mistakes on your copy. Also mark where the student is at the end of one minute. To figure words correct per minute (WCPM), subtract the number of mistakes from the total number of words read in one minute.

WCPM

Corrective feedback

If... students cannot read fluently at a rate of 95–105 WCPM,
then... make sure they practice with text at their independent reading level. Provide additional fluency practice by pairing nonfluent readers with fluent readers.

If... students already read at 120 WCPM,
then... have them read a book of their choice independently.

Small Group Time

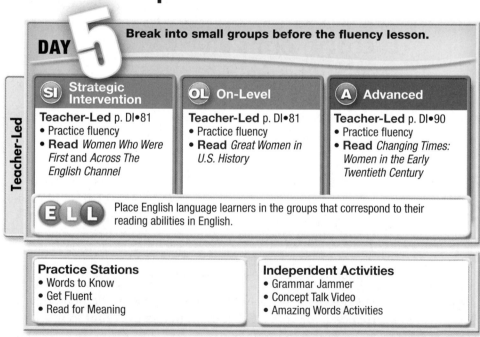

DAY 5 — Break into small groups before the fluency lesson.

Teacher-Led

SI Strategic Intervention	**OL** On-Level	**A** Advanced
Teacher-Led p. DI•81 • Practice fluency • **Read** *Women Who Were First* and *Across The English Channel*	**Teacher-Led** p. DI•81 • Practice fluency • **Read** *Great Women in U.S. History*	**Teacher-Led** p. DI•90 • Practice fluency • **Read** *Changing Times: Women in the Early Twentieth Century*

ELL Place English language learners in the groups that correspond to their reading abilities in English.

Practice Stations
• Words to Know
• Get Fluent
• Read for Meaning

Independent Activities
• Grammar Jammer
• Concept Talk Video
• Amazing Words Activities

Name _____

The Duck Olympics

Henry always dreamed of swimming in the Duck Olympics. He   10
practiced his strokes every day. Sometimes the ocean current was very   21
strong. Once he almost drowned.   26

Jerry was also trying out for the Olympics.   34

"You'll never be able to win because your feet are too small," Jerry   47
told Henry.   49

Henry didn't need to be reminded of his problem.   58

"I'm still going to try," Henry replied.   65

"Why bother? It's a waste of your time," Jerry said.   75

All his life, Henry was always in last place. It was true that his feet   90
were very small for a duck, but why shouldn't he try?   101

Henry's teacher Bert helped Henry improve his strokes.   109

"Keep kicking your feet," he would shout.   116

Henry listened to everything Bert said. Bert had trained many other   127
ducks. One even made it to the Olympics.   135

Henry continued practicing. Another swimmer would have given up   144
a long time ago.   148

When the day of the tryouts came, Henry was nervous. Other ducks   160
had their instructors pushing them too.   166

"On your mark, get ready, swim!" shouted the head duck.   176

Henry moved his feet faster than he ever did before. He zoomed   188
past Jerry and swam straight to the finish line.   197

"You made it to the Olympics!" shouted Bert.   205

Henry quacked for joy.   209

MONITOR PROGRESS • Check Fluency

Assessment

Check fact and opinion

Fact and Opinion Use "Bessie Coleman" on p. 149m to check students' understanding of fact and opinion.

1. Why was it surprising that Bessie became a pilot? Support your conclusion with evidence from the text. She was raised during a time when African American females did not have many opportunities. Flying schools in the United States would not even teach an African American to fly.

2. Is this sentence a fact or an opinion? "She shocked Americans." How do you know it might be a fact or an opinion? It is an opinion. It is the author's feeling or judgment that Bessie's flying shocked Americans. It cannot be proved true or false.

3. Name two facts that you learned about Bessie Coleman from this passage. Bessie was eight years old when the Wright Brothers flew the first airplane. Bessie learned to fly in France.

If... students are unable to answer the comprehension questions, **then...** use the Reteach lesson in the *First Stop* book.

Bessie Colman

When the Wright Brothers invented and flew the first airplane in 1903, Bessie Coleman was eight years old. There wasn't TV or radio then, and poor families like Bessie's probably didn't see a newspaper regularly. So it is likely that Bessie didn't know about the Wright Brothers' success immediately.

But when she did finally hear about it, what did Bessie think? Did she realize that she might fly too someday? That idea may have seemed impossible then.

Bessie came from a large, poor Texas family. Both of her parents had been slaves when they were young. Most of her brothers and sisters still worked in cotton fields.

Bessie was smart. She was good at math. She even went to college for a year. In those days, most African-Americans didn't get that chance. Did Bessie think about flying while she was in college?

During World War I, two of Bessie's brothers were soldiers. In 1919, they told her about women pilots in France. Their stories gave Bessie a goal. She would become a pilot!

Yet in 1919, no American flying school would teach an African-American woman to fly. That didn't stop Bessie. She found a way to get to France, thousands of miles away! There she learned to fly.

When she returned to America, Bessie flew in air shows. She shocked Americans. There was great prejudice against women and African Americans then. At first, many people didn't believe that Bessie was really a pilot. But then they saw her fly!

Objectives

- Communicate inquiry results.
- Administer spelling test.
- Use and understand contractions.

Research and Inquiry
Communicate

Present ideas   Have students share their inquiry results by presenting their information and giving a brief talk on their research.

Listening and speaking   Remind students how to be good speakers and how to communicate effectively with their audience.

- Speak clearly.
- Speak at an appropriate volume and pace.
- Use correct sentence structure.
- Make eye contact with the audience.

Remind students of these tips for being a good listener.

- Wait until the speaker has finished before raising your hand to ask a relevant question or make a comment.
- Be polite, even if you disagree.

Spelling Test
Suffixes -er, -or, -ess, -ist

Spelling test   To administer the spelling test, refer to the directions, words, and sentences on p. 121c.

Conventions
Extra Practice

Teach   Remind students that contractions are formed by combining two words. An apostrophe shows the location of omitted letters.

Guide practice   Have students work in pairs to practice the contractions *he's, they've, wasn't, haven't, should've,* and *could've.* The first partner should say a sentence containing the contraction, and then the second partner should say a different sentence containing the original two words.

Daily Fix-It   Use Daily Fix-It numbers 9 and 10 in the right margin.

On their own   Write these sentences. Have students look back in *America's Champion Swimmer: Gertrude Ederle* to find the correct contractions to fill in the blanks. Remind them that contractions are formed by combining two words. Students should complete the *Let's Practice It! DVD.*

> 1. **Many people thought Trudy _____ swim the English Channel. (couldn't)**
>
> 2. **It _____ matter to Trudy what people said. (didn't)**
>
> 3. **"_____ get started," Trudy said. (Let's)**
>
> 4. **The boat made sure she _____ get lost. (didn't)**
>
> 5. **Trudy's trainer was sure that she _____ finish the swim. (couldn't)**

Daily Fix-It

9. Beths race is next, and her coatch is talking to her. (*Beth's; coach*)

10. The winer will go to the finals in new york. (*winner; New York*)

Let's Practice It!
TR DVD • 256

Objectives
- Proofread revised drafts of auto-biographies, including correct use of contractions.
- Publish and present a final draft.

Writing—Autobiography

Review revising

Remind students that yesterday they revised their autobiographies, paying particular attention to paragraph organization and use of vivid details. Today they will proofread their compositions.

MINI-LESSON

Proofread for Contractions

◼ **Teach** When we proofread, we look closely at our work, searching for errors in mechanics such as spelling, capitalization, punctuation, and grammar. Today we will focus on contractions.

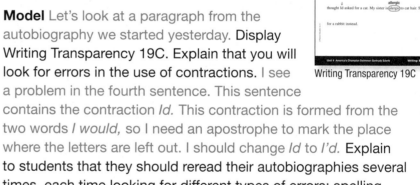

Writing Transparency 19C

◼ **Model** Let's look at a paragraph from the autobiography we started yesterday. Display Writing Transparency 19C. Explain that you will look for errors in the use of contractions. I see a problem in the fourth sentence. This sentence contains the contraction *Id*. This contraction is formed from the two words *I would,* so I need an apostrophe to mark the place where the letters are left out. I should change *Id* to *I'd*. Explain to students that they should reread their autobiographies several times, each time looking for different types of errors: spelling, punctuation, capitalization, and grammar.

Proofread

Display the Proofreading Tips. Ask students to proofread their compositions, using the Proofreading Tips and paying particular attention to contractions. Circulate around the room answering students' questions. When students have finished editing their own work, have pairs proofread one another's autobiography.

Proofreading Tips

✔ Be sure that all contractions are used correctly.
✔ Check for correct spelling, capitalization, punctuation, and grammar.
✔ Use correct indentation when beginning new paragraphs in your autobiography.

Present Have students incorporate revisions and proof–reading edits into their autobiography to create a final draft.

Give students two options for presenting: an oral presentation to the class or a bound pamphlet. For oral presentations, encourage students to use gestures to act out the events that they are describing. Students creating bound pamphlets should find or make appropriate illustrations for their autobiography as well as a cover page. When students have finished, have each student complete a self-evaluation form.

ROUTINE — Quick Write for Fluency — Team Talk

1. **Talk** Pairs discuss what they learned about writing about their own experiences this week.

2. **Write** Each partner writes a few sentences summarizing what they learned.

3. **Share** Each partner reads the sentences to the other.

Routines Flip Chart

Teacher Note

Student self-evaluation Make copies of the Self-Evaluation form from the *Let's Practice It! DVD* and hand out to students.

ELL

English Language Learners
Poster preview
Prepare students for next week by using Week 5, ELL Poster 20. Read the Poster Talk-Through to introduce the concept and vocabulary. Ask students to identify and describe objects and actions in the art.

Selection summary Send home the summary of *Fly, Eagle, Fly!: An African Tale,* in English and students' home languages, if available. Students can read the summary with family members.

Preview NEXT WEEK

What behaviors are unique for different animals? Tell students that next week they will be reading about an eagle that thinks it is a chicken.

Weekly Assessment

Use pp. 109–114 of *Weekly Tests* to check:

✔ **Phonics** Suffixes (-er, -or, -ess, -ist)

✔ **Comprehension Skill** Fact and Opinion

✔ **Lesson Vocabulary**

✔ Review **Comprehension Skill** Generalize

celebrate	medals
continued	stirred
current	strokes
drowned	

Weekly Tests

A

Advanced

OL

On-Level

SI

Strategic Intervention

Differentiated Assessment

Use pp. 109–114 of *Fresh Reads for Fluency and Comprehension* to check:

✔  **Comprehension Skill** Fact and Opinion

✔ Review **Comprehension Skill** Generalize

✔ **Fluency** Words Correct Per Minute

Fresh Reads for Fluency and Comprehension

Managing Assessment

Use *Assessment Handbook* for:

✔ **Weekly Assessment Blackline Masters for Monitoring Progress**

✔ **Observation Checklists**

✔ **Record-Keeping Forms**

✔ **Portfolio Assessment**

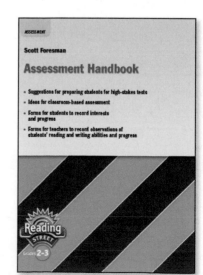

Assessment Handbook

Teacher Notes

Pacing Small Group Instruction

15–20 min

5-Day Plan

DAY 1	• Reinforce the concept • Read Leveled Readers Concept Literacy Below Level
DAY 2	• ◉ Fact and Opinion • ◉ Questioning • Read Student Edition pp. 124–131
DAY 3	• ◉ Multiple-Meaning Words • Read Student Edition pp. 132–139
DAY 4	• Practice Retelling • Read Student Edition pp. 144–147
DAY 5	• Reread for fluency • Reread Leveled Readers

3- or 4-Day Plan

DAY 1	• Reinforce the concept • Read Leveled Readers • ◉ Fact and Opinion • ◉ Questioning • Read Student Edition pp. 124–131
DAY 2	• ◉ Multiple-Meaning Words • Read Student Edition pp. 132–139
DAY 3	• Practice Retelling • Read Student Edition pp. 144–147
DAY 4	• Reread for fluency • Reread Leveled Readers

3-Day Plan: Eliminate the shaded box.

SI *Strategic Intervention*

DAY 1

Build Background

■ **Reinforce the Concept** Reinforce the weekly question *What unique traits does it take to be the first to do something?* People overcome many challenges in order to be the first to do something. One example of someone who was "first" at something was George Washington, the first president of the United States. Discuss the words on the concept map on p. 117. This week we are going to learn about "firsts" that American women have accomplished. Who were some American women who were the first to do something? *(Students may mention female athletes, astronauts, or politicians.)* What qualities would a person have in order to be the first to do something? *(Students may mention bravery, independence, and willingness to work hard.)*

Preview Decodable Practice Reader 19A

■ **Before Reading** Review the words on p. 25 of Decodable Practice Reader 19A. Then have students blend these words from the text: *discuss, blurted, silent, canvases, admire, whistle, sleek,* and *eager.* Be sure students understand the meaning of such words as *sleek* and *eager.* Guide students through the text by doing a picture walk.

Objectives
• Participate in teacher-led discussions by answering questions with appropriate detail.

Concept Literacy Reader

- **Read** *Women Who Were First!*

- **Before Reading** Preview the book with students, focusing on key concepts and vocabulary. Then have them set a purpose for reading.

- **During Reading** Read the first two pages aloud while students track along with the print. Then have students finish reading the book with a partner.

- **After Reading** After students finish reading, ask: What kinds of jobs did these women have? *(judge, pilot, astronaut, athlete, explorer)*

Below-Level Reader

- **Read** *Across the English Channel*

- **Before Reading** Have students use the illustrations to preview the book. Then have students set a purpose for reading.

- **During Reading** Read pp. 3–5 aloud. Then do a choral reading of pp. 6–9. If students are able, have them read and discuss the remainder of the book with a partner. Ask: What conditions does a swimmer face in the English Channel? *(strong currents; strong winds; rough, cold waters)*

- **After Reading** Ask students to look at and discuss the concept map. Connect the Below-Level Reader to the weekly question *What unique traits does it take to be the first to do something?* What kind of person is able to swim the English Channel? *(He or she must be strong and able to swim for many hours at a time.)*

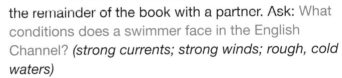
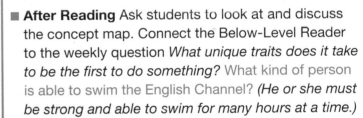

MONITOR PROGRESS

If... students have difficulty reading the selection with a partner,

then... have them follow along as they listen to the Leveled Readers DVD-ROM.

If... students have trouble understanding why it is an accomplishment to swim the English Channel,

then... reread pp. 3–4 and discuss where the Channel is and how wide it is.

Objectives
- Participate in teacher-led discussions by answering questions with appropriate detail.

SI Strategic Intervention

Reinforce Comprehension

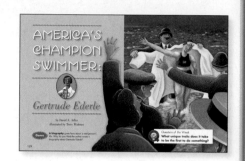

Skill Fact and Opinion Review with students the *Envision It! Skill* material on fact and opinion. Then use p. 120 to review the definitions of fact and opinion. A statement of fact can be proved to be true or false. A statement of opinion tells someone's beliefs.

Strategy Questioning Review the definition of questioning. Remind students to ask themselves questions about people, places, and events as they read. For additional support, refer students to *Envision It! Strategy* p. EI•23.

Read *America's Champion Swimmer: Gertrude Ederle* on pp. 124–131. As students read, have them apply the comprehension skill and the comprehension strategy to the biography.

- Why did Trudy's father teach her to swim? *(She nearly drowned because she didn't know how to swim, so he wanted to keep her safe.)*

- What is the sentence "Gertrude Ederle almost drowned"—a statement of fact or opinion? *(fact)*

- What is the sentence "Swimming is the best exercise"—a statement of fact or opinion? *(opinion)*

- What is the sentence "Basketball is more fun than tennis"? *(opinion)*

- What clue words help you identify the opinions in the last two statements? *(best, more fun than)*

- What is the sentence "The English Channel separates France and England"— fact or opinion? *(fact)* What makes it a fact? *(It can be proved to be true or false.)*

Use the During Reading Differentiated Instruction for additional support for struggling readers.

MONITOR PROGRESS

If... students have difficulty reading along with the group,
then... have them follow along as they listen to the AudioText.

Objectives
- Draw conclusions from facts presented in text.
- Support assertions with textual evidence.

 **Strategic Intervention**

DAY 3

Reinforce Vocabulary

Reread for Fluency Use Decodable Practice Reader 19A.

Decoding Multisyllabic Words Write *reporter* on the board and model how to use meaningful parts to read it. First, I cover the suffix and read the base word: *re port, report.* Then I blend the base word and the suffix to read the whole word: *report er, reporter.* The suffix *-er* means "someone who does something," so *reporter* means "someone who reports."

Use the Multisyllabic Word routine on p. 2 of *Routines Flip Chart* to help students read these other words from the biography: *photographer, determined, editorial, lanolin, foghorns,* and *athletic.*

Multiple-Meaning Words/Context Clues Write the word *current* on the board. I know the word *current* can mean "up to date," as in "I want the current issue of this magazine, not the old issues." However, in the dictionary, I see that another of the definitions is "something that flows, such as a river or another body of water." That definition makes sense with the words and sentences around *current* on p. 130.

Read *America's Champion Swimmer: Gertrude Ederle* on pp. 132–139. Review *Words!* on pp. W•7 and W•10. Encourage students to use context clues to figure out the meaning of any multiple-meaning words. Ask: Which definition of the word *stroke* makes more sense in the biography: "a movement of the arms and legs while swimming" or "a mark made by a pencil or pen"? *(The biography is of a famous swimmer, so the first definition about swimming makes sense.)*

Use the During Reading Differentiated Instruction for additional support for struggling readers.

MONITOR PROGRESS

If... students have difficulty reading along with the group,

then... have them follow along as they listen to the AudioText.

Objectives
• Use context to distinguish among multiple meaning words.
• Use context to determine the relevant meaning of unfamiliar words.

 **Strategic Intervention**

Practice Retelling

■ **Retell** Guide students in using the Retelling Cards to list events in Gertrude Ederle's life in order.

- Who is this biography about? *(Gertrude Ederle)*

- Why is this person famous? *(She made a record-breaking swim.)*

If students struggle, model a fluent retelling.

■ **Before Reading** "Women Athletes" on pp. 144–147, read aloud the genre information about online directories on p. 144. An online directory is like a table of contents or an index. It can help you find information about a topic. This selection will explain a search for information about women athletes.

Read the rest of the panel. Then have students find the cursor on each reproduced computer screen and read the name of the link that was chosen.

■ **During Reading** Have students perform a choral reading of the selection. When you get to the article about Wilma Rudolph, point out the subheads. Subheads can help you locate specific information quickly. What are the subheads in this article? *(They are* Name, Birthdate, Birthplace, Family Background, *and* Achievements.*)*

■ **After Reading** Have students share their reactions to the selection. Then guide them through the Reading Across Texts and Writing Across Texts activities, prompting if necessary.

- Who are these two women athletes? *(Gertrude Ederle and Wilma Rudolph)*

- What did each woman accomplish? *(Both became famous, successful athletes at a time when few women played sports.)*

- How are they alike? How are they different? *(Both won medals at the Olympics. One was a swimmer; the other was a track star.)*

MONITOR PROGRESS

If... students have difficulty reading along with the group,
then... have them follow along as they listen to the AudioText.

Objectives
- Understand how communication changes when moving from one genre of media to another.

Concept Literacy Reader

■ **Model** Model the fluency skill of appropriate phrasing for students. Ask students to listen carefully as you read aloud the first two pages of *Women Who Were First!* Have students note the difference between grouping together words in a way that makes sense and reading in a word-by-word manner.

Women Who Were First!

■ **Fluency Routine**

1. Have students reread passages from *Women Who Were First!* with a partner.

2. For optimal fluency, students should reread three to four times.

3. As students read, monitor fluency and provide corrective feedback. Have students note the grouping of your words and the rise and fall of your voice.

See *Routines Flip Chart* for more help with fluency.

■ **Retell** Have students retell *Women Who Were First!* Prompt students as necessary.

Below-Level Reader

■ **Model** Ask students to listen carefully as you read aloud the first two pages of *Across the English Channel,* emphasizing appropriate phrasing.

Across the English Channel

■ **Fluency Routine**

1. Have students reread passages from *Across the English Channel* with a partner or individually.

2. For optimal fluency, students should reread three to four times.

3. As students read, monitor fluency and provide corrective feedback. Discuss how stressing important words creates a more natural rhythm.

See *Routines Flip Chart* for more help with fluency.

■ **Retell** For additional practice, have students retell *Across the English Channel* page by page, using the illustrations. Prompt students' retellings as necessary with questions:

- What are the challenges of swimming across the English Channel?

- What did you learn about the English Channel from reading this book?

MONITOR PROGRESS

If... students have difficulty reading fluently,

then... provide additional fluency practice by pairing nonfluent readers with fluent ones.

Objectives
- Read aloud grade-level appropriate text with fluency.

Small Group Time

5-Day Plan

DAY 1	• Expand the concept • Read On-Level Reader
DAY 2	• Fact and Opinion • Questioning • Read Student Edition pp. 124–131
DAY 3	• Multiple-Meaning Words • Read Student Edition pp. 132–139
DAY 4	• Practice Retelling • Read Student Edition pp. 144–147
DAY 5	• Reread for fluency • Reread On-Level Reader

3- or 4-Day Plan

DAY 1	• Expand the concept • Read On-Level Reader • Fact and Opinion • Questioning • Read Student Edition pp. 124–131
DAY 2	• Multiple-Meaning Words • Read Student Edition pp. 132–139
DAY 3	• Practice Retelling • Read Student Edition pp. 144–147
DAY 4	• Reread for fluency • Reread On-Level Reader

3-Day Plan: Eliminate the shaded box.

OL On-Level — DAY 1

Build Background

■ **Expand the Concept** Connect to the weekly question *What unique traits does it take to be the first to do something?* Then expand the concept. A person who becomes the first to accomplish something has special qualities. He or she probably doesn't listen to people who say "It can't be done" or "You'll never do that." Discuss the meaning of the words on the concept map on p. 117.

On-Level Reader

Great Women in U.S. History

■ **Before Reading** *Great Women in U.S. History,* have students preview the book by looking at the title, cover, and pictures.

• What is the topic of this book? *(the achievements of American women)*

• Why is it important to learn about women's successes? *(People used to think that many jobs and careers were for men only.)*

Have students create a three-column chart with the headings *Name, Reason for Fame,* and *Date.* Explain that students will complete their three-column charts as they read.

■ **During Reading** Read aloud the first three pages of the book as students follow along. Then have them finish reading the book on their own. Remind students to add names, accomplishments, and dates and events to their three-column charts as they read. Ask: What qualities or characteristics did these women have to have in order to be first at something? *(They worked hard and had persistent, determined attitudes.)*

■ **After Reading** Have partners compare their three-column charts.

• Which woman did you most enjoy reading about? Why? *(Encourage students to support their choices by using evidence from the text.)*

• How does the topic relate to the weekly question *What unique traits does it take to be the first to do something? (The women described in the text were intelligent and worked hard. As a result, they accomplished many "firsts.")*

Objectives
• Participate in teacher-led discussions by answering questions with appropriate detail.

 On-Level

DAY 2

Expand Comprehension

◉ **Skill Fact and Opinion** Use p. 120 to review the definitions of fact and opinion. For additional review, see Fact and Opinion in *Envision It! Skill.* I will look for clue words that signal opinions, such as *believed, felt, must, should, most,* and *best.*

◉ **Strategy Questioning** Review the definition of questioning, and encourage students to ask questions as they read. For additional support, use the Extend Thinking questions during reading or refer students to p. EI•23 of *Envision It! Strategy.*

Read *America's Champion Swimmer: Gertrude Ederle* on pp. 124–131. As students read, have them look for facts and opinions.

- On p. 129, what opinions do people give about Gertrude Ederle? *(Newspaper reporters say she is brave and skilled. Her mother says she is ordinary and not a show-off.)* What clue word do you notice? *(most)*

- On p. 129, what facts does the author give about Gertrude Ederle? *(She won three medals at the Olympics, and her team outscored all the other teams.)*

Objectives
- Draw conclusions from facts presented in text.
- Support assertions with textual evidence.

America's Champion Swimmer: Gertrude Ederle **DI•83**

OL On-Level DAY 3

Expand Vocabulary

◉ Multiple-Meaning Words/Context Clues
Remind students that they can use context clues (the words and phrases around a word) to help them figure out the meaning of a particular word in a text. The selection we are reading has some terms related to swimming, and those may at first be unfamiliar and hard to understand. As I read, I will think about context clues when I notice words that have more than one meaning. The context clues will help me understand which meaning is the right one for this biography.

Read *America's Champion Swimmer: Gertrude Ederle* on pp. 132–139. Encourage students to look for multiple-meaning words throughout the selection and to use context clues if they are available.

- What are some different meanings of the word *channel?* *("pathway of information," as in TV channel; "pathway of water")*

- Where does *channel* appear in this biography? *(in references to the English Channel)*

- Based on the words and sentences around *channel,* what does the word mean in this biography? *("pathway of water")* Have students refer to a dictionary if necessary.

- In the sentence "She beat the men's record by almost two hours," does *beat* mean *hit* or *stirred* or *defeated? (defeated)* How do you know? *(Substituting each of those words into the sentence results in only one sentence that makes sense—she defeated the men's record.)*

Objectives
- Use context to distinguish among multiple meaning words.
- Use context to determine the relevant meaning of unfamiliar words.

OL On-Level

DAY 4

Practice Retelling

■ **Retell** To assess students' comprehension, use the Retelling Cards. Monitor retelling and prompt students as needed.

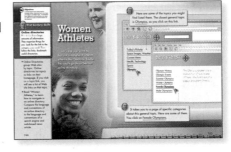

■ **Before Reading** "Women Athletes" on pp. 144–147, read aloud the genre information about online directories on p. 144. Explain that online directories can help students find information for research papers. Have students preview "Women Athletes" and set a purpose for reading. Ask:

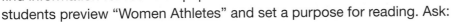

- What features do you see that are different from stories you have read? *(Students should point out the topics and headings.)*

- Why are some words in red type? *(so the reader can easily find important or interesting parts)*

■ **During Reading** Have students read along with you while tracking the print.

- How is an online directory organized? *(in broad topics and specific categories)*

- How is this online information similar to and different from a biography? *(The online information is briefer and lacks a beginning, middle, and end.)*

■ **After Reading** Have students share their reaction to "Women Athletes." Then have them write a paragraph comparing and contrasting Wilma Rudolph and Gertrude Ederle.

Objectives
- Understand how communication changes when moving from one genre of media to another.

On-Level DAY **5**

On-Level Reader

■ **Model** Read aloud p. 3 of the On-Level Reader *Great Women in U.S. History,* emphasizing appropriate phrasing. If you wish, read a few more sentences in a word-by-word fashion, without grouping words logically, to show how difficult it is to understand text that is not read with appropriate phrasing.

Great Women in U.S. History

■ **Fluency Routine**

1. Have students reread passages from *Great Women in U.S. History* with a partner.

2. For optimal fluency, students should reread passages three to four times.

3. As students read, monitor fluency and provide corrective feedback. Have students note the grouping of words into phrases and the rise and fall of the reader's voice. Then discuss how reading with a natural rhythm is much more pleasing than reading word by word.

See *Routines Flip Chart* for more help with fluency.

■ **Retell** For additional practice, have students use headings and photographs as a guide to retell *Great Women in U.S. History.* Prompt students as necessary.

• Who are the three women that the book describes? *(Babe Didrikson Zaharias, Amelia Earhart, and Eleanor Roosevelt)*

• Why do people still remember them today? *(Babe Didrikson Zaharias was a fantastic athlete. Amelia Earhart flew planes, which was even more dangerous then than it is now. Eleanor Roosevelt was successful in politics.)*

Objectives
• Read aloud grade-level appropriate text with fluency.

Build Background

- **Extend the Concept** Extend the weekly question *What unique traits does it take to be the first to do something?* What qualities must someone have to be the first to do something? *(be independent, ignore doubters)* How might those qualities be positive or negative? *(often positive, but can be negative if person cares only about winning)*

Advanced Reader

- **Before Reading** *Changing Times: Women in the Early Twentieth Century,* have students look at the illustrations in the book and use them to predict what will happen in the text. After that, help students set a purpose for reading.

- **During Reading** Have students read the Advanced Reader independently. How was life different for women in the early 1900s? *(Fewer women worked outside the home. At that time, women did not even have the same rights that men had.)*

- **After Reading** Have students review the concept map and explain how *Changing Times* helps students answer the weekly question *What unique traits does it take to be the first to do something?* Prompt as necessary. Of the "firsts" that you read about in this book, which one interested you the most? Why? *(Students should use information from the text to support their answers.)*

- **Creative Thinking** Challenge students to reflect on what they learned.

  - What risks did the women in the book take by being first? In your opinion, were the risks worth it?

  - How might the world be different today if women did not have the right to vote?

  - What accomplishments do you think women will achieve in this century?

- **Now Try This** Assign "Now Try This" at the end of the Advanced Reader.

Changing Times: Women in the Early Twentieth Century

Pacing Small Group Instruction

5-Day Plan

DAY 1	• Extend the concept • Advanced Reader
DAY 2	• Fact and Opinion • Questioning • Read Student Edition pp. 124–131
DAY 3	• Multiple-Meaning Words • Read Student Edition pp. 132–139
DAY 4	• Literary Nonfiction: Biography • Read Student Edition pp. 144–147
DAY 5	• Reread for fluency • Reread Advanced Reader

3- or 4-Day Plan

DAY 1	• Extend the concept • Advanced Reader • Fact and Opinion • Questioning • Read Student Edition pp. 124–131
DAY 2	• Multiple-Meaning Words • Read Student Edition pp. 132–139
DAY 3	• Literary Nonfiction: Biography • Read Student Edition pp. 144–147
DAY 4	• Reread for fluency • Reread Advanced Reader

3-Day Plan: Eliminate the shaded box.

Objectives
• Participate in teacher-led discussions by answering questions with appropriate detail.

A Advanced DAY **2**

Extend Comprehension

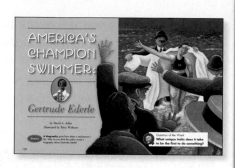

Skill Fact and Opinion Explain that biographies often blend facts and opinions. A biography about an athlete might state that the athlete was the most talented athlete of his or her time and then support that opinion with facts about what competitions he or she won and what records he or she set. Remind students that words such as *felt, in my opinion, must,* and *worst* often signal opinions.

• Think of the book that you just read, *Changing Times.* In your opinion, what change has been most beneficial for women in the United States?

• What fact or facts from the book support your opinion?

Strategy Questioning Review the definition of the strategy of questioning. Remind students to ask themselves questions as they read the rest of the selection.

Read *America's Champion Swimmer* on pp. 124–131.

• Based on pp. 126–127, what do you think made Gertrude so determined to swim well?

• What is your opinion of Gertrude so far? What facts in the biography helped you come to that conclusion?

• What questions do you have about the rest of the selection?

■ **Critical Thinking** Urge students to evaluate opinions as they read.

• Gertrude's mother said Gertrude was "just a plain home girl." What do you think the mother meant by this? Was she calling her daughter ugly? *(No. She was saying that Gertrude was polite and did not brag about her abilities, even though she was talented.)*

• What facts from the text tell you that Gertrude was not just a good swimmer but a great swimmer? *(She beat records set by male athletes. She won three Olympic medals. Her team at the Olympics won more points than all the other countries' teams combined.)*

Objectives
• Draw conclusions from facts presented in text.
• Support assertions with textual evidence.

A Advanced

DAY **3**

Extend Vocabulary

◉ Multiple-Meaning Words/Context Clues

Read a sentence containing a multiple-meaning word, such as "Her team won more points than all the other countries' swimming teams combined."

- What are some meanings of the word *point*? *("a sharp end," as in the point of a pencil; "to motion to something," as in pointing with your finger; "a unit of counting in the score of the game," as in winning a game 6 points to 5)*

- How can I use the phrases and sentences around the word *point* to figure out which meaning is correct? *(The sentence is about a competition, so the third definition sounds correct.)*

Read *America's Champion Swimmer: Gertrude Ederle* on pp. 132–139. Challenge students to find multiple-meaning words throughout the selection. For example, ask:

- What does the author mean by *clubs* in the first sentence? *("a group or organization with a certain purpose")*

- What does the author mean by *current* on p. 130? *("the flow of a river or other body of water")*

A Advanced

- **Before Reading** "Women Athletes" on pp. 144–147, read the panel information on online directories. Then have students use the text features to set a purpose for reading. Finally, have students read "Women Athletes" on their own.

- **During Reading** Have students read the selection. Point out that the user begins with a list of general topics and then clicks on links to find specific information. *How is an online directory different from a biography, such as America's Champion Swimmer: Gertrude Ederle? (With the directory, the user chooses which information to access, while the reader of the biography usually reads the information from beginning to end.)* As they read, have students note other elements of online directories that make them different from print materials.

"Women Athletes"

- **After Reading** Have students discuss Reading Across Texts. Then have them do Writing Across Texts independently.

Objectives
- Understand how communication changes when moving from one genre of media to another.

A Advanced

- **Reread for Fluency** Have students silently reread passages from the Advanced Reader *Changing Times: Women in the Early Twentieth Century.* Then have them reread aloud with a partner or individually. As students read, monitor fluency and provide corrective feedback. If students read fluently on the first reading, they do not need to reread three to four times. Assess the fluency of students in this group using p. 117.

- **Retell** Have students summarize the main idea and key details from the Advanced Reader *Changing Times: Women in the Early Twentieth Century.*

- **Now Try This** Have students complete their "Pioneers in the Classroom!" projects.

Changing Times: Women in the Early Twentieth Century

Objectives
- Read aloud grade-level appropriate text with fluency.

The ELL lessons are organized by strands. Use them to scaffold the weekly curriculum of lessons or during small group time instruction.

Academic Language

Students will hear or read the following academic language in this week's core instruction. To help them internalize new vocabulary, provide a simple definition or concrete example. Then ask students to suggest an example or synonym of the word and identify available cognates.

Skill Words	fact *(hecho)*	multiple-meaning words
	opinion *(opinión)*	heading
	suffix *(sufijo)*	
	contraction *(contracción)*	
Concept Words	courage *(coraje)*	subhead trait
	champion *(campeón)*	famous *(famoso)*

*Spanish cognates in parentheses

Concept Development

What unique traits does it take to be the first to do something?

■ **Preteach Concept**

• **Prior Knowledge** Have students turn to pp. 116–117 in the Student Edition. Call attention to the picture of the astronaut and tap into students' knowledge of the first moon walk. Where is this person? What is he doing? Why do you think he wanted to be the first person on the moon? How do you think he felt?

• **Discuss Concept** Elicit students' knowledge and experience of being the first to do something. What do you think it was like being the very first president of the United States? What kind of special talents or skills do you think you need to be the first person to do something? Supply background information.

• **Poster Talk-Through** Read aloud the Poster Talk-Through on ELL Poster 19 and walk through the Day 1 activities.

■ **Daily Concept and Vocabulary Development** Use the daily activities on ELL Poster 19 to build concept and vocabulary knowledge.

Objectives
• Speak using grade-level content area vocabulary in context to internalize new English words and build academic language proficiency.

Content Objectives

• Use concept vocabulary related to being the first person to do something.

Language Objectives

• Express ideas in response to art and discussion.

• Internalize academic vocabulary.

Daily Planner	
DAY 1	• Concepts and Oral Vocabulary • Listening (Read Aloud)
DAY 2	• Concepts • Vocabulary • Phonics and Spelling • Multiple-Meaning Words
DAY 3	• Concepts • Vocabulary • Fact and Opinion • *America's Champion Swimmer: Gertrude Ederle*
DAY 4	• Concepts • Vocabulary • ELL/ELD Readers
DAY 5	• Concepts • Vocabulary • Heading and Subhead • Revising

*See the ELL Handbook for ELL Workshops with targeted instruction.

Concept Talk Video

Use the Concept Talk Video Routine (*ELL Handbook,* p. 477) to build background knowledge about unique traits. For more listening practice, see *Use Classroom Resources* (*ELL Handbook,* pp. 406–407).

Language Objectives

- Understand and use basic vocabulary.
- Learn meanings of grade-level vocabulary.

Cognates

For Spanish speakers, point out that the word for *medals* is spelled *medallas* in Spanish. medals *(medallas)*. Reinforce the concept that Spanish and English share many words that are the same or similar.

Basic Vocabulary

■ **High-Frequency Words** Use the ELL Vocabulary Routine on p. 471 of the *ELL Handbook* to systematically teach newcomers the first 300 sight words in English. Students who began learning ten words per week at the beginning of the year are now learning words 181–190 (*ELL Handbook,* p. 452). P. 446 of the handbook contains a bank of strategies that you can use to ensure students' mastery of high-frequency words.

Lesson Vocabulary

■ **Preteach** Use this routine to introduce the Lesson Vocabulary:

1. Distribute copies of this week's Word Cards (*ELL Handbook,* p. 137).
2. Display ELL Poster 19 and reread the Poster Talk-Through.
3. Using the poster illustrations, model how a word's meaning can be expressed with other similar words: Her teacher placed the ribbon with the round, gold object, or medal, around her neck.
4. Use these sentences to reveal the meaning of the other words.

   - Even though she was tired, she *continued* to train. (kept going or doing)
   - The *current* was too rough for the swimmers. (movement of water)
   - The surfer can *drown* if they cannot swim. (died from lack of air while under water)
   - The champion proudly displayed his *medals.* (prizes)
   - I *stirred* the soup on the stove. (moved around with a spoon)
   - The swimmer practiced her *strokes* over and over. (arm movements)
   - We wanted to *celebrate* our victory. (do something enjoyable for a special occasion)

Objectives

- Use visual, contextual, and linguistic support to enhance and confirm understanding of increasingly complex and elaborated spoken language.

 English Language Learners

■ **Reteach** Have students work in pairs. Distribute Word Cards to each pair. Write the following sentence frames on the board. Have one partner select a Word Card without the other student seeing it. The player with the card gives clues about the word using other words, phrases, sentences, and gestures but not the word itself. The guesser tries to identify the word quickly, as the player with the word adds clues without showing or saying the word. Time the play and have partners take turns, so that all can present and identify words.

■ **Writing** Have students turn to p. 122 in the Student Edition. Point to the picture of the medals. These are medals. The team received medals for winning. Then have students say the word and repeat your sentence or make up their own. Repeat this routine with the other words on p. 122. Write the following sentence frames on the board and have students complete them:

1. The team wanted to _____ after they won the game. (celebrate)

2. Lucy _____ to swim even though she was tired. (continued)

3. The swift _____ kept pushing her back to the shore. (current)

4. The swift water nearly caused the swimmer to _____. (drown)

5. The team received _____ for their victory. (medals)

6. The swimmer's fast _____ pushed her through the water. (strokes)

7. Rey _____ the soup mix in the hot water. (stirred)

 Leveled Support

Beginning Have students draw pictures that illustrate three of the vocabulary words. Then have them label each picture with the word. Provide prompts if necessary: Did you ever see a medal? What did it look like? How do you move your arms when you swim? Show me. That is called a stroke.

Intermediate/Advanced Have students use selection vocabulary to complete each sentence. Then have them read the sentences aloud.

Advanced High Have students generate new sentences with the vocabulary words.

Language Objectives
• Produce drawings, phrases, or short sentences using Lesson Vocabulary.

ELL Teacher Tip
• Have Beginning students keep a vocabulary notebook to define new English vocabulary using their home language. Students will expand their vocabularies by making semantic maps for these two words: celebrate, stirred. For celebrate, show pictures of a party, a parade, and a holiday celebration. Elicit the words for these pictures in students' home languages. Then write the English equivalents in the semantic map as examples of how we celebrate. Do the same for stirred, showing pictures of people stirring foods. Have students write their new vocabulary in their notebook.

ELL Workshop
Provide opportunities for students to give directions using newly acquired high-frequency words, concrete vocabulary, and key words and expressions. Give Directions (ELL Handbook, pp. 398–399) supports students in this task.

Objectives
• Use strategic learning techniques such as concept mapping, drawing, memorizing, comparing, contrasting, and reviewing to acquire basic and grade-level vocabulary.

Content Objectives

- Monitor and adjust oral comprehension.

Language Objectives

- Discuss oral passages.
- Use a graphic organizer to demonstrate listening comprehension.

Graphic Organizers

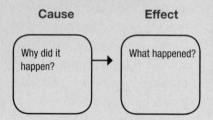

ELL Teacher Tip

Support students with understanding implicit ideas by filling out the cause-and-effect graphic organizer together. Review the difference between a cause and an effect. We are going to list Ellen Ochoa's traits, or ways of acting or thinking. In the first box on the left, let's write Liked to Learn. That is one of Ellen's traits. What happened because she liked to learn? That's right, she did well in school. Let's write that in the box on the right. Continue scaffolding with questions and think-alouds.

ELL English Language Learners

Listening Comprehension

First to Reach a Goal

What traits helped Ellen Ochoa reach her goal? As a child, she had a strong imagination. She imagined that she was an astronaut exploring space. Ellen also had a great desire to learn. She studied hard in school. Math and science were her favorite subjects. Ellen went to college to study these subjects and earned many degrees. Ellen also was curious about many things. She found out how tools worked. Then she tried to improve them. She invented tools that are very helpful to scientists.

Ellen had a good career as an inventor. But she wanted more. She wanted to be an astronaut. In 1990, NASA chose her to train to be an astronaut. In April 1993, her childhood dream came true! Ellen went into space on the Space Shuttle *Discovery*. She became the first Hispanic American woman in space.

Ellen spent nine days on *Discovery*. This space flight was the first of many for Ellen. Since her first flight, she has logged hundreds of hours in space. She also won many awards. One was a Distinguished Service Medal for her good work. Ellen helped develop the International Space Station. That was an important job. Ellen is still at work in space exploration to this day.

Prepare for the Read Aloud The modified Read Aloud above prepares students for listening to the oral reading "First in Space: Ellen Ochoa" on p. 117b.

■ **First Listening: Listen to Understand** Write the title of the Read Aloud on the board. This story is about a woman's dream of being an astronaut. What traits in her personality helped her make her dream come true? What important work did she do as an astronaut? Afterward, ask the questions again and have students share their answers.

■ **Second Listening: Listen to Check Understanding** Use the Cause-and-Effect graphic organizer (*ELL Handbook,* p. 489). Re-label the box on the left *Ellen's Traits* and the box on the right *Results*. List traits such as *liked to learn; liked to invent*. List results such as *did well in school; invented science tools*.

Objectives

- Demonstrate listening comprehension of increasingly complex spoken English by following directions, retelling or summarizing spoken messages, responding to questions and requests, collaborating with peers, and taking notes commensurate with content and grade-level needs.

 **ELL** English Language Learners

Phonics and Spelling

- **Suffixes -er, -or, -ist** Copy and distribute p. 296 from the *ELL Handbook.*

- **Preteach** Write these words on the board: *swimmer, actor; tourist.* Remind students that a *suffix* is a word part added to the end of a base word to change its meaning.

- **Teach/Model** Circle the suffixes *-er, -or,* and *-ist* in the words on the board. Then underline the base words. Each of these suffixes changes the meaning of the base word to mean "a person who does this action." What is a swimmer? (a person who swims) An actor? A tourist?

- **Assess** Have students list words for suffixes *-er, -or,* and *-ist.* Discuss how the suffix changes the meaning of the base word. If students have difficulty grasping this language structures, have them work with peers with more advanced proficiency to understand the suffixes.

Vocabulary Skill: Multiple-Meaning Words

- **Preteach and Model** Have students read the sentences on pp. 129–130 in the Student Edition with words *points* and *point.* These words look the same but have different meanings. You need to use other words in the sentence, or context clues, to figure out the meaning. What does *points* means on p. 129? (type of reward) What does *point* means on p. 130? (a place to be) Listen to these sentences:

  The mattress on my bed is hard and my back hurts. (not soft)
  I read the whole book in one day, but it was hard to stay awake. (not easy)

  The sentences gave clues to the meaning of the word *hard* in each one.

- **Practice** Have students use a dictionary to find the different meanings of the following words: *raise, wore, I.* Have them say one sentence using the word with one meaning, and then one with the other meaning.

 Leveled LS Support

  Beginning/Intermediate Have students create a picture dictionary to show the words and their different meanings.

  Advanced/Advanced High Challenge students to use at least two of the words in sentences that show both of their meanings.

Content Objectives

- Identify suffixes *-er, -or, -ist.*

- Identify and use context to understand multiple-meaning words.

Language Objectives

- Apply phonics and decoding skills to spelling.

- Understand how the addition of a suffix changes the base or root word.

Transfer Skills

Spanish Pronunciation In Spanish, the letters *-er* are pronounced like *air* in English. As a result, Spanish speakers may pronounce words like *seller* and *teacher* as *sell-air* and *teach-air.*

Monosyllabic Languages Speakers of monosyllabic languages such as Cantonese, Hmong, Korean, and Vietnamese may have difficulty understanding that words with suffixes are single words. Have them practice saying and writing words with suffixes as single words.

ELL Teaching Routine

For more practice with suffixes, use the Multisyllabic Word Strategy Routine (*ELL Handbook,* p. 473).

ELL English Language Learners

Comprehension
Fact and Opinion

■ **Preteach** Use p.120 in the Student Edition to review facts and opinions. A fact can be proven true or false. An opinion tells someone's beliefs or feelings. It cannot be proven true or false. Questioning can help you distinguish between fact and opinion. Have students turn to Envision It! on p. El•21 in the Student Edition. Read the definition of *questioning.* Then read the steps involved in questioning before, during, and after reading. When you read informational text, ask yourself if the information is fact or opinion. To find out if it is a fact, ask, How could this statement be proven? You can prove facts by observation or research. To find out if the information is an opinion, ask, Is the author expressing feelings about an idea or event? Is this a statement that cannot be proven? If the answer to either question is yes, then the statement is an opinion.

■ **Reteach** Give each student a copy of the Picture It! (*ELL Handbook,* p. 139). Have students reread the passage and identify facts and opinions. Model how to ask questions about one fact and one opinion in the passage that would help students identify other facts and opinions. Then have students create questions about another fact and opinion in the passage.

Beginning/Intermediate Have students discuss questions with a partner. The more proficient partner will write the questions and share them with the class.

Advanced/Advanced High Have students write one fact and one opinion about swimming. Then have them tell how the fact could be proven.

MINI-LESSON

Social Language

Have students return to Envision It! on p. El•7 in the Student Edition. Explain that people use casual, or informal, words when they are talking to their friends. Who do think is using informal words in this picture? What clues tell you that? Explain that more serious, or formal, words are used when giving instructions. Which words are formal in this page? Why do you think that? Explain that people say "Wow, this is awesome!" to express happiness. What words do you use to express happiness?

Objectives
• Understand the general meaning, main points, and important details of spoken language ranging from situations in which topics, language, and contexts are familiar to unfamiliar. 4.C Develop basic sight vocabulary, derive meaning of environmental print, and comprehend English vocabulary and language structures used routinely in written classroom materials.

Content Objectives
• Distinguish between fact and opinion.
• Recognize word clues and expressions that signal opinions.

Language Objectives
• Formulate questions to distinguish between facts and opinions.
• Speak using academic vocabulary.

ELL Workshop
Provide students with the opportunity to orally express their opinions and ideas. *Express Opinions (ELL Handbook,* pp. 416–417) supports student practice.

Mini-Lesson
Have students turn to p. 120 in the Student Edition. Review fact and opinion and have them read the passage. What opinion is the author expressing? Do you agree with the author's opinion? Have students express their own opinions and feelings about swimming. Students can respond using words, phrases, or complete sentence.

Reading Comprehension
America's Champion Swimmer: Gertrude Ederle

Student Edition pp. 124–125

■ **Frontloading** Have students look through *America's Champion Swimmer: Gertrude Ederle,* pp. 116–131 in the Student Edition, and find evidence for what they think makes it look like biography, a kind of writing that is about a real person's life. Distribute copies of the English summary of *America's Champion Swimmer: Gertrude Ederle (ELL Handbook,* p. 139). Have students read the summary aloud with you. Have them ask questions about any ideas or unfamiliar words. Use the pictures in the story to support students in reading the challenging language. If you've sent home copies of the summary, the support of peers at home to develop background knowledge that will help students with the language.

Sheltered Reading Ask questions such as the following to guide students' comprehension. Have them find evidence from the text to support their answers.

- **pp. 129–130:** What traits did Trudy have as a swimmer? (courage, determination to succeed) Why did she want to be the first woman to swim the English Channel? (to prove that women could be as strong as men)

- **pp. 131–135:** What problems did Trudy have as she swam the Channel? (strong current, cold water, rain, wind, high waves, stiff leg) What made her succeed with all these problems? (courage, not giving up)

- **pp. 136–139:** Look at the picture of Gertrude in the parade on p. 136. What can you conclude about Gertrude's success in swimming the channel? (that she gets to the end) (a parade)

■ **Fluency: Appropriate Phrasing** Remind students to divide sentences into phrases as they read. This will help them better understand the text. Model appropriate phrasing by reading aloud the first paragraph on page 119. Have students read chorally with you or listen to a recording based on their proficiency level. For more practice, use the Fluency: Choral Reading Routine (*ELL Handbook,* p. 474).

After Reading Guide students in summarizing the text using the Retelling Cards. Have Beginning students arrange the cards in order of events. Intermediate and Advanced students can describe beginning, middle, and end events.

Content Objectives
- Monitor and clarify comprehension.
- Make and adjust predictions.

Language Objectives
- Read aloud with appropriate phrasing.
- Summarize text using visual support.

Audio Support
Have students listen to *America's Champion Swimmer: Gertrude Ederle* using the main selection eText online or the Audio Text CD. to build and reinforce their language attainment.

Objectives
- Use visual and contextual support and support from peers and teachers to read grade-appropriate content area text, enhance and confirm understanding, and develop vocabulary, grasp of language structures, and background knowledge needed to comprehend increasingly challenging language.

Comprehension:
Helen Wills Moody

- **Before Reading** Distribute copies of the ELL and ELD Readers, *Helen Wills Moody: America's Tennis Champion,* to students at their reading level.

  - **Preview** Read the title aloud with students. This is a biography about a woman who was a tennis champion. Invite students to look through pictures and read the captions and labels. Have them predict how Helen became a champion based on the picture clues and their prior knowledge.

  - **Set a Purpose for Reading** Let's read to find out how Helen became a tennis champion.

- **During Reading** Follow this Reading Routine for both reading groups.

  1. Read the entire Reader aloud slowly.

2. Read pp. 1–4, pausing to build background knowledge or model comprehension. Have Beginning students finger-point as you read.
Use the questions in the chart below to check students' comprehension.

3. Have pairs reread pp. 1–4, alternating pages as they read aloud.

4. Repeat steps 2–3 above for pp. 5–8 of the Reader.

- **After Reading** Use the exercises on the inside back cover of each Reader and have students share their writing. In a whole-group discussion, ask students, What are some important facts about Helen? What is your opinion of her? Why? Record answers on the board; invite students to point to pictures and information to support their answers.

ELD Reader

- **pp. 2–3** What did Helen love to do? Read the sentence that tells you. (Helen loved painting and tennis.)

- **pp. 4–5** Who did Helen practice with? (Hazel Wightman; men)

- **pp. 6–8** How long did it take Helen to win against Mallory? (33 minutes)

Writing Copy one fact about Helen from the Reader. Then write one sentence that tells your opinion of Helen. Use this sentence frame: I think Helen Wills Moody was _____.

ELL Reader

- **pp. 2–3** Who did Helen play tennis with? (her father)

- **pp. 4–5** How old was Helen when she won her first championship? (16) What was Helen's rank in tennis in 1922? (third best female tennis player in the U.S.)

- **pp. 6–8** What happened when Helen played against the best-ranked female tennis player in the world? (Helen won easily.) How did Helen change tennis fashion? (She was the first to wear a short skirt.)

Study Guide Distribute copies of the ELL Reader Study Guide (*ELL Handbook,* p. 142). Scaffold comprehension of distinguishing facts from opinions by helping students look back through the Reader in order to answer questions on the back cover. (**Answers** See *ELL Handbook,* pp. 209–212.)

Objectives

- Respond orally to information presented in a wide variety of print, electronic, audio, and visual media to build and reinforce concept and language attainment.

 **ELL** *English Language Learners*

Conventions
Contractions

■ **Preteach** Display these sentences: <u>I'm</u> playing soccer. <u>You're</u> on the same team. <u>We're</u> going to win the game today. The underlined words are contractions. A contraction is a shortened form of two words. *I'm* is a contraction of *I am.* You're is a contraction of *you are.* What two words are in the contraction *we're*? In each contraction, an apostrophe (point to the apostrophe) takes the place of one or more letters that are missing. What letter is missing in each contraction? **(a)**

■ **Teach/Model** Present these examples and discuss.

	Contractions
<u>I</u> and <u>will</u>	<u>I'll</u> try harder.
<u>should</u> and <u>have</u>	You <u>should've</u> called home.
<u>will</u> and <u>not</u>	We <u>won't</u> be at home today.

■ **Oral and Written Language** Have students rephrase these sentences using contractions: <u>She will</u> hide. <u>I do not</u> see her. I <u>will not</u> stop looking. They <u>should have</u> eaten lunch at school. <u>You have</u> eaten your sandwich. We <u>are not</u> going to the movies today. Have students write the sentences with the contraction.

■ **Reteach** Review the chart in **Teach/Model.** Cover up the first column and have students provide the two words that make up the contraction. Cover up the second column and have them provide the contraction.

■ **Practice** Have students practice using these contractions in oral and written sentences.

 Beginning/Intermediate Have students underline the words that make up the contraction in each sentence. Have them say the sentences with contractions.
Advanced/Advanced High Have students rewrite the sentences with contractions and underline the contractions.

Content Objectives
- Identify contractions.
- Understand function of apostrophe in contractions.

Language Objectives
- Practice using contractions in speaking.
- Write sentences using contractions.

 Transfer Skills

Contractions Ask students if there are contractions in their home language. (In Spanish, a + *el* = *al* and *de* + as = *das.*) Explain that an English contraction uses an apostrophe to replace the missing letters.

Grammar Jammers

For more practice with contractions, use the Grammar Jammers for this target skill. See the Grammar Jammers Routine (*ELL Handbook,* p. 478) for suggestions on using this learning tool.

Objectives
- Speak using a variety of grammatical structures with increasing accuracy and ease as more English is acquired.

Support for English Language Learners

Content Objectives

- Identify vivid details.
- Use vivid details to describe a person's traits.

Language Objectives

- Use vivid language in writing.
- Share feedback for editing and revising.

ELL Workshop

Students may use classroom resources to respond to questions they have about their writing. *Use Classroom Resources (ELL Handbook,* pp. 406–407) provides extra support.

Writing Headings and Subheads

■ **Introduce** Write *heading and subheads* on the board. Headings and subheads are used to help organize the text in story or a book. The heading tells what the following text will be about. The subhead is under the heading. The subhead tells you that more detailed information will be in the following text. Display the Writing Model and read it aloud. Point to the heading and subhead. What does the heading tell you about the text? What does the subhead tell you?

> **Writing Model**
>
> **Gertrude's Early Years**
> **Visiting Germany**
> It wasn't until she was seven that she had her first adventure in the water. While visiting her grandmother in Germany, Trudy fell into a pond and nearly drowned.

■ **Practice** Distribute the ELD/ELL Reader Helen *Wills Moody* (3.4.4). Have students write headings and subheads that match the information on the page. Remind students that a heading tells you what the page will be about. The subhead tells about a small section on the page.

■ **Write** Have students use basic vocabulary to write a paragraph about something they learned how to do when they were younger. Have them include a heading and subhead to help organize the information.

Beginning/ Intermediate What did you learn to do when you were young? Explain that their response can be the heading. Have them write a sentence about the topic. Guide them to create a subhead from the sentence.

Advanced/Advanced High Have students include two subheads in their paragraph. Explain that if they include more detail in the paragraph, the subheads will be easier to write.

Objectives

- Write using newly acquired basic vocabulary and content-based grade-level vocabulary. Write using a variety of grade-appropriate sentence lengths, patterns, and connecting words to combine phrases, clauses, and sentences in increasingly accurate ways as more English is acquired. Narrate, describe, and explain with increasing specificity and detail to fulfill content area writing needs as more English is acquired.

Fly, Eagle, Fly!:
An African Tale

My Planning Guide

This Week's ELL Overview

Grade 3 • Unit 4 • Week 5
Fly, Eagle, Fly!: An African Tale
150a–187b
and DI•116–DI•125

ELL Handbook

- Maximize Literacy and Cognitive Engagement
- Research Into Practice
- Full Weekly Support for Every Selection

Fly, Eagle, Fly!: An African Tale

- Multi-Lingual Summaries in Five Languages
- Selection-Specific Vocabulary Word Cards
- Frontloading/Reteaching for Comprehension Skill Lessons
- ELD and ELL Reader Study Guides

- Transfer Activities
- Professional Development

Daily Leveled ELL Notes

ELL notes appear throughout this week's instruction and ELL Support is on the DI pages of your Teacher's Edition. The following is a sample of an ELL note from this week.

English Language Learners

Beginning Give students a story map and have them sketch what happened in the beginning, middle, and end of the story. Have them use their story map to guide their retelling.

Intermediate Have students use brief sentences to retell the story.

Advanced Have students listen as another student retells the story. Then have listeners respond with details they would add or leave out.

Advanced High Have students create an outline to jot down the main events of the story. Then have them use the outline to guide their retelling.

ELL by Strand

The ELL lessons on this week's Support for English Language Learners pages are organized by strand. They offer additional scaffolding for the core curriculum. Leveled support notes on these pages address the different proficiency levels in your class. See pages DI•116–DI•125.

ELL Guy
Dr. Jim Cummins

The Three Pillars of ELL Instruction

ELL Strands	Activate Prior Knowledge	Access Content	Extend Language
Vocabulary pp. DI•117–DI•118	Preteach	Reteach	Leveled Writing Activities
Reading Comprehension p. DI•122	Frontloading	Sheltered Reading	Summarizing
Phonics, Spelling, and Word Analysis p. DI•120	Preteach	Teach/Model	Practice
Listening Comprehension p. DI•119	Prepare for the Read Aloud	First Listening	Second Listening
Conventions and Writing p. DI•124	Teach/Model	Leveled Practice Activities	Reteach
Concept Development p. DI•116	Activate Prior Knowledge	Develop Concept	Daily Activities

This Week's Practice Stations Overview

Six Weekly Practice Stations with Leveled Activities can be found at the beginning of each week of instruction. For this week's Practice Stations, see pp. 150h–150i.

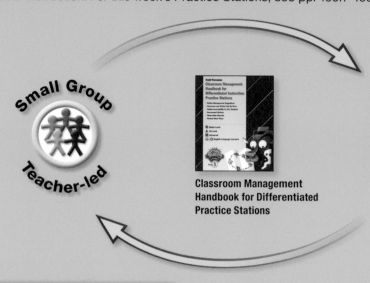

Small Group
Teacher-led

Classroom Management Handbook for Differentiated Practice Stations

Practice Stations

Daily Leveled Center Activities

⬤ Below　　◻ Advanced

△ On-Level　　ⓔⓛⓛ

Practice Stations Flip Charts

	Word Wise	Word Work	Words to Know	Let's Write!	Read For Meaning	Get Fluent
Objectives	• Spell words with suffixes -er, -or, -ess, and -ist.	• Identify and pronounce words with suffixes -er, -or, -ess, and -ist.	• Determine the meanings of multiple-meaning words.	• Write an autobiography telling about your life.	• Identify fact and opinion in expository text.	• Read aloud with appropriate phrasing.
Materials	• *Word Wise* Flip Chart Activity 20 • Teacher-made word cards • dictionary • pencils • paper	• *Word Work* Flip Chart Activity 20 • Teacher-made word cards • paper • pencil	• *Words to Know* Flip Chart Activity 20 • Teacher-made word cards • paper • pencil	• *Let's Write!* Flip Chart Activity 20 • paper • pencils	• *Read for Meaning* Flip Chart Activity 20 • Leveled Readers • paper • pencils	• *Get Fluent* Flip Chart Activity 20 • Leveled Readers

This Week on Reading Street!

 Question of the Week

What behaviors are unique to different animals?

One of a Kind

Daily Plan

Don't Wait Until Friday

Whole Group

- ⊙ Cause and Effect
- ⊙ Unknown Words
- Fluency/Rate
- Writing/Conventions
- Research and Inquiry

MONITOR PROGRESS | **Success Predictor**

Day 1	Day 2	Day 3	Day 4	Day 5
Check Oral Vocabulary	Check Word Reading	Check Retelling	Check Fluency	Check Oral Vocabulary

Small Group

Teacher-Led

- Reading Support
- Skill Support
- FLuency Practice

Practice Stations

Independent Activities

Customize Literacy More support for a balanced literacy appoach, see pp. CL•1–CL•45.

Customize Writing More support for a customized writing approach, see pp. CW•11–CW•20.

Whole Group

- Writing: Writing for Tests
- Conventions: Prepositions
- Spelling: Syllables VCCCV

Assessment

- Weekly Tests
- Day 5 Assessment
- Fresh Reads

You Are Here! Unit 4 Week 5

This Week's Reading Selections

Main Selection
Genre: **Folk Tale**

Paired Selection
Folk Tale

Decodable Readers

Leveled Readers

ELL and ELD Readers

Resources on Reading Street!

	Build Concepts	Phonics	Comprehension
Whole Group	 Let's Talk About pp. 150–151	 Student Edition pp. 152–153 Decodable Readers  Sound–Spelling Cards	 Envision It! Skills/ Strategies Comprehension Skills Lesson pp. 154–155
Go Digital	• Concept Talk Video	• Interactive Sound-Spelling Cards • Decodable eBooks	• Envision It! Animations • eSelections
Small Group and Independent Practice	Fly, Eagle, Fly!: An African Tale pp. 158–159 ELL and ELD Readers Leveled Readers Decodable Readers	Decodable Readers Practice Stations Flip Chart	 Fly, Eagle, Fly!: An African Tale pp. 158–159 ELL and ELD Readers Leveled Readers Envision It! Skills/ Strategies  RWN Cover Practice Stations Flip Chart
Go Digital	• eReaders • eSelections • Decodable eBooks	• Letter Tile Drag and Drop • Decodable eBooks	• Envision It! Animations • eSelections • eReaders
Customize Literacy	• Leveled Readers • Decodable Readers	• Decodable Readers	• Envision It! Skills and Strategies • Handbook • Leveled Readers
Go Digital	• Concept Talk Video • Decodable eBooks • eReaders	• Decodable eBooks	• Envision It! Animations • eReaders • Decodable eBooks

Question of the Week
What behaviors are unique to different animals?

Vocabulary

Envision It!
Word Cards

Vocabulary Skills Lesson
pp. 156–157

- Envision It! Word Cards
- Vocabulary Activities

Envision It!
Word Cards

Fly, Eagle, Fly!: An African
Tale pp. 158–159

Practice Stations
Flip Chart

Words!

RWN Cover

- Envision It! Word Cards
- Vocabulary Activities
- eSelection

- Envision It! Word Cards

- Vocabulary Activities

Fluency

Let's Learn It!
pp. 182–183

Decodable and
Leveled Readers

- eSelection
- Decodable eBooks
- eReaders

Fly, Eagle, Fly!: An African
Tale pp. 158–159

Practice Stations
Flip Chart

Leveled
Readers

ELL and ELD
Readers

- eSelection
- eReaders

- Leveled Readers
- Decodable Readers

- eReaders
- Decodable eBooks

Conventions and Writing

Let's Write It!
pp. 174–175

Decodable
Readers

- Grammar Jammer
- Online Journal

RWN Cover

Fly, Eagle, Fly!: An African
Tale pp. 158–159

Practice
Stations
Flip Chart

- Grammar Jammer
- Online Journal

- Reader's and Writer's Notebook

- Grammar Jammer
- Online Journal

You Are Here!
Unit 4
Week 5

My 5-Day Planner for Reading Street!

Don't Wait Until Friday

MONITOR PROGRESS

	Check Oral Vocabulary **Day 1** pages 150j–155f	**Word Reading** **Day 2** pages 156a–167d

Get Ready to Read	**Concept Talk,** 150j
	Oral Vocabulary, 151a
	    armor, agile, snout, protrude
	Listening Comprehension,
	    Read Aloud, 151b
	Phonics/Word Analysis, 152a–153b
	READ Decodable Practice Reader, 153a–153b
		Concept Talk, 156a
		Oral Vocabulary, 156b
		    extraordinary, scenery
		Phonics/Word Analysis, 156c
		    Syllables VCCV
		Literary Terms, 156d
		    Sensory Details
		Story Structure, 156d
		    Rising Action

Read and Comprehend	**Comprehension Skill,**
	    ⊙ Cause and Effect, 154a
	Comprehension Strategy,
	    ⊙ Monitor and Clarify, 154a
	READ Comprehension, 154–155
	Model Fluency, Rate, 000–000
	Introduce Lesson Vocabulary, 155a
	    scrambled, gully, echoed, valley, reeds,
	    clutched, thatch
		Vocabulary Skill,
		    ⊙ Unknown Words, 156e
		Vocabulary Strategy,
		    Dictionary/Glossary, 000–000
		Lesson Vocabulary, 156–157 scrambled, gully,
		    echoed, valley, reeds, clutched, thatch
		READ Vocabulary, 156–157
		Model Fluency, Rate, 156–157
		READ Main Selection
		    Fly, Eagle, Fly! An African Tale, 158–167a

Language Arts	**Research and Inquiry,**
	    Identify Questions, 155b
	Spelling,
	    Syllables VCCV, 155c
	Conventions,
	    Prepositions, 155d
	Handwriting,
	    Cursive Letter t, 155d
	Writing, Writing for Tests, 153e–153f
		Research and Inquiry,
		    Navigate/Search, 167b
		Conventions, Prepositions, 167c
		Spelling,
		    Syllables VCCV, 167c
		Writing,
		    Writing for Tests: Word Choice, 167d

You Are Here! Unit 4 Week 5

What behaviors are unique to different animals?

Check Retelling	Check Fluency	Check Oral Vocabulary
Day 3 pages 168a–175c	**Day 4** pages 176a–183e	**Day 5** pages 183f–183q
Concept Talk, 168a **Oral Vocabulary**, 168b 　pesky, unfurl **Phonics/Word Analysis**, 168c–168d **Decodable Story**, 168d **Comprehension Check**, 168e **Check Retelling**, 168f	**Concept Talk**, 176a **Oral Vocabulary**, 176b 　coil, intersection **Phonic/Word Analysis**, 176c–176f **Decodable Story**, 176f **Genre: Folk Tale**, 176g	**Concept Wrap Up**, 183f **Check Oral Vocabulary**, 183g 　armor, agile, snout, protrude, 　extraordinary, scenery, pesky, 　unfurl, coil, intersection **Amazing Ideas**, 183g Review ⦿ Cause and Effect, 183h Review ⦿ Unknown words, 183h Review Phonics/Word Analysis, 183i Review Literary Terms, 183i
READ Main Selection, 　*Fly, Eagle, Fly! An African Tale,* 　168–171a **Retelling**, 172–173 **Think Critically**, 173a **Model Fluency**, Rate, 173b **Research and Study Skills**, 173c	**READ Paired Selection,** 　"Purple Coyote", 176–181a **Let's Learn It!**, 182–183a 　Fluency: Rate 　Vocabulary: Unknown Words 　Listening and Speaking: Book 　Review	**Fluency Assessment**, Rate, 183j–183k **Comprehension Assessment,** 　⦿ Cause and Effect, 183l–183m
Research and Inquiry, 　Navigate/Search, 173d **Conventions,** 　Prepositions, 173e **Spelling**, Syllables VCCV, 173e **Let's Write It!,** 　Writing for Tests, 174–175a **Writer's Craft**, Time–order transition 　words, 175b–175c	**Research and Inquiry,** 　Synthesize, 183d **Conventions,** 　Prepositions, 183c **Spelling,** 　Syllables VCCV, 183c **Writing**, Writing for Tests: 　Revising, 183d–183e	**Research and Inquiry,** 　Communicate, 183n **Conventions,** 　Prepositions, 183o **Spelling Test,** 　Syllables VCCV, 183o **Writer's Craft,** 　Prepositions, 183p **Quick Write for Fluency**, 183q

Week 5

Grouping Options for Differentiated Instruction
Turn the page for the small group time lesson plan.

Planning Small Group Time on Reading Street!

SMALL GROUP TIME RESOURCES

Look for this Small Group Time box each day to help meet the individual needs of all your children. Differentiated Instruction lessons appear on the DI pages at the end of each week.

DAY 1

Teacher-Led

SI Strategic Intervention	OL On-Level	A Advanced
Teacher Led • Reinforce the Concept • **Read Concept** Literacy Reader or Below-Level Reader	**Teacher Led** • Explain the Concept Read On-Level Reader	**Teacher Led** • Explain the Concept • **Read** Advanced Reader

ELL Place English language learners in the groups that correspond to their reading abilities in English.

Practice Stations	**Independent Activities**
• Read for Meaning • Get Fluent • Word Work	• Concept Talk Video • *Reader's and Writer's Notebook* • Inquiry and Research

ELL

Mealtime in Madagascar

ELL Reader

Mealtime in Madagascar
by Jim Harrison
illustrated by Eldon Doty

ELD Reader

ELL Poster

You Are Here!
Unit 4
Week 5

Day 1

SI Strategic Intervention	**Reinforce the Concept,** DI•101–DI•102 **Read Decodable Reader,** and **Concept Literacy Reader** or **Below-Level Reader**
OL On-Level	**Expand the Concept,** DI•107 **Read On-Level Reader**
A Advanced	**Extend the Concept,** DI•112 **Read Advanced Reader**
ELL English Language Learners	• **Concepts and Oral Vocabulary** • **Listening (Read Aloud)** DI•116–DI•125

Question of the Week
What behaviors are unique to different animals?

 **SI** Strategic Intervention

What Can Animals Do?
By Meish Goldish
Concept Literacy Reader

Swimming Like Buck
by Evan Allen
illustrated by Bob Brugger

Below-Level

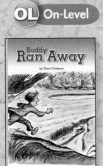
Buddy Ran Away
by Theo Feldman
illustrated by Tom LaBaff

OL On-Level

On-Level

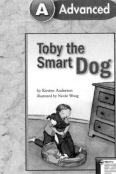
Toby the Smart Dog
by Kirsten Anderson
illustrated by Nicole Wong

A Advanced

Advanced Reader

Decodable Practice Readers Units 4-6
• Practice phonics skills
• Blending practice
• Reread for fluency

Decodable Readers

Fly, Eagle Fly!: An African Tale, pp. 158–159

Purple Coyote
by Cornette
illustrated by Rochut

"Purple Coyote" pp. 176–177

Small Group Weekly Plan

Week 5

Day 2	Day 3	Day 4	Day 5
Reinforce Comprehension, DI•103 **Read Main Selection**	**Reinforce Vocabulary,** DI•104 **Read Main Selection**	**Reinforce Comprehension,** Practice Retelling, DI•105 **Read Paired Selection**	**Practice Fluency,** DI•106 **Reread Decodable Reader,** and **Concept Literacy Reader** or **Below-Level Reader**
Expand Comprehension, DI•108 **Read Main Selection**	**Expand Vocabulary,** DI•104 **Read Main Selection**	**Reinforce Comprehension,** Practice Retelling, DI•110 **Read Paired Selection**	**Practice Fluency,** DI•111 **Reread On-Level Reader**
Extend Comprehension, DI•113 **Read Main Selection**	**Extend Vocabulary,** DI•114 **Read Main Selection**	**Extend Comprehension,** Practice Retelling, DI•115 ~~Read Paired Selection~~	**Practice Fluency,** DI•115 **Reread Advanced Reader**
• Concepts • Vocabulary • Phonics and Spelling DI•116–DI•125	• Concepts • Vocabulary • Comprehension DI•116–DI•125	• Concepts •Vocabulary **Read ELL Reader** DI•116–DI•125	• Concepts • Vocabulary DI•116–DI•125

Practice Stations for Everyone on Reading Street!

Word Wise
Suffixes -er, -or, -ess, and -ist

Objectives
• Spell words with suffixes -er, -or, -ess, and -ist.

Materials
• *Word Wise* Flip Chart Activity 20
• Teacher-made word cards
• dictionary • pencils • paper

Differentiated Activities

⬤ Choose ten word cards. Make a four-column chart. Use -er, -or, -ess, and -ist as headings. Write your words in the correct column. Write sentences with one word from each column.

▲ Choose twelve word cards. Make a four-column chart with -er, -or, -ess, and -ist as headings. List each word in the correct column. Write sentences using two words from each column.

⬛ Choose fifteen word cards and use -er, -or, -ess, and -ist as headings in a four-column chart. List the words in the columns. Write sentences using three words from each column.

Technology
• Online Dictionary

Word Work
Suffixes -er, -or, -ess, and -ist

Objectives
• Identify and pronounce words with suffixes -er, -or, -ess, and -ist.

Materials
• *Word Work* Flip Chart Activity 20
• Teacher-made word cards
• paper • pencil

Differentiated Activities

⬤ Choose ten word cards. Group your words by suffix. Write them in lists. Say each word. Add other words you know with these suffixes to your lists. Circle the suffix in each word.

▲ Choose twelve word cards, and group your words by suffix. Write lists of words that have the same suffix. Say each word. Add other words with the same suffixes to your lists.

⬛ Choose fifteen word cards, and group your words by suffix. Write lists of words that share a suffix. Say each word. Add other words with these suffixes to your lists.

Technology
• Modeled Pronunciation Audio CD

Words to Know
Multiple-meaning words

Objectives
• Determine the meanings of multiple-meaning words.

Materials
• *Words to Know* Flip Chart Activity 20
• Teacher-made Word Cards
• paper • pencil

Differentiated Activities

⬤ Choose three word cards. Write the words. Use a dictionary to find two meanings for each word. Write two sentences for each word to show its different meanings.

▲ Choose four word cards, and write the words. Use a dictionary to find two meanings for each word. Write two sentences for each word to show its multiple meanings.

⬛ Choose five word cards, and write the words. Use a dictionary to find the multiple meanings of each word. Write at least two sentences for each word to show its multiple meanings.

Technology
• Online Dictionary

You Are Here! Unit 4 Week 5

Use this week's materials from the Reading Street Practice Stations Kit to organize this week's stations.

Key

- Below
- On-Level
- Advanced

Let's Write!
Autobiography

Objectives
- Write an autobiography telling about your life.

Materials
- *Let's Write!* Flip Chart Activity 20
- paper
- pencils

Differentiated Activities

● Write an autobiography that tells about some of the important events in your life. Include facts about your life your readers may not know. Use paragraphs to organize the events you tell about.

▲ Write an autobiography that tells about some of the important events in your life. Include information about yourself others may not know. Use a separate paragraph for each of the events.

■ Write an autobiography that tells about some of the important events in your life. Include interesting details about yourself others may not know. Organize the events into paragraphs.

Technology
- Online Graphic Organizers

Read for Meaning
Fact and opinion

Objectives
- Identify fact and opinion in expository text.

Materials
- *Read for Meaning* Flip Chart Activity 20
- Leveled Readers
- paper
- pencils

Differentiated Activities

● Choose and read one of the books your teacher provides. Find a fact and an opinion in the book. Write a sentence telling the opinion. Write a sentence stating the fact. Write the difference between a fact and an opinion.

▲ Choose and read one of the books your teacher provides, and think about the facts and opinions the author includes. Write two sentences that give facts from the selection. Write two sentences that give opinions.

■ As you read the book you chose, distinguish between the facts and opinions the author provides. Write a paragraph telling about some of the facts and opinions you read in the selection.

Technology
- Leveled Reader Database

Get Fluent
Practice fluent reading

Objectives
- Read aloud with appropriate phrasing.

Materials
- *Get Fluent* Flip Chart Activity 20
- Leveled Readers

Differentiated Activities

● Work with a partner. Choose a leveled reader. Take turns reading a page from the book. Think about the topic of the book. As you read, match your rate to what you are reading. Provide feedback to your partner.

▲ Work with a partner. Choose a leveled reader. Take turns reading a page from the book. Think about the topic of the book. As you read, match your rate to what you are reading. Provide feedback to your partner.

■ Work with a partner. Choose a leveled reader. Take turns reading a page from the book. Think about the topic of the book. As you read, match your rate to what you are reading. Provide feedback to your partner.

Technology
- Leveled Reader Database
- Reading Street Readers CD-ROM

Week 5

Objectives
- Introduce the weekly concept.
- Develop oral vocabulary.

Today at a Glance

Oral Vocabulary
armor, agile, snout, protrude

Phonics/Word Analysis
Syllables VCCCV

Comprehension
◉ Cause and effect
◉ Monitor and clarify

Reading
"Birds of Prey"

Fluency
Rate

Lesson Vocabulary
Tested vocabulary

Research and Inquiry
Identify questions

Spelling
Syllables VCCCV

Conventions
Prepositions

Handwriting
Cursive letter *f*

Writing
Writing for tests: Summary

Concept Talk

Question of the Week

What behaviors are unique to different animals?

Introduce the concept

To further explore the unit concept of One of a Kind, this week students will read, write, and talk about the behaviors that are unique to different animals. Write the Question of the Week on the board.

ROUTINE **Activate Prior Knowledge** **Team Talk**

 Think Have students think about different animals and the ways they behave that are unique to them.

 Pair Have pairs of students discuss the Question of the Week.

 Share Call on a few students to share their ideas and comments with the group. Guide the discussion and encourage elaboration with prompts such as:

- What behavior is unique to your favorite animal?
- Why do you think the animal behaves that way?

Routines Flip Chart

Anchored Talk

Develop oral vocabulary

Have students turn to pp. 150–151 in their Student Editions. Look at each of the photos. Then, use the prompts to guide discussion and create the *Unique behaviors of animals* concept map. Remind students to ask and answer questions with appropriate details.

- What do bats look like? What do they do? (Bats have long snouts and wings. They hang upside down.) Let's begin the concept map with *Animal, Behavior,* and *Characteristics.* Characteristics are what the animal looks like. Behaviors are how the animal acts.

Objectives
• Speak clearly and to the point while making eye contact, changing how fast, loud, and clearly you speak to in discussions and offer ideas that build on the ideas of others.

Oral Vocabulary

Let's Talk About

Unique Animal Behaviors
• Describe unique animals.
• Pose and answer questions about why animals exhibit unique behaviors.
• Discuss what behaviors are unique to specific animals.

READING STREET ONLINE
CONCEPT TALK VIDEO
www.ReadingStreet.com

You've learned **1 8 6** Amazing Words so far this year!

150   151

Student Edition pp. 150–151

Writing on Demand

Writing Fluency
Ask students to respond to the photos on pp. 150–151 by writing as well as they can and as much as they can about animals' unique behaviors.

• What is the lizard doing? (It is balancing on a branch.) What word can you use to describe its actions? (You could call its action *agile*.) Every animal's behavior can be described using an adjective. Let's add *Description* to the map.

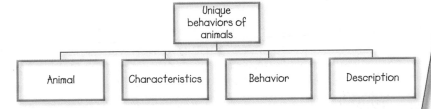

ELL

English Language Learners
ELL support Additional ELL support and modified instruction is provided in the *ELL Handbook* and in the ELL Support lessons on pp. D1•116–D1•125.

Listening comprehension
English learners will benefit from additional visual support to understand the key terms in the concept map. Use the pictures on pp. 150–151 to scaffold understanding.

Connect to reading
Tell students that this week they will be reading about unique behaviors of different animals. Encourage students to add concept-related words to this week's concept map.

Frontload for Read Aloud Use the modified Read Aloud on p. D1•119 of the ELL Support Lessons to prepare students to listen to "Where Are the Alligators?" (p. 151b).

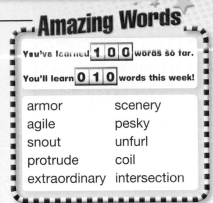

ELL **Preteach Concepts** Use the Day 1 instruction on ELL Poster 20 to assess and build background knowledge, develop concepts, and build oral vocabulary.

ELL Poster 20

Fly, Eagle, Fly! **150–151**

Objectives
- Develop listening comprehension.
- Develop oral vocabulary.

Check Oral Vocabulary
SUCCESS PREDICTOR

Oral Vocabulary
Amazing Words

Introduce Amazing Words

"Where Are the Alligators?" on p. 151b is about American alligators and their behaviors. Tell students to listen for this week's Amazing Words—*armor, agile, snout,* and *protrude*—as you read.

Model fluency

As you read "Where Are the Alligators?" model appropriate rate by reading at a speed that will improve the listener's comprehension.

Teach Amazing Words

Amazing Words Oral Vocabulary Routine

armor
agile
snout
protrude

1 **Introduce** Write the word *armor* on the board. Have students say the word aloud with you. In "Where Are the Alligators?" we learn about animals that look like lizards in a suit of *armor.* What does *armor* mean? Supply a student-friendly definition.

2 **Demonstrate** Have students answer questions to demonstrate understanding. What is armor usually made of? How is an alligator's skin like armor?

3 **Apply** Have students give examples of the ways armor protects. See pp. OV•2 to teach *agile, snout,* and *protrude.*

Routines Flip Chart

Apply Amazing Words

To build oral language, lead the class in a discussion about the meaning of the Amazing Words. Remind students to listen attentively to speakers and to build on the ideas of others in a discussion.

Don't Wait Until Friday

MONITOR PROGRESS Check Oral Vocabulary

During discussion, listen for students' use of Amazing Words.

If... students are unable to use the Amazing Words to discuss the concept,

then... use Oral Vocabulary Routine Card in the Routines Flip Chart to demonstrate words in different contexts.

Day 1 Check Oral Vocabulary	**Day 2** Check Word Reading	**Day 3** Check Retelling	**Day 4** Check Fluency	**Day 5** Check Oral Vocabulary	Success Predictor

Where Are the Alligators?

What looks like a lizard in a suit of armor? The American alligator! The American alligator is one of the largest reptiles in the world. Most grow to about 10 feet long and weigh about 500 pounds. But some male alligators can be twice that length and weigh twice as much!

American Alligators live in only a few states. Most live in Florida and Louisiana, but they can live in Texas too. Alligators in Texas live in the Rio Grande River. Most of the alligators in Florida live in swamps and rivers in an area called the Everglades.

American alligators are excellent swimmers. They have agile bodies, so they move easily through water. The snout and tail of an alligator is the perfect shape for digging holes in the bottoms of swamps and rivers. The alligators dig out plants they find to make the holes deeper. They push the mud to the side to make the holes wider. Some gator holes are as small as bathtubs. Others can be as large as swimming pools!

Alligators use these holes mostly for shelter. When the weather gets too cold, they stay in the holes and sleep. And when the weather gets too dry, and the rivers and swamps become too shallow, then the alligators stay in their holes until it rains again and the water level rises.

What makes an alligator different from a crocodile? Well, for one thing, they live in different places. It is very rare to find a crocodile in any of America's rivers. Crocodiles live mostly in the Nile River in Egypt and in other areas of Africa.

Alligators look different from crocodiles too. For one thing, alligators have snouts that are short and rounded, while crocodiles have long and pointed snouts. Also, crocodiles have big teeth that protrude upward from their bottom jaws. An alligator's teeth protrude downward from the top. Alligators have about 80 teeth, and they are very sharp! When they lose a tooth, another grows in its place.

For many, many years, American alligators were in danger of disappearing. People hunted them, and many were killed. But other people worked hard to save the alligators. Today no one can hunt alligators because there are laws that protect them.

Now that alligators are protected, there are many more around. You can find them in water and you can find them on land. You might see them lying in the sun by a riverbank. You might see their snouts sticking out of the water. Alligators breathe air, so they swim close to the surface. You might hear an alligator, too, especially if it is angry. Alligators roar like lions and sound very fierce!

Oral Vocabulary

Success Predictor

Objectives
- Use word analysis to recognize words with syllable pattern VCCCV.
- Read and build words with syllable pattern VCCCV.

Skills Trace
⊙ Syllables VCCCV
Introduce U4W5D1
Practice U4W5D3; U4W5D4
Reteach/Review U4W5D5; U5W1D4
Assess/Test Weekly Test U4W5
Benchmark Test U4

Word Analysis
⊙ Syllables VCCCV

> **ROUTINE** **Word Parts Strategy**
>
> **1** **Connect** Connect today's lesson to previously learned syllabication patterns CVC and VCCV. Write *super* and *supper.* You already can read words like these. Read these words. Today you'll learn to spell and read words with the syllabication pattern VCCCV.
>
> **2** **Model** Write *pilgrim.* When I say the word *pilgrim,* I hear two syllables. I see two vowels. Identify each vowel by writing *V* below it. I see three consonants between the vowels: *l, g, r.* Identify each consonant by writing *C* below it. Divide the word into syllables. *(pil/grim)* I divide the syllables between the *l* and *g* because *gr* is a blend and should not be split. I put the parts, or syllables, together to read the whole word: *pilgrim.* Write *surprise, farther, monster, mischief, dolphin,* and *hungry.* Model how to read each word by identifying the vowels and the consonants in the VCCCV pattern. Discuss how to divide the words into syllables. Remind students to not split blends or digraphs.
>
> **3** **Guide practice** Have students read each word with you. Identify the VCCCV pattern, divide the word into syllables, and then read the word.
>
> | complex | sample | explore | merchant | address |
> | contrast | inspect | central | purchase | simply |
>
> **4** **Review** What do you know about reading words with the syllable pattern VCCCV? Identify the VCCCV pattern. Then divide between the blend or digraph and the other consonant.

Routines Flip Chart

Model Have students turn to p. 152 in their Student Editions. Each word on this page has the VCCCV pattern. In the first word, the letters *u, n, d, r, e* make the VCCCV pattern. I know *dr* is a blend. I divide the word between the *n* and *d,* and say the syllables together to read *hundreds.*

Guide practice For each word in Words I Can Blend, ask students to identify the VCCCV pattern, divide the word into syllables, and say the word.

If... students have difficulty reading a word,
then... model reading the parts and then the whole word, and then ask students to read it with you.

Objectives
• Read aloud words that have syllable pattern VCCCV

Envision It! Sounds to Know

sandwich

VCCCV

READING STREET ONLINE
SOUND-SPELLING CARDS
www.ReadingStreet.com

Phonics

Syllable Pattern VCCCV

Words I Can Blend

h u n d r e d s

c h i l d r e n

c o m p l e t e

e x p l a i n

i n s t e a d

Sentences I Can Read

1. Hundreds of children go to school in my town.
2. Did you complete the test?
3. Explain why we are going tomorrow instead of today.

I Can Read!

Children in my apartment complex have a concrete area where we play. Sometimes we complain that there simply is not enough room there, but we get constant use out of it anyway.

A man came to inspect the area last week. He explained they are going to destroy the old playground and improve the area. That's what Mom said, anyway.

I can't wait until it is complete and we have an outstanding new place to play.

You've learned!
Syllable Pattern VCCCV

152

153

Student Edition pp. 152–153

Decode and Read

Read words independent of context

After students can successfully decode the words on p. 152 in their Student Editions, point to words in random order and ask students to read them naturally.

Read words in context

Have students read each of the sentences on p. 152. Have them identify words with the VCCCV syllable pattern.

Team Talk Pair students and have them take turns reading each of the sentences aloud.

Chorally read the I Can Read! passage on p. 153 with the students. Then have them read the passage aloud to themselves.

On their own

For additional practice, use *Reader's and Writer's Notebook* p. 291.

INTERACT
with
TEXT

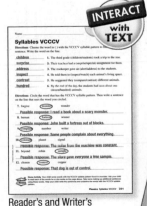

Reader's and Writer's
Notebook p. 291

Differentiated Instruction

SI Strategic Intervention

Syllable pattern VCCCV To understand how to divide a word with the VCCCV syllable pattern, struggling readers may need extra help recognizing blends, such as *dr, st, pl,* and digraphs, such as *th, sh,* and *ch.* Give them a variety of words *(hundred, wishful, monster)* to practice breaking into syllables.

Vocabulary Support

You may wish to explain the meaning of these words.

complex hard to understand

merchant someone who buys and sells goods for a living

contrast to compare two things to show their differences

Academic Vocabulary

syllable a word part that contains a single vowel sound

ELL

English Language Learners
Contrastive Analysis Chart See also the Contrastive Analysis Chart in the *First Stop* book.

Language Transfer Consonant blends with *l* and *r* are difficult for speakers of some Asian languages. Pronounce each syllable in VCCCV words and have students practice pronouncing them after you.

Objectives

- Apply knowledge of VCCCV syllable patterns to decode unknown multisyllabic words when reading.
- Decode and read words in context and independent of context.
- Practice fluency with oral rereading.

Decodable Practice Reader 20A
Syllables VCCCV

Read words independent of context

Have students turn to the first page. Have students read each word.

Read high-frequency words

Have students read the high-frequency words *friends, a, very, they, to, you, were, one, would, was, into, do,* and *want* on the first page.

Preview Decodable Practice Reader

Have students read the title and preview the story. Tell them that they will read words with the syllable pattern VCCCV.

Read words in context

Pair students for reading and listen as they read. One student begins. Students read the entire story, switching readers after each page. Partners reread the story. This time the other student begins. Make sure that students are monitoring their accuracy when they decode words.

Decodable Practice Reader 20A

Corrective feedback

If... students have difficulty reading a word,
then... refer them to the Sound-Spelling Cards to identify the word parts. Have them read the word parts individually and then together to say the word.

- What is the new word?
- Is the new word a word you know?
- Does it make sense in the story?

Check decoding and comprehension

Have students retell the story to include characters, setting, and events. Then have students find words in the story that have the syllabication pattern VCCCV. Students should supply *Constance, ostrich, Sandra, actress, constant, complain, Mildred, distress, frustrated, monster, control, inspect, complete, surprise, hungry, instant, hundred, impressed, exclaimed.*

Reread for Fluency

Have students reread Decodable Practice Reader 20Λ to develop automaticity decoding words with the VCCCV syllable pattern.

> ### ROUTINE Oral Rereading
>
> 1. **Read** Have students read the entire book orally.
> 2. **Reread** To achieve optimal fluency, students should reread the text three or four times.
> 3. **Corrective Feedback** Listen as students read. Provide corrective feedback regarding their fluency and decoding.

Routines Flip Chart

English Language Learners
Syllables VCCCV
Beginning Write several words with the VCCCV syllable pattern from the Decodable Practice Reader on the board, such as *ostrich, actress, constant,* and *complain.* Point to each word as you say it aloud. Then identify the letters that make the VCCCV syllable pattern by writing *V* under the vowels and *C* under the consonants. Identify the blend and model how to divide each word. Have students say the syllables and then put the parts together to say the word with you. Repeat the procedure for other words with the VCCCV syllable pattern, such as *Constance, distress, inspect,* and *hungry.*

Intermediate After reading, have students find words with the VCCCV syllable pattern, write them, and draw a line between the syllables. For example: *os/trich, con/stant, mon/ster,* and *hun/dred.*

Advanced/Advanced High After reading the story, have students choose 4 or 5 words with the VCCCV syllable pattern and write a sentence for each word.

Objectives

- Identify cause and effect to aid comprehension.
- Monitor and clarify to aid comprehension.
- Read grade-level text with appropriate rate.

Skills Trace

◎ Cause and Effect

Introduce/Teach U3W5D1; U4W5DI; U6W2D1

Practice U3W5D2; U3W5D3; U3W5D4; U4W5D2; U4W5D3; U4W5D4; U6W2D2; U6W2D3; U6W2D4

Reteach/Review U3W5D5; U4W3D2; U4W3D3; U4W5D5; U5W1D2; U5W1D3; U6W2D5; U6W4D2; U6W4D3

Assess/Test

Weekly Tests U3W5; U4W5; U6W2
Benchmark Tests U6

Skill ↔ Strategy
◉ Cause and Effect
◉ Monitor and Clarify

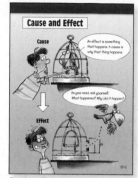

Student Edition p. EI•3

Introduce cause and effect

Envision It!

A cause is a reason something happens. An effect is what happens. *Because* and *so* are clue words that show cause-and-effect relationship. If I am late because my alarm doesn't go off, what is the cause? (My alarm doesn't go off.) What is the effect? (I am late.) Have students turn to p. EI•3 in the Student Edition to review cause and effect. Then read "Birds of Prey" with students.

Model the skill

Think Aloud

Today we're going to read about eagles. Have students follow along as you read. In the last sentence of the first paragraph I read, I see the clue word *because*. I know that the cause comes after that word. The cause is that eagles have large pupils. What effect do the large pupils have? (Eagles can spot their prey from long distances.)

Guide practice

Have students finish reading "Birds of Prey" on their own. After they read, have them use a graphic organizer like the one on p. 154 and identify causes and effects from the passage.

Strategy check

Monitor and Clarify Remind students that if they find anything confusing in "Birds of Prey" they should stop and reread to clarify their understanding.

Student Edition p. EI•21

Model the strategy

Think Aloud

Envision It!

When I first read about how eagles build their nests in full tress or on cliffs, I wondered why they didn't build them closer to the ground. I reread the passage to clarify my understanding. Now I understand that eagles build their nests in high places to protect the young chicks from other animals. Have students review the stratcgy of monitor and clarify on p. FI•21 of the Student Edition.

On their own

Tell students to ask questions and seek clarification about other texts they read. Use p. 292 in the *Reader's and Writer's Notebook* for additional practice with cause and effect.

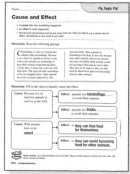

Reader's and Writer's
Notebook p. 292

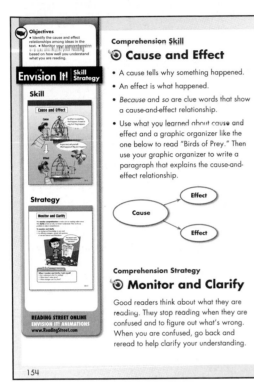

Student Edition pp. 154–155

Objectives
- Identify the cause and effect relationships among ideas in the text. • Monitor your comprehension based on how well you understand what you are reading.

Envision It! | Skill Strategy

Skill

Cause and Effect

Strategy

Monitor and Clarify

READING STREET ONLINE
ENVISION IT! ANIMATIONS
www.ReadingStreet.com

Comprehension Skill

Cause and Effect
- A cause tells why something happened.
- An effect is what happened.
- *Because* and *so* are clue words that show a cause-and-effect relationship.
- Use what you learned about cause and effect and a graphic organizer like the one below to read "Birds of Prey." Then use your graphic organizer to write a paragraph that explains the cause-and-effect relationship.

Cause → Effect
Cause → Effect

Comprehension Strategy

Monitor and Clarify
Good readers think about what they are reading. They stop reading when they are confused and to figure out what's wrong. When you are confused, go back and reread to help clarify your understanding.

154

Birds of Prey

Eagles are large birds of prey that are members of the falcon family. Like all birds of prey, eagles have very large hooked beaks, strong legs, and powerful talons or claws. Another advantage that eagles have is their keen eyesight. Eagles can spot their prey from very long distances because they have large pupils.

Eagles are different from many other birds of prey. They are larger, have a more powerful build, and have heavier heads and bills. Most eagles are larger than any other birds of prey apart from vultures.

Eagles build their nests in tall trees or on high cliffs so that their young chicks are protected from other animals. In recent years, eagles have fallen prey to their environment. Many eagles have moved away from the heavily populated areas in the United States or disappeared entirely because of human expansion.

Skill What clue word is in this paragraph? What cause and effect does it show?

Strategy Are you having trouble understanding how eagles are different from other birds of prey? Go back and reread this paragraph aloud.

Your Turn!

Need a Review? See *Envision It! Handbook* for help with cause and effect and monitoring and clarifying.

Ready to Try It? As you read *Fly, Eagle, Fly!*, use what you've learned about cause and effect and monitoring and clarifying to understand the text.

155

Skill
because; eagles can spot prey from long distances because of their large pupils.

Strategy
Have students reread any portion of the selection they don't understand.

Academic Vocabulary
transition words words like *because, so,* and *then* that show how one idea or event relates to another

Model Fluency
Rate

Model fluent reading
Have students listen as you read paragraphs 1–3 of "Birds of Prey" with appropriate rate. Explain that as the excitement builds, your rate increases to reflect the feeling of the text.

ROUTINE Paired Rereading

1. **Select a passage** For "Birds of Prey," use the whole passage.
2. **Reader 1** Students read the entire passage, switching readers at the end of each paragraph.
3. **Reader 2** Partners reread the passage. This time the other student begins.
4. **Reread** For optimal fluency, have partners continue to read three or four times.
5. **Corrective Feedback** Listen as students read. Provide feedback about their rate and encourage them to adjust rate to reflect the feeling of the text.

Routines Flip Chart

ELL

English Language Learners
Cause and Effect Write on the board: The baby bird wanted to grow up so she tried to fly. The bird fell because she wasn't ready to fly. Circle the words *so* and *because*. Then ask volunteers to help you label the position of the cause and the effect in each sentence. Make sure students understand that the cause comes before the word *so* and after the word *because*.

Objectives
- Activate prior knowledge of words.
- Identify questions for research.

Vocabulary
Tested Vocabulary

Lesson vocabulary

Have students complete sentences by filling in the blanks with lesson words.

Activate prior knowledge

Display the lesson words and discuss what students already know about these words. Then write incomplete sentences on the board, such as those below. Have students identify the lesson word that completes each sentence and makes sense in context. Students may need to check the glossary.

- From the top of the mountain, we could see the _____ below. (valley)
- The flow of the rain water made a _____ in our front yard. (gully)
- When I yelled for Juan, my call _____ through the auditorium. (echoed)
- When I realized I had overslept, I _____ out of bed and threw on my clothes. (scrambled)
- The _____ that grew along the pond rustled in the wind. (reeds)
- The roof of the hut was made from _____. (thatch)
- I _____ the handlebars tightly as I rode my bike down the trail. (clutched)

At the end of the week, students can review these fill-in-the-blank sentences or create their own with a partner.

Preteach Academic Vocabulary

 Academic Vocabulary Write the following words on the board:

outline	preposition
prepositional phrase	syllable
folk tale	transition words

Have students share what they know about this week's Academic Vocabulary. Use the students' responses to assess their prior knowledge. Preteach the Academic Vocabulary by providing a student-friendly description, explanation, or example that clarifies the meaning of each term. Then ask students to restate the meaning of the Academic Vocabulary term in their own words.

Research and Inquiry
Identify Questions

Teach

Discuss the Question of the Week: *What behaviors are unique to different animals?* Tell students they will research the instincts and behaviors of a chosen animal and write a journal article about it. They will present their findings to the class on Day 5.

Model

 I would like to learn more about bears. I'll start by brainstorming a list of questions about bears. I know they hibernate, but I don't know when or why or what they do to prepare for hibernation. Some possible questions could be *When do bears hibernate? Why do they hibernate? When do bears prepare for hibernation?*

Guide practice

After students have brainstormed inquiry questions, explain that tomorrow they will conduct research using their questions. Help students identify keywords that will guide their search. Tell students they will write an outline later in the week.

On their own

Have students work individually, in pairs, or in small groups to write an inquiry question.

Weekly Inquiry Project

Day 1 Identify Questions

Day 2 Navigate/Search

Day 3 Analyze

Day 4 Synthesize

Day 5 Communicate

Academic Vocabulary

Outline a plan that shows how research information is organized

Small Group Time

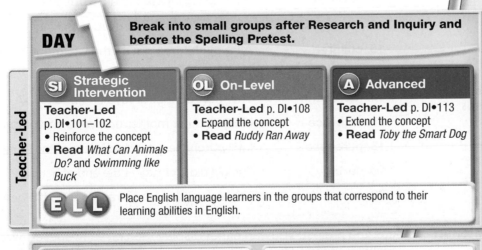

DAY 1

Break into small groups after Research and Inquiry and before the Spelling Pretest.

Teacher-Led

SI Strategic Intervention

Teacher-Led p. DI•101–102
• Reinforce the concept
• **Read** *What Can Animals Do?* and *Swimming like Buck*

OL On-Level

Teacher-Led p. DI•108
• Expand the concept
• **Read** *Ruddy Ran Away*

A Advanced

Teacher-Led p. DI•113
• Extend the concept
• **Read** *Toby the Smart Dog*

ELL Place English language learners in the groups that correspond to their learning abilities in English.

Practice Stations
• Read for Meaning
• Get Fluent
• Word Work

Independent Activities
• Concept Talk Video
• *Reader's and Writer's Notebook*
• Amazing Words Activities

English Language Learners
Multilingual Vocaublary
Students can apply knowledge of their home languages to acquire new English vocabulary by using the Multilingual Vocabulary Lists (*ELL Handbook*, pp. 433–446).

Objectives
- Spell words with syllable pattern VCCCV.
- Define and correctly use prepositions.
- Write words and phrases using the lowercase cursive letter *f*.

Spelling Pretest
Syllables VCCCV

Introduce
Tell students to think of words that have the spelling pattern VCCCV. This week we will spell words with the spelling pattern VCCCV.

Pretest
Use these sentences to administer the spelling pretest. Say each word, read the sentence, and repeat the word.

1.	**monster**	I was a **monster** for Halloween.
2.	**surprise**	Your **surprise** made me happy.
3.	**hundred**	Review the notes one **hundred** times.
4.	**complete**	Make sure you **complete** your chores.
5.	**control**	Please **control** the volume of your voice.
6.	**sample**	Here is a free **sample** of our new CD.
7.	**instant**	We will be back in an **instant**.
8.	**inspect**	They **inspect** the elevator twice a year.
9.	**pilgrim**	A **pilgrim** is a kind of traveler.
10.	**contrast**	Her clean room is a sharp **contrast** to her sister's dirty room.
11.	**explode**	Fireworks **explode**, so never play with them.
12.	**district**	What voting **district** are you?
13.	**address**	Who do I **address** the envelope to?
14.	**substance**	Yeast is a **substance** used in baking.
15.	**children**	A lot of **children** are on the playground.

Challenge words

16.	**merchant**	The **merchant** sells toys and books.
17.	**embrace**	Molly and her mother **embrace** each morning.
18.	**purchase**	I will **purchase** a new backpack at the store.
19.	**curtsy**	The girl did a **curtsy** at the end of her performance.
20.	**contract**	The men signed a **contract** to build the new office.

Self-correct
After the pretest, you can either display the correctly spelled words or spell them orally. Have students self-correct their pretests by rewriting misspelled words correctly.

On their own
For additional practice, use the *Let's Practice It! DVD*.

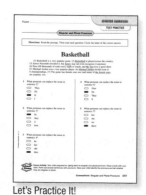

Let's Practice It!
TR DVD•257

Conventions
Prepositions

Teach

Display Grammar Transparency 20, and read aloud the explanation and examples in the box. Point out the preposition *on* in the prepositional phrase *on a cliff.*

Model

Model combining the sentences and putting a prepositional phrase from the second sentence into the first sentence to complete numbers 1 and 2. Apply the definitions for prepositions and prepositional phrases to show how you determined the preposition and prepositional phrase.

Grammar Transparency 20

Guide practice

Guide students to complete item 3. Remind them to find the prepositional phrase and insert it in the other sentence. Record the correct responses on the transparency.

Daily Fix-It

Use Daily Fix-It numbers 1 and 2 in the right margin.

Connect to oral language

Have students read sentences 4 and 5 on the transparency and choose the correct preposition to complete each sentence.

Handwriting
Cursive Letter *f*

Model letter formation

Display the lowercase cursive letter *f*. Follow the stroke instruction pictured to model letter formation.

Model letter slant and spacing

Explain that writing legibly means the letters slant the same way. They may slant to the left, to the right, or straight up or down, but they should not slant in different ways. Also explain that writing legibly means there should be more space between words than between letters in a word. Model writing the proper letter slant and spacing with this sentence: *I flew first class to find my friends in France.*

Guide practice

Have students write the words *fifteen fireflies, fifty frogs,* and *funny fish.* Circulate around the room, guiding students.

Academic Vocabulary

A **preposition** is a word that shows a relationship between a noun and another word.

A **prepositional phrase** is the combination of a preposition and the noun to which it relates.

Daily Fix-It

1. Tamara and me couldnt find Dad's coin with an eagle's picture. (*I; couldn't*)
2. Its worth a lot of mony. (*It's; money*)

ELL

English Language Learners
Leveled support: Prepositions
Write the following prepositions on the board: *on, under, above, in, behind,* and *between.*

Beginning Use an object such as a book to demonstrate each preposition. For example, put the book on a desk and say *The book is **on** the desk.*

Intermediate Have students work with a partner to draw pictures to show the meaning of each preposition.

Advanced/Advanced High Have students use each preposition in a sentence.

Supporting Handwriting Provide extra practice writing lowercase cursive letter *f* with words such as *fluffy, fearful,* and *flavorful.*

Objectives

- Understand and identify the features of a summary.

Writing for Tests—Summary
Introduce

MINI-LESSON

Read Like a Writer

INTERACT with TEXT

Name

Summary of Why the Dog Wags His

Long ago, all the animals could speak and understood all the secrets of how things worked in the world. One special animal, Dog, knew all the secrets of the King. One day, the Dog told the other animals to follow him because he was going to reveal all the King's secrets. So, many animals followed Dog to the cave.

Dog spoke for a long incredible secrets. Next, the palace to report to the King what Dog did. After, the King decided to teach Dog a lesson by taking away the Dog's power to speak. Ever since then, when Dog wants to say something he wags his tail—not his tongue.

1. Read the summary. Who are the main characters?
The Dog, Raven, and the King are the main characters.

2. What happens at the end of the story?
The King takes away the Dog's power to speak.

Writing 293

Reader's and Writer's Notebook p. 293

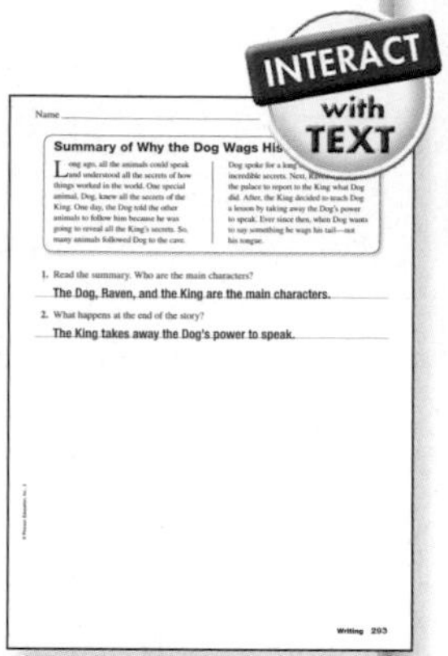

■ **Introduce** This week you will write a **summary**. A summary is a short retelling of a piece of writing, such as an article or a story.

Genre	Summary
Trait	Word Choice
Mode	Narrative

■ **Examine Model Text** Let's read an example of a summary written in response to a writing prompt on a test. Have students read "Summary of Why the Dog Wags His Tail" on p. 293 of their *Reader's and Writer's Notebook.*

■ **Key Features** A summary is shorter than the original story and includes only the most important information. Ask students to identify some of the most important information from the story in the model.

Summaries are usually presented in a logical order. Time-order transition words are used to help explain the order of events. Have students circle the time-order transition words in the passage.

MINI-LESSON

5 Day Planner
Guide to Mini-Lessons

DAY 1	Read Like a Writer
DAY 2	Time-Order Transition Words
DAY 3	Evaluation
DAY 4	Using Strong Verbs
DAY 5	Revising: Conventions

Review key features Review the key features of summaries with students. You may want to post key the key features in the classroom for students to reference as they work on their summaries.

Key Features of a Summary

- retells a piece of writing
- includes only the most important information
- shorter than the original

ROUTINE

Quick Write for Fluency   Team Talk

1 Talk Have pairs take a few minutes to discuss the features of a summary.

2 Write Each person writes one sentence about one of the features.

3 Share Partners share their sentences with one another.

Routines Flip Chart

Wrap Up Your Day

✔ **Build Concepts** Have students discuss what behaviors are unique to different animals.

✔ **Oral Vocabulary** Have students use the Amazing Words they learned in context sentences.

✔ **Homework** Send home this week's Family Times Newsletter in the *Let's Practice It!* DVD.

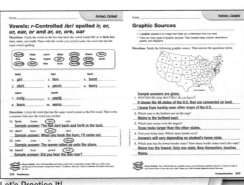

Let's Practice It!
TR DVD•258–259

Academic Vocabulary

A **transitional word** is a word that helps explain the order of events.

ELL

English Language Learners
Retelling Have students practice orally retelling a story.

Beginning Give students a story map and have them sketch what happened in the beginning, middle, and end of the story. Have them use their story map to guide their retelling.

Intermediate Have students use brief sentences to retell the story.

Advanced/Advanced High Have students create an outline to jot down the main events of the story. Then have them use the outline to guide their retelling.

Preview DAY 2

Tell students that tomorrow they will read about an eagle that thinks it is a chicken.

Objectives
- Expand the weekly concept.
- Develop oral vocabulary.

Today at a Glance

Oral Vocabulary
extraordinary, scenery

Phonics
Syllables VCCCV

Literary Terms
Sensory details

Story Structure
Rising action

Lesson Vocabulary
◉ Unknown words

Fluency
Rate

Reading
"Eagle Watching"
Fly, Eagle, Fly!

Research and Inquiry
Navigate/Search

Spelling
Syllables VCCCV

Conventions
Prepositions

Writing
Writing for tests: Summary

Concept Talk

 Question of the Week

What behaviors are unique to different animals?

Expand the concept

Remind students of the weekly concept question. Tell students that today they will begin reading *Fly, Eagle, Fly!: An African Tale.* As they read, encourage students to think about the behaviors that are unique to eagles and chickens.

Anchored Talk

Develop oral vocabulary

Use the photos on pp. 150–151 and the Read Aloud "Where Are the Alligators?" to talk about the Amazing Words: *armor, agile, snout,* and *protrude.* Add these and other concept-related words to the concept map to develop students' knowledge of the topic. Discuss the following questions. Remind students to listen attentively to other students and to answer with appropriate detail. Encourage students to build on the ideas of others when they answer.

- Does the word *snout* describe a characteristic or a behavior?
- What kind of behavior could be described as *agile*?
- What purpose does skin like *armor* serve?

Oral Vocabulary
Amazing Words

Amazing Words

armor	scenery
agile	pesky
snout	unfurl
protrude	coil
extraordinary	intersection

Teach Amazing Words

Amazing Words Oral Vocabulary Routine

1 Introduce Write the Amazing Word *extraordinary* on the board. Have students say it aloud with you. Relate *extraordinary* to the photographs on pp. 150–151 and "Where Are the Alligators?" What makes each animal picture *extraordinary*? What behaviors of alligators are *extraordinary*? Have students determine the definition of the word. (Something that is *extraordinary* is very unusual and deserves attention.)

2 Demonstrate Have students answer questions to demonstrate understanding. Why are the bats' hanging upside down to sleep *extraordinary*? What *extraordinary* behavior or characteristic does your favorite animal have?

3 Apply Have students apply their understanding by using the word in a personal context.

See p. OV•5 to teach *scenery*.

Routines Flip Chart

Apply Amazing Words

As students read "Eagle Watching" on p. 157, have them think about the behaviors of eagles that are *extraordinary* and the *scenery* the characters experience as they go to watch eagles.

Connect to reading

Help students establish a purpose for reading. Explain that today students will read about an eagle that is trained to act like a chicken. As they read, they should think about how the Question of the Week and the Amazing Words *extraordinary* and *scenery* apply to the folktale.

ELL **Reinforce Vocabulary** Use the Day 2 instruction on ELL Poster 20 to teach lesson vocabulary and the lesson concept.

ELL

English Language Learners
Cognates Spanish-speaking students might find it helpful to connect the Amazing Word *extraordinary* to the Spanish cognate *extraordinario*.

ELL Poster 20

Objectives
• Apply knowledge of the VCCCV syllable pattern to decode words in context and independent of context.

Check Word Reading
SUCCESS PREDICTOR

Word Analysis
◉ Syllables VCCCV

Review

Review the syllable pattern VCCCV, reminding students that when dividing words into syllables, they should not split blends or digraphs.

Read words independent of context

Display these words. Have the class decode the words. Then point to the words in random order and ask students to read them quickly.

district	address	complain	control
purchase	extreme	further	dolphin

Model identifying the VCCCV syllabication pattern, reading the syllables, and then reading the word. Then ask students to read the word with you.

Read words in context

Display these sentences. Have the class read the sentences.

Team Talk Have pairs take turns reading the sentences naturally.

The **children** got into a lot of **mischief.**
The **monster** liked to eat ham **sandwiches.**
My uncle is **employed** at an **orchard.**

Don't Wait Until Friday

MONITOR PROGRESS | **Check Word Reading**

Words with Syllables VCCCV

Write the following words and have the class read them. Notice which words students miss during the group reading. Call on individuals to read some of the words.

explain	improve	simply	instruct	**Spiral Review** Row 2 reviews words with VCV and VCCV patterns.
super	supper	hoper	hopper	
subject	abstain	captive	although	Row 3 contrasts words with VCCV and VCCCV patterns.

If... students cannot read words with the VCCCV syllable pattern at this point,

then... use the Small Group Time Strategic Intervention lesson, p. D1•103, to reteach the VCCCV syllable pattern. Continue to monitor students' progress using other instructional opportunities during the week. See the Skills Trace on p. 154a.

Day 1	Day 2	Day 3	Day 4	Day 5	
Check Oral Vocabulary	Check Word Reading	Check Retelling	Check Fluency	Check Oral Vocabulary	Success Predictor

Literary Terms
Sensory Details

Teach sensory details

Tell students that sensory details are words that help the reader see, smell, taste, hear, or feel what is described. Writers use sensory details to bring things and events to life for readers. Sensory details appear in all kinds of writing, from nonfiction to fiction to poetry.

Model sensory details

 Think Aloud Listen as I read these sentences from "Lulu Wants to Grow Up." *Suddenly she slipped. Lulu tumbled down.* What sense do the sentences appeal to—sight, smell, hearing, taste, or touch? Which words make you "see" what happened to Lulu? **(The sentences appeal to the sense of sight. The words *slipped* and *tumbled* make the reader "see" what happened.)**

Guide practice

Read aloud p. 160 of *Fly, Eagle, Fly!* Pause at the end of each paragraph and have students identify the senses to which the descriptions appeal. Ask volunteers to share what they imagined as you read.

On their own

Have students read p. 161, paying attention to the sensory details the author uses to bring the story to life.

Story Structure
Rising Action

Teach rising action

The plot of a story is its series of related events that show the characters in action. After the characters and the problem are introduced, then the character must face the conflict. This is called the rising action.

Model the strategy

 Think Aloud When I read pages 164–165 of *Fly, Eagle, Fly!*, I see that the friend faces the problem of proving that the eagle is not a chicken. The rising action begins as the friend tries to get the eagle to fly and it won't. The rising action will continue as the friend thinks of different ways to solve the problem.

Guide practice

Read pp. 166–167 and guide students in identifying the rising action. Explain that each time, the friend takes the bird higher but has the same results.

On their own

Explain that the friend will keep trying different ways to get the eagle to fly. Point out that these attempts lead to the climax, or turning point, of the story.

Check Word Reading

Success Predictor

DAY 2 Read and Comprehend

40–45 min

Objectives

- Use a dictionary or glossary to find meanings, syllabication, and pronunciation of unknown words.
- Read grade-level text with appropriate rate.

Vocabulary Strategy for 🔊 Unknown Words

Student Edition p. W•14

Teach unknown words

Envision It!

Explain to students that as they read they will encounter unknown words. If they are not able to use word parts or context to determine meanings, they should use a dictionary or glossary to look up the meaning. Remind students that dictionaries and glossaries list the meanings of words in alphabetical order. They also show the syllabication and pronunciation of the words. Refer students to *Words!* on p. W•14 in the Student Edition for additional practice.

Model the strategy

Write on the board: *Loud eagle cries often echoed across the valley.*

Think Aloud

I can't figure out the meaning of *echoed* from the context, so I will use a dictionary or glossary to look up the word. When I look up *echoed* in a dictionary, I see that it means that a sound is "repeated because it reflects off a surface." Now I understand that the cries of the eagles were repeated off the sides of the hills that made the valley. If I don't know how many syllables are in the word, or how the word is pronounced, I can find that information, too. Dictionaries and glossaries divide each word into syllables and show the pronunciation of each word in parentheses right after it. The pronunciation key at the bottom of each spread helps me figure out how to pronounce the word.

Guide practice

Write this sentence on the board: *Rashid scrambled to the front of the line for lunch.* Have students try to determine the meaning of the word *scrambled* from context clues. If they cannot determine the meaning, have them use a dictionary or glossary to find the definition. Have students tell the number of syllables and the pronunciation of *scrambled,* as well. For additional support, use *Envision It! Vocabulary Cards* or *Tested Vocabulary Cards.*

On their own

Read "Eagle Watching" on page 157. Have students use a dictionary to determine the meanings of the lesson vocabulary. For additional practice use *Reader's and Writer's Notebook* p. 292.

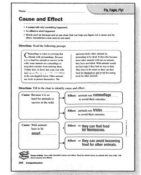

Reader's and Writer's Notebook, p. 292

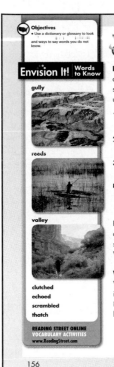

Objectives
• Use a dictionary or glossary to look ___ and ways to say words you do not know.

Envision It! Words to Know

gully

reeds

valley

clutched
echoed
scrambled
thatch

READING STREET ONLINE VOCABULARY ACTIVITIES
www.ReadingStreet.com

Vocabulary Strategy for

Unknown Words

Dictionary/Glossary You can use a dictionary or glossary to find the meaning, syllable division, and pronunciation of an unknown word.

1. Find the entry word and pronunciation in the dictionary or glossary.

2. Look at the pronunciation key and each syllable to pronounce the word correctly.

3. Read all of the definitions. Which meaning best fits the your sentence?

4. Try that meaning in the sentence. If it doesn't make sense, try another meaning of the word.

Read "Eagle Watching" on page 157. Use a dictionary or glossary to find the meanings, syllable divisions, and pronunciations of the Words to Know.

Words to Write Reread "Eagle Watching." What kind of animals are you interested in studying? Write about your interest. Use words from the Words to Know list in your answer.

Eagle Watching

José and his father scrambled up the side of the gully. Near the top of the gully was their favorite eagle-watching spot. José and his father looked for the bald eagles that lived in the area. First, they used their binoculars to scan the tops of the trees. Eagles usually perch in high places so that they can look for food. Next, José and his father listened for the eagles. Loud eagle cries often echoed across the valley.

In the valley below where José and his father hid was a large lake. The eagles swooped over the reeds and thatch along the lake's edge, skimmed over the surface, and dipped down and snatched a fish out of the water. Then the eagles flew away with the fish clutched in their sharp talons, or claws. They carried the fish back to their nests, high in the tall trees or on the cliffs. It was an amazing sight, and José never got tired of watching it.

Your Turn!

 Need a Review? For help with using a dictionary or glossary to find the meaning and pronunciation of unknown words, see *Words!*

 Ready to Try It? Read *Fly, Eagle, Fly!* on pp. 158–171.

156   157

Student Edition pp. 156–157

Reread for Fluency
Rate

Model fluent reading   Read paragraph 1 of "Eagle Watching," keeping an even rate. Tell students that your rate reflects the content and aids understanding.

ROUTINE **Paired Reading**

1. **Select a passage** For "Eagle Watching," use the whole passage.

2. **Reader 1** Students read the entire passage, switching readers at the end of each paragraph.

3. **Reader 2** Partners reread the passage. This time the other student begins.

4. **Reread** For optimal fluency, have partners continue to read three or four times.

5. **Corrective Feedback** Listen as students read. Provide feedback about their rate and encourage them to adjust rate based on the content of the selection.

Routines Flip Chart

Lesson Vocabulary

clutched grasped something tightly

echoed the repeating of a sound caused by its reflecting off a hard surface

gully a ditch made by heavy rains or running water

reeds tall grasses that grow in wet places

scrambled made your way, especially by climbing or crawling quickly

thatch roofing material made of straw

valley an area of low land that lies between hills or mountains

Differentiated Instruction

SI **Strategic Intervention**

Dictionary Have students work in pairs to look up two unknown words in a dictionary. Review alphabetical order and guide words to help students complete the task. Invite groups to share definitions with the class.

ELL

English Language Learners
Cognates Point out the Spanish cognates in this week's lesson vocabulary: *echo/hacer eco, valley/valle.*

Objectives

- Understand the elements of folk tales.
- Use illustrations to preview and predict.
- Set a purpose for reading.

Student Edition pp. 158–159

Build Background

Discuss eagles

Team Talk Have students turn to a partner and discuss the Question of the Week and these questions about eagles.

- What do eagles look and sound like?
- How do eagles behave?
- What kinds of things do eagles eat?

Connect to selection

Have students discuss their answers with the class. Possible responses: Eagles are huge birds that often have white heads. Their calls sound like cries or screeches, and they soar way up in the sky. Eagles are predators, so they catch small animals and fish in their claws.

Prereading Strategies

Genre Explain that **folk tales** are stories that are created by an anonymous storyteller and handed down orally from generation to generation until someone records them. Often there are several versions of one folk tale. Folk tales express themes about human nature, often through animals. Characters usually aren't well developed but instead represent an aspect of human nature or are used to move the plot along.

Preview and predict Have students preview the title and illustrations to predict what the selection will be about.

Set purpose Have students set their own purpose for reading this selection. To help students set a purpose, ask them to think about how eagles normally behave.

Strategy Response Log

Have students use p. 26 in the *Reader's and Writer's Notebook* to identify the characteristics of folk tales.

Small Group Time

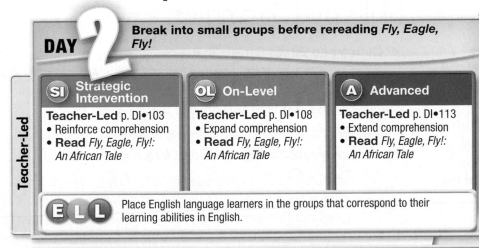

DAY 2 — Break into small groups before rereading *Fly, Eagle, Fly!*

SI Strategic Intervention
Teacher-Led p. DI•103
• Reinforce comprehension
• **Read** *Fly, Eagle, Fly!: An African Tale*

OL On-Level
Teacher-Led p. DI•108
• Expand comprehension
• **Read** *Fly, Eagle, Fly!: An African Tale*

A Advanced
Teacher-Led p. DI•113
• Extend comprehension
• **Read** *Fly, Eagle, Fly!: An African Tale*

ELL Place English language learners in the groups that correspond to their learning abilities in English.

Practice Stations
• Words to Know
• Get Fluent
• Word Wise

Independent Activities
• Background Building Audio
• *Reader's and Writer's Notebook*
• Research and Inquiry

Differentiated Instruction

 Strategic Intervention
Work with students to set a purpose for reading, or if time permits, have students work with partners to set purposes.

 Advanced
Have students share with partners one of their favorite folk tales, explaining the plot and describing the main idea of the tale.

Multidraft Reading
To assist struggling readers and to deepen reading for all, apply multidraft reading protocols. For each reading, have students set the purpose indicated.

• **First reading**—Literal comprehension: discuss Guide Comprehension questions to monitor and clarify understanding.
• **Second reading**—Application of skills: answer higher-order thinking skills questions to develop deeper understanding of text and make connections to the real world.

English Language Learners
Build background To build background, review the selection summary in English (*ELL Handbook*, p. 145). Use the Retelling Cards to provide visual support for the summary.

A farmer went out one day to search for a lost calf. The little herd boys had come back without it the evening before. And that night there had been a terrible storm.

He went to the valley and searched. He searched by the riverbed. He searched among the reeds, behind the rocks, and in the rushing water.

He wandered over the hillside and through the dark and tangled forests where everything began, then out again along the muddy cattle tracks.

He searched in the long thatch grass, taller than his own head. He climbed the slopes of the high mountain with its rocky cliffs rising to the sky. He called out all the time, hoping that the calf might hear, but also because he felt so alone. His shouts echoed off the cliffs. The river roared in the valley below.

He climbed up a gully in case the calf had huddled there to escape the storm. And that was where he stopped. For there, on a ledge of rock, close enough to touch, he saw the most unusual sight—an eagle chick, very young, hatched from its egg a day or two before and then blown from its nest by the terrible storm.

He reached out and cradled it in both hands. He would take it home and care for it. And home he went, still calling, calling in case the calf might hear.

He was almost home when the children ran out to meet him. "The calf came back by itself!" they shouted. He was very pleased. He showed the eagle chick to his wife and children, then placed it carefully in the warm kitchen among the hens and chicks and under the watchful eye of the roosters.

"The eagle is the king of the birds," he said, "but we shall train it to be a chicken."

160 161

Student Edition pp. 160–161

Guide Comprehension
Skills and Strategies

Teach cause and effect

 Cause and Effect Explain that a cause is why something happens and an effect is what happens. Ask the following question to help students identify the cause of the action: Why does the farmer go to the riverbed and valley? (He needs to find the calf that was lost.)

If... students are unable to answer the question,
then... model recognizing cause and effect.

Model the skill

Think Aloud In the first sentence on page 160, I read that the farmer went "to search for a lost calf." I know that "what happened" is the farmer goes out to search. Is that the cause or effect? (effect) If I ask myself why that happened, I know that the calf getting lost causes him to conduct a search.

On their own

Have students reread pp. 160–161 to identify further causal relationships. For additional practice, use *Let's Practice It! DVD*.

Let's Practice It!
TR DVD•260

Extend Thinking
Think Critically

Higher-order thinking skills

 Cause and Effect • Analysis Reread page 161. What happens to make the farmer feel pleased? Possible response: The calf returns on its own.

Background Knowledge • Synthesis On these pages we learn that the farmer finds an eagle and plans to train it to be a chicken. Based on what you know about eagles, do you think his plan will work? Possible response: The plan won't work because it will go against the eagle's true nature.

Genre • Synthesis What makes this passage seem like a folk tale so far? Possible response: The characters don't have names, and the animals seem to be most important to the plot of the story.

Differentiated Instruction

 **Strategic Intervention**

Cause and effect Tell students that cause and effect is often signaled by clue words, such as *because* and *so*. Write this sentence from the story: *He called out all the time . . . because he felt so alone.* Help students identify the cause (he felt so alone) and the effect (he called out all the time).

Connect to Science

Often fledglings, or small birds that are just learning to fly, seem like they need human intervention. However, experts agree that these creatures have the best chance of survival if they are left alone. The mother bird will watch over them and continue to feed and protect them even after they are out of the nest.

ELL

English Language Learners
Activate prior knowledge Remind students of your discussion about eagles and their behavior. What do you know about chickens? Do eagles and chickens behave the same or differently? Will the farmer have problems teaching the eagle to be a chicken? Have students talk to partners about the differences between eagles and chickens.

Objectives

• Monitor and clarify to improve comprehension.

So the eagle lived among the chickens, learning their ways. His children called their friends to see the strange bird. For as it grew, living on the bits and pieces put out for the chickens, it began to look quite different from any chicken they had ever seen.

Student Edition pp. 162–163

Guide Comprehension
Skills and Strategies

Teach monitor and clarify

 Monitor and Clarify Have students read p. 162 and look at the illustrations. Ask students why the eagle is living among the chickens and acting like them. (The farmer planned to teach the eagle to be a chicken.)

If... students have difficulty answering the question,
then... model how to monitor and clarify information in the text.

Model the strategy

Think Aloud When I read about the eagle acting like a chicken, I am confused. I know that the farmer said the eagle was the king of birds. To clarify why the eagle is acting this way, I will return to page 161 and reread the last two paragraphs. What plan does the farmer have for the eagle? (He wants to teach it to be a chicken.) Do the eagle's actions make sense now? (Yes)

On their own

Have students reread p. 162 and have them generate questions to clarify the text. Have students use textual evidence to support, adjust, or correct their comprehension.

Extend Thinking
Think Critically

Higher-order thinking skills

 **Monitor and Clarify • Synthesis** What parts of the folk tale do you find confusing? What can you do to monitor and clarify your understanding? **Possible response:** Rereading, summarizing, and reviewing text and illustrations can help clarify understanding.

Cause and Effect • Analysis Why does the eagle live with the chickens and start acting like the chickens? **Possible response:** The farmer places the eagle with the chickens and hopes to teach it to act like a chicken.

Review **Draw Conclusions • Synthesis** Read the text on page 162 and look at the illustration. Why do people have a reaction to the eagle? **Possible responses:** It looks different from all the other birds. It isn't behaving as an eagle is expected to.

<mark>Objectives</mark>

- Draw conclusions about characters and events in the text.

The farmer's children helped his friend catch the bird. It was fairly heavy but he lifted it above his head and said: "You are not a chicken but an eagle. You belong not to the earth but to the sky. Fly, Eagle, fly!"

The bird stretched out its wings as the farmer and his family had seen it do before. But it looked about, saw the chickens feeding, and jumped down to scratch with them for food.

"I told you it was a chicken," the farmer said, and roared with laughter.

One day a friend dropped in for a visit. He and the farmer sat at the door of the kitchen hut. The friend saw the bird among the chickens. "Hey! That's not a chicken. It's an eagle!"

The farmer smiled at him and said, "Of course it's a chicken. Look—it walks like a chicken, it talks like a chicken, it eats like a chicken. It *thinks* like a chicken. Of course it's a chicken."

But the friend was not convinced. "I will show you that it is an eagle," he said.

"Go ahead," said the farmer.

164

165

Student Edition pp. 164–165

Guide Comprehension
Skills and Strategies

Teach draw conclusions

Review **Draw Conclusions** Ask students why they think the eagle refuses to fly.

If... students have difficulty responding,
then... use the model to help them draw conclusions.

Model the skill

 Think Aloud I know it is the eagle's nature to fly, but so far in the story, the farmer has let the chickens raise the eagle. The eagle thinks it is a chicken, and the chickens don't fly. Therefore, I think the eagle refuses to fly because it has never seen the chickens do it.

On their own

Have students reread pp. 164–165 and use textual evidence to draw another conclusion about one of the characters or events in the story. Remind them that drawing conclusions can help them clarify their understanding. For additional practice with drawing conclusions, use the *Let's Practice It! DVD*.

INTERACT with TEXT

Teacher's Resource DVD-ROM•261

Extend Thinking
Think Critically

Higher-order thinking skills

Review **Draw Conclusions • Evaluation** The farmer concludes that the eagle is a chicken because it walks, talks, eats, and thinks like a chicken. Does his conclusion make sense? Explain. Possible response: It doesn't make sense because the eagle is still an eagle, no matter how it acts or thinks.

 Monitor and Clarify • Analysis Reread what the friend says to the eagle on page 165. Why does the friend want to prove the eagle is an eagle? Use facts and details from the story to support your answer. Possible response: I read that he believes that the eagle belongs to the sky. In other words, it is going against its nature to be on the ground all the time.

Sensory Details • Analysis Remind students that sensory details appeal to the senses and create vivid images in readers' minds. Read aloud the last paragraph on p. 165. Ask: Do the details make you see, feel, hear, taste, or smell something? Explain which words appeal to your senses. Possible response: The words *roared with laughter* appeal to the sense of hearing and sight. They create an image of a man laughing loudly and doubling over with laughter from his amusement.

Objectives
• Monitor and clarify to improve comprehension.

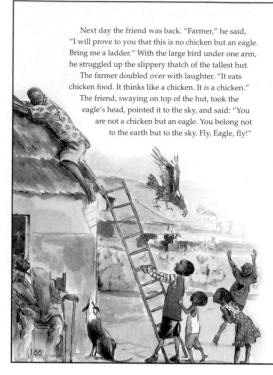

Next day the friend was back. "Farmer," he said, "I will prove to you that this is no chicken but an eagle. Bring me a ladder." With the large bird under one arm, he struggled up the slippery thatch of the tallest hut. The farmer doubled over with laughter. "It eats chicken food. It thinks like a chicken. It *is* a chicken." The friend, swaying on top of the hut, took the eagle's head, pointed it to the sky, and said: "You are not a chicken but an eagle. You belong not to the earth but to the sky. Fly, Eagle, fly!"

Again the great bird stretched out its wings. It trembled and the claws that clasped his hand opened. "Fly, Eagle, fly!" the man cried.

But the bird scrambled out of his hands, slid down the thatch, and sailed in among the chickens.

There was much laughter.

Very early next morning, on the third day, the farmer's dogs began to bark. A voice was calling outside in the darkness. The farmer ran to the door. It was his friend again. "Give me one more chance with the bird," he begged.

"Do you know the time? It's long before dawn. Are you crazy?"

"Come with me. Fetch the bird."

Reluctantly the farmer went into the kitchen, stepping over his sleeping children, and picked up the bird, which was fast asleep among the chickens. The two men set off, disappearing into the darkness.

166

167

Student Edition pp. 166–167

Guide Comprehension
Skills and Strategies

Teach monitor and clarify

Monitor and Clarify After students read pp. 166–167, ask them why the friend is so determined to prove that the eagle is actually an eagle. Tell students to pay special attention to the friend's words.

If... students have difficulty identifying the reason,
then... use the model to help them clarify the text.

Model the strategy

Think Aloud

At first, I thought the friend just wanted to prove the farmer wrong. But after I reread the friend's words, I realize he keeps repeating the same words to the eagle. He tells the bird it is an eagle and explains that it belongs to the sky, not the earth. I think he is determined to help the eagle realize what it really is and where it actually belongs.

On their own

Have students reread pp. 166–167 and practice fix-up strategies to help them monitor, adjust, and correct their understanding of the story.

Extend Thinking
Think Critically

Higher-order thinking skills

 Monitor and Clarify • Analysis On page 166 the friend takes the bird to the roof of the tallest hut. There must be a reason he does that. What do you think it is? **Possible response: He hopes that being up high will seem familiar to the bird and inspire it to fly.**

Review Draw Conclusions • Synthesis Why does the farmer think that it is funny when the eagle refuses to fly? **Possible response: He thinks it is funny because he believes he has succeeded in changing the eagle's true nature. He thinks the friend's actions are pointless.**

Prior Knowledge • Synthesis • Text to Text Did you learn anything new about eagles in *Fly, Eagle, Fly!* and in "Eagle Watching"? How do the eagles in the two stories compare? **Possible response: I learned how eagles actually catch their food. The eagles act differently. In "Eagle Watching," they soar high in the sky and catch fish to eat, whereas the eagle in the story eats chicken food and stays on the ground.**

Check Predictions Have students look back at the predictions they made earlier and discuss whether they were accurate. Then have students preview the rest of the selection and either adjust their predictions accordingly or make new predictions.

If you want to teach this selection in two sessions, stop here.

Differentiated Instruction

 Strategic Intervention

Monitor and clarify Have students work in small groups to summarize the main events of the selection. From their summaries, determine whether they need to apply fix-up strategies to improve comprehension.

 Advanced

Investigate eagles Have students work in pairs to investigate the natural habitats and behaviors of eagles. Have students present their findings to the class, using visuals to add interest to their presentations.

ELL

English Language Learners
Oral language: Intonation Tell students that the intonation of dialogue is determined by the end punctuation. Point out that intonation signals questions, exclamations, and statements. Demonstrate reading different types of sentences from p. 167. Have students identify them as questions, exclamations, or statements based on intonation.

Monitor and clarify Tell students they should keep asking themselves questions to make sure they understand the story. Write these questions: Whom or what is the story about? Where does the story happen? What happens in the beginning, middle, and end?

Objectives

- Find pertinent information from encyclopedias.
- Recognize and correctly use prepositions and prepositional phrases.
- Practice correctly spelling words with the syllable pattern VCCCV.

Research and Inquiry
Navigate/Search

Teach Have students generate a research plan for gathering relevant information about their topic. Suggest that students search encyclopedias—either print, electronic, or online versions—using their inquiry questions and keywords. Tell them to skim and scan each book or site for information that helps answer their inquiry question or leads them to specific information that will be useful. Bolded or italicized words may be clues to the kind of information the Web site source will provide. Have students look for visual aids such as photographs, illustrations, graphs, and diagrams. Remind students to take notes as they gather information.

Model **Think Aloud** While looking for information on bears and hibernation, I found that black bears start preparing for hibernation in the summer by eating carbohydrate-rich diets. I will use keywords from this information, such as *diets,* to lead me to more specific information. One fact I found explains that bears eat a lot of berries.

Guide practice Have students continue their review of sources they identified. Tell students to make sure to skim and scan for further keywords that might lead to more information. Remind students that they can use graphic organizers and outlines to take simple notes.

On their own Have students sort their notes into an organizer as they prepare their journal entry. Suggest that they organize their notes by main ideas and supporting details.

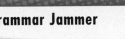
Conventions
Prepositions

Teach

Write *An eagle flew* and *An eagle flew from the tall trees* on the board. Point out the preposition *from*. A preposition shows a relationship between a noun or pronoun and the other words in a sentence. Underline *from the tall trees.* This is a prepositional phrase, which is a group of words that begins with a preposition and ends with a noun or pronoun.

Guide practice

Have students complete the sentence frames orally by adding a preposition and prepositional phrase.

> **Eagles fly** ——————.
>
> **Chickens scratch** ——————.
>
> **Farmers plant** ——————.

Daily Fix-It

Use Daily Fix-It numbers 3 and 4 in the right margin.

Connect to oral language

Have students look for examples of prepositions and prepositional phrases in *Fly, Eagle, Fly!* (*over the hillside and through the dark and tangled forests*, p. 160; *sailed in among the chickens*, p. 167)

On their own

For additional practice, use the *Reader's and Writer's Notebook* p. 295.

Reader's and Writer's Notebook p. 295

Daily Fix-It

3. The bald eagle live high on top the cliff. (*lives, top of*)
4. It is one of the bigest birds in the wirld. (*biggest, world*)

Spelling
Syllables VCCCV

Teach

Remind students that their spelling words for this week have the syllable pattern VCCCV. Model how to spell the word *surprise*. First write the letter *s*. Then write the first vowel, *u*. Write the group of three consonants, *rpr*, and the last vowel, *i*. Finally, write the last letters, *se*.

Guide practice

Have students write each spelling word and identify and underline the VCCCV syllable pattern in it.

On their own

For additional practice, use the *Reader's and Writer's Notebook* p. 296.

Reader's and Writer's Notebook p. 296

English Language Learners

Conventions To provide students with practice on prepositions, use the modified grammar lessons in the *ELL Handbook* and the Grammar Jammer online: www.TexasReadingStreet.com

Fly, Eagle, Fly! **167c**

Writing for Tests—Summary
Preparing for Test Writing

Introduce the prompt

Remind students that yesterday they learned about the key features of a summary. Tell them today they will practice writing for tests by creating a summary that addresses the prompt. Read aloud the writing prompt.

Writing Prompt

Think about a tale you know well. Now write a summary of the plot, telling the events in time order.

MINI-LESSON

Time-Order Transition Words

- When we write summaries we want to include only the most important information. We also want to present that information in the order that it happens in the story.

- Explain that a story sequence chart can help students identify the important parts of a story in the order that they happen. Display a story sequence chart and complete it with a well-known story as the example. Discuss what happened first in the story, and write the most important information in the first Events box. Then identify two more important events and write them in the next two Events boxes. Then discuss what happens last in the story and write the information in the last Events box.

- Many summaries include time-order transition words. Time-order transition words help us organize our writing and reading. The words tell when things happened or in what order. Examples of time-order transition words include *first, then, next, last, meanwhile,* and *finally.*

Discuss Rubric

Discuss the Writing Rubric found on p. 297 in the *Reader's and Writer's Notebook.* Go over the criteria for each trait under each score. Remind students that this is the rubric that will be used to evaluate the summaries they write.

Sample Test

Direct students to get paper and pencil ready to take a writing test. Display the writing prompt for students and give them appropriate time to write to it. Remind students to allow themselves a couple of minutes after writing to reread what they've written and make changes or additions.

Prompt

Think about a tale you know well. Now write a summary of the plot, telling the events in time order.

ROUTINE Quick Write for Fluency   Team Talk

1. **Talk** Have pairs discuss time-order transition words.

2. **Write** Have students write two to three sentences using time-order transition words.

3. **Share** Have students read their own writing to their partner.

Routines Flip Chart

Wrap Up Your Day

✔ **Build Concepts** What did you learn about how the farmer's friend tried to prove that the eagle was not a chicken?

✔ **Cause and Effect** What caused the farmer and his family to laugh when the man tried to get the eagle to fly?

✔ **Monitor and Clarify** How can you figure out what the words *claws* and *clasped* mean?

Differentiated Instruction

SI Strategic Intervention

Outline Some students may find it easier to create an outline of the main events of the story they are summarizing before they start writing. They can use the outline to help them organize the events they'll be summarizing.

Reader's and Writer's Notebook p. 297

Teacher Tip

If students have trouble with time management, discuss tips for managing time during tests before you begin the actual writing test. List the tips on the board for students to refer to.

Preview DAY 3

Tell students that tomorrow they will read about what happens when the man takes the eagle to the mountains.

Objectives
- Expand the weekly concept.
- Develop oral vocabulary.

Today at a Glance

Oral Vocabulary
pesky, unfurl

Phonics/Word Analysis
Syllables VCCCV

Comprehension Check/Retelling
Discuss questions

Reading
Fly, Eagle, Fly!

Think Critically
Retelling

Fluency
Rate

Research and Study Skills
Outlining and summarizing

Research and Inquiry
Analyze

Conventions
Prepositions

Spelling
Syllables VCCCV

Writing
Writing for tests: Summary

Concept Talk

Question of the Week

What behaviors are unique to different animals?

Expand the concept

Remind students of the weekly concept question. Discuss how the question relates to an eagle acting like a chicken. Remind students to make pertinent comments in a discussion. Tell students that today they will read about how the friend tries again to teach the eagle to act like an eagle. Encourage students to think about the actions of the eagle that are extraordinary.

Anchored Talk

Develop oral vocabulary

Use illustrations to review pp. 158–167 of *Fly, Eagle, Fly!* Discuss the Amazing Words *extraordinary* and *scenery*. Add these and other concept-related words to the concept map. Use the following questions to develop students' understanding of the concept. Remind students to ask and answer questions with appropriate detail and to give suggestions based on the ideas of others.

- What animals' behaviors and characteristics are *extraordinary*?
- How does the *scenery* and environment affect animals' behaviors and characteristics?

Oral Vocabulary
Amazing Words

Amazing Words

armor	scenery
agile	pesky
snout	unfurl
protrude	coil
extraordinary	intersection

Amazing Words Oral Vocabulary Routine

Teach Amazing Words

1 Introduce Write the word *pesky* on the board. Have students say it with you. Yesterday, we read about a farmer who trains an eagle to be a chicken. His *pesky* friend tries to prove him wrong and teach the eagle to fly. Have students determine a definition of *pesky*. (A pesky person is troublesome or irritating.)

2 Demonstrate Have students answer questions to demonstrate understanding. Why might chickens be thought of as *pesky*? (Possible response: They make a mess or are in the way.)

3 Apply Have students apply their understanding by listing possible synonyms of *pesky*.

See p. OV•2 to teach *unfurl*.

Routines Flip Chart

Apply Amazing Words

As students read pp. 158–171 of *Fly, Eagle, Fly!* have them consider how the Amazing Words *pesky* and *unfurl* apply to the friend and his quest to teach the eagle to fly.

Connect to reading

Help students establish a purpose for reading. Explain that today students will read about the friend's final attempt to teach the eagle to fly. As they read, students should think about how the Question of the Week and the Amazing Words *pesky* and *unfurl* apply to this attempt.

ELL Expand Vocabulary Use the Day 3 instruction on ELL Poster 20 to help students expand vocabulary.

ELL Poster 20

Word Analysis
Build Words

Model word building

Now we are going to build words with the syllabication pattern VCCCV. Write *central* and identify the VCCCV pattern. Watch me change the vowel *e* in the first syllable to the vowel *o,* and the vowel *a* in the second syllable to the vowel *o.* Model how to pronounce the new word *control.*

Guide practice

Write *hardly* and have the class decode it with you. Remind students that the letter *y* is sometimes considered a vowel. Have students spell *hardly* with their letter tiles. Monitor students' work.

Corrective feedback

For corrective feedback, model the correct spelling and have students correct their tiles.

- Change the *h* to *p* and the *d* to *t.* Say the new word.

- Change the vowel *a* to the vowel *o.* Say the new word.

- Change the vowel *o* to the vowel *e.* Say the new word.

p	a	r	t	l	y
p	o	r	t	l	y
p	e	r	t	l	y

Fluent Word Reading

Model

Write *dolphin.* I can identify the VCCCV pattern in *dolphin.* I divide the word between the *l* and *p,* say each syllable, and put the parts together to say *dolphin.*

Guide practice

Write the words below. Look for the word parts you know. When I point to the word, we'll read it together. Allow one second per word part previewing time for the first reading.

| huddle | contract | orphan | explain | enclose | complain |

On their own

Have students read the list above three or four times, until they can read one word per second.

Decode and Read

Read words independent of context

Have students turn to p. 57 in *Decodable Practice Reader 3.2* and find the first list of words. Each word in this list has the VCCCV syllabication pattern. Let's read these words. Be sure that students identify the correct pattern.

Next, have students read the high-frequency words.

Preview Decodable Practice Passage

Have students read the title and preview the story. Tell them that they will read words with the VCCCV syllable pattern.

Read words in context

Chorally read the story along with the students. Have students identify words in the story that have the VCCCV syllable pattern. Make sure that students are monitoring their accuracy when they decode words.

Team Talk Pair students and have them take turns reading the story aloud to each other. Monitor students as they read to check for proper pronunciation and appropriate pacing.

Decodable Practice Passage 20B

Differentiated Instruction

 Advanced

Build words Have students come up with their own addition and deletion questions and build new words.

DAY 3 Get Ready to Read

Objectives
- Identify cause and effect to aid comprehension.
- Monitor and clarify to aid comprehension.
- Use a dictionary or glossary to determine meanings of unknown words.

Comprehension Check

Have students discuss each question with a partner. Ask several pairs to share their responses.

☑ **Genre • Evaluation**

Does *Fly, Eagle, Fly!* have the characteristics of a folk tale? Explain. Possible response: It does have the characteristics of a folk tale because the characters aren't developed but move the plot along. It expresses an important message about human nature through animal characters.

☑ **Cause and effect • Analysis**

Why does the friend work so hard to prove that the eagle is not a chicken? He understands the importance of the eagle living as it is supposed to live, majestically and in the sky.

☑ **Monitor and clarify • Synthesis**

How are all of the friend's attempts to teach the eagle to fly similar? Use facts and details from the story to support your answer. He tries to get the eagle up off the ground in each attempt. Every time he tries, he takes the bird higher.

☑ **Unknown words**

Use the interaction between the farmer and the friend to define the word *convince.* Check your definition in a dictionary or glossary. The word *convince* means "to make somebody sure or certain of something."

☑ **Connect text to text**

In *Fly, Eagle, Fly!* the friend tries three times to get the eagle to fly. Many folk tales feature patterns of three. Think of another tale that has a character that tries three times to do something. Possible response: The tales *The Three Rings, Goldilocks and the Three Bears,* and *The Three Little Pigs* all feature patterns of three.

Strategy Response Log

Have students revisit p. 26 in the *Reader's and Writer's Notebook* to add additional information about folk tales.

INTERACT with TEXT

Check Retelling

Have students retell the story of *Fly, Eagle, Fly!*

If... students leave out important details,
then... have students look back through the illustrations in the selection.

Small Group Time

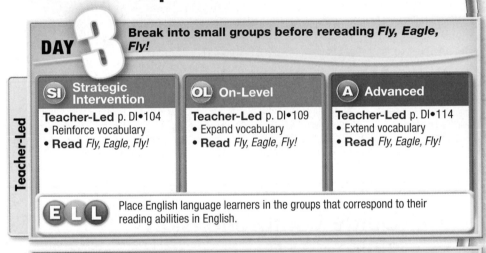

DAY 3 Break into small groups before rereading *Fly, Eagle, Fly!*

Teacher-Led

(SI) Strategic Intervention
Teacher-Led p. DI•104
• Reinforce vocabulary
• **Read** *Fly, Eagle, Fly!*

(OL) On-Level
Teacher-Led p. DI•109
• Expand vocabulary
• **Read** *Fly, Eagle, Fly!*

(A) Advanced
Teacher-Led p. DI•114
• Extend vocabulary
• **Read** *Fly, Eagle, Fly!*

ELL Place English language learners in the groups that correspond to their reading abilities in English.

Practice Stations
• Let's Write
• Get Fluent
• Word Work

Independent Activities
• AudioText of *Fly, Eagle, Fly!*
• *Reader's and Writer's Notebook*
• Research and Inquiry

English Language Learners
Check retelling To support retelling, review the multilingual summary for *Fly, Eagle, Fly!* with the appropriate retelling cards to scaffold understanding.

Objectives

• Use a dictionary to determine the meanings of unknown words.

"Where are we going?" asked the farmer sleepily.

"To the mountains where you found the bird."

"And why at this ridiculous time of the night?"

"So that our eagle may see the sun rise over the mountain and follow it into the sky where it belongs."

They went into the valley and crossed the river, the friend leading the way. The bird was very heavy and too large to carry comfortably, but the friend insisted on taking it himself.

"Hurry," he said, "or the dawn will arrive before we do!"

The first light crept into the sky as they began to climb the mountain. Below them they could see the river snaking like a long, thin ribbon through the golden grasslands, the forest, and the veld, stretching down toward the sea. The wispy clouds in the sky were pink at first and then began to shimmer with a golden brilliance.

Sometimes their path was dangerous as it clung to the side of the mountain, crossing narrow shelves of rock and taking them into dark crevices and out again. They were both panting, especially the friend who was carrying the bird.

Student Edition pp. 168–169

Guide Comprehension
Skills and Strategies

Teach unknown words

 Unknown Words Have students use a dictionary to determine the meaning of the word *veld* in the last paragraph on p. 168.

If... students are unable to figure out the meaning of *veld*, **then...** model using a dictionary to figure out the unknown word.

Model the skill

Think Aloud When I look up *veld* in the dictionary, I look first at the guide words to find the right page. I know that *veld* comes between words that start with *va* and *vi*. The dictionary definition of *veld* is "open country in South Africa, with grass or bushes but few trees." Does that definition make sense here?

On their own

Have students find the word *crevices* (p. 169) in a dictionary and figure out the meaning of the word. (narrow splits or cracks) For additional practice, use *Reader's and Writer's Notebook* p. 298.

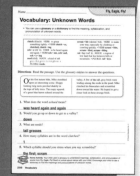

Reader's and Writer's Notebook p. 298

Extend Thinking
Think Critically

Higher-order thinking skills

 Unknown Words • Synthesis What does the word *insisted* in paragraph 5 on page 168 mean? How does it connect, in general, to the actions of the friend? Possible response: *Insisted* means "to state or demand something despite disagreement." It connects to the friend's repeated attempts to teach the eagle to fly despite the people laughing at him and the bird refusing to leave the ground.

Review **Draw Conclusions • Analysis** Why is the friend so determined to teach the eagle to fly? Possible response: He understands the importance of the bird realizing its true nature and doing what it is meant to do.

Monitor and Clarify • Analysis How does the friend's plan to take the bird to the top of the mountain relate to his other attempts to teach the eagle to fly? Possible response: He again wants to bring the eagle to a high place. This time it is even higher than lifting the bird in the air or taking it onto a roof.

Differentiated Instruction

SI **Strategic Intervention**

Unknown words Tell students that *insisted* means "to state or demand something despite disagreement" and "to request urgently." Read the sentence on p. 168 and ask students which meaning fits best in this context.

Connect to Science

There are many species of backyard birds common to Texas. They include the mourning dove, the western screech-owl, the black-chinned and ruby-throated hummingbird, and many types of woodpeckers. As urban areas continue to sprawl, however, the habitats of these birds are being threatened.

English Language Learners
Monitor and clarify Read p. 168 and model monitoring and clarifying: I don't understand why they are taking such a long journey with the bird. I will review the page. I see that the friend says the bird will see the sun and follow it into the sky where the bird belongs. That's why they are climbing so high. He wants to take the bird to the top of the mountain to teach it to fly. Have students review or reread to clarify understanding as needed.

At last he said, "This will do." He looked down the cliff and saw the ground thousands of feet below. They were very near the top.

Carefully the friend carried the bird onto a ledge of rock. He set it down so that it looked toward the east, and began talking to it.

The farmer chuckled. "It talks only chickens' talk."

But the friend talked on, telling the bird about the sun, how it gives life to the world, how it reigns in the heavens, giving light to each new day.

"Look at the sun, Eagle. And when it rises, rise with it. You belong to the sky, not to the earth."

At that moment the sun's first rays shot out over the mountain, and suddenly the world was ablaze with light.

The golden sun rose majestically, dazzling them. The great bird stretched out its wings to greet the sun and feel the life-giving warmth on its feathers. The farmer was quiet. The friend said, "You belong not to the earth, but to the sky. Fly, Eagle, fly!"

He clambered back to the farmer.

All was silent. Nothing moved. The eagle's head stretched up; its wings stretched outwards; its legs leaned forward as its claws clutched the rock.

And then, without really moving, feeling the updraft of a wind more powerful than any man or bird, the great eagle leaned forward and was swept upward, higher and higher, lost to sight in the brightness of the rising sun, never again to live among the chickens.

Student Edition pp. 170–171

Guide Comprehension
Skills and Strategies

Teach cause and effect

🔊 **Cause and Effect** Ask students to tell what happens at the end of the story and to identify why it happens. (The eagle flies because the friend helps it remember where it belongs.)

If... students cannot answer the questions,
then... model identifying causal relationships.

Model the skill

Think Aloud

At the end of the story, the eagle flies away toward the sun. That is the effect. Now, I think about the cause, or why the eagle flies away. If the friend had never come along, the eagle would likely have lived with the chickens forever. What role does the friend play in causing the eagle to fly? (He gives the eagle the opportunity to see where it belongs.)

On their own

Have students reread p. 171 and identify the cause of the farmer being quiet.

Extend Thinking
Think Critically

Higher-order thinking skills

 Cause and Effect • Analysis The eagle's true nature is to fly free. The farmer's friend repeatedly gives the eagle the opportunity to realize its nature. What final effect do these causes have? Possible response: The eagle leaves the chickens and flies toward the sun.

Review **Draw Conclusions • Synthesis** What message does the folk tale express through the actions of the characters and the events? How can you apply that message to your life? Possible response: The folk tale expresses the idea that we all have a true nature and that we just need to find that nature to "soar." If we really know ourselves, we can be our best by simply being who we are and doing what we do.

Comprehension Check

Spiral review

Sequence of Events • Analysis Do you think the friend would have been successful in getting the eagle to fly if he had taken it to the top of the mountain right away instead of first lifting it above his head and then taking it to the roof? Why or why not? Possible response: Yes, because at the top of the mountain the eagle had a much better view of the world beyond rather than just the chickens below.

Character • Evaluation Are the characters like real people or do they just move the action along in the folk tale? Explain. Possible response: They just move the action along. Readers do not know much about any of the characters. In fact, the characters don't even have names.

Check Predictions Have students return to the predictions they made earlier and confirm whether they were accurate.

If you want to teach this selection in two sessions, stop here.

Differentiated Instruction

SI **Strategic Intervention**
Monitor and clarify When students finish the selection, ask them to tell a partner what *Fly, Eagle, Fly!* is about. Have them explain its important points in four or five sentences.

A **Advanced**
Theme Have students identify the theme of the folk tale and write it in their own words. Then have them describe a time when they applied the theme in their own lives.

ELL

English Language Learners
Homonyms Tell students that some words have the same pronunciation and spelling but have different meanings. Point out the word *rose* in paragraph 7 on p. 171. Explain that *rose* can be the name of a flower and it can also mean "the past tense of *rise*." Read the sentence aloud. Help students determine the meaning of the word.

Objectives

- Identify cause and effect to aid comprehension.
- Monitor and clarify to check understanding.

Check Retelling
SUCCESS PREDICTOR

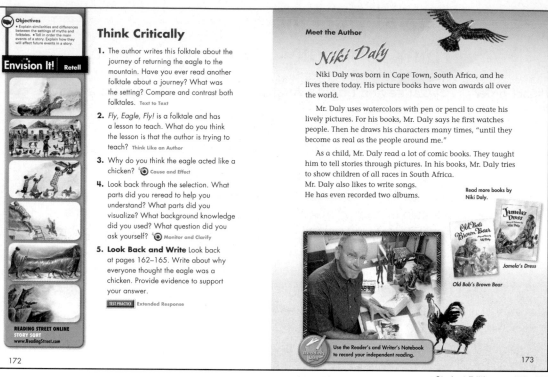

Think Critically

1. The author writes this folktale about the journey of returning the eagle to the mountain. Have you ever read another folktale about a journey? What was the setting? Compare and contrast both folktales. **Text to Text**

2. *Fly, Eagle, Fly!* is a folktale and has a lesson to teach. What do you think the lesson is that the author is trying to teach? **Think Like an Author**

3. Why do you think the eagle acted like a chicken? **Cause and Effect**

4. Look back through the selection. What parts did you reread to help you understand? What parts did you visualize? What background knowledge did you used? What question did you ask yourself? **Monitor and Clarify**

5. **Look Back and Write** Look back at pages 162–165. Write about why everyone thought the eagle was a chicken. Provide evidence to support your answer.

   TEST PRACTICE Extended Response

Meet the Author

Niki Daly

Niki Daly was born in Cape Town, South Africa, and he lives there today. His picture books have won awards all over the world.

Mr. Daly uses watercolors with pen or pencil to create his lively pictures. For his books, Mr. Daly says he first watches people. Then he draws his characters many times, "until they become as real as the people around me."

As a child, Mr. Daly read a lot of comic books. They taught him to tell stories through pictures. In his books, Mr. Daly tries to show children of all races in South Africa. Mr. Daly also likes to write songs. He has even recorded two albums.

Read more books by Niki Daly.

Jamela's Dress

Old Bob's Brown Bear

Use the Reader's and Writer's Notebook to record your independent reading.

Student Edition pp. 172–173

Retelling

Envision It! Have students work in pairs to retell the selection, using the Envision It! Retelling Cards as prompts. Have students sequence and summarize the plot's main events. Remind students that they should accurately describe the main topic and important ideas and use key vocabulary in their retellings. Monitor students' retellings.

Scoring rubric

Top-Score Response A top-score response makes connections beyond the text, describes the main topic and important ideas using accurate information, and draws conclusions from the text. For a complete rubric see the *First Stop* book.

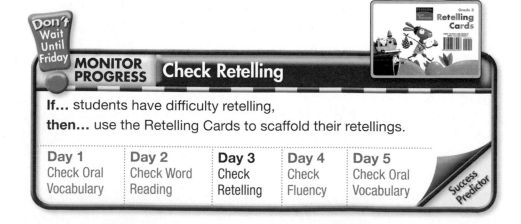

Don't Wait Until Friday

MONITOR PROGRESS Check Retelling

Grade 3 Retelling Cards

If... students have difficulty retelling,

then... use the Retelling Cards to scaffold their retellings.

Day 1	Day 2	Day 3	Day 4	Day 5
Check Oral Vocabulary	Check Word Reading	Check Retelling	Check Fluency	Check Oral Vocabulary

Success Predictor

Think Critically

Text to text

1. Possible response: I read the tale of Johnny Appleseed. He wanted to plant apple trees across America before it was settled. The setting is similar to *Fly, Eagle, Fly!* because they both take place in outdoor settings. They are different because *Fly, Eagle, Fly!* takes place in the mountains of Africa, and Johnny Appleseed's journey is set in the wilderness and prairies of the Midwestern United States.

Think like an author

2. Possible response: The author is trying to teach the lesson that it is important for us to be true to our own nature, even if others try to change us.

Cause and effect

3. Possible response: The eagle acted like a chicken because the farmer trained it to live like a chicken.

Monitor and clarify

4. Possible responses: I reread to find out why the eagle chick was all alone on the ledge. I visualized the eagle stretching its wings and being swept away by the wind. I knew that eagles fly. I asked why the friend talked to the eagle at the end of the story.

Writing on Demand

5. **Look Back and Write** To build writing fluency, assign a 10–15 minute time limit.

Suggest that students use a prewriting strategy, such as brainstorming or using a graphic organizer, to organize their ideas. Remind them to establish a topic sentence and support it with facts, details, or explanations. As students finish, encourage them to reread their responses, revise for organization and support, and proofread for errors in grammar and conventions.

Scoring rubric

> **Top-Score Response** A top-score response uses details to tell why everyone believed the eagle was a chicken.
>
> **A top-score response should include:**
>
> • a description of people's reactions, including the farmer's
>
> • a description of the friend's protest and people's reaction to it
>
> • an explanation for the people's reasoning

Check Retelling

Success Predictor

Objectives
- Read grade-level text with appropriate rate.
- Reread for fluency.
- Outline and summarize.

Model Fluency
Rate

Model fluent reading

Have students turn to p. 169 of *Fly, Eagle, Fly!* Have students follow along as you read the page. Tell them to listen to how fast you read and pay attention to your pauses and how they correlate to punctuation and content.

Guide practice

Have students follow along as you read the page again. Then have them reread the page as a group without you until they read with the right rate and with no mistakes. Continue in the same way for p. 171.

Reread for Fluency

Corrective feedback

If... students are having difficulty reading at the correct rate, **then...** prompt:

- Do you think you need to slow down or read more quickly?

- Read the sentence more quickly. Now read it more slowly. Which helps you understand what you are reading?

- Tell me the sentence. Read it at the rate that would help me understand it.

ROUTINE **Paired Reading**

1. **Select a passage** For *Fly, Eagle, Fly!,* use p. 167.

2. **Reader 1** Students read the entire passage, switching readers at the end of each paragraph.

3. **Reader 2** Partners reread the passage. This time the other student begins.

4. **Reread** For optimal fluency, have partners continue to read three or four times.

5. **Corrective Feedback** Listen as students read. Provide feedback about their rate and encourage them to adjust their rate based on punctuation and content.

Routines Flip Chart

Research and Study Skills
Outlining and Summarizing

Teach

Tell students that good readers summarize to check their understanding of a text. When students summarize nonfiction, they tell the main ideas in their own words. When they summarize fiction, they tell what happened in a story. Outlines, like summaries, list the main ideas of a text. However, outlines are visually organized to show the main ideas and the details that support those ideas. Outlines can be used to better understand a text and to organize students' own writing. Draw a basic outline:

I. Main idea

   A. Important detail

      1. Support

- A **summary** tells the main ideas or ideas of a nonfiction text. It leaves out unimportant details. For a story, a summary tells what happened, listing the main events, the goals of the characters, how they tried to reach them, and whether they were successful.

- An **outline** visually organizes main ideas and supporting details. It can be used to map a text or to organize writing.

Discuss these questions:

Guide practice

What should you include in a summary of a story? (an explanation of the main events, goals of the characters, and how they reached them)

Why would an outline help you with your own writing? (It allows you to organize your main ideas and make sure you have enough support for each idea.)

On their own

Have students review complete p. 299 of the *Reader's and Writer's Notebook.*

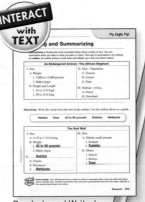

Reader's and Writer's Notebook p. 299

Advanced

Summarize Have students read a magazine or encyclopedia article about animal instincts. Challenge them to write a two- to three-sentence summary of the article.

ELL

English Language Learners

Summarize Give English learners the opportunity to practice their summarizing skills orally. Ask them to tell you the main things that happened in *Fly, Eagle, Fly!* Invite students to illustrate their summaries to further solidify understanding.

Objectives
- Analyze data for usefulness.
- Identify and correctly use prepositions.
- Spell frequently misspelled words correctly.

Research and Inquiry
Analyze

Teach

Tell students that once they gather information, they need to summarize the information in their own words and then consider whether the information they gathered has led them to a better question or to a specific area of inquiry.

Model

Think Aloud Originally, I thought that learning about when bears start preparing for hibernation was the most important information, but I learned from my research that how they prepare for hibernation is both well documented and fascinating. I will refocus my inquiry question to include information from my online research. Now my inquiry question is *How do bears prepare for hibernation?*

Guide practice

Have students analyze their findings. They may need to refocus their inquiry question to better fit the information they found. Remind students that if they have difficulty improving their focus they can ask a reference librarian or a local expert for guidance.

Remind students that they can add to their graphic organizers and outlines as they research.

On their own

Have students write brief summaries of the information they gathered and share their summaries with partners. Have partners pose questions that arise from the summaries to further direct investigation.

Conventions
Prepositions

Review

Remind students that this week they learned about prepositions.

- A preposition shows a relationship between a noun or pronoun and the other words in a sentence.
- A prepositional phrase is a group of words that begins with a preposition. It ends with a noun or pronoun called the object of the preposition.

Daily Fix-It

Use Daily Fix-It numbers 5 and 6 in the right margin.

Connect to oral language

Have students complete each sentence with a prepositional phrase.

> Gary walked _____.
>
> I followed it _____.
>
> A little bird flew _____.

On their own

For additional support, use the *Let's Practice It! DVD.*

Let's Practice It!
TR DVD•262

Spelling
Syllables VCCCV

Frequently misspelled words

The words *Christmas* and *went* are words that students often misspell. These words are difficult because of the syllable pattern. Think carefully before you write these words. Have students practice writing the words *Christmas* and *went* by writing sentences using each word. Ask pairs of students to exchange sentences and check for any misspellings.

On their own

For additional support, use the *Reader's and Writer's Notebook* p. 300.

Reader's and Writer's
Notebook p. 300

Differentiated Instruction

SI Strategic Intervention

Prepositions Create sentences to describe the location of classroom objects. Example: *The books are on the bookshelves. The Word Wall is beside the window.* On blank index cards, write the subject and verb of each sentence (e.g., *The books are*). On separate cards, write the prepositional phrase (e.g., *on the bookshelves*). Mix the cards and have students match the cards to make sentences.

Daily Fix-It

5. Jamal has saw a movie bout eagles. (*seen; about*)
6. They builds nests with sticks and leafs. (*build; leaves*)

Objectives
- Understand the criteria for writing an effective summary.

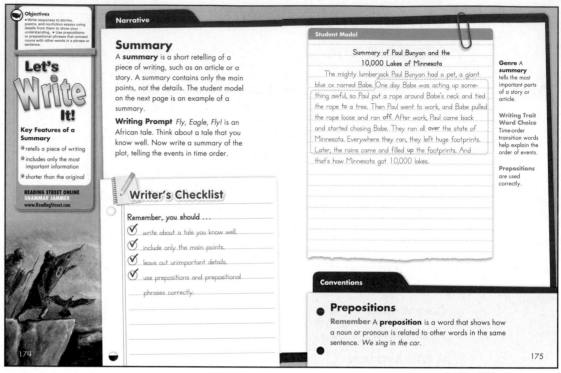

Student Edition pp. 174–175

Let's Write It!
Summary

Teach

Use pp. 174–175 in the Student Edition. Direct students to read the key features of summaries that appear on p. 174. Remind students that they can refer to the information in the Writer's Checklist as they write their own summaries.

Read the student model on p. 175. Point out the key features of summaries in the model.

Connect to conventions

Remind students that prepositions show a relationship between a noun or pronoun and the other words in a sentence. Point out the correct use of prepositions in the model.

Writing for Tests
Evaluation

Display rubric Have students return to the Scoring Rubric from p. 297 of the *Reader's and Writer's Notebook* that you reviewed on Day 2. Go over the criteria for each trait under each score. Then explain to students that they will use this rubric to evaluate the summaries they wrote yesterday.

Scoring Rubric: Writing for Tests: Summary

	4	3	2	1
Focus/Ideas	Strong summary; only uses important information	Good summary; mostly uses important information	Summary has some main ideas and too many details	Does not understand summary form
Organization	Important ideas are in correct sequence	Sequence of events is generally correct	Sequence of events isn't always clear	No clear sequence of events
Voice	Shows understanding of the main ideas	Shows understanding of topic	Lacks understanding of topic	Does not understand topic
Word Choice	Uses strong action verbs and time-order words	Uses some strong action verbs and time-order words	Few or no strong verbs or time-order words	Poor word choice
Sentences	Clear sentences of different lengths and types	Sentences of a few lengths and types	Sentences of similar length and type	No variety of sentence length and type
Conventions	Few, if any, errors; correct use of prepositions	Several small errors; use of prepositions	Many errors; weak use of prepositions	Many serious errors; incorrect or no use of prepositions

English Language Learners
Prepositions Have students practice the meaning of prepositions by playing a question game using prepositions as clues. For example, "Is it on the desk?"

Objectives
• Evaluate writing using a rubric.

Writing for Tests – Evaluation

Evaluation

■ **Introduce** Explain that when you evaluate writing with a rubric, you are evaluating different traits in the writing. Have students read aloud a few of the six traits in the rubric.

Evaluate a Trait Tell students that they will evaluate their sample writing test based on one of the six traits in the rubric. We will focus on trait 2, organization. Remind students that the information presented in the summary should be in the correct sequence. According to the rubric, we want to make sure that the information summarized is in the correct sequence. In your summary, you should have first written about what happens first in the story. Then you should have written about the events that happen next and what happens at the end.

Apply Scoring Have students review their summaries to make sure that the important ideas are in the correct sequence. Then, using the rubric as a guide, have them assess their organization on a scale from 4 to 1.

Direct students to continue evaluating their summaries based on the other five traits on the rubric. Remind students that they may receive different number scores for each of the different traits, but that is all right. Lower or higher scores for different traits can help them see where their strengths lie, and where they might need to focus more attention and effort.

ROUTINE Quick Write for Fluency — Team Talk

1. **Talk** Pairs talk about why presenting information in the correct sequence is important.

2. **Write** Students write one to two sentences using prepositional phrases to explain why presenting information in the correct sequence is important.

3. **Share** Students read their sentences to their partner. Partners check each other's writing for correct use of prepositional phrases.

Routines Flip Chart

Differentiated Instruction

SI Strategic Intervention

Sequence Give students photographs, drawings, or images from a magazine of something that happens in a sequence. Then have them use the pictures to tell about the sequence of events.

Wrap Up Your Day

✔ **Build Concepts** Have students discuss what unique behaviors helped the eagle fly away.

✔ **Cause and Effect** What finally caused the eagle to fly away?

✔ **Monitor and Clarify** What does "updraft of the wind" mean?

Preview DAY 4

Tell students that tomorrow they will read about a coyote that is an unusual color.

Objectives
- Expand the weekly concept.
- Develop oral vocabulary.

Today at a Glance

Oral Vocabulary
coil, intersection

Phonics
Syllables VCCCV

Genre
Folktale: Trickster tale

Reading
"Purple Coyote"

Let's Learn It!
Fluency: Rate
Vocabulary: Dictionary/Glossary
Listening and speaking: Book Review

Research and Inquiry
Synthesize

Conventions
Prepositions

Spelling
Syllables VCCCV

Writing
Writing for tests: Summary

Concept Talk

Question of the Week

 What behaviors are unique to different animals?

Expand the concept

Remind students that this week they have read about an eagle whose behavior was unique to chickens. Tell students that today they will read a trickster tale about a coyote that has turned purple.

Anchored Talk

Develop oral vocabulary

Use illustrations to review pp. 168–171 of *Fly, Eagle, Fly!* Discuss the Amazing Words *pesky* and *unfurl.* Add these and other concept-related words to the concept map. Use the following questions to develop students' understanding of the concept. Remind students to ask and answer questions with appropriate detail and to build on other students' answers.

- What animal do you think of as *pesky*?
- What kind of animal might need to *unfurl*?

Strategy Response Log

INTERACT with TEXT

Have students review the characteristics of a folktale on p. 26 of the *Reader's and Writer's Notebook.* Then have them compare *Fly, Eagle, Fly!* to another example of a folktale that they have read or know about.

Oral Vocabulary
Amazing Words

Amazing Words

armor	scenery
agile	pesky
snout	unfurl
protrude	coil
extraordinary	intersection

Teach Amazing Words

Amazing Words   Oral Vocabulary Routine

1 Introduce Write the word *coil* on the board. Have students say it aloud with you. We read about the friend and the farmer climbing a road that *coils* around and up a mountain. What was the road like? (It was winding and steep. It wrapped around the mountain.) Have students provide a definition. (Something that coils winds in circles.)

2 Demonstrate Have students answer questions to demonstrate understanding. What kind of animal *coils* itself? (snake)

3 Apply Have students apply their understanding. Why might a snake *coil* itself?

See p. OV•2 to teach *intersection.*

Routines Flip Chart

Apply Amazing Words

As students read "Purple Coyote" on pp. 176–181, have them think about the unique behaviors of the coyote and how the Amazing Words relate to the selection.

Connect to reading

Help students establish a purpose for reading. Tell students that today they will read about the unique behavior of a purple coyote. Have them think about how the Question of the Week and the Amazing Words *coil* and *intersection* apply to the trickster tale.

ELL Produce oral language Use the Day 4 instruction on ELL Poster 20 to extend and enrich language.

ELL Poster 20

Objectives
- Identify and read words with suffixes *-er, -or, -ess, -ist.*
- Identify and read words with prefixes *pre-, mid-, over-, by-,* and *de-.*
- Identify and read words with *r*-controlled vowel sounds.
- Read words fluently independent of context.

Word Analysis Review Review
⦿ Suffixes

Review suffixes

To review suffixes *-er, -or, -ess,* and *-ist,* write *golfer, sculptor, heiress,* and *tourist.* You studied words like these last week. What do you know about how to read a word with a suffix? (Cover the suffix, read the base word, then uncover the suffix and read the parts together.) Have students identify the suffixes and read the words. Review with students that the suffixes *-er, -or, -ess, -ist* mean "one who does something," so they change the base word's meaning to "one who does (base word)." Have students discuss the meaning of each word.

If students are unable to identify the suffix and tell the meaning of each word, refer them to Sound-Spelling Cards 165, 166, 171, and 176.

Guide practice

Draw a four-column chart. When I say a word, listen for the suffix. Hold up the number of fingers to tell me which suffix you hear and the column to place the word in: *cyclist, collector, actress, teacher, narrator, baker, manager, duchess, lioness, flutist, investor, internist, defender, shepherdess, machinist, auditor.* Write each word in the appropriate column. Then have students read the words. Ask volunteers to identify the suffix and tell the meaning of the word.

1 er	2 or	3 ess	4 ist
teacher	collector	actress	cyclist
baker	narrator	duchess	flutist
manager	investor	lioness	internist
defender	auditor	shepherdess	machinist

On their own

For additional practice, use the *Let's Practice It! DVD*

Let's Practice It!
TR DVD●263

Fluent Word Reading
Spiral Review

Read words independent of context

Display these words. Tell students that they can already decode some words on this list. Explain that they should know other words because they appear often in reading.

Have students read the list three or four times until they can read at the rate of two to three seconds per word.

Word Reading

stars	pretest	said	port	for
decorate	roared	midnight	to	overtime
their	biweekly	short	before	precut
storm	decode	chores	they	watched

Corrective feedback

If... students have difficulty reading whole words,
then... have them use sound-by-sound blending for decodable words or chunking for words that have word parts, or have them say and spell high-frequency words.

If... students cannot read fluently at a rate of two to three seconds per word,
then... have pairs practice the list until they can read it fluently.

Differentiated Instruction

 Strategic Intervention

Suffixes To assist students having difficulty identifying the suffix and explaining how the suffix changes the meaning of the base word, focus on only one suffix at a time. Write words with the suffix -*er* on separate cards. Model identifying the suffix and telling the word's meaning (*teacher*, suffix -*er*, one who teaches) Repeat with words with suffixes -*or*, -*ess*, and -*ist*.

Spiral Review

These activities review

- previously taught high-frequency words *watched*, *to*, *said*, *their*, *they*.
- *r*-controlled vowels (*ar*, *or*, *ore*, *oar*); prefixes (*pre-*, *mid-*, *over-*, *bi-*, *de-*).

English Language Learners
Fluent word reading Have students listen to a more fluent reader say the words. Then have them repeat the words.

Objectives
- Read words fluently in context.
- Apply knowledge of sound-spellings to decode unknown words when reading.
- Practice fluency with oral rereading.

Check Word Reading

🏆 **SUCCESS PREDICTOR**

Read words in context

Display these sentences. Call on individuals to read a sentence. Then randomly point to review words and have students read them. To help you monitor word reading, high-frequency words are underlined and decodable words are italicized.

Don't Wait Until Friday

MONITOR PROGRESS — Sentence Reading

We <u>watched</u> the ship leave the *port* at *midnight.*

<u>They</u> finished <u>their</u> *chores* after studying for the *biweekly pretest.*

The *stars* shone *for* a *short* time *before* the *storm roared* in.

He worked *overtime* <u>to</u> *decode* the message.

Mom <u>said</u> to *decorate* the *precut* tree.

If... students are unable to read an underlined high-frequency word,

then... read the word for them and spell it, having them echo you.

If... students have difficulty reading an italicized decodable word,

then... guide them in using sound-by-sound blending or chunking.

Success Predictor

Reread for Fluency

Have students reread the sentences to develop automaticity decoding words.

 ROUTINE **Oral Rereading**

 Read Have students read all the sentences orally.

Reread To achieve optimal fluency, students should reread the sentences three or four times.

Corrective Feedback Listen as students read. Provide corrective feedback regarding their fluency and decoding.

Routines Flip Chart

Decode and Read

Read words independent of context

Have students turn to p. 59 in *Decodable Practice Reader 3.2* and find the first list of words. Each word in this list has the VCCCV syllabication pattern. Let's read these words. Be sure that students identify the VCCCV syllable pattern.

Next, have students read the high-frequency words.

Preview Decodable Practice Passage

Have students read the title and preview the story. Tell them that they will read words with the VCCCV syllable pattern.

Read words in context

Chorally read the story along with the students. Have students identify words in the story that have the VCCCV syllable pattern. Make sure that students are monitoring their accuracy when they decode words.

Team Talk Pair students and have them take turns reading the story aloud to each other. Monitor students as they read to check for proper pronunciation and appropriate pacing.

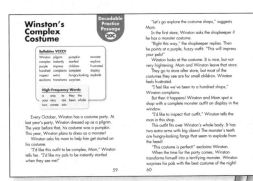

Decodable Practice Passage 20C

Differentiated Instruction

 Advanced

Decodable words Have students write their own sentences using some of the decodable words found in the sentences on p.176e.

Sentence Reading

Success Predictor

Genre
Folk Tale: Trickster Tale

Introduce the genre

Explain to students that what we read is structured differently depending on the author's reasons for writing and what kind of information he or she wishes to convey. Different types of texts are called genres. Tell them that the trickster tale is one type of genre.

Discuss the genre

Ask students what they know about trickster tales. Then discuss the elements of trickster tales with students. Explain: A trickster tale is a kind of folk tale. Like folk tales, trickster tales have simple plots and undeveloped characters, and they share a lesson about human nature. The characters are sometimes animals that act like humans. The settings are often outside time—they could be anywhere at any time. A trickster tale is special because it has a character who tries to trick the main character.

On the board, draw a two-column chart like the one below. In the first column, list literary elements. In the second, record a brief description of how each appears in trickster tales. Ask the following questions. Remind students to answer questions with appropriate detail.

• What are the plots and characters in trickster tales like? Possible response: The plots of trickster tales are simple. The characters are undeveloped, flat, or stock. Trickster tales feature a character who tries to trick the main character.

• What kinds of settings do trickster tales usually have? Possible response: They could be anywhere at any time.

• What kinds of themes do trickster tales have? Possible response: Trickster tales often teach lessons about human behavior.

Trickster Tales	
plot	simple
characters	stock, features a trickster
settings	outside time, universal
themes	about human nature

Guide practice

Have students work in pairs to review other elements of folk tales with which they are familiar. Have them list additional elements in the chart.

Connect to reading

Tell students that they will now read a trickster tale about a coyote that has turned purple. Have students think about what they might learn from a trickster tale.

Small Group Time

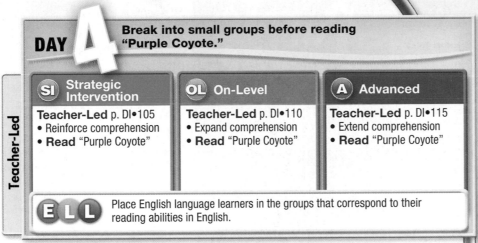

DAY 4

Break into small groups before reading "Purple Coyote."

Teacher-Led

SI Strategic Intervention	**OL** On-Level	**A** Advanced
Teacher-Led p. DI•105 • Reinforce comprehension • **Read** "Purple Coyote"	**Teacher-Led** p. DI•110 • Expand comprehension • **Read** "Purple Coyote"	**Teacher-Led** p. DI•115 • Extend comprehension • **Read** "Purple Coyote"

ELL Place English language learners in the groups that correspond to their reading abilities in English.

Practice Stations
• Read for Meaning
• Get Fluent
• Words to Know

Independent Activities
• AudioText: "Purple Coyote"
• *Reader's and Writer's Notebook*
• Inquiry and Research

Objectives
- Identify the characteristics of a folk tale.
- Compare and contrast settings.

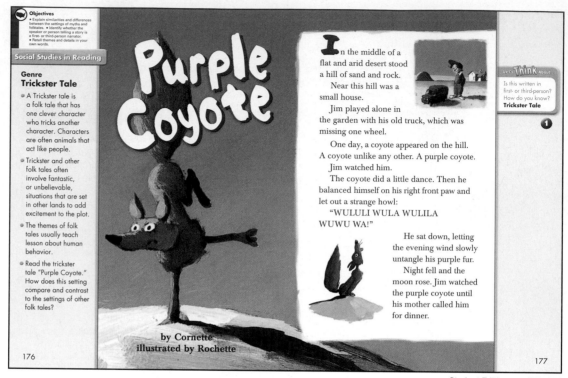

Student Edition pp. 176–177

Guide Comprehension

Teach the genre

Folk Tale: Trickster Tale Have students read the information about trickster tales and preview pp. 176–177 of "Purple Coyote." Point out that a trickster tale is a type of folk tale. Ask: What is "fantastic" about the coyote? What about the story is unexpected?

If... students are unable to identify the fantastic and unexpected elements of the story,
then... use the model to guide students in answering the questions.

Model the skill

Think Aloud

On page 176, I learn that trickster tales often have fantastic characters and unexpected events. I know that coyotes aren't usually purple. In fact, I don't know of any purple animals. The coyote's color is fantastic. When I preview the page, I see his song in all capital letters. Coyote howls don't sound like that, so his howl is unexpected.

On their own

Have students record other unexpected or fantastic events as they read pp. 176–177.

Extend Thinking
Think Critically

Higher-order thinking skills

Setting • Analysis Is the desert setting like most deserts you have read about? **Possible response:** Yes; it is flat, arid, and sandy.

Compare and Contrast • Synthesis Does the setting remind you of the setting in a myth you have read? How are the settings alike and different? **Possible responses:** This story and "How the Desert Tortoise Got its Shell" both take place in a desert. In this folk tale, the flat and arid desert stands on a hill of sand and rock. In the myth "How the Desert Tortoise Got Its Shell," there are many desert plants and a dry riverbed in addition to the sand.

 Let's Think About...

● **Possible response:** The tale is written in the third person because it uses the words *Jim, he,* and *his.* If it were written in the first person, it would use words such as *I, me,* and *mine.*

Differentiated Instruction

 Strategic Intervention

Compare and contrast Remind students that when they compare, they tell how things are alike. When they contrast, they tell how things are different. Write these clue words on the board:

*Compare: similar, like, same
Contrast: unlike, differ, different*

 Advanced

Folk tales Write the word *universal* on the board. Explain that it means something is applicable to all situations. Have students discuss in small groups the qualities of folk tales and trickster tales that make them universal.

Academic Vocabulary

folk tale a fictional story that is a traditional tale handed down from one generation to another

English Language Learners
Cognates Spanish students may better understand the fantastic element of the trickster tale if you introduce the cognate for the title—*Coyote Púrpura.* **Ask:** What is unusual about a purple coyote?

Objectives

- Use ideas to make and confirm predictions about the tale.
- Draw conclusions about characters' actions.
- Compare and contrast plots.

The next day, Jim didn't play with his truck, which had lost a second wheel.

He went to wait for the coyote at the bottom of the hill.

The purple coyote appeared. He did his little dance, balanced himself on his right front paw, and let out his "WULULI WULA WULILA WUWU WA!"

Jim climbed up the hill.

It wasn't very hard, as the hill was neither high nor steep.

He went up to the animal, greeted him and asked, "Why are you purple? That's not normal for a coyote!"

"I won't tell you!" answered the coyote.

"Why not?"

"Because it's a secret! But you can ask me questions if you want."

Let's Think About
What details in the plot make it a fantastic situation? **Trickster Tale**

❷

178

Jim thought hard. He looked the purple coyote straight in the eyes and asked, "Did you eat too many blueberries?"

"I never eat blueberries," the coyote replied.

Every afternoon, the purple coyote returned to the hill, did his little dance, balanced himself on his right front paw, and howled:

"WULULI WULA WULILA WUWU WA!"

Every afternoon, Jim joined the coyote, greeted him, and asked him a question. "Did you put purple dye on your fur?"

"No," answered the coyote.

"Were you born purple?"

"No."

"Did you catch purple-itis?"

"No."

"Did you catch purple fever?"

"No."

The days went by. Jim began to lose patience.

"I don't care if I never find out why you're purple!" he shouted at the coyote.

Let's Think About
Who do you think is the clever character? Who will be tricked? Why? **Trickster Tale**

❸

179

Student Edition pp. 178–179

Guide Comprehension

Teach the genre

Folk Tale: Trickster Tale Have students preview the illustrations, the questions, and the text on pp. 178–179. Have students use the information they gather to make predictions about what will happen on these pages.

If... students are not able to make predictions,
then... use the model to guide the thinking process.

Model the skill

Think Aloud When I look at the pictures, I see the boy walking up the hill toward the coyote. I think he will talk to the coyote. I think the boy wants to find out why the coyote does that silly song and dance. Since it is a trickster tale, I think the coyote will talk back.

On their own

Have students record their predictions based on the clues they found during previewing. Then, when they finish, have them revisit their predictions to see whether they were accurate.

Extend Thinking
Think Critically

Higher-order thinking skills

Draw Conclusions • Evaluation Why do you think the coyote refuses to tell the boy why he is purple? Possible response: He wants the boy to guess why he is purple because he wants to trick the boy.

Compare and Contrast • Synthesis How are the plots in *Fly, Eagle, Fly!* and "Purple Coyote" alike? What do the characters in each tale do to solve their problems? Possible responses: The plots are alike because the characters repeat actions to solve the problem. In *Fly, Eagle, Fly!* the friend tries three times to get the eagle to fly. In "Purple Coyote," the boy asks question after question to find out why the coyote is purple.

Let's Think About...

● Possible responses: The coyote couldn't have been purple, stood on one paw, sung his song, or talked back. Also, the boy could not have approached the coyote.

● Possible responses: The coyote is the clever character. The boy will be tricked because the coyote seems like he has a plan.

Differentiated Instruction

 Strategic Intervention

Draw conclusions Explain that students must think about all of the elements of the story, including the genre, to put together information to form conclusions. Have students work with partners to list evidence that will help them conclude why the coyote doesn't want to tell the boy his secret.

 Advanced

Compare and contrast Have students write about the similarities and differences between *Fly, Eagle, Fly!* and "Purple Coyote." Tell students to think about the general attributes of the texts to make their comparisons.

English Language Learners
Build Academic Vocabulary
Have pairs of students practice using key words, such as *similar, like, unlike,* and *different,* to compare and contrast the plots of *Fly, Eagle, Fly!* and "Purple Coyote."

Objectives
- Paraphrase theme.
- Identify supporting details.
- Compare and contrast settings.

In his anger, he thought about not coming up the hill anymore, but his curiosity was too strong.

"Tell me instead why you do that dance and why you howl in that funny way," he asked.

The coyote smiled. "That's my second secret," he said.

Jim tried very hard to keep calm. He acted as though he didn't care. "That's a stupid secret," he said. "Anyone can dance and howl like that! Look!"

Jim did a little dance, then leaned over on his right arm and howled a piercing "WULULI WULA WULILA WUWU WA!"

All at once, Jim turned purple.

As for the coyote, he got his color back. He was once again the color of desert and sand.

"Well done!" said the coyote. "You've discovered my two secrets in one try! You've given me back my natural color. Now I can leave. Goodbye, Jim!"

He disappeared into the vast desert.

Jim was now all purple and all by himself.

Night had fallen on the hill when a little raccoon came up to him.

"Hello," the raccoon said.

"Hello!" replied the purple kid.

"Did you see?" said Jim. "I'm purple all over."

"Yes," said the small animal.

"It's my secret," Jim went on. "Do you want to find out why?"

"No."

Let's Think About...

How is this Coyote similar to the Coyote in the myth "Catch It and Run"? **Trickster Tale**

④

Let's Think About...

Explain the interaction between Jim and the coyote. What changes did they undergo? **Trickster Tale**

⑤

Let's Think About...

Summarize the theme and supporting details from the story in your own words. What does this show about human behavior? **Trickster Tale**

⑥

Let's Think About...

Reading Across Texts Compare and contrast the settings in the two folk tales *Fly, Eagle, Fly!* and *Purple Coyote.* How are they alike and different?

Writing Across Texts Make a Venn diagram that compares and contrasts the settings in each of these folk tales.

180

181

Student Edition pp. 180–181

Guide Comprehension

Teach the genre

FolkTale: Trickster Tale Have students preview pp. 180–181. Ask: How has the purple coyote tricked the boy?

If... students have difficulty answering the question,
then... use the model to guide students' thinking.

Model the skill

 Think Aloud When I preview these pages, I look at the illustrations. I see that now the coyote is a normal color and the boy is purple. I think the coyote tricked the boy so that he could return to his normal color.

On their own

Have students finish the selection and discuss what the coyote did to trick the boy.

Extend Thinking
Think Critically

Higher-order thinking skills

Theme • Synthesis When is it good to be curious? Possible responses: When you want to find out how something works or you want to learn more about someone.

Draw Conclusions • Evaluation What kind of character is the raccoon? He is smart and knows how to stay out of trouble.

Let's Think About...

4 Possible responses: Both coyotes are very clever and they trick other characters to get their way.

5 Possible responses: At first Jim was nice to the coyote when he kept asking why he was purple. But after a while, Jim lost patience and shouted at the coyote.

6 Possible responses: The theme is that curiosity can cause trouble. The boy is curious about the coyote, so he ignores his common sense and tries to uncover the coyote's secret. In the end, his curiosity hurts him. This tale shows that sometimes people don't know when to stop asking questions.

Reading Across Texts

Have students review *Fly, Eagle, Fly!* and make notes about the setting. Then, have them make notes about the setting of "Purple Coyote." Instruct students to review these notes to find similarities and differences between the two settings.

Writing Across Texts

Have students record their notes about the setting in the Venn diagram. Then, challenge students to write a brief paragraph that compares and contrasts the settings of these folk tales.

Connect to Social Studies

The coyote often appears in Native American folk tales as a trickster. In these stories, he interacts with people or other animals as a cunning, greedy, vain, foolish, and powerful character.

ELL

English Language Learners
Theme Help students identify theme by asking: What lesson did you learn from this story? Have students state the theme in their own words with the sentence starter *I learned that* _____.

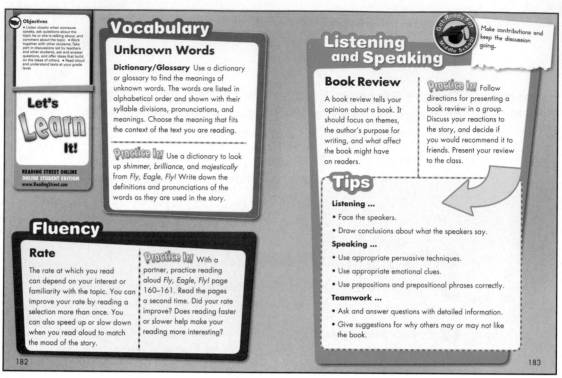

Vocabulary

Unknown Words

Dictionary/Glossary Use a dictionary or glossary to find the meanings of unknown words. The words are listed in alphabetical order and shown with their syllable divisions, pronunciations, and meanings. Choose the meaning that fits the context of the text you are reading.

Practice It! Use a dictionary to look up *shimmer*, *brilliance*, and *majestically* from *Fly, Eagle, Fly!* Write down the definitions and pronunciations of the words as they are used in the story.

Fluency

Rate

The rate at which you read can depend on your interest or familiarity with the topic. You can improve your rate by reading a selection more than once. You can also speed up or slow down when you read aloud to match the mood of the story.

Practice It! With a partner, practice reading aloud *Fly, Eagle, Fly!* page 160–161. Read the pages a second time. Did your rate improve? Does reading faster or slower help make your reading more interesting?

Listening and Speaking

Book Review

A book review tells your opinion about a book. It should focus on themes, the author's purpose for writing, and what affect the book might have on readers.

Practice It! Follow directions for presenting a book review in a group. Discuss your reactions to the story, and decide if you would recommend it to friends. Present your review to the class.

Tips

Listening ...
- Face the speakers.
- Draw conclusions about what the speakers say.

Speaking ...
- Use appropriate persuasive techniques.
- Use appropriate emotional clues.
- Use prepositions and prepositional phrases correctly.

Teamwork ...
- Ask and answer questions with detailed information.
- Give suggestions for why others may or may not like the book.

182   183

Student Edition pp. 182–183

Fluency
Rate

Guide practice

Use the Student Edition activity as an assessment tool. Make sure the reading passage is at least 200 words in length. As students read aloud with partners, walk around to make sure their rate is appropriate and that it changes to reflect content and punctuation.

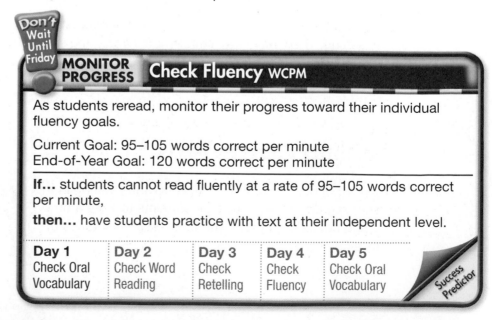

Don't Wait Until Friday

MONITOR PROGRESS   Check Fluency WCPM

As students reread, monitor their progress toward their individual fluency goals.

Current Goal: 95–105 words correct per minute
End-of-Year Goal: 120 words correct per minute

If... students cannot read fluently at a rate of 95–105 words correct per minute,

then... have students practice with text at their independent level.

Day 1	Day 2	Day 3	Day 4	Day 5
Check Oral Vocabulary	Check Word Reading	Check Retelling	Check Fluency	Check Oral Vocabulary

Success Predictor

Vocabulary
Unknown Words

Teach dictionary/ glossary

 Dictionary/Glossary Write these sentences on the board: The scientist proved his brilliance when he made the major discovery. The brilliance of the afternoon sun nearly blinded us.

Remind students that a word may have more than one definition. When they look up a word in the dictionary or glossary, they need to look at the context of the word to determine which definition the author intended.

Guide practice

Have students look up *brilliance, shimmer,* and *majestically* in a dictionary or glossary. Help them use the context of the story to determine the intended meaning for each word.

On their own

Walk around the room, making sure students are able to locate the words in a dictionary or glossary and identify their intended meanings. Have students identify the number of syllables in each word and use the pronunciation key to help them figure out how to say each word correctly.

Listening and Speaking
Book Review

Teach

Tell one member of each group that when group members review a book, they need to tell their reaction to the story and whether they would recommend it to a friend. Explain that when they present their reviews, they should speak coherently with appropriate rate, volume, enunciation, and conventions of language, and they should make eye contact with their audience.

Guide practice

Have each chosen group member restate to the group the oral instructions for how to review a book and how to deliver the review. Encourage group members to listen attentively, to ask and answer questions, and to provide suggestions that build upon the ideas of others.

On their own

Have group members follow the multi-step oral instructions to prepare and give their book reviews.

Express Opinions

Reiterate to students that book reviews are a way to express an opinion. Remind students that when giving an opinion, they need to provide reasons and support for that opinion. They should cite evidence from the actual text being reviewed in order to support their opinions in this case.

ELL

English Language Learners
Unknown words After students find the word in the dictionary, assist them by helping them identify synonyms of the words to replace in context. For example, in the first sentence replace *brilliance* with both *skill* and *light,* and then have students raise their hands to indicate which meaning is intended.

Success Predictor

Objectives
- Synthesize data to prepare presentation.
- Review prepositions.
- Spell words with the syllable pattern VCCCV correctly.

Research and Inquiry
Synthesize

Teach

Have students synthesize their research findings and results. Students should use their summaries to help write their journal entries. Suggest that students might also find that their graphic organizers are a helpful reference source when writing their journal entries.

Guide practice

Have students review their graphic organizers and summaries to prepare to write their journal entries. If students are using illustrations, suggest that they use drawing paper for the illustrations and then paste the illustrations into their journals.

On their own

Have students write a brief explanation of their research findings. Then have them organize and combine information for their presentation.

Conventions
Prepositions

Test practice   Remind students that grammar skills, such as prepositions, are often assessed on important tests. Remind students that a preposition shows the relationship between a noun or pronoun and the other words in the sentence. A prepositional phrase adds more important details by telling exactly where something occurs or how things are related.

Daily Fix-It   Use Daily Fix-It numbers 7 and 8 in the right margin.

On their own   For additional practice, use the *Reader's and Writer's Notebook* p. 301.

Reader's and Writer's Notebook p. 301

Spelling
Syllables VCCCV

Practice spelling strategy   Give pairs of students index cards on which the spelling words have been written. Have one student read a word while the other writes it. Then have students switch roles. Have them use the cards to check their spelling and correct any misspelled words.

On their own   For additional practice, use the *Let's Practice It! DVD.*

Let's Practice It! TR DVD•264

Writing—Writing for Tests

MINI-LESSON

Using Strong Verbs

■ Yesterday we evaluated our test writing sample based on a writing rubric. Today we will prepare to write to another writing prompt.

■ Discuss the importance of word choice in writing. Strong verbs can create sounds or images for a reader. Using strong verbs in your writing will make it more interesting and lively. As you write, think about how you can use strong verbs to make your writing better.

■ Write the following sentence on the board: *Emily walked home from school.* Model how to improve the sentence with strong verbs. The verb *walk* does not tell me much. I can use a different verb in the sentence to show exactly how Emily walked home from school. The sentence *Emily strolled home from school* is more specific. It tells the reader exactly how Emily walked.

Sample test   Direct students to get paper and pencil ready to take a writing test. Display the new writing prompt for students and allow them appropriate time to write to the prompt. Tell students to spend some time thinking about the key features of the writing product before beginning to write. Remind students to allow themselves a couple of minutes after writing to reread what they've written and make changes or additions.

Writing Prompt

Write a summary of the plot of your favorite animated movie.

ROUTINE — Quick Write for Fluency — Team Talk

1. **Talk** Pairs discuss how to use stronger verbs when writing sentences.

2. **Write** Students write one sentence using the verb *ran,* then write two other sentences replacing the word *ran* with stronger verbs such as *sprinted, jogged,* or *dashed.*

3. **Share** Students share what they wrote with their partners and each checks the other's writing for strong verb choices.

Routines Flip Chart

Wrap Up Your Day

✔ **Build Concepts** Have students discuss why the coyote was purple.

✔ **Oral Vocabulary** Monitor students' use of oral vocabulary as they respond: What extraordinary scenery would you see in a desert?

✔ **Text Features** Discuss how the illustrations help students understand the text.

Write Guy
Jeff Anderson

Powerful Words, Powerful Verbs

If students have trouble distinguishing complete sentences from fragments, have them ask this question: "Who or what did something? What did they do?" Students can have fun making a complete statement by adding together subjets *(David)* and powerful verbs *(laughed, talked, punched):* David laughed.

Differentiated Instruction

 Strategic Intervention

Strong verbs Have students use a dictionary or thesaurus to find interesting verbs to use in their summaries.

English Language Learners
Word choice Pair an English learner with a proficient English speaker to discuss pictures of people or animals in books or magazines. Have them use strong verbs to describe what the people or animals are doing.

Preview DAY 5

Remind students to think about what it means to be unique.

DAY 5 Wrap Up your Week

10–15 min

Objectives
- Review the weekly concept.
- Review oral vocabulary.

Today at a Glance

Oral Vocabulary
Review

Phonics
Syllables VCCCV

Comprehension
◉ Cause and effect

Lesson Vocabulary
◉ Unknown Words

Literary Terms
Sensory details

Assessment
Fluency
Comprehension

Research and Inquiry
Communication

Spelling
Syllables VCCCV

Conventions
Prepositions

Writing
Summary

Check Oral Vocabulary
SUCCESS PREDICTOR

Concept Wrap Up

Question of the Week

What behaviors are unique to different animals?

Review the concept

Have students look back at the reading selections to find examples that best demonstrate unique animal behaviors.

Review Amazing Words

Display and review this week's concept map. Remind students that this week they have learned ten amazing words related to unique animal behaviors. Have students use the Amazing Words and the concept map to answer the question *What behaviors are unique to different animals?*

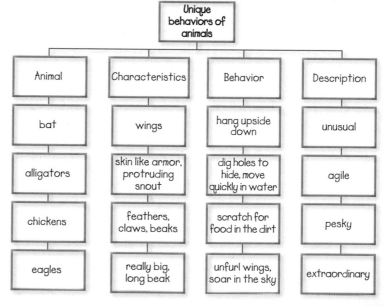

Concept map:

Unique behaviors of animals

Animal	Characteristics	Behavior	Description
bat	wings	hang upside down	unusual
alligators	skin like armor, protruding snout	dig holes to hide, move quickly in water	agile
chickens	feathers, claws, beaks	scratch for food in the dirt	pesky
eagles	really big, long beak	unfurl wings, soar in the sky	extraordinary

ELL Check concepts and language Use the Day 5 instruction on ELL Poster 20 to monitor students' understanding of the lesson concept.

ELL Poster 20

Amazing Ideas

Connect to the Big Question

Have pairs of students discuss how the Question of the Week connects to the Big Question: *What does it mean to be unique?* Tell students to use the concept map and what they have learned from this week's Anchored Talks and reading selections to form an Amazing Idea—a realization or "big Idea" about being One of a Kind. Remind partners to ask and answer questions with appropriate details and give suggestions that build on each other's ideas. Then ask each pair to share their Amazing Idea with the class.

Amazing Ideas might include these key concepts:

- Even when we act like others, we each still have qualities that are special to only us.
- Sometimes animals' behaviors are unique, but their outcome is the same.
- The way animals and people act, as well as the way they look, makes them unique.

Write about it

Have students write a few sentences about their Amazing Idea, beginning with "This week I learned…"

Amazing Words

armor	scenery
agile	pesky
snout	unfurl
protrude	coil
extraordinary	intersection

Don't Wait Until Friday

MONITOR PROGRESS | **Check Oral Vocabulary**

Have individuals use this week's Amazing Words to describe unique animal behaviors. Monitor students' ability to use the Amazing Words and note which words you need to reteach.

If… students have difficulty using the Amazing Words,

then… reteach using the Oral Vocabulary Routine, pp. 151a, 156b, 168b, 176b, OV•2.

Day 1	Day 2	Day 3	Day 4	**Day 5**
Check Oral Vocabulary	Check Word Reading	Check Retelling	Check Fluency	Check Oral Vocabulary

Success Predictor

ELL

English Language Learners
Concept map Work with students to add new words to the concept map.

Check Oral Vocabulary **Success Predictor**

Comprehension **Review**
🎯 Cause and Effect

Teach cause and effect

Envision It!

Review the definitions of *cause* and *effect* on p. 154. Remind students that words such as *because* and *so* signal cause-and-effect relationships. For additional support have students review p. EI•3 on cause and effect.

Guide practice

Have partners identify an example of cause and effect in "Lulu Wants to Grow Up" on p. 155. Then have pairs tell which of the events is a cause and which is an effect. Have students explain using the words *so* or *because.*

On their own

For additional practice with cause and effect, use *the Let's Practice it! DVD.*

Student Edition p. EI•3

Let's Practice it! TR DVD, 265

Vocabulary **Review**
🎯 Unknown Words

Teach unknown words

Remind students to use a dictionary or glossary to help them understand the meanings of unknown words.

Guide practice

Review with students how to find the correct meaning of *huddled* using a dictionary or glossary. Explain that there may be more than one definition for the word. Remind students that they can also find the number of syllables and the pronunciation for a word.

On their own

Have students write sentences for the lesson vocabulary words. Tell students to be sure to include context clues to indicate the intended definition of the word. Invite volunteers to share their sentences with the class. Have students tell how they used the dictionary or glossary to determine the number of syllables and the pronunciation of each word.

Word Analysis Review
Syllables VCCCV

Teach Syllables VCCCV

Write the following sentences on the board. Have students read each one, first quietly to themselves and then aloud as you track the print.

1. Should I explain why you don't walk on wet concrete?
2. All of the partners have contracts to sell the orchard's apples.
3. My conscience stopped me from making the purchase.
4. We attended a surprise function at the district office.
5. One hundred dolphins were simply having fun.

Team Talk Have students discuss with a partner which words have the VCCCV syllable pattern. Ask them to identify the syllables and read the words. Then call on individuals to share with the class.

Literary Terms Review
Sensory Details

Teach sensory details

Have students reread pp. 164–167 of *Fly, Eagle, Fly!* Remind students that sensory details help them see, hear, taste, smell, or feel the thing the author describes.

Guide practice

Read aloud p. 167 to students. Tell them to close their eyes and pay attention to what they imagine as you read. Discuss how the author uses sensory details to create vivid images and which senses those details address.

On their own

Have students make a concept web with *Sensory details* listed in the center circle and each of the five senses listed in the outer circles. Then, have students record words and details from the story in the circles with the appropriate senses.

English Language Learners

Articulation tip If students have trouble pronouncing blends and digraphs in VCCCV syllable patterns, demonstrate how to pronounce them by slowly repeating words. Have students practice saying them until they develop confidence.

Sensory details Reinforce the connection between words and senses by asking students to interact with the text. Read the first sentence on p. 167, *Again the great bird stretched out its wings.* Then ask students to mimic the action. If necessary, show them by stretching out your arms. Continue the exercise with the next sentence, having students demonstrate trembling.

Objectives
• Read grade-level text with fluency.

Assessment

Check words corrected per minute

Fluency Make two copies of the fluency passage on page 183k. As the student reads the text aloud, mark mistakes on your copy. Also mark where the student is at the end of one minute. To check the student's comprehension of the passage, have him or her retell what was read. To figure words correct per minute (WCPM), subtract the number of mistakes from the total number of words read in one minute.

WCPM

Corrective feedback

If... students cannot read fluently at a rate of 95–105 WCPM,
then... make sure they practice with text at their independent reading level. Provide additional fluency practice by pairing nonfluent readers with fluent readers.

If... students already read at 120 WCPM,
then... they do not need to reread three or four times.

Small Group Time

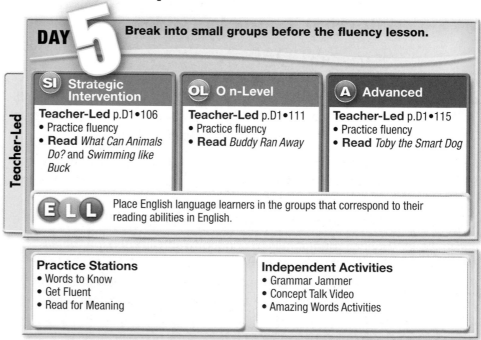

DAY 5 Break into small groups before the fluency lesson.

SI Strategic Intervention	**OL** On-Level	**A** Advanced
Teacher-Led p.DI•106	**Teacher-Led** p.DI•111	**Teacher-Led** p.DI•115
• Practice fluency	• Practice fluency	• Practice fluency
• **Read** *What Can Animals Do?* and *Swimming like Buck*	• **Read** *Buddy Ran Away*	• **Read** *Toby the Smart Dog*

ELL Place English language learners in the groups that correspond to their reading abilities in English.

Practice Stations
• Words to Know
• Get Fluent
• Read for Meaning

Independent Activities
• Grammar Jammer
• Concept Talk Video
• Amazing Words Activities

Teacher-Led

Bats Are Special

Andy and Dora were exploring the valley with their parents when it   12
started to rain.   15

"Let's look for a place to stay dry," Mom said.   25

"There's a cave just over the gully," Dad added.   34

"Aren't bats in caves?" Dora asked in a frightened voice.   44

"You shouldn't be afraid of bats. They're really cool," Andy replied.   55

"How cool can they be? They can't even see!" Dora exclaimed.   66

"Are you kidding? Bats can't see color, but they can see in the dark   80
better than you or me," Andy said. "They also use echoes to help them   94
hunt for insects," Andy added.   99

"What about vampire bats?" Dora asked.   105

"They can be found in Mexico, Central America, and South   115
America," Andy answered. "Unlike Dracula, they only need about   124
2 tablespoons of blood a day. That amount doesn't hurt the animal it   137
takes the blood from," Andy added.   142

"Did you know that the smallest bat weighs less than a penny?"   154
Mom said.   165

"I'd like to see one of those," Dora said excitedly.   166

"You'd have to go to Thailand. They're called bumblebee bats," her   177
father added.   179

"Let's hurry to the cave," Dora said as she scrambled ahead.   190

"I thought you were afraid," Andy shouted.   197

"Not anymore! Bats are too special to be afraid of," Dora laughed.   209

Check cause and effect

Assessment

◉ Cause and Effect Use "Armadillos" on p. 183m to check students' understanding of cause and effect.

1. What did you learn from the passage? **Possible Response: I learned about armadillos' features and their habits.**

2. What causes an armadillo to pull its legs under its armor to hide? Is there a clue word to help you identify the cause? **Possible response: Being frightened causes it to hide. The clue is** *because.*

3. If an armadillo is really frightened, what will it likely do? **Possible response: It will jump up to scare the attacker or might even fight with its claws.**

If… students are unable to answer the comprehension questions, **then…** use the Reteach lesson in the *First Stop* book.

Armadillos

Are you curious about armadillos? These weird-looking critters are covered with big, tough scales. They even have scales on their faces and long, skinny tails. The scales look like armor that ancient knights wore. Armadillos need to protect themselves, so they use their armor. They quickly pull their legs under the armor and hide because they are frightened.

What happens when you poke an armadillo hiding in its armor? It usually fakes being dead. But if you scare it enough, it might jump straight up and scare you back.

Most of the day, armadillos live in burrows because they are shy and do not want to be seen. A burrow is a hole or tunnel. Armadillos have sharp claws that help them to dig burrows and to catch food. They also use their claws to fight anything that attacks them. Armadillos will fight only when hiding, jumping, or playing dead doesn't work.

Armadillos come out at night to hunt for dinner. They eat bugs, small animals, and some plants. Some armadillos also eat small worms that live in dead, rotting animals! Yuck! Armadillos have a strong sense of smell, so they use it to find food in the dark night. Rotting animals must be easy to smell.

How big do armadillos grow? The kind found in the United States can be 30 inches long. There are giant armadillos in South America that grow five feet long and can weigh over 60 pounds. That's as big as some dogs!

⏱ 10–15 min

Research and Inquiry
Communicate

Present ideas   Have students share their inquiry results by presenting their journals and giving a brief talk on their research. Have students display any outlines and graphic organizers they created on Days 2 and 3.

Listening and speaking   Remind students how to be good speakers and how to communicate effectively with their audience.

- Speak coherently, using an appropriate rate and volume.
- Maintain eye contact with the audience.
- Respond to relevant questions with appropriate details.

Remind students of these tips for being a good listener.

- Listen attentively without interrupting the speaker.
- Jot down relevant questions and ask them after the speaker finishes.
- Be polite, even if you disagree.

Spelling Test
Syllables VCCCV

Spelling test To administer the spelling test, refer to the directions, words, and sentences on page 155c.

Conventions
Prepositions

Teach Remind students that prepositions show a relationship between a noun or pronoun and the other words in a sentence. A preposition is the first word in a group of words called a prepositional phrase. A prepositional phrase ends with a noun or pronoun and adds important detail to writing.

Guide practice Have students add a preposition to complete the sentence frames.

My cat is _____ the chair. (on, behind)

Marta is sitting _____ Jeff and Kara. (between)

The bird flew _____ the sky. (across, through)

Daily Fix-It Use Daily Fix-It numbers 9 and 10 in the right margin.

On their own Write these sentences. Have students look back in *Fly, Eagle, Fly!* to find the correct preposition to fill in the blanks. Students should complete the *Let's Practice It! DVD.*

1. He searched _____ the riverbed. (by)

2. He searched _____ the reeds, _____ the rocks, and _____ the rushing water. (behind, among, in)

3. He wandered _____ the hillside. (over)

4. His shouts echoed _____ the cliffs. (off)

Let's Practice It! TR DVD•266

Daily Fix-It

9. An eagle sudenly appeared on the Ridge. (*suddenly; ridge*)

10. The eagles flight took us by suprise. (*eagle's; surprise*)

Objectives
- Proofread for correct use of prepositions and prepositional phrases.
- Evaluate timed-writing sample.

Writing for Tests

Review Evaluating

Remind students that yesterday they learned more about the key features of summaries and wrote to a second prompt. Today they will evaluate their writing from yesterday.

MINI-LESSON

Revising Strategy: Conventions

■ Yesterday we wrote a summary of the plot of our favorite animated movie. Part of effectively writing for tests is using some of the test-taking time to revise and edit what we've written. The goal is to make the writing as clear as possible. Today we will focus on making sure we used prepositions and prepositional phrases correctly.

■ Remind students that prepositional phrases add important details to writing by telling exactly where something occurs or how two things are related. Some words can be prepositions or not, depending on their use in a sentence. Remind them that a preposition is part of a phrase and is followed by a noun or a pronoun. It can not stand alone. Write these sentences on the board: *The eagle flew down. The eagle flew down the mountain. Down* is not a preposition in the first sentence. *Down* is a preposition in the second sentence.

Look for places where you have used or could use a prepositional phrase. Remind students of some common prepositions, such as *of, for, on, down, at*, and so on. Tell students to make sure that their prepositional phrases make sense and that they include both a preposition and an appropriate noun.

Display the following Revising Tips for students.

Revising Tips

✔ Make sure that you include prepositions that make sense in your summary.

✔ Review your writing to make sure that is clear and focused.

✔ Check that your prepositional phrases are appropriate to the summary.

Evaluate Have students spend a few minutes editing and revising the sample test-writing piece they wrote on Day 4, paying particular attention to using prepositions and prepositional phrases correctly. When students have finished editing in the allotted time, have them use the Scoring Rubric from their *Reader's and Writer's Notebook* p. 297 that they used in Day 3. This time they should use it to evaluate the sample test-writing they just revised.

ROUTINE Quick Write for Fluency — Team Talk

1. **Talk** Pairs discuss what they learned about writing summaries.
2. **Write** Students write a paragraph explaining three things they learned about writing summaries.
3. **Share** Partners read one another's paragraphs.

Routines Flip Chart

Teacher Note

Student self-evaluation Make copies of the Self-Evaluation form from the *Let's Practice It! DVD* and hand out to students.

English Language Learners

Poster preview Prepare students for next week by using Week 1, ELL Poster 21. Read the Poster Talk-Through to introduce the concept and vocabulary. Ask students to identify and describe objects and actions in the art.

Selection summary Send home the summary of *Suki's Kimono,* in English and the students' home languages, if available. Students can read the summary with family members.

Preview NEXT WEEK

Tell students that next week they will review this unit's skills and the Question of the Week: *What behaviors are unique to different animals?*

Objectives

- Describe the characteristics of a limerick.
- Describe the characteristics of a free verse poem.
- Identify language that appeals to the senses.
- Describe how different types of poetry create imagery.
- Write a limerick or free verse poem.

Student Edition pp. 184–185

Guide Comprehension
Literary Terms

Teach limericks

Limericks Review the definition of limericks on p. 184. Remind students that limericks are usually silly or funny and might contain some repetitive words. Limericks always have five lines in a verse, specific lines that rhyme, and a specific number of beats per line. Review that rhymes are words that have the same ending sounds, and that the beat pattern gives the rhyme cadence, or a regular rhythm. Read the first verse of "Limericks" aloud, tapping your hand on a table for each of the beats. Point out that the number of beats does NOT match the number of words in the limerick.

Guide practice

Write the second verse of the poem "Limericks" on the board. Number each line 1 through 5. Then ask volunteers to name the numbers of the lines that rhyme (1, 2, and 5; 3 and 4). Ask other volunteers to count the number of beats in each line. Then ask a volunteer to find an example of repetition in the limerick.

On their own

Have students take turns reading "Limericks" aloud. Tell students to pay attention to the rhyming patterns and beat as they read. Point out that sometimes the rhymes are forced as in *lady* and *steady.*

Guide Comprehension
Literary Terms

Teach free verse poems

Free Verse Poems Review the definition of free verse poems on p. 184. Remind students that free verse poems do not rhyme, nor do they have cadence or a regular rhythm. Free verse poems sound more like everyday speech and often express a strong emotion.

Guide practice

Make a two-column chart with the headings "Limericks" and "Po-Shan Monastery." Fill in the chart by asking about characteristics of limericks and free verse poems. Make sure to include questions about rhyme, cadence, and repetition.

On their own

Have students write a free verse poem about a funny or interesting person they know. Have them share their poems with the rest of the class.

Teach imagery

Imagery Review the idea that authors use imagery to help their readers see, hear, feel, smell, and touch what is happening in the poem. Point out that imagery can be found in limericks and free verse poems, and that it is the author's choice of words that helps the readers create pictures in their minds.

Guide practice

Have students discuss the imagery in the poems on pp. 184–185. Ask them to identify specific phrases that helped them create pictures in their minds.

On their own

Have partners practice reading each poem several times.

Let's Think About...

● The limericks have a specific length and rhyming pattern shared by all limericks. They use sensory words that create imagery for the reader. In the first limerick, we can "see" the long nose that hangs down to the girl's toes. In the second limerick, we can "smell" and "taste" the buns that the man feeds to his sons.

● The free verse poem contains no rhymes and has no rhythm. It sounds like the writer is just speaking to the reader. The imagery is created by the choice of words used by the writer. We can "see" the farm, situated between the mountains, and the farmer, looking at his crops and feeling contented.

Differentiated Instruction

 Strategic Intervention

Limericks Read a number of different short poems to students (including limericks). Have students pick out the poems that are limericks. Have them explain what makes them a limerick.

 Advanced

Limericks Have student pairs write their own limericks and read them to the rest of the class. Suggest topics that students might write about, such as people they've met, places they've been to, or fun things they've done.

ELL

English Language Learners
Rhyming words Make sure English language learners understand rhyme by writing the following on the board: *fish/ wish, dream/team,* and *bumper/ jumper.* Have students identify the parts of the words that sound the same. Then ask students to name other words that rhyme.

Objectives
- Identify rhyming words.
- Read poetry fluently.
- Write a short rhyming poem.

Student Edition pp. 186–187

Guide Comprehension
Literary Terms

Teach rhyme

Rhyming Poems Remind students that rhyme is when two or more words have the same ending sounds. Have students supply examples. Then explain that a poet sometimes builds a poem out of pairs of rhyming lines, which are called couplets.

Guide practice

Have students identify the rhymes in each of the couplets in "Me." Then have them notice that the couplets are of different lengths, but each pair has the same number of beats.

On their own

Ask students to write a short rhyming poem that uses couplets. You may want to narrow their choices by suggesting topics such as pets, favorite foods, or something they are good at. Encourage students to include imagery in their poems by using words that appeal to the senses.

Extend Thinking
Think Critically

Higher-order thinking skills

Rhyme • Analysis How does the rhythm of rhyming couplets affect the way you read "Me"? Possible response: The lines have a rhythm, so once you get in the groove, the couplets are easy to read. Also, after you read the first line and know what the last word is, you can anticipate what the rhyming word might be in the next line.

Limerick • Analysis How is the rhyming pattern of the poem "Me" different than the rhyming pattern of a limerick? In the poem "Me," the rhyming pattern is rhyming couplets, but in a limerick, there is a fifth line that rhymes with the first two lines.

Rhyme vs Free Verse • Synthesis What kind of poem is "By Myself"? Explain your answer. The poem starts off as a free verse poem because the first two lines do not rhyme. But after that, it uses rhyming couplets. Since most of the lines of the poem are like that, it is a rhyming poem.

Practice Fluent Reading

Have partners take turns reading "Me" aloud. Before they begin, have them discuss the main feeling, or emotion, expressed in the poem. For example, does it express wonder, joy, pride, love, or something else? Then have students attempt to show this feeling as they read. After students finish, have them listen to the AudioText of the poem. What emotion does the reader express? Does it echo the one they tried to express in their own readings?

Writing Poetry

Have students write their own poems modeled on "By Myself." Students can use that poem's first two and last five lines, and then supply their own endings to lines 3–10. When students have finished, invite them to read their works aloud.

 Strategic Intervention

Rhyme Have students make a list of the rhyming words found in the poems on pp. 186–187 to start a rhyming journal. Ask them to write other words that rhyme with the words on their list and add to it whenever they hear or think of another rhyming word.

 Advanced

Write a poem Point out that the poem "Me" used the rhyming scheme (couplets) and cadence of a famous poem that begins *I think that I shall never see/A poem lovely as a tree.* Ask students to find another poem that they like and use its rhyming scheme and cadence to write their own versions, like the author of "Me" did.

English Language Learners
Monitor understanding Read "Me" and "By Myself" aloud. Make sure students understand who the poems are about and what message the authors are trying to give the reader. Have students look back at the text to clarify their understanding if necessary.

Weekly Assessment

Use pp. 115–120 of *Weekly Tests* to check:

✔ **Phonics** Syllables VCCCV

✔ ⊙ **Comprehension Skill** Cause and Effect

✔ **Lesson Vocabulary**

✔ **Review** **Comprehension Skill**
Draw Conclusions

clutched	scrambled
echoed	thatch
gully	valley
reeds	

Weekly Tests

Advanced

On-Level

Strategic Intervention

Differentiated Assessment

Use pp. 115–120 of *Fresh Reads for Fluency and Comprehension* to check:

✔ ⊙ **Comprehension Skill** Cause and Effect

✔ **Review** **Comprehension Skill** Draw Conclusions

✔ **Fluency** Words Correct Per Minute

Fresh Reads for Fluency and Comprehension

Managing Assessment

Use *Assessment Handbook* for:

✔ **Weekly Assessment Blackline Masters for Monitoring Progress**

✔ **Observation Checklists**

✔ **Record-Keeping Forms**

✔ **Portfolio Assessment**

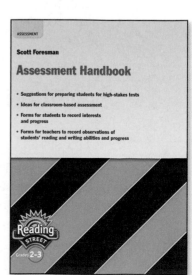

Assessment Handbook

Teacher Notes

Pacing Small Group Instruction

15–20 min

5-Day Plan

DAY 1	• Reinforce the concept • Read Leveled Readers Concept Literacy Below Level
DAY 2	• ◉ Cause and Effect • ◉ Monitor and Clarify • Read Student Edition pp. 158–164
DAY 3	• ◉ Unknown Words • Read Student Edition pp. 165–171
DAY 4	• Practice Retelling • Read Student Edition pp. 176–181
DAY 5	• Reread for fluency • Reread Leveled Readers

3- or 4-Day Plan

DAY 1	• Reinforce the concept • Read Leveled Readers • ◉ Cause and Effect • ◉ Monitor and Clarify • Read Student Edition pp. 158–164
DAY 2	• ◉ Unknown Words • Read Student Edition pp. 165–171
DAY 3	• Practice Retelling • Read Student Edition pp. 176–181
DAY 4	• Reread for fluency • Reread Leveled Readers

3-Day Plan: Eliminate the shaded box.

SI *Strategic Intervention* **DAY 1**

Build Background

■ **Reinforce the Concept** Discuss the weekly question *What behaviors are unique to different animals?* Different animals behave in different ways. These behaviors are part of what make every kind of animal unique. For example, when turtles sense danger, they hide in their shells. What other kinds of unique animal behaviors can you think of? *(Students may say that only spiders make webs and that only beavers build dams.)* Discuss the words on the concept map on p. 151. This week we are going to read a folk tale about an eagle that is raised with chickens. What problems do you think this might cause? *(The eagle might act like a chicken or might try to eat the chickens.)* Do you know any folk tales or stories that have a similar plot? *(Students may mention "The Ugly Duckling," in which a bird raised with ducks turns out to be a swan.)*

Preview Decodable Practice Reader 20A

■ **Before Reading** Review the words in Decodable Practice Reader 20A. Then have students blend these story words: *ostrich, actress, window, crate, distress, frustrated, slumped, moaned,* and *hundred.* Guide students through the text by doing a picture walk.

Objectives
• Participate in teacher-led discussions by answering questions with appropriate detail.

DAY 1

Concept Literacy Reader

■ **Read** *What Can Animals Do?*

■ **Before Reading** Preview the book with students, focusing on key concepts and vocabulary. Then help them set a purpose for reading.

■ **During Reading** Read the first two pages aloud while students track along with the print. Then have students finish reading the book with a partner.

■ **After Reading** After students finish reading, ask: What unique ability does each animal in the book display?

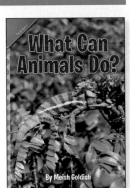

Below-Level Reader

■ **Read** *Swimming Like Buck*

■ **Before Reading** Help students use the illustrations to preview the book. Then help them set a purpose for reading.

■ **During Reading** Read the first three pages aloud. Then do a choral reading of the next four pages. If students are able, have them read and discuss the remainder of the book with a partner.

■ **After Reading** Discuss students' reactions to *Swimming Like Buck.*

• What do ducks do well?

• How is Buck's style of swimming different from most other ducks'?

Ask students to look at and discuss the concept map. Connect the Below-Level Reader to the weekly question *What behaviors are unique to different animals?* What unique qualities help ducks swim well? *(webbed feet, back location of feet, oiled feathers)*

MONITOR PROGRESS

If... students have difficulty reading the selection with a partner,
then... have them follow along as they listen to the Leveled Readers DVD-ROM.

If... students have trouble understanding why the other ducks make fun of Buck,
then... reread p. 5 and discuss what is unusual about his swimming style.

Objectives
• Participate in teacher-led discussions by answering questions with appropriate detail.

Strategic Intervention

Reinforce Comprehension

Skill Cause and Effect Review with students the *Envision It! Skill* material on cause and effect. Then use p. 194 to review the definitions of cause and effect. A cause tells why something happened. An effect is what happened. *Because* and *so* are clue words signaling cause and effect. To explain that a squirrel was causing your dog to bark, what cause-and-effect statements would you make? *(My dog is barking because a squirrel is nearby; a squirrel is here, so my dog is barking.)*

Strategy Monitor and Clarify Review the definitions of monitor and clarify. Remind students to pay attention to their level of understanding as they read and also to clarify sections of the folk tale as they read. Students can clarify by rereading, adjusting their reading rates, asking themselves questions as they read, or requesting help. For additional support, refer students to *Envision It! Strategy* p. EI•21.

Read *Fly, Eagle, Fly!* on pp. 158–164. Have partners read together, applying the comprehension skill to the folk tale.

- What does the farmer find above the gully? *(He finds a newly hatched eaglet.)*

- What does he decide to do with it? *(He decides to raise it as a chicken.)*

- How does the eagle act around the chickens? *(It acts the same way they do, staying on the ground and pecking at the bits and pieces that the family gives it instead of flying high and hunting animals.)*

Use the During Reading Differentiated Instruction for additional support for struggling readers.

> **MONITOR PROGRESS**
>
> **If...** students have difficulty reading along with the group,
> **then...** have them follow along as they listen to the AudioText.

Objectives
- Identify explicit cause and effect relationships among ideas in texts.
- Monitor comprehension.

SI *Strategic Intervention* DAY 3

Reinforce Vocabulary

Reread for Fluency Use Decodable Practice Reader 20A.

◉ **Decoding Multisyllabic Words** Write *ostrich* and model how to use nonmeaningful parts to read it. First I divide the word into chunks: *os trich.* I ask myself if I see any parts I know. I don't. So I look up the word in a dictionary, using the first three letters to guide me: there are the Os. Look for *ost...*

ostrich: An *ostrich* is a large, flightless bird. Use the Multisyllabic Word routine on p. 2 of *Routines Flip Chart* to help students read these words from the folk tale: *scrambled, gully, echoed, valley,* and *clutched.*

◉ **Unknown Words/Dictionary or Glossary** Write the word *valley* on the board. First I divide the word into chunks: *val ley.* I don't see any word parts I know, so I will look up the word in a dictionary. It says a *valley* is a long, low place that usually includes a river. The folk tale says that the farmer searched in the valley. Now I know he was searching in a low place near a river.

Read *Fly, Eagle, Fly!* on pp. 165–171. Review *Words!* on p. W•14. Then have students finish reading *Fly, Eagle, Fly!* Encourage students to use the glossary or a dictionary to figure out the meaning of any unknown words. Based on the definition in the glossary, who can show me what the bird must have done when it scrambled out of the farmer's hands? *(Students should demonstrate the quick movements of scrambling.)*

Use the During Reading Differentiated Instruction for additional support.

MONITOR PROGRESS

If... students have difficulty reading along with the group,

then... have them follow along as they listen to the AudioText.

Objectives
• Use a dictionary or glossary to determine meanings of unknown words.

SI Strategic Intervention
DAY 4

Practice Retelling

- **Retell** Guide students in using the Retelling Cards to retell the folk tale. Monitor retelling and prompt students as needed.

  - Who are the main characters in the story?

  - Tell me what this story is about in a few sentences.

  - What is the author trying to teach us?
    (Some students may say that a wild animal cannot act like a tame animal for long. Others may say that animals and people should be themselves rather than trying to act like those around them.)

  If students struggle, model a fluent retelling.

- **Before Reading** "Purple Coyote" on pp. 176–181, read aloud the genre information on p. 194 about the trickster tale. A trickster tale is a folk tale in which one character fools others. Like other folk tales, trickster tales entertain and also show how people and animals behave. As I read, I will try to figure out which animal is the trickster. Read the rest of the panel. Then have students read the introduction to the selection.

- **During Reading** Have students perform a choral reading of the selection. Encourage them to create different voices for the coyote, the boy, and the raccoon. How can we make the coyote sound tricky? How should the raccoon sound—smart, sarcastic, or bored? How should the boy sound?

- **After Reading** Have students share their reactions to the selection. Then guide them through the Reading Across Texts and Writing Across Texts activities, prompting if necessary with these questions:

  - What animals do the two tales describe?

  - How would you describe each animal?

  - How are the tales alike? How are they different?

MONITOR PROGRESS

If... students have difficulty reading along with the group,
then... have them follow along as they listen to the AudioText.

Objectives
- Compare settings in myths and traditional folktales.

Concept Literacy Reader

■ **Model** Demonstrate the fluency skill of rate for students. Ask students to listen carefully as you read aloud the first two pages of *What Can Animals Do?* Have students note the care you take to read slowly enough to be understandable and yet quickly enough to maintain listener interest.

What Can Animals Do?

■ **Fluency Routine**

1. Have students reread passages from *What Can Animals Do?* with a partner.

2. For optimal fluency, students should reread three to four times.

3. As students read, monitor fluency and provide corrective feedback. Encourage students to read slowly enough to be understood and quickly enough so that they and their listeners do not lose interest.

See *Routines Flip Chart* for more help with fluency.

■ **Retell** Have students retell *What Can Animals Do?* Prompt students as necessary.

Below-Level Reader

■ **Model** Ask students to listen carefully as you read aloud the first two pages of *Swimming Like Buck,* emphasizing rate.

Swimming Like Buck

■ **Fluency Routine**

1. Have students reread passages from *Swimming Like Buck* with a partner or individually.

2. For optimal fluency, students should reread three to four times.

3. As students read, monitor fluency and provide corrective feedback. Discuss how grouping words into phrases helps maintain a natural pace and rhythm.

See *Routines Flip Chart* for more help with fluency.

■ **Retell** For additional practice, have students retell *Swimming Like Buck* page by page using the illustrations. Prompt students as necessary with questions like these:

• What happened after Buck joined the swim team?

• What did you learn about differences from reading this book?

MONITOR PROGRESS

If... students have difficulty reading fluently,

then... provide additional fluency practice by pairing nonfluent readers with fluent ones.

Objectives
• Read aloud grade-level appropriate text with fluency.

Small Group Time

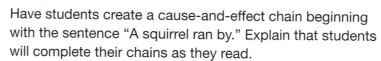

Pacing Small Group Instruction

15–20 min

5-Day Plan

DAY 1	• Expand the concept • Read On-Level Reader
DAY 2	• ◉ Cause and Effect • ◉ Monitor and Clarify • Read Student Edition pp. 158–164
DAY 3	• ◉ Unknown Words • Read Student Edition pp. 165–171
DAY 4	• Practice Retelling • Read Student Edition pp. 176–181
DAY 5	• Reread for fluency • Reread On-Level Reader

3- or 4-Day Plan

DAY 1	• Expand the concept • Read On-Level Reader • ◉ Cause and Effect • ◉ Monitor and Clarify • Read Student Edition pp. 158–164
DAY 2	• ◉ Unknown Words • Read Student Edition pp. 165–171
DAY 3	• Practice Retelling • Read Student Edition pp. 176–181
DAY 4	• Reread for fluency • Reread On-Level Reader

3-Day Plan: Eliminate the shaded box.

OL On-Level — DAY 1

Build Background

■ **Expand the Concept** Connect to the weekly question *What behaviors are unique to different animals?* Then expand the concept. Some unique behaviors come from instinct. Some come from training. People can train an animal to use its instincts in helpful ways. Discuss the meaning of the words on the concept map on p. 151.

On-Level Reader

Buddy Ran Away

■ **Before Reading** *Buddy Ran Away,* have students preview the book by looking at the title, cover, and pictures.

• What is the topic of this book? *(a dog that ran away)*

• What behavior does the illustration on page 4 show? *(It shows how dogs like to chase smaller animals.)*

Have students create a cause-and-effect chain beginning with the sentence "A squirrel ran by." Explain that students will complete their chains as they read.

■ **During Reading** Read aloud the first three pages of the book as students follow along. Then have them finish reading the book on their own. Remind students to add effects and causes to their chains as they read. Ask: What are some effects of a beagle's ability to sniff out scents? *(The ability causes them to be effective hunters; it can get them lost because they get distracted when following a scent; it can help them find their way.)*

■ **After Reading** Have partners compare their charts.

• What instinct caused Buddy to run away and allowed him to find his way home? *(his instinct to follow scent trails)*

• How does the story relate to the weekly question *What behaviors are unique to different animals? (It shows how beagles naturally behave. Another kind of animal—even another dog—might not have behaved in the same way.)*

Objectives
• Participate in teacher-led discussions by answering questions with appropriate detail.

OL On-Level

DAY 2

Expand Comprehension

◉ **Skill Cause and Effect** Use p. 194 to review the definitions of cause and effect. For additional review, see the Cause and Effect entry in *Envision It! Skill*. *Causes* are the reasons why something happens, and *effects* are the things that happen. For example, if I untie my shoe (cause), I might trip over my shoelace (effect). Some cause-and-effect statements use clue words such as *because* or *so*, but others do not.

Cause and Effect

◉ **Strategy Monitor and Clarify** Review the definitions of monitor and clarify, and encourage students to monitor and clarify sections of the folk tale as they read. You may not know much about how eagles and chickens behave, so you will need to monitor your understanding of the folk tale as you read. You can clarify by rereading parts of the folk tale, asking yourself questions about it, reading more slowly, asking a classmate for help, or asking me for help. For additional support, use the Extend Thinking questions during reading or refer students to p. EI•21 of *Envision It! Strategy*.

Read *Fly, Eagle, Fly!* on pp. 158–164. Then have students begin reading aloud. As they read, have them look for causes and effects explained in the folk tale.

- Why did the farmer call the eagle a chicken? *(He had trained it to act like a chicken, so he came to think of it as a chicken.)*

- Why did the eagle act like a chicken? *(because it was raised among chickens and learned their behaviors)*

- What effects do you think the farmer's actions will have? *(Some students may say that the eagle will continue to act like a chicken because those are the behaviors it knows. Others may say that the eagle will eventually realize it is an eagle.)*

Objectives
- Identify explicit cause and effect relationships among ideas in texts.
- Monitor comprehension.

DAY 3

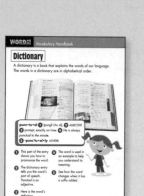

Expand Vocabulary

🔘 **Unknown Words/Dictionary or Glossary**
Write the word *clutched* as you say it aloud.
Draw a line between the base word and the
suffix. Then ask:

- Where does *clutched* appear in this folk tale?
  *(where it says "the eagle's claws clutched the
  rock")*

- What are some dictionary definitions of the
  word *clutch? ("group of eggs," "held on to")*

- What do you think the word means in this folk tale? *(An eagle comes from an
  egg, but I don't think that makes sense in this sentence. The eagle could hold
  onto the rock. In this context,* clutched *must mean "held on to.")*

Read *Fly, Eagle, Fly!* on pp. 158–164. Then have students finish reading the
selection, encouraging them to use a dictionary or glossary to find out the
meanings of other unknown words.

- What does the word *convinced* mean on p. 164? Use a dictionary if you can't
  figure it out based on the words and sentences around the word. *(persuaded)*

- What does *roared* mean on p. 165? *("gave a loud laugh")*

 On-Level

DAY **4**

Practice Retelling

■ **Retell** To assess students' comprehension, use the Retelling Cards. Monitor retelling and prompt students as needed.

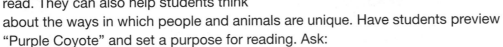

■ **Before Reading** "Purple Coyote" on pp. 176–181, read aloud the genre information on p. 176 about trickster tales. Explain that trickster tales can be fun to read. They can also help students think about the ways in which people and animals are unique. Have students preview "Purple Coyote" and set a purpose for reading. Ask:

- Based on the information in the side column, what would you expect this story to be about? *(a person or animal playing a trick on another person or animal)*

- How would you expect the animals in this tale to act? Would they be like real animals in the wild? *(No, the information in the side column says that animals in folk tales often act like people. The coyote will probably be able to talk. Based on the first picture, it may even be able to dance.)*

■ **During Reading** Have students read along with you while tracking the print. Ask:

- Who are the characters mentioned on the first few pages? *(Jim and the purple coyote)*

- Why do you think the coyote behaves so strangely? *(He will probably try to trick Jim.)*

■ **After Reading** Have students share their reaction to "Purple Coyote." Then have them create and act out a trickster tale explaining how a school rule came to be.

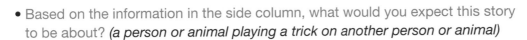

Objectives
- Compare settings in myths and traditional folktales.

Small Group Time

On-Level Reader

■ **Model** Read aloud the first page of the On-Level Reader *Buddy Ran Away,* emphasizing the use of an appropriate reading rate. If you wish, demonstrate inappropriate rates by reading some parts too quickly or too slowly.

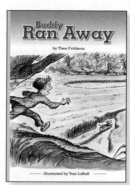

Buddy Ran Away

■ **Fluency Routine**

1. Have students reread passages from *Buddy Ran Away* with a partner.

2. For optimal fluency, students should reread passages three to four times.

3. As students read, monitor fluency and provide corrective feedback. Have students take care to read neither too quickly nor too slowly to be understood.

See *Routines Flip Chart* for more help with fluency.

■ **Retell** For additional practice, have students use illustrations as a guide to retelling *Buddy Ran Away.* Prompt students as necessary with questions like these:

• Why did Buddy run away? *(He was chasing a rabbit.)*

• How did Sam feel without Buddy? *(extremely sad)*

• How did Sam help Buddy find his way home? *(He left a scent trail by throwing small pieces of clothing out of the car window on the way home.)*

Objectives
• Read aloud grade-level appropriate text with fluency.

A Advanced **DAY 1**

Build Background

- **Extend the Concept** Explain that the weekly question is *What behaviors are unique to different animals?* Then extend the concept. How do dogs typically behave? *(They dig in dirt, follow scents, grab food, and chase rabbits and squirrels.)* What behaviors must dogs be trained to do? *(respond to their names, follow commands, perform tricks, sit, stay, roll over, shake hands)*

Advanced Reader

- **Before Reading** *Toby the Smart Dog,* tell students to look at the front cover. Based on the title and artwork, what do you think this book will be about? *(The book will probably describe behaviors of dogs.)* Have students look at the illustrations in the book and use them to predict what will happen in the text. Then help them set a purpose for reading.

Toby the Smart Dog

- **During Reading** Have students read the Advanced Reader independently, and encourage them to think critically. For example, ask:

  - How does Charlie want Toby to behave? *(He wants Toby to respond to his name, obey commands, and perform tricks.)*

  - How does Toby respond at first? *(Toby follows his instincts instead of Charlie's commands.)*

- **After Reading** Have students review the concept map and explain how *Toby the Smart Dog* helps them answer the weekly question *What behaviors are unique to different animals?* Prompt as necessary.

  - How does Toby's behavior change over time? *(At first Toby obeys instincts, but he learns to obey humans.)*

  - Which of Toby's actions come from instinct? *(digging up the flowers)*

  - Which of Toby's actions come from training? *(coming when called, obeying commands)*

- **Now Try This** Pair students, and have each pair write down a brief retelling of the story from Toby's point of view. Pairs should work on their retellings throughout the week.

Objectives
- Participate in teacher-led discussions by answering questions with appropriate detail.

Pacing Small Group Instruction

15–20 min

5-Day Plan

DAY 1	• Extend the concept • Read Advanced Reader
DAY 2	• Cause and Effect • Monitor and Clarify • Read Student Edition pp. 158–164
DAY 3	• Unknown Words • Read Student Edition pp. 165–171
DAY 4	• Folk Tale: Trickster Tale • Read Student Edition pp. 176–181
DAY 5	• Reread for fluency • Reread Advanced Reader

3- or 4-Day Plan

DAY 1	• Extend the concept • Read Advanced Reader • Cause and Effect • Monitor and Clarify • Read Student Edition pp. 158–164
DAY 2	• Unknown Words • Read Student Edition pp. 165–171
DAY 3	• Folk Tale: Trickster Tale • Read Student Edition pp. 176–181
DAY 4	• Reread for fluency • Reread Advanced Reader

3-Day Plan: Eliminate the shaded box.

A | Advanced | **DAY 2**

Extend Comprehension

Skill Cause and Effect Explain that folk tales sometimes explain the causes and effects of behaviors. Think of the book that you just read, *Toby the Smart Dog.* If you were to explain Toby's behavior using cause and effect, what statement would you make? *(Toby used to act on instinct alone, but because Charlie trained him, he learned to obey.)*

Strategy Monitor and Clarify Review the definition of the strategy of monitor and clarify. Then remind students to monitor their understanding as they read the rest of the selection. If you don't monitor your understanding, you may come to the end of a page and realize that you don't understand what you have just read. As you read, keep track of how well you are following events in the text. If you need to, reread parts of the text, read more slowly, or stop to look up a word in a dictionary or glossary. You may also ask a classmate or me for help. During reading, use the Extend Thinking questions and the During Reading Differentiated Instruction for additional support.

Read *Fly, Eagle, Fly!* on pp. 158–164. Have students begin reading *Fly, Eagle, Fly!,* tracking causes and effects as they read. Ask: Based on the first three pages, how do you think the eaglet will respond to being raised as a chicken? When, if ever, do you think it will remember its eagle nature?

■ **Critical Thinking** Encourage students to reflect on what they have read.

- What qualities do people believe that eagles have? *(strength, speed, independence)*

- What qualities do people believe that chickens have? *(They are slow and depend on others.)*

- How do these beliefs affect your understanding of the story? *(Students may say that it is better—but more dangerous—to be an eagle.)*

Objectives
- Identify explicit cause and effect relationships among ideas in texts.
- Monitor comprehension.

Extend Vocabulary

◉ Unknown Words/Dictionary or Glossary
Read a sentence containing a difficult word, such as "He climbed up a *gully,* in case a calf had huddled there to escape the storm."

- How does the dictionary define *gully*? *(It is a deep trench caused by running water.)*

- Why would a calf try to escape a storm by climbing up a gully? *(On top of a gully is high ground that might be safe from flooding.)*

Read *Fly, Eagle, Fly!* on pp. 165–171. Challenge students to use a dictionary or glossary to define unknown words throughout the selection. For example, ask:

- Page 160 includes the sentence "He searched among the reeds, behind the rocks, and in the rushing water." Look up the word *reed* in the dictionary. What does it mean? *(a tall, thin plant)* Why do you think reeds often grow in valleys? *(The dictionary says reeds grow in riverbeds and shallow water, and riverbeds are often part of valleys.)*

- Page 161 includes the sentence "He reached out and cradled it in both hands." Are you likely to find the word *cradled* in the dictionary? *(No. The definition would be under the word* cradle, *without the suffix.)* Which dictionary definition makes more sense in this story—"a piece of furniture in which a baby sleeps" or "held gently"? *("held gently")*

Objectives
- Use a dictionary or glossary to determine meanings of unknown words.

Small Group Time

DAY **4**

- **Before Reading** "Purple Coyote" on pp. 176–181, read the panel information on trickster tales. Then have students use the text features, including the time line and statistics, to set a purpose for reading. After that, have students read "Purple Coyote" on their own.

- **During Reading** Have students read the selection. Point out that a trickster tale tells why people or animals behave as they do. What does this trickster tale seem to say about humans? *(We're not as smart as we think we are!)* As they read, have students think about other trickster tales they've read.

- **After Reading** Have students discuss Reading Across Texts. Then have them complete the Writing Across Texts activity independently.

"Purple Coyote"

Objectives
- Compare settings in myths and traditional folktales.

A Advanced DAY **5**

- **Reread for Fluency** Have students silently reread passages from the Advanced Reader *Toby the Smart Dog.* Then have them reread aloud with a partner or individually. As students read, monitor fluency and provide corrective feedback. If students read fluently on the first reading, they do not need to reread three to four times. Assess the fluency of students in this group using p. 183j.

- **Retell** Have students monitor and clarify the causes and effects featured in the Advanced Reader *Toby the Smart Dog.*

- **Now Try This** Have students complete their retellings. Remind them to consult the Advanced Reader to make sure they have recorded events in the proper order. Have them share their retellings with classmates.

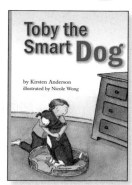

Toby the Smart Dog

Objectives
- Read aloud grade-level appropriate text with fluency.

 English Language Learners

The ELL lessons are organized by strands. Use them to scaffold the weekly curriculum of lessons or during small group time instruction.

Academic Language

Students will hear or read the following academic language in this week's core instruction. As students encounter the vocabulary, provide a simple definition or concrete example. Then ask students to suggest an example or synonym of the word and identify available cognates.

Skill Words	cause (*causa*)	phrase (*frase*)
	effect (*efecto*)	singular (*sílaba*)
	preposition (*preposición*)	transition (*transición*)
Concept Words	behavior	eagle
	unique (*único*)	

Spanish cognates in parentheses

Concept Development

What behaviors are unique to different animals?

■ **Preteach Concept**

- **Prior Knowledge** Have students turn to pages 150–151 in the Student Edition. Call attention to the picture of the different animals and tap into students' knowledge of unusual-looking animals. Can you name what kind of animals these are? What do you notice about the lizard's eyes? Can you think of why a lizard would have eyes like that? How could they help it blend in to the branch?

- **Discuss Concept** Elicit students' knowledge and experience of unique behaviors of different animals. Why do some animals fly? Why do others crawl? Why do you think different animals have different kinds of behaviors? How does this help the different animals? Supply background information as needed.

- **Poster Talk-Through** Read aloud the Poster Talk-Through on ELL Poster 20 and work through the Day 1 activities.

■ **Daily Concept and Vocabulary Development** Use the daily activities on ELL Poster 20 to build concept and vocabulary knowledge.

Objectives

- Use prior knowledge and experiences to understand meanings in English. Internalize new basic and academic language by using and reusing it in meaningful ways in speaking and writing activities that build concept and language attainment. Learn new language structures, expressions, and basic and academic vocabulary heard during classroom instruction and interactions.

Content Objectives

- Use concept vocabulary related to animals and their behaviors.

Language Objectives

- Express ideas in response to art and discussion.

Daily Planner

DAY 1	• Concepts and Oral Vocabulary • Listening (Read Aloud)
DAY 2	• Concepts • Vocabulary • Phonics and Spelling • Unknown Words
DAY 3	• Concepts • Vocabulary • Cause and Effect • Read *Fly, Eagle, Fly! An African Tale*
DAY 4	• Concepts • Vocabulary • ELL/ELD Readers
DAY 5	• Concepts • Vocabulary • Time-Order Transition Words

See the ELL Handbook for ELL Workshops with targeted instruction.

Concept Talk Video

Use the Concept Talk Video Routine (*ELL Handbook,* page 477) to build background knowledge about unique behavior in animals. For more listening practice, see *Use Classroom Resources* (*ELL Handbook,* pages 406–407).

Support for English Learners

Language Objectives

- Understand and use basic vocabulary.
- Learn meanings of grade-level vocabulary.

Cognates

For Spanish speakers, point out that the word *valley* has a Spanish cognate, *valle*. Explain that both words look almost the same but the *ll* sound is pronounced differently in Spanish and English. Have students practice repeating the word pair, focusing on the different pronunciations of the double l.

ELL English Language Learners

Basic Vocabulary

■ **High-Frequency Words** Use the ELL Vocabulary Routine on p. 471 of the *ELL Handbook* to systematically teach newcomers the first 300 sight words in English. Students who began learning ten words per week at the beginning of the year are now learning words 191–200 (*ELL Handbook,* p. 452). Page 446 of the handbook contains a bank of strategies that you can use to ensure students' mastery of high-frequency words.

Lesson Vocabulary

■ **Preteach** Preteach the Lesson Vocabulary using this routine:

1. Distribute copies of this week's Word Cards (*ELL Handbook,* page 143).

2. Display ELL Poster 20 and reread the Poster Talk-Through.

3. Using the poster illustrations, model how a word's meaning can be expressed with other similar words: Tall, green plants, or reeds, are often found in wet areas.

4. Use these sentences to reveal the meaning of the other words.

- When the girl shouted loudly near the cliffs, her voice *echoed* back to her. **(sound that comes back to you)**

- When it rains, water flows through the *gully*. **(deep ditch cut by water)**

- Some long, thin *reeds* grow in this wet area. **(tall grass in shallow water)**

- They *scrambled* up the mountain using their hands. **(to move hurriedly)**

- They *clutched* the rocks as they climbed so they wouldn't fall. **(to hold tightly)**

- Many people in warm climates make thatched roofs out of *grass*. **(plants used for making roofs)**

- They looked down from the hill into the *valley*. **(area between hills)**

Objectives

- Expand and internalize initial English vocabulary by learning and using high-frequency English words necessary for identifying and describing people, places, and objects, by retelling simple stories and basic information represented or supported by pictures, and by learning and using routine language needed for classroom communication.

 English Language Learners

■ **Reteach** Have students answer questions about any English words in the reading or language arts lesson that they want to understand better. Elicit questions about any words they wish to use in school. If students do not ask any questions, ask them questions that will help them read, write, and use the English words better. Examples:

- Which suffix is used in three of the selection vocabulary words? (-*ed* in *clutched, echoed,* and *scrambled*)

- What do we know about action words that end in -ed? (They are in the past tense.)

- Which two words are things people might do when climbing a mountain? (*clutched* and *scrambled*)

- Which two words refer to plants? (*reeds* and *thatched*)

■ **Writing** Use a T-Chart to help children internalize new vocabulary by having them write the words and their meanings. Write the vocabulary words on the board. Give students a T-Chart and have them copy the vocabulary words in the left column. Then ask them to write a synonym for each word or draw a picture to illustrate it in the right column. When students have completed the task, have them take turns reading the words and their synonyms or sharing their pictures.

 Leveled Support

Beginning Have students draw and label pictures to show the meanings of *gully, valley, reeds, and thatch.* Have them use gestures to show *scrambled, echoed, and clutched.*

Intermediate Ask students to use pictures to illustrate some words and synonyms or phrases to define others.

Advanced Encourage students to use synonyms or short definitions to show the meaning of each vocabulary word.

Advanced High Challenge students to use as many vocabulary words as they can in meaningful sentences.

Language Objectives

- Produce drawings, phrases, or short sentences using Lesson Vocabulary.

ELL Teacher Tip

- Research shows that students who acquire a strong grasp of academic vocabulary will become successful learners. Instruction in academic vocabulary should be explicit and systematic. It is very important to offer students many different types of opportunities to practice academic vocabulary, for example, graphic organizers, definitions, sentence completion, and questions and answers.

Graphic Organizers

Vocabulary Word	Synonym
valley	area between hills

ELL Workshop

Provide opportunities for students to give directions using newly acquired abstract and content-based vocabulary. *Give Directions* (*ELL Handbook,* pages 398–399) supports students in this task.

Objectives

- Internalize new basic and academic language by using and reusing it in meaningful ways in speaking and writing activities that build concept and language attainment. Share information in cooperative learning interactions. Demonstrate comprehension of increasingly complex English by participating in shared reading, retelling or summarizing material, responding to questions, and taking notes commensurate with content area and grade level needs. Ask and give information ranging from using a very limited bank of high-frequency, high-need, concrete vocabulary, including key words and expressions needed for basic communication in academic and social contexts, to using abstract and content-based vocabulary during extended speaking assignments;

Support for English Language Learners

Content Objectives
- Monitor and adjust oral comprehension.

Language Objectives
- Discuss oral passages.
- Use a graphic organizer to take notes.

Graphic Organizers

Mini-Lesson

Before reading the passage, have students turn to p. EI•9 in the Student Edition. What do the pictures tell about this selection? (space) What details do you see that support that main idea? (stars, moon, planet) Explain that details are important to understand what you hear. Listen for the details about alligators and crocodiles in this story.

ELL Teacher Tip
- Reread the selection a third time and pause to help students focus on information that they can add to the Venn diagram.

ELL Workshop

As you give directions for using the graphic organizer, you might use *Follow Directions* (*ELL Handbook,* pp. 398–399) to support students in comprehending increasingly complex spoken directions.

Listening Comprehension

> **The American Alligator**
>
> The American alligator is one of the largest reptiles in the world. Most American alligators grow to about 10 feet long. They weigh about 500 pounds. The American alligator can be found in Florida, Louisiana, and Texas.
>
> American alligators are excellent swimmers. Their snout and tail are shaped for digging holes at the bottom of swamps and rivers. Some holes are the size of a bathtub. Other holes can be as big as a swimming pool. Alligators use the holes for shelter.
>
> What is the difference between an alligator and a crocodile? Alligators and crocodiles live in different places. Crocodiles live mostly in the Nile River in Egypt and in other areas of Africa. Alligators have short and rounded snouts. Crocodiles have long and point snouts. Alligators have teeth in their upper jaws. Crocodiles have teeth in their lower jaws.
>
> For many years, American alligators were in danger of disappearing. Today no one can hunt alligators because there are laws to protect them. You can see alligators on land and in the water. If you listen, you might hear their fierce roar.

Prepare for the Read Aloud The modified Read Aloud above prepares students for listening to the oral reading "Where Are the Alligators?" on p. 151b.

■ **First Listening: Listen to Understand** Write the title of the Read Aloud on the board. This teaches us about alligators. Listen carefully to learn more about alligators. What do alligators look like? Where do they live? Afterward, ask the questions again and have students share their answers.

■ **Second Listening: Listen to Check Understanding** Using a Venn diagram (*ELL Handbook,* p. 488), work with students to track information about alligators and crocodiles. Label the left circle "Alligators." Label the right circle "Crocodiles." Record the facts in the appropriate sections.

Objectives
- Demonstrate listening comprehension of increasingly complex spoken English by following directions, retelling or summarizing spoken messages, responding to questions and requests, collaborating with peers, and taking notes commensurate with content and grade-level needs.

ELL *English Language Learners*

Phonics and Spelling

- **Syllables VCCCV** Use Sound-Spelling Card 146 to teach words with VCCCV.

- **Preteach** Write *sandwich* on the board and draw a small picture. This is a sandwich /s/ /a/ /n/ /d/ /w/ /i/ /ch/. Point out that there are two vowel sounds in *sandwich* and therefore two syllables. How many consonants do you see between the vowels *a* and *i*? (three) *nd* is a consonant blend so these letters stay together when we divide a word into syllables. Now let's divide sandwich into syllables: sand / wich.

- **Teach/Model** Write *monster* on the board. Underline the three consonants between the vowels *o* and *e*. There are three consonants between two vowels. Each vowel sound means one syllable, so we know there are two syllables. What is the first syllable? (mon) What is the second syllable? (ster)

- **Practice** Write the following words on the board: *surprise, control, and pilgrim.* Have students write the words and show the syllable divisions.

For more practice with syllables VCCCV, see the *ELL Handbook*, p. 238.

Vocabulary Skill: Unfamiliar Words

- **Preteach/Model** Have students turn to p. 159 of the Student Edition. Read aloud the first sentence in the last paragraph. *Reluctantly* is a difficult word. When I come across a word I don't know, I use the dictionary to find out what it means. Let's look up *reluctantly*. Use a dictionary to look up the word and read the definition aloud. So the farmer didn't want to go into the kitchen and pick up the bird. Model using *reluctantly* in a different context, for example, *He turned in the test reluctantly.*

- **Practice** Write this sentence on the board: *The path took them into dark crevices.* Have students look up the word *crevices* in a dictionary.

Beginning/Intermediate Help students use the dictionary to locate the word *crevice*. Point out the definition and use simple language to help students understand it. Ask them to write the word and draw a picture to illustrate it.

Advanced/Advanced High Ask students to use the dictionary to find the meaning of *crevice*. Working individually, have students write the word with its definition beside it. Challenge them to write an original sentence using the word. Then students can take turns reading their sentences aloud.

Content Objectives

- Identify words with syllables VCCCV.
- Identify unknown words.
- Break words with VCCCV into syllables.

Language Objectives

- Apply phonics and decoding skills to vocabulary.
- Use a dictionary to find the meanings of unknown words.

Transfer Skills

Speakers of monosyllabic languages such as Cantonese, Hmong, Khmer, Korean, and Vietnamese may have difficulty understanding that multisyllabic words are single words. Help students practice saying and writing words with VCCCV as single words. Provide them with guided practice pronouncing the multisyllablic words.

Unknown Words

Students whose home languages use a different alphabet or symbols may have difficulty locating unknown words in the dictionary. Display the English alphabet to provide these students with additional support.

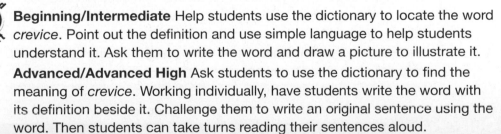

Objectives
- Practice producing sounds of newly acquired vocabulary such as long and short vowels, silent letters, and consonant clusters to pronounce English words in a manner that is increasingly comprehensible.

Content Objectives

- Identify an effect as something that happens.

- Determine the cause or why a thing happens.

Language Objectives

- Use *if... then* clauses to talk about cause and effect.

- Use sentences with *if... then* to talk about things that happen in the classroom.

ELL Workshop

Encourage students to ask questions to monitor their understanding of instruction of comprehension skills. Use *Ask Clarifying Questions* (*ELL Handbook,* p. 405–406) for practice.

ELL English Language Learners

Comprehension
Cause and Effect

- **Preteach** An effect is something that happens. A cause is why that thing happens. *I fell on the ground* is an effect. It is something that happened to me. *I tripped on a rock* is the cause. It is why I fell on the ground. Have students turn to Envision It! on p. EI•3 in the Student Edition. Read aloud the text together. Have students identify what happens (the bird flies out of the cage) and why it happens (because the boy opens the cage door). Have students raise their hands to be called on to answer the questions.

- **Reteach** Distribute copies of the Picture It! (*ELL Handbook,* p. 144). Explain to students that understanding cause and effect helps make better readers. Before reading the passage aloud, tell students to listen for cause and effect clue words (**Answers** Cause: Lulu can see better than most animals. She flies quickly. Effect: she is a good hunter; Cause: Lulu can see fish underwater. Lulu has strong legs. Effect: Lulu can catch fish.)

 Leveled Support

Beginning/Intermediate Have students underline clue words, such as *so, because* and *thanks to.*

Advanced/Advanced High Pair students together. Have one student read either part of a sentence that shows a cause. Have the other scan the passage and read the effect. For example, Student 1: "She has giant claws." Student 2: "She can hold prey."

MINI-LESSON

Basic Classroom Language

Have students expand and internalize initial English vocabulary by learning and using language needed for classroom communication. What do you do when you know an answer to a question and you want to be called on? (raise my hand) Have students demonstrate raising a hand. Have students complete the Envision It! activity from the Preteach section above. Have them practice raising their hand to be a called on when they know the answers.

Objectives

- Expand and internalize initial English vocabulary by learning and using high-frequency English words necessary for identifying and describing people, places, and objects, by retelling simple stories and basic information represented or supported by pictures, and by learning and using routine language needed for classroom communication. Learn new language structures, expressions, and basic and academic vocabulary heard during classroom instruction and interactions.

 English Language Learners

Reading Comprehension
Fly, Eagle, Fly!

Student Edition pp. 158–159

■ **Frontloading** Read aloud the title and talk about how eagles fly. Ask students to model soaring like an eagle. Do chickens fly? Show me how a chicken flies. Let's look through the book and see how these birds behave. Guide students on a picture walk through *Fly, Eagle, Fly!* Ask them what the man does to the eagle and have them predict what the eagle will do. During reading, pause and invite students to adjust their predictions. Provide students with a three-column chart to fill out as they read the selection. Supply these headings: *What the man does, Predictions, and Revised Predictions.*

■ **Sheltered Reading** Have students read pp. 158–171 and take notes about what they read on each page. Then ask questions such as the following to guide students' comprehension:

- p. 161: What does the man find? (an eagle chick)

- p. 162: What animals does the eagle chick live with? (chickens) What does the eagle chick eat? (corn or chicken food) Do you think wild eagles eat chicken food? Why or why not? (Answers will vary.)

- p. 164: What does the farmer say about the eagle? (It thinks it's a chicken. Of course it's a chicken.) Do you think that an eagle is a chicken because it is raised with chickens? Explain your answer. (Accept all reasonable answers.)

- p. 166: Why does the farmer's friend take the eagle up on the roof? (He wants it to fly.) What does the eagle do? (slides down the thatch to the ground)

- p. 169: Where do the men take the eagle? (to the top of the mountain) Why? (so it'll soar like an eagle) What happens to the bird? (It leans forward and is swept upward.)

■ **Fluency: Read at the appropriate rate** Remind students that it is important to maintain a reading rate similar to the rate at which they speak. Read the first paragraph on p. 164 at an appropriate rate. Point out how your intonation changes when you read the exclamation. Have pairs of students read the paragraph aloud to each other using their intonation to express exclamation. For more practice, use the Fluency: Paired Reading Routine (*ELL Handbook,* p. 474).

■ **After Reading** Give small groups of students a Retelling Card. Have groups line up in story order and take turns summarizing their section of the story.

Content Objectives

- Monitor and adjust comprehension.

- Make and revise predictions.

Language Objectives

- Read grade-level text at the appropriate rate.

- Summarize text using visual support.

Graphic Organizers

What the man does	Predictions	Revised Predictions

Objectives

- Distinguish sounds and intonation patterns of English with increasing ease. Speak using learning strategies such as requesting assistance, employing non-verbal cues, and using synonyms and circumlocution (conveying ideas by defining or describing when exact English words are not known). Express opinions, ideas, and feelings ranging from communicating single words and short phrases to participating in extended discussions on a variety of social and grade-appropriate academic topics.

ELL/ELD Reader 3.4.5

Comprehension:
Mealtime in Madagascar

■ **Before Reading** Distribute copies of the ELL and ELD Readers, *Mealtime in Madagascar,* to students at their reading level.

• **Preview** Read the title aloud with students: This is a book about animals in Madagascar. Invite students to look through the pictures and name what they see. Have them use the pictures and their prior knowledge to help them make predictions about the animals.

• **Set a Purpose for Reading** Let's read to figure out where each animal lives and what it eats.

■ **During Reading** Follow the Reading Routine for both reading groups.

1. Read the entire Reader aloud slowly.

2. Read pp. 2–9, pausing to build background or model comprehension. Have Beginning students finger-point as you read. Use the questions in the chart to check students' comprehension.

3. Have students do a choral rereading of pp. 2–9.

4. Repeat steps 2–4 above for pp. 10–12 of the Reader.

■ **After Reading** Use the exercises on the inside back cover of each Reader and invite students to share their writing. In a whole-group discussion, ask students Where does each animal live and what does it eat? Record their answers on the board and invite them to point to pictures in the book to support their answers.

ELD Reader

■ **pp. 2–3** What does Ringo, the lemur, eat? Read aloud the sentence that gives you the answer. (p. 2 leaves, fruit, and insects)

■ **pp. 4–9** What do chameleon's do when they are angry? (p. 8 become big)

Writing On page 10, it says *Suddenly, Fred could not see Tina!* This is the effect. Find the sentence on this page that tells the cause. Copy the sentence. Then read it aloud to your partner.

ELL Reader

■ **pp. 2–3** Name three animals that live in a forest in Madagascar. (chameleon, lemur, fossa) Which of these animals eats other animals? (fossa)

■ **pp. 4–9** Which animal has a long tongue? (chameleon) What can the chameleon do with its tongue? (catch flies) How do lemurs use their long tails? (to see each other)

Study Guide Distribute copies of the ELL Reader Study Guide (*ELL Handbook*, p. 148). Scaffold comprehension of cause and effect by helping students look back through the Reader to complete the organizer. Review their responses together. (**Answers** See *ELL Handbook*, pp. 209–212.)

Objectives

• Understand the general meaning, main points, and important details of spoken language ranging from situations in which topics, language, and contexts are familiar to unfamiliar. Demonstrate listening comprehension of increasingly complex spoken English by following directions, retelling or summarizing spoken messages, responding to questions and requests, collaborating with peers, and taking notes commensurate with content and grade-level needs. Share information in cooperative learning interactions. Write using newly acquired basic vocabulary and content-based grade-level vocabulary.

 **English Language Learners**

Conventions
Prepositions

■ **Teach/Model** Remind students that prepositions tell where things are. Ask questions about classroom objects, such as Where is the pencil? (It's on the desk.) Where is the chair? (It's under the table.) Prepositions can also tell where things were in the past or where things or people are going. Where are you from? (I am from Texas.) Where did you go yesterday? (I went to the store.) Underline *on, under, from*, and *to* as students identify the prepositional phrase for you.

■ **Practice** Write commands, such as the following, on index cards: *Walk to the door. Take a book from the shelf. Write on the board. Stand beside your desk* Call students individually to the front of the room. Give each student a card. Have the student read the card silently and perform the command.

Beginning Have Beginning students pick a card. Help them read the card, and then have the student perform the command.

Intermediate Have students work with partners. One partner picks a card and performs the command. The other tells what the command is.

Advanced Have partners make their own set of command cards. Then partners take turns picking a card and performing the command. Have students identify the preposition in each sentence.

Advanced High Have pairs of students make their own set of command cards. One student can pick a card and perform the command. Have the other describe what the partner did, for example, *Ben stood beside his desk.*

■ **Reteach** For additional practice, have students work together to complete the following sentence frames: The book is _____ the desk. The pencil is _____ the book. The chair is _____ the desk.

Content Objectives

- Identify prepositions in a sentence.
- Understand that prepositions tell where things are.

Language Objectives

- Use prepositions to tell where something is.
- Write sentences with prepositions.

 Transfer Skills

Continue to monitor word order in sentences that contain prepositions. Make sure that students place the relevant noun after every preposition. Continue to provide sentences that contain errors in preposition usage.

ELL Workshop

Students may need extra practice using language structures heard during classroom interactions. *Use Prepositions and Adjectives in Your Speaking (ELL Handbook, pp. 426–427)* provides extra support.

Objectives

- Internalize new basic and academic language by using and reusing it in meaningful ways in speaking and writing activities that build concept and language attainment. Learn new language structures, expressions, and basic and academic vocabulary heard during classroom instruction and interactions. Speak using a variety of grammatical structures, sentence lengths, sentence types, and connecting words with increasing accuracy and ease as more English is acquired. Employ increasingly complex grammatical structures in content area writing commensurate with grade level expectations such as (i) using correct verbs, tenses, and pronouns/antecedents; (ii) using possessive case (apostrophe -s) correctly; and, (iii) using negatives and contractions correctly.

Support for English Language Learners

Content Objectives

- Identify time-order transition words in a text.

Language Objectives

- Write paragraphs using time-order transition words.

- Share feedback for editing and revising.

ELL Teaching Routine

For practice spelling words related to animal behavior use the Spelling Routine (*ELL Handbook,* p. 476).

ELL Workshop

Have students collaborate with peers to discuss ideas before writing. *Discuss with Classmates* (*ELL Handbook,* pages 418–419) provides assistance with discussion.

ELL English Language Learners

Writing Time-Order Transition Words

■ **Introduce** Display the paragraph model and read it aloud. Tell students that time-order transition words help readers know what happens and the order in which it happens. What happens first in this paragraph? (The man comes very early.) Then what happens? (He takes the eagle up the mountain.) Finally, what happens? (The bird is swept into the air.) Underline *first, then, at last,* and *finally.* These are examples of time-order transition words.

Writing Model

First, the man came very early the next morning. Then, he took the eagle up the mountain. They climbed and climbed. At last, they reached the top. The man set the bird down at the edge of the cliff. Finally, the sun began to rise and the eagle was swept away into the air.

■ **Practice** Write the following sentences on the board. Help students use the time-order words to determine what happens and in what order it happens. Have students take turns reading the sentences in order.

Next, he brought the eagle chick home.
In the end, the eagle chick thought it was a chicken.
Then, the eagle chick lived with the man's chickens.
First, the man found an eagle chick.

■ **Write** Have students use time-order words to write about animal behavior. They can use pp. 158–171 in the Student Edition, *Fly, Eagle, Fly!,* ELL/ELD Reader *Mealtime in Madagascar,* or their graphic organizers to give them ideas. Have students share their ideas aloud cooperatively when they are finished writing.

 Beginning Have students copy the following time-order words on their paper: *first, next, then, at last.* Then they can draw pictures beside each word to illustrate animal behavior.

Intermediate Have students use time-order words to label their graphic organizers from *Mealtime in Madagascar.* Encourage partners to write complete sentences using these words and the information in their organizer.

Advanced/Advanced High Have students work independently to write paragraphs about animal behavior. Tell them to use time-order words to help organize their writing. Then pairs can exchange papers and provide feedback for editing and revising.

Objectives

- Edit writing for standard grammar and usage, including subject-verb agreement, pronoun agreement, and appropriate verb tenses commensurate with grade-level expectations as more English is acquired. Internalize new basic and academic language by using and reusing it in meaningful ways in speaking and writing activities that build concept and language attainment.

Interactive
Review Week

☑ Choose skills and strategies to **review** based on progress-monitoring.

☑ Focus on **target skills** or use the **flexible plan** to adjust instruction.

☑ Provide opportunities for interacting with texts—underlining, highlighting, and circling **model text** in the *Reader's and Writer's Notebook*.

☑ Develop student's understanding of genre and text structure using the **Strategy Response Log** in the *Reader's and Writer's Notebook*.

Reader's & Writer's Notebook

This Unit's Interactive Writing Review

Daily Quick Writes for Fluency

	Talk	Write	Share
Day 1	Pairs discuss the information in the sports timelines in *The Man Who Invented Basketball* and "My Turn at Bat."	Students write short timelines about their own experience playing sports, using singular and plural pronouns.	Partners read each other's timelines, checking for the correct use of singular and plural pronouns.
Day 2	Have pairs discuss the amazing places described in *Hottest, Coldest, Highest, Deepest* and "Paul Bunyan and the Great Lakes."	Students write a few sentences describing one of these amazing places. Students should include subject and object pronouns in their sentences.	Partners read their sentences to each other, making sure that subject and object pronouns are used correctly.
Day 3	Pairs discuss the objects that are collected in *Rocks in His Head* and "Marvelous Marble Mania."	Students write a paragraph about what they and their friends collect, using possessive pronouns correctly.	Partners read each other's paragraphs, checking for the correct use of possessive pronouns.
Day 4	Pairs discuss what they've learned about the accomplishments of women athletes in the two selections this week.	Each student writes a few sentences summarizing the accomplishments of a particular woman athlete. Students should include contractions in their sentences.	Students read their sentences to their partners, and check for the correct use of contractions.
Day 5	Have pairs discuss the special features of the animals in *Fly, Eagle, Fly!* and "Purple Coyote."	Students write a few sentences describing one of these unusual animals, using prepositions correctly.	Partners read each other's sentences and check them for correct use of prepositions.

Resources for Interactive Writing Review

Reader's and Writer's Notebook

Writing Rubrics and Anchor Papers

Digital Resources
- Grammar Jammer
- Online Journal
Teacher Resource DVD-ROM

For 21st Century Writing practice, see the **Classroom Profile** Project in Unit 4, Volume 1.

For Process Writing practice, see the **Story** Lesson in Unit 4, Volume 2.

47026

Review on **Reading Street!**

 Big Question
What does it mean to be unique?

Daily Plan

Review	Day 1 How do talents make someone unique?	Day 2 What makes nature's record holders unique?	Day 3 Why is it valuable to have unique interests?	Day 4 What unique traits does it take to be the first to do something?	Day 5 What behaviors are unique to different animals?
• Concept Talk • Oral Vocabulary • Comprehension • Vocabulary • Fluency • Phonics • Conventions					

Customize Literacy
More support for a balanced literacy approach, see CL•1– CL•45.

Customize Writing
More support for a customized writing approach, see CW•11– CW•20.

Assessment
• Unit 4 Benchmark Test
• Assessment Handbook

You Are Here!
Unit 4
Week 6

Review this Unit's Reading Selections

Man Who Invented Basketball
Genre: **Biography**

Hottest, Coldest, Highest, Deepest
Genre: **Expository Text**

Rocks in His Head
Genre: **Biography**

Gertrude Ederle
Genre: **Biography**

Fly, Eagle, Fly!
Genre: **Folk Tale**

My Planning Guide

Resources on Reading Street!

	Build Concepts	Phonics	Comprehension
Day 1 **Review Week 1** ❓ How do talents make someone unique?	 Retelling Cards Routines Flip Chart	 Reader's and Writer's Notebook Sound-Spelling Cards	 Student Edition pp. 28–29
Day 2 **Review Week 2** ❓ What makes nature's record holders unique?	 Retelling Cards Routines Flip Chart	 Reader's and Writer's Notebook Sound-Spelling Cards	 Student Edition pp. 62–63
Day 3 **Review Week 3** ❓ Why is it valuable to have unique interests?	 Retelling Cards Routines Flip Chart	 Reader's and Writer's Notebook Sound-Spelling Cards	 Student Edition pp. 94–95
Day 4 **Review Week 4** ❓ What unique traits does it take to be the first to do something?	 Retelling Cards Routines Flip Chart	 Reader's and Writer's Notebook Sound-Spelling Cards	 Student Edition pp. 124–125
Day 5 **Review Week 5** ❓ What behaviors are unique to different animals?	 Retelling Cards Routines Flip Chart	 Reader's and Writer's Notebook Sound-Spelling Cards	 Student Edition pp. 158–159

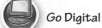 **Go Digital**
- Big Question Video
- Concept Talk Video
- Interactive Sound-Spelling Cards
- eSelection
- Envision It! Animations

Big Question
What does it mean to be unique?

Vocabulary	Fluency	Conventions and Writing
 Student Edition pp. 28–29	Reader's and Writer's Notebook	Reader's and Writer's Notebook
 Student Edition pp. 62–63	Reader's and Writer's Notebook	Reader's and Writer's Notebook
 Student Edition pp. 94–95	Reader's and Writer's Notebook	Reader's and Writer's Notebook
 Student Edition pp. 124–125	Reader's and Writer's Notebook	Reader's and Writer's Notebook
 Student Edition pp. 158–159	Reader's and Writer's Notebook	Reader's and Writer's Notebook

- eSelection
- Vocabulary Activities

- eSelection
- Let's Practice It! DVD
- eReaders

- Grammar Jammer
- Online Journal

Week 6

You Are Here! Unit 4 Week 6

My 5-Day Planner for Reading Street!

	Review Week 1	Review Week 2
	Day 1 pages IR8–IR17	**Day 2** pages IR18–IR27
Get Ready to Read	**Concept Talk**, IR8 How do talents make someone unique? **Oral Vocabulary**, IR9 *mock, idle, potential, ecstatic, thrill, audition, necessary, result, succeed, rise, verge*	**Concept Talk**, IR18 What makes nature's record holders unique? **Oral Vocabulary**, IR19 *evergreens, lumber, competitors, plunged, valuable, champ, sprinter, acrobat, weaken, ranger*
Read and Comprehend	**Comprehension**, IR10–IR15 ◉ Skill: Generalize ◉ Strategy: Summarize **Vocabulary Skill**, IR12–IR15 Unfamiliar Words **Fluency**, IR15 Read with Accuracy	**Comprehension**, IR20–IR25 ◉ Skill: Graphic Sources ◉ Strategy: Important Ideas **Vocabulary Skill**, IR22–IR25 Unknown Words **Fluency**, IR25 Read with Appropriate Phrasing
Language Arts	**Phonics and Spelling**, IR16 Irregular Plurals **Conventions**, IR17 Singular and Plural Pronouns **Quick Write for Fluency**, IR17 **Wrap Up Your Day**, IR17	**Phonics and Spelling**, IR26 *r*-Controlled Vowels **Conventions**, IR27 Subject and Object Pronouns **Quick Write for Fluency**, IR27 **Wrap Up Your Day**, IR27

You Are Here!
Unit 4
Week 6

Big Question
What does it mean to be unique?

Review Week 3	Review Week 4	Review Week 5
Day 3 pages IR28–IR37	**Day 4** pages IR38–IR47	**Day 5** pages IR48–IR57
Concept Talk, IR28 ❓ Why is it valuable to have unique interests? **Oral Vocabulary,** IR29 *hobby, project, leftover, murmur, ancestor, ornament, descendent, forge, compartment*	**Concept Talk,** IR38 ❓ What unique traits does it take to be the first to do something? **Oral Vocabulary,** IR39 *ordinary, imagination, assemble, magnificent, organize, erect, suspend, accompany*	**Concept Talk,** IR48 ❓ What behaviors are unique to different animals? **Oral Vocabulary,** IR49 *armor, agile, snout, protrude, extraordinary, scenery, pesky, unfurl, coil, intersection*
Comprehension, IR30–IR35 ◉ Skill: Fact and Opinion ◉ Strategy: Inferring **Vocabulary Skill,** IR32–IR35 Multiple-Meaning Words **Fluency,** IR35 Read with Expression	**Comprehension,** IR40–IR45 ◉ Skill: Fact and Opinion ◉ Strategy: Questioning **Vocabulary Skill,** IR42–IR45 Multiple-Meaning Words **Fluency,** IR45 Read with Appropriate Phrasing	**Comprehension,** IR50–IR55 ◉ Skill: Cause and Effect ◉ Strategy: Monitor and Clarify **Vocabulary Skill,** IR52–IR53 Unknown Words **Fluency,** IR55 Read with Appropriate Rate
Phonics and Spelling, IR36 Prefixes *pre-, mid-, over-, out-, bi-, de-* **Conventions,** IR37 Possessive Pronouns **Quick Write for Fluency,** IR37 **Wrap Up Your Day,** IR37	**Phonics and Spelling,** IR46 Suffixes *-er, -or, -ess, -ist* **Conventions,** IR47 Contractions **Quick Write for Fluency,** IR47 **Wrap Up Your Day,** IR47	**Phonics and Spelling,** IR56 Syllables VCCCV **Conventions,** IR57 Prepositions **Quick Write for Fluency,** IR57 **Wrap Up Your Day,** IR57

Week 6

Turn the page for grouping suggestions to differentiate instruction.

Differentiate Instruction on Reading Street!

	Review Week 1 **Day 1** pages IR8–IR17	Review Week 2 **Day 2** pages IR18–IR27
SI Strategic Intervention	**Reteach and Review** • Concept Talk • Oral Vocabulary • Writing on Demand • Irregular Plurals • Generalize • Unfamiliar Words • Read with Accuracy • Spelling • Singular and Plural Pronouns • Quick Write for Fluency	**Reteach and Review** • Concept Talk • Oral Vocabulary • Writing on Demand • r-Controlled Vowels • Graphic Sources • Unknown Words • Read with Appropriate Phrasing • Spelling • Subject and Object Pronouns • Quick Write for Fluency
OL On-Level	**Review** • Writing on Demand • Generalize • Unfamiliar Words • Read with Accuracy • Quick Write for Fluency	**Review** • Writing on Demand • Graphic Sources • Unknown Words • Read with Appropriate Phrasing • Quick Write for Fluency
A Advanced	**Extend** • Generalize • Unfamiliar Words • Quick Write for Fluency	**Extend** • Graphic Sources • Unknown Words • Quick Write for Fluency
ELL English Language Learners	**Reteach and Review** • Concept Talk • Oral Vocabulary • ELL Poster • Irregular Plurals • Generalize • Unfamiliar Words • Read with Accuracy • Spelling • Singular and Plural Pronouns • Quick Write for Fluency	**Reteach and Review** • Concept Talk • Oral Vocabulary • ELL Poster • r-Controlled Vowels • Graphic Sources • Unknown Words • Read with Appropriate Phrasing • Spelling • Subject and Object Pronouns • Quick Write for Fluency

You Are Here!
Unit 4
Week 6

Reading Street
Intervention Kit

Big Question
What does it mean to be unique?

Review Week 3	Review Week 4	Review Week 5
Day 3 pages IR28–IR37	**Day 4** pages IR38–IR47	**Day 5** pages IR48–IR57

Reteach and Review
- Concept Talk
- Oral Vocabulary
- Writing on Demand
- Prefixes *pre-, mid-, over-, out-, bi-, de-*
- Fact and Opinion
- Multiple-Meaning Words
- Read with Expression
- Spelling
- Possessive Pronouns
- Quick Write for Fluency

Reteach and Review
- Concept Talk
- Oral Vocabulary
- Writing on Demand
- Suffixes *-er, -or, -ess, -ist*
- Fact and Opinion
- Multiple-Meaning Words
- Read with Appropriate Phrasing
- Spelling
- Contractions
- Quick Write for Fluency

Reteach and Review
- Concept Talk
- Oral Vocabulary
- Writing on Demand
- Syllables VCCCV
- Cause and Effect
- Unknown Words
- Read with Appropriate Rate
- Spelling
- Prepositions
- Quick Write for Fluency

Review
- Writing on Demand
- Fact and Opinion
- Multiple-Meaning Words
- Read with Expression
- Quick Write for Fluency

Review
- Writing on Demand
- Fact and Opinion
- Multiple-Meaning Words
- Read with Appropriate Phrasing
- Quick Write for Fluency

Review
- Writing on Demand
- Cause and Effect
- Unknown Words
- Read with Appropriate Rate
- Quick Write for Fluency

Extend
- Fact and Opinion
- Multiple-Meaning Words
- Quick Write for Fluency

Extend
- Fact and Opinion
- Multiple-Meaning Words
- Quick Write for Fluency

Extend
- Cause and Effect
- Unknown Words
- Quick Write for Fluency

Reteach and Review
- Concept Talk
- Oral Vocabulary
- ELL Poster
- Prefixes *pre-, mid-, over-, out-, bi-, de-*
- Fact and Opinion
- Multiple-Meaning Words
- Read with Expression
- Spelling
- Possessive Pronouns
- Quick Write for Fluency

Reteach and Review
- Concept Talk
- Oral Vocabulary
- ELL Poster
- Suffixes *-er, -or, -ess, -ist*
- Fact and Opinion
- Multiple-Meaning Words
- Read with Appropriate Phrasing
- Spelling
- Contractions
- Quick Write for Fluency

Reteach and Review
- Concept Talk
- Oral Vocabulary
- ELL Poster
- Syllables VCCCV
- Cause and Effect
- Unknown Words
- Read with Appropriate Rate
- Spelling
- Prepositions
- Quick Write for Fluency

week 6

Objectives
- Review the weekly concept.
- Connect the weekly selection to the Big Question.

Today at a Glance

Oral Vocabulary
mock, idle, potential, ecstatic, thrill, audition, necessary, result, succeed, rise, verge

◉ Comprehension
Generalize

◉ Vocabulary
Unfamiliar words

Fluency
Accuracy

Word Analysis
Irregular plurals

Spelling
Irregular plurals

Conventions
Singular and plural pronouns

Writing
Quick write for fluency

Concept Talk

 Question of the Week
How do talents make someone unique?

Revisit the concept

Today students will explore how the Unit 4 Big Question connects to *The Man Who Invented Basketball*. Remind students of the Question of the Week for *The Man Who Invented Basketball*.

ROUTINE   Activate Prior Knowledge   Team Talk

1. **Think** Have students think about how talents make a person unique.

2. **Pair** Have pairs of students discuss how the Question of the Week relates to the life and accomplishments of James Naismith.

3. **Share** Call on a few students to share their idea with the group. Guide the discussion and encourage elaboration with prompts such as:

   • What were some of James Naismith's talents?

   • What were some things James accomplished by using his talents?

Routines Flip Chart

Anchored Talk

Connect to the Big Question

Remind students of the Unit 4 Big Question, *What does it mean to be unique?* Use the prompts below to discuss what it means to be unique, and how our talents can make us unique. Remind students to listen attentively to other students and to make pertinent comments and answer questions with appropriate detail. Encourage students to build on the ideas of others when they answer.

• What kinds of results can a person get by using his or her unique talents?

• How is every person unique?

• In what way could a talent make someone unique?

Oral Vocabulary
Amazing Words

Review Amazing Words

Display the Amazing Words. Remind students that the words are related to the week's concept, how talents make someone unique.

Amazing Words — Oral Vocabulary Routine

1 Review Ask students for definitions of the words, starting at the top of the list. Listen for accurate definitions Prompt students to connect the words to the unit concept of One of a Kind whenever possible.

2 Demonstrate Have students use two or more Amazing Words in the same sentence. Guide the discussion by providing an example that shows the meaning of each word. *An audition is a way to show your talent and potential.* Follow this pattern to the end of the list, covering as many of the eleven words as possible.

3 Apply Assign the words in random order and have students come up with new sentences for them. *To show you are becoming more comfortable using these Amazing Words, think up more new sentences for them.*

Routines Flip Chart

Apply Amazing Words

Have students use the Retelling Cards for *The Man Who Invented Basketball* to talk about the Amazing Words.

Connect to reading

Tell students that today they will be reading about a famous horseback rider and rereading passages from *The Man Who Invented Basketball.* As they read, ask students to think about the characters' talents.

[Insert Retelling Card, ISBN 47684]

Retelling Card

ELL Build Background Use ELL Poster 16 to review the week 1 lesson concept and to practice oral language. Point out and read the question: How do talents make someone unique?

Amazing Words

mock	audition
idle	necessary
potential	result
ecstatic	succeed
thrill	rise
	verge

Writing on Demand

Writing Fluency

Ask students to write as well as they can and as much as they can about what makes someone one of a kind.

 Poster 16

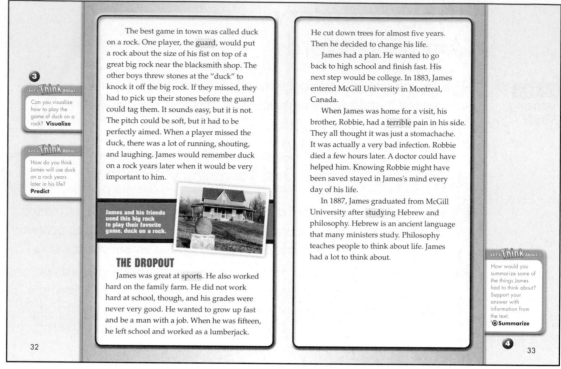

Student Edition pp. 32–33

Guide Comprehension
Skills and Strategies

Review
Generalize

Generalize Use the information on p. 24 to review how to make a generalization. Remind students that a general statement tells how some things are all alike or mostly alike. Discuss how you can use several examples to come up with a generalization.

Guide practice

Read aloud the first paragraph on p. 32. Have students identify a generalization in this paragraph. Possible response: The best game in town was called duck on a rock. What is a generalization you can make from the details in this paragraph about how people felt when playing duck on a rock? Possible response: People always ran around, shouted, and had a good time playing duck on a rock.

On their own

Have pairs of students reread pp. 32–35 and use the information on these pages to make a generalization about James's attitude toward hard work and when it was necessary to work hard.

Extend Thinking
Think Critically

Higher-order thinking skills

 Generalize • Synthesis Look back and use information from page 39 to make a generalization about James Naismith. Possible response: James Naismith wanted to help people by doing his different jobs as teacher, minister, and sports doctor, rather than making money from being famous.

Text to Self • Synthesis James's memory of the game he played as a child gave him ideas later for how to invent basketball. If someone asked you to invent a game, from where would you get your ideas? Possible response: I would think about games I play with my brother and sister and fun things my friends and I do during gym class.

Text to World • Evaluate James Naismith invented basketball because people needed a fun game that could be played indoors. Can you think of another example of something that was invented to meet a need? Possible response: Thomas Edison invented the light bulb so people could see more easily in the dark.

Differentiated Instruction

 Strategic Intervention

For students having difficulty creating accurate general statements, have them choose between an accurate and an inaccurate general statement. Discuss why students chose one over the other. For example, "James Naismith never loved sports" versus "James Naismith always loved sports."

A **Advanced**

Discuss with students how some general statements can be too extreme and are therefore inaccurate. Direct students to generate one accurate and one inaccurate general statement. For example, "James never got good grades" and "James always hated school."

 Multidraft Reading

To assist struggling readers and to deepen reading for all, apply multidraft reading protocols. For each reading, have students set the purpose indicated.

- **First reading**—Literal comprehension: discuss Guide Comprehension questions to monitor and clarify understanding.

- **Second reading**—Application of skills: answer higher-order thinking skills questions to develop deeper understanding of text and make connections to the real world.

Objectives

- Review unfamiliar words and context clues.

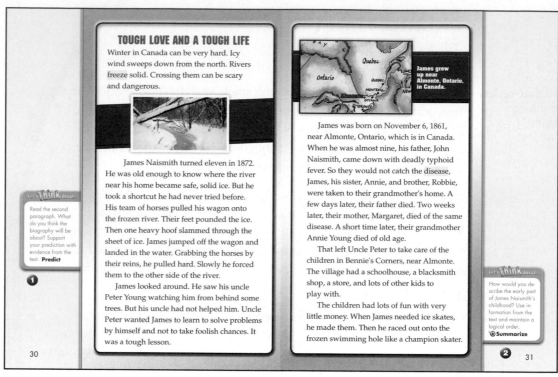

Student Edition pp. 30–31

Guide Comprehension
Skills and Strategies

Review Unfamiliar Words

Unfamiliar Words Have students use context to determine the relevant meaning of unfamiliar words. Review the instruction on unfamiliar words on p. 26. Remind students that they will often come across unfamiliar words as they are reading. Tell them they should look at context clues, or the words and sentences around the unfamiliar word to see if the author has included any clues as to the new word's meaning.

Guide practice

Point out the word *reins* on page 30. Have students identify clues that might help them understand this word. Point out that the text shows that reins are connected to horses. James pulls on them, and with the reins James controls the horses. Then work with students to help determine the meaning of the word.

On their own

Use the *Let's Practice It! DVD* for additional practice with unfamiliar words.

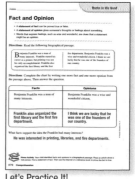

Let's Practice It!
TR DVD•270

Extend Thinking
Think Critically

Higher-order thinking skills

 Unfamiliar words • Evaluate Write the following sentences on the board: "James felt *jittery* crossing the ice. He was nervous that it would crack." Then have students guess the meaning of the word *jittery.* Have them explain what context clue helped them figure out the word's meaning. Possible response: "worried"; the word nervous in the next sentence

 Generalize • Analysis Have students identify a generalization in the first paragraph of p. 30. Possible response: *Winters in Canada can be very hard.*

Text to Self • Synthesis Have you ever done something dangerous like James and learned a lesson yourself? Possible response: Yes, my mom told me to be keep my bike on the sidewalk. I didn't listen and almost got hit by a car!

Text to World • Synthesis James drives a team of horses in the snow when he is eleven and makes his own ice skates to go skate on the frozen pond. Think about children today and the things they do in cold weather. Are their experiences similar to James's experience or different? Possible response: Children today do not drive teams of horses around. They travel with their parents in cars. They also buy their skates at the store instead of making them and usually skate in indoor skating rinks instead of on ponds.

Differentiated Instruction

SI Strategic Intervention

Write the following sentence on the board: *One heavy hoof* slammed *through the sheet of ice.* Then create a 3-column chart on the board. Write the underlined word in the left column. As a class, discuss context clues. Write these in the middle column. Move on to students' ideas about the meaning of the word. Write these in the right-hand column. Then test whether the different ideas make sense in the sentence.

A Advanced

Have students use unfamiliar words that the class has defined to write their own sentences. Tell students to include context clues that hint at their meaning.

Objectives

• Review generalizing.
• Review summarizing.
• Review using context clues to figure out the meaning of unfamiliar words.
• Read aloud fluently with accuracy.

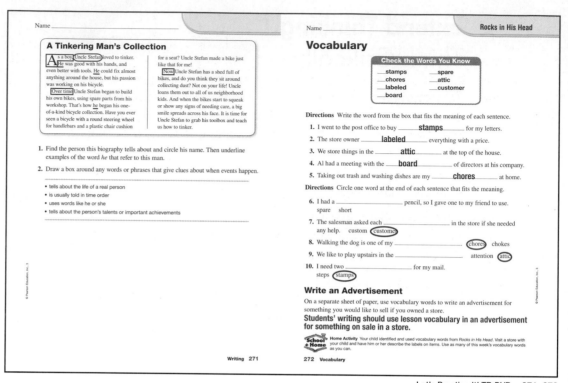

Let's Practice It! TR DVD • 271–272

Guide Comprehension
Skills and Strategies

Review generalizing

What details from the story support this generalization: Margie Goldstein is one of the very best riders. Possible response: She has been Rider of the Year, an all-time money winner, and an Olympic champion.

Remind students of generalizing clue words such as *all, always, never, most, many, some, sometimes,* and *usually.* Have students look for some of these clue words in the story.

Review summarizing

Have students summarize information in the text while maintaining meaning and logical order. How would you summarize this story in two or three sentences? Possible response: Margie Goldstein had a way with animals. She loved horses. She became a very good rider.

Review unfamiliar words

Use context to determine the relevant meaning of unfamiliar words. In the seventh paragraph, the author uses the word *obstacles*. What context clues could you use to help you figure out what this word means? Possible response: The sentence says that horses jump over water, fences, rock walls, and other *obstacles*. Fences and rock walls and water are all things in the horse's way, so I think that *obstacles* means "things that are in the way."

If students are familiar with the word *obstacles,* find a different word and work with students to use context to understand what the word means. Such words might include *stables, arenas,* and *disaster.*

Review generalizing

Make a generalization about these details: A horse can jump over stone walls, hedges, fences, and many other obstacles. Possible response: Horses can jump over many different obstacles.

Reread for Fluency

Model fluent reading

Help students read aloud grade-level appropriate text fluently, with accuracy and comprehension. Remind students that when they read, it is important to read with accuracy in order to understand what they are reading. Model reading the first paragraph of "Margie Goldstein, Rider of the Year" on p. 171 aloud with accuracy. Have students track the print as you read.

Pair students and have them read "Margie Goldstein, Rider of the Year."

ROUTINE Paired Reading

1. **Reader 1 Begins** Students read the entire story, switching readers at the end of each paragraph.
2. **Reader 2 Begins** Partners reread the story. This time the other student begins.
3. **Reread** For optimal fluency, have partners continue to read three or four times.
4. **Provide Feedback** Listen to students read and provide corrective feedback regarding their accuracy.

Routines Flip Chart

Objectives

- Read irregular plurals.
- Spell irregular plurals correctly.
- Review singular and plural pronouns.
- Write a sports time line.

Word Analysis— Review
Irregular Plurals

Review — Review irregular plurals using Sound-Spelling Card 140.

Read words independent of context — Use the *Let's Practice It! DVD.* Point out that students know how to read these words. Then tell students they will all read the words in each row together. Allow several seconds previewing time for the first reading.

If... students cannot read all the words in a row consecutively without an error,
then... return to the first word in the row, and have students reread all the words in the row. Repeat until students can read the words fluently.

Read words in context — Use the passage on the *Let's Practice It! DVD.* Point out that there are many words in the passage that students already know how to read. Have students read the passage together.

If... students have difficulty reading irregular plurals,
then... guide them in using the word parts strategy. Have students read each sentence. Repeat until students can read the sentences fluently.

Let's Practice It!
TR DVD•269

Spelling
Irregular Plurals

Review irregular plurals — Write *halves, wolves,* and *mice.* Point out that these words are plurals. Remind students that they have learned how to spell irregular plurals.

Spelling strategy — Review irregular plurals by having students follow the spelling strategy for these words.

> **Step 1: Mark the letters that give you a problem.**
>
> **Step 2: Find words you know with the same letters.**
>
> **Step 3: Use your problem words and the word you know in a sentence.**

On their own — Use p. 302 in the *Reader's and Writer's Notebook* for additional practice with irregular plurals.

Reader's and Writer's
Notebook p. 302

Conventions
Singular and Plural Pronouns

Reader's and Writer's
Notebook p. 303

Review
Singular and plural pronouns

- **Pronouns** take the place of nouns.
- Pronouns that take the place of singular nouns are **singular pronouns,** such as *I, me, he, she, him, her,* and *it.*
- Pronouns that take the place of plural nouns are **plural pronouns,** such as *we, us, they,* and *them.*

Guide practice

Read the following sentences. Have students identify the pronouns.

1. Thanks for reading **us** a funny story.
2. **It** made the class laugh out loud.

On their own

For additional practice, use the *Reader's and Writer's Notebook* p. 303.

ROUTINE **Quick Write for Fluency** **Team Talk**

1. **Talk** Pairs discuss the information in the sports time lines in *The Man Who Invented Basketball* and "My Turn at Bat."

2. **Write** Students write short time lines about their own experience playing sports, using singular and plural pronouns.

3. **Share** Partners read each other's time lines, checking for the correct use of singular and plural pronouns.

Routines Flip Chart

Wrap Up Your Day

Preview DAY 2

Tell students that tomorrow they will review *Hottest, Coldest, Highest, Deepest.*

✔ **Build Concepts** How did James Naismith's talents make him unique?

✔ **Generalize** What makes a sport enjoyable to play?

✔ **Unfamiliar Words** How can you determine what an unfamiliar word means?

✔ **Homework** Send home this week's Family Times newsletter in the *Let's Practice It!* DVD.

Objectives
- Review the weekly concept.
- Connect the weekly selection to the Big Question.

Today at a Glance

Oral Vocabulary
evergreen, lumber, competitor, plunge, valuable, champ, sprinter, acrobat, weaken, ranger

Phonics
Vowels *r*-controlled

Comprehension
⊙ Graphic sources

Vocabulary
⊙ Unknown words

Fluency
Appropriate phrasing with punctuation cues

Spelling
Vowels: *r*-controlled

Conventions
Subject and object pronouns

Writing
Quick write for fluency

Concept Talk

 Question of the Week

What makes nature's record holders unique?

Revisit the concept

Today students will explore how the Unit 4 Big Question connects to *Hottest, Coldest, Highest, Deepest*. Remind students of the Question of the Week for *Hottest, Coldest, Highest, Deepest*.

ROUTINE **Activate Prior Knowledge** **Team Talk**

 Think Have students think about the qualities that make nature's record holders unique.

 Pair Have pairs of students discuss how the Question of the Week applies to the places in nature in *Hottest, Coldest, Highest, Deepest*.

 Share Call on a few students to share their ideas with the group. Guide the discussion and encourage elaboration with prompts such as:

- What are some ways we can decide if something in nature is unique?
- What might be unique about a very large lake?

Routines Flip Chart

Anchored Talk

Connect to the Big Question

Remind students of the Unit 4 Big Question, *What does it mean to be unique?* Use the prompts below to discuss how thinking about things that are One of a Kind can help us understand what it means to be unique. Remind students to ask and answer questions with appropriate detail, building on the ideas of others.

- How can you tell if something in nature is unique?
- Is one way of being unique the best way? Why or why not?
- How can an evergreen tree be unique?

Oral Vocabulary
Amazing Words

Review Amazing Words

Display the Amazing Words. Remind students that the words are related to the week's concept, nature's record holders.

Amazing Words

evergreen	champ
lumber	sprinter
competitor	acrobat
plunge	weaken
valuable	ranger

Amazing Words Oral Vocabulary Routine

1 Review Ask students for definitions of the words, starting at the top of the list. Listen for accurate definitions. Prompt students to connect the words to the unit concept of One of a Kind whenever possible.

2 Demonstrate Have students use two or more Amazing Words in the same sentence. Guide the discussion by providing an example that shows the meaning of each word. *The ranger who guided our park tour gave us valuable tips for staying on the marked trails.* Follow this pattern to the end of the list, covering as many of the ten words as possible.

3 Apply Assign the words in random order and have students come up with more sentences for them. *To show that you are becoming more comfortable using these Amazing Words, think up more new sentences for them.*

Routines Flip Chart

Writing on Demand

Writing Fluency
Ask students to write as well as they can and as much as they can about what makes nature's record holders unique.

Apply Amazing Words

Have students use the Retelling Cards for *Hottest, Coldest, Highest, Deepest* to talk about the Amazing Words.

Connect to reading

Tell students that today they will be reading about banning the penny and rereading passages from *Hottest, Coldest, Highest, Deepest.* As they read, ask students to think about things that are unique.

Retelling Card

ELL Build Background Use ELL Poster 17 to review the week 2 lesson concept and to practice oral language. Point out and read that question: *What makes nature's record holders unique?*

ELL Poster 17

Objectives
- Review graphic sources.
- Make text connections.

The world's **highest** waterfall is Angel Falls, in Venezuela. It is 3,212 feet high.

Angel Falls is more than seventeen times higher than Niagara Falls (180 feet), in New York State. Victoria Falls, in Zimbabwe, Africa, carries more water than any other waterfall. It is 355 feet high.

Angel Falls 3,212 ft.

Victoria Falls 355 ft.

Empire State Building 1,250 ft.

Niagara Falls 180 ft.

The **deepest** spot in the ocean is the Marianas Trench, in the Philippines. It is 36,202 feet deep.

The average depth of the world's oceans is about 3 miles, or 16,000 feet. The lowest spot on dry land is the shore of the Dead Sea, 1,100 feet below sea level.

The world's **most active** volcano is Sangay, in Ecuador. Since 1937 it has erupted once every 24 hours on average. It once erupted more than 400 times in a single day.

Other very active volcanoes include Colima, in Mexico (it has erupted regularly since 1560); Aso, in Japan (erupting since 533); and Mount Etna, in Italy (erupting regularly since 1500 B.C.).

Student Edition pp. 72–73

Guide Comprehension
Skills and Strategies

Review Graphic Sources

🔎 **Graphic Sources** Review the definition of graphic sources on p. 58. Remind students that graphic sources are ways of showing information visually. Explain that maps and charts are two kinds of graphic sources. Remind students that looking at graphic sources before they read can help them predict what the text will be about.

Guide practice

Point to the graph on p. 72. Have students tell what information the chart displays visually. Asks whether Victoria Falls is taller or shorter than the Empire State Building.

On their own

Have students use the information in the chart to make a list of the heights of Angel Falls, Victoria Falls, Niagara Falls, and the Empire State Building in order from lowest to highest.

Extend Thinking
Think Critically

Higher-order thinking skills

 Graphic Sources • Synthesis Look at the chart on page 72. Where on the chart would you expect to see a waterfall that is 1,000 feet high? between Angel Falls and Victoria Falls

Text to Self • Analysis In Sangay, the volcano erupts almost everyday. Have you ever been around something that was always noisy? How did it make you feel? Possible response: The people next door were fixing their house. There was a lot of noise every day. It was awful!

Text to World • Evaluation How do you think knowing about nature's record holders helps scientists? Possible response: Scientists can use information about extreme places to learn about other places that are similar, but not as extreme.

 SI Strategic Intervention

Graphic sources Scaffold students' discussion of the chart on p. 72 by providing a simple chart with a picture of a six-inch pencil, a ruler, and a yardstick, each labeled with its height. Ask students to tell which item is tallest and to explain how they used the chart to answer the question.

A Advanced

Have students create another book page about the most extreme temperature change in the United States in one day, which occurred in Browning, Montana, between January 23 and 24, 1916. During a 24-hour period, the temperature went from 44° F to –56° F. Encourage students to include an illustration, a map, and a chart.

 Multidraft Reading

To assist struggling readers and to deepen reading for all, apply multidraft reading protocols. For each reading, have students set the purpose indicated.

- **First reading**—Literal comprehension: discuss Guide Comprehension questions to monitor and clarify understanding.

- **Second reading**—Application of skills: answer higher-order thinking skills questions to develop deeper understanding of text and make connections to the real world.

Objectives
• Use a dictionary or glossary to understand unknown words.
• Make text connections.

The **most extreme tides** occur in the Bay of Fundy, in Nova Scotia, Canada. There the water level rises and falls more than 50 feet every 6 hours.

The tide here comes in so fast that it can overtake a person trying to outrun it.

100 ft.
Mt. Rainier record
1-year snowfall

The **snowiest** place on Earth is Mount Rainier, in Washington State. One year, more than 1,200 inches of snow fell there.

Mount Rainier is covered in snow the whole year. Some of the snow has formed glaciers, masses of ice that slowly move down the mountain under their own weight.

6 ft.
Adult man

3 ft.
Typical annual
New York City
snowfall

74

75

Student Edition pp. 74–75

Guide Comprehension
Skills and Strategies

Review
Unknown
Words

☉ **Unknown Words** Review the strategy for finding the meaning of unknown words on p. 60. Remind students that if they come across an unknown word when they read, they can use a dictionary or glossary to determine the meaning, syllabication, and pronunciation of the word.

Guide
practice

Point to the word *tide* on p. 74 and have students use a dictionary or glossary to find its pronunciation, syllabication, and meaning. Ask students how to pronounce the word. (/tīd/) Then ask how they could tell how many syllables it has. (Look at the pronunciation markings. There are no spaces between letters, so it is one syllable.) Then ask what the meaning is. ("the rise and fall of the ocean every twelve hours")

On their
own

Use the *Let's Practice It! DVD* for additional practice with unknown words.

Let's Practice It!
TR DVD•274

Extend Thinking
Think Critically

Higher-order thinking skills

 Unknown Words • Analysis Some of the words you read have endings that are not shown in the dictionary. How can you figure out which part of the word to use? What word would you look up to find the meaning of *snowiest* on page 75? Possible response: I can look for the base word first and then see if I need to include an ending. For *snowiest*, the base word is *snow*, but I can tell it is describing something so I want the word as an adjective; I will look up *snowy*.

 Graphic Sources • Synthesis How does seeing the typical annual New York City snowfall in the chart on page 75 help us understand the record snowfall in one year in Mount Rainier? Possible response: The amount of annual snowfall in New York City is very small compared to the amount of snow that fell in one year in Mount Rainier. Comparing the two snowfalls helps us understand how much snow fell in Mount Rainier in a year.

Text to World • Analysis We read on page 74 that the Bay of Fundy has the most extreme tides. What might happen to boats in the bay at low tide? Possible response: The boats in the bay might be on dry ground or stuck in very shallow water.

Text to Self • Evaluate Would you rather see the extreme tides in the Bay of Fundy or Mount Rainier, the snowiest place on Earth? Explain your response. Possible response: I would rather see the tides in the Bay of Fundy, because they are very unusual. Mount Rainier is probably very cold.

Differentiated Instruction

SI Strategic Intervention

Unknown words Review clues that help students understand which part of speech to look up when defining an unknown word: a noun names a person, place, or thing; a verb shows action; an adjective tells more about a noun; an adverb tells more about a verb.

A Advanced

Unknown words Give students nine cards. Have them each choose (or assign) three words for the selection. Have them write each word on one card, its definition on another, and the pronunciation and syllabication on another. Have students mix up the cards and give them to a partner to sort. Then have students use the words in sentences that show understanding of meaning.

Objectives
• Review graphic sources.
• Review important ideas.
• Review unknown words.
• Read aloud fluently using appropriate phrasing.

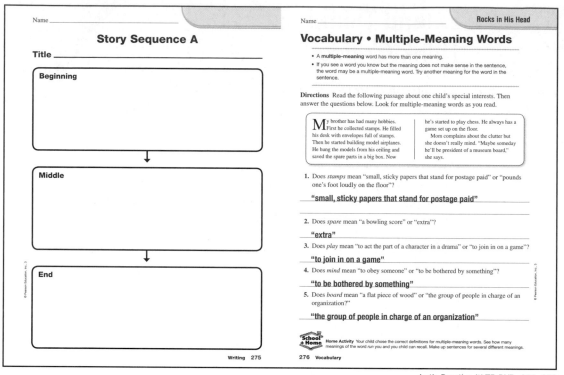

Let's Practice It! TR DVD•275–276

Guide Comprehension
Skills and Strategies

Review Graphic sources

What does the chart show? Possible response: It shows the cost of making some different kinds of coins.

Tell students that the chart uses columns and rows to display information visually. Point to the title "The Cost of Making Coins" and the column heads, *Coin* and *Cost,* and explain that students can use this information to understand what the chart shows.

Review Important ideas

What is an important idea in the text? How can you tell? Possible response: An important idea is that some people think pennies should be banned because it costs more than one cent to make a penny. I can tell because almost every paragraph talks about pennies. I also see that the title says "Ban the Penny?" and the chart shows the cost of making coins, emphasizing how much it costs to make a penny.

Review Unknown words

Use a dictionary to find the meaning, syllabication, and pronunciation of *mixture* in paragraph 4 on page 275. Which meaning is correct in this sentence? How do you know? **The correct meaning is "something that has been mixed." I know because it makes sense in the sentence.** How do you pronounce the word? **/miks//chèr/, with an accent on the first syllable**

Review Graphic sources

Look at the chart. Which coins cost more to make than they are worth? **the penny and the nickel**

Ask students to explain the order in which the coins are listed in the left column. (They are listed from the coin with the lowest monetary value, the penny, to the coin with the highest value, the Sacajawea dollar.)

Reread for Fluency

Model fluent reading

Read the first two paragraphs of "Ban the Penny?" aloud, using punctuation marks to aid in appropriate phrasing. Remind students that phrasing, or grouping words together, helps listeners understand the meaning of spoken words.

ROUTINE **Oral Rereading**

1. **Read** Have students read the first paragraph of "Ban the Penny?" orally.

2. **Reread** To achieve optimal fluency, students should reread the text three or four times.

3. **Corrective Feedback** Listen as students read. Provide corrective feedback about their phrasing, paying special attention to grouping words by pausing at punctuation marks.

Routines Flip Chart

Objectives

- Decode words with *r*-controlled vowels.
- Spell words with *r*-controlled vowels correctly.
- Review subject and object pronouns.
- Write about amazing places.

Phonics — Review

r-Controlled Vowels

Review

Review the *r*-controlled vowel sound /ėr/ spelled *ir, er, ur, ear, or;* /är/ spelled *ar;* and /ôr/ spelled *or, ore, oar,* using Sound-Spelling Cards 62, 67, 72, 87, 91, 92, 93, and 104.

Read words independent of context

Use the *Let's Practice It! DVD.* Point out that students know how to blend these words. Then tell students they will all read the words in each row together. Allow several seconds previewing time for the first reading.

If... students cannot blend all the words in a row consecutively without an error,
then... return to the first word in the row, and have students reread all the words in the row. Repeat until students can read the words fluently.

Read words in context

Use the passage on the *Let's Practice It! DVD.* Point out that there are many words in the passage that students already know how to read. Have students read the passage together.

If... students have difficulty reading the *r*-controlled vowel sounds /ėr/, /är/, or /ôr/,
then... guide them in using sound-by-sound blending. Have students read each sentence. Repeat until students can read the sentences fluently.

Let's Practice It!
TR DVD•273

Spelling
r-Controlled Vowels

**Review
r-Controlled vowels**

Write *thirsty, certain, earn,* and *worm.* Point out the /ėr/ sound. Write *start.* Point out that it has the /är/ sound. Write *horn, sore,* and *board.* Point out the /ôr/ sound. Remind students that they have learned how to spell words with these sounds.

Spelling strategy

Tell students that even short words can be hard to spell until you discover where they come from. Example: *heard*

The spelling of *heard* makes sense when you remember that *heard* is the past tense of *hear. Hear* is a meaning helper for *heard.*

On their own

Use p. 304 in the *Reader's and Writer's Notebook* for additional practice with *r*-controlled vowels.

Reader's and Writer's
Notebook p. 304

Conventions
Subject and Object Pronouns

Review
Subject and object pronouns

- A pronoun used as the subject of a sentence is called a **subject pronoun.** (*I, you, he, she, it, we, they*)

- A pronoun used after a verb or as the object of a preposition is called an **object pronoun.** (*me, you, him, her, it, us, them*)

Guide practice

Read the sentences. Have students identify each pronoun and say whether it is a subject pronoun or an object pronoun.

> **1. I** have visited the Sacramento River. [subject]
>
> **2.** Mary talked to **us** about her birthday. [object]

On their own   For additional practice, use the *Reader's and Writer's Notebook* p. 305.

Reader's and Writer's Notebook p. 305

ROUTINE **Quick Write for Fluency** **Team Talk**

1. **Talk** Have pairs discuss the amazing places described in *Hottest, Coldest, Highest, Deepest* and "Paul Bunyan and the Great Lakes."

2. **Write** Students write a few sentences describing one of these amazing places. Students should include subject and object pronouns in their sentences.

3. **Share** Partners read their sentences to each other, making sure that subject and object pronouns are used correctly.

Routines Flip Chart

Wrap Up Your Day

✔ **Build Concepts** What makes Mount Everest unique?

✔ **Graphic Sources** What can you learn about rivers from the graphics in *Hottest, Coldest, Highest, Deepest?*

✔ **Unknown Words** Where can you find the meanings of words you don't know?

Preview DAY 3

Tell students that tomorrow they will review *Rocks in His Head.*

Objectives
- Review the weekly concept.
- Connect the weekly selection to the Big Question.

Today at a Glance

Oral Vocabulary
hobby, murmur, project, leftover, ancestor, ornament, descendant, compartment, forge

Vocabulary
◉ Multiple-meaning words

Comprehension
◉ Fact and opinion

Fluency
Expression

Phonics/Word Analysis
Prefixes *(pre-, mid-, over-, out-, bi-, de-)*

Spelling
Prefixes *pre-, mid-, over-, out-, bi-, de-*

Conventions
Possessive pronouns

Writing
Quick write for fluency

Concept Talk

 Question of the Week
Why is it valuable to have unique interests?

Revisit the concept

Today students will explore how the Unit 4 Big Question connects to *Rocks in His Head.* Remind students of the Question of the Week for *Rocks in His Head.*

> **ROUTINE** **Activate Prior Knowledge** **Team Talk**
>
> **Think** Have students think about why it is valuable to have unique interests.
>
> **Pair** Have pairs of students discuss how the Question of the Week applies to the main character in *Rocks in His Head.*
>
> **Share** Call on a few students to share their ideas with the group. Guide the discussion and encourage elaboration with prompts such as:
>
> • What was unique about the father's interest in rocks?
>
> • How did his interest become valuable to him?

Routines Flip Chart

Anchored Talk

Connect to the Big Question

Remind students of the Unit 4 Big Question, *What does it mean to be unique?* Use the prompts below to discuss how being unique can be valuable. Encourage students to ask and answer questions with appropriate detail.

• Who are some people you think are unique? What is unique about them?

• What can having a unique hobby add to a person's life?

• What might a person with unique interests have to offer to others?

Go Digital! | Big Question Video | Concept Talk Video

Whole Group

Oral Vocabulary
Amazing Words

Review Amazing Words

Display the Amazing Words. Remind students that the words are related to the week's concept, having one of a kind interests.

Amazing Words

hobby	ornament
murmur	descendant
project	compartment
leftover	forge
ancestor	

Writing on Demand

Writing Fluency

Ask students to write as well as they can and as much as they can about the importance of unique interests.

Amazing Words — Oral Vocabulary Routine

1. **Review** Ask students for definitions of the words, starting at the top of the list. Listen for accurate definitions. Prompt students to connect the words to the unit concept of One of a Kind whenever possible.

2. **Demonstrate** Have students use two or more Amazing Words in the same sentence. Guide the discussion by providing an example that shows the meaning of each word. People sometimes decorate using *ornaments* that they create from *leftover* scraps of material. Follow this pattern to the end of the list, covering as many of the nine words as possible.

3. **Apply** Assign the words in random order and have students come up with more new sentences for them. To show that you are becoming more comfortable using these Amazing Words, think up more new sentences for them.

Routines Flip Chart

Apply Amazing Words

Have students use the Retelling Cards for *Rocks in His Head* to talk about the Amazing Words.

Retelling Card

Connect to reading

Tell students that today they will be reading about the first woman in space and rereading passages from *Rocks in His Head.* As they read, ask students to think about how unique interests are valuable.

ELL Build background Use ELL Poster 18 to review the week 3 lesson concept and to practice oral language. Point out and read a question: *Why is it valuable to have unique interests?*

ELL Poster 18

Objectives
• Review fact and opinion..
• Make text connections.

He had to build more shelves for the rocks, up the west wall of the station.

Then people stopped coming for gas. They stopped coming to play chess, and they even stopped coming to look at the rocks and minerals. They were all too busy looking for work.

One day my father picked up the chess set and carefully packed it in a big box. He took down each mineral, wrapped it in newspaper, and carefully placed it in a wooden box.

When his friends came with a truck to help us move, they said, "Watch out for those wooden boxes. He's got rocks in his boxes, now."

"Yessir," said my father. "That's just what I got in there. Take a look at this one."

The house we moved to was old and falling apart. My father said he'd have it fixed up in no time.

But before he started in on the repairs, we had to take those rocks up to the attic, where he'd already built tiny little wooden shelves.

My father did fix up the old house, and after he finished each repair, he went up to the attic with his rocks. He spent a lot of time reading about rocks, too.

"If you think those rocks are ever going to do you any good," said my mother, "you've got rocks in your head."

"Maybe I have," said my father. "Maybe I have." He reached into his pocket. "Take a look at this one."

My father spent a lot of time looking for any job he could find. Most jobs lasted only a day or two.

On rainy days when my father could find no other work, he'd take the bus to the science museum. They had a whole room full of glass cases containing many rocks. Sometimes he'd spend the whole day in that room.

100

101

Student Edition pp. 100–101

Guide Comprehension
Skills and Strategies

Review Fact and opinion	**Fact and Opinion** Review the definitions of fact and opinion on p. 90. Remind students that a statement of fact can be proved true or false. An opinion gives someone's thoughts or feelings. Tell students that they can draw conclusions about facts by looking for clues in the text.
Guide practice	Point out that in the last paragraph on p. 101 the narrator says that the science museum had "a whole room full of glass cases containing many rocks." Ask students what conclusion they can draw from this fact. Have them support their answer with textual evidence.
On their own	Have students look back at *Rocks in His Head* on pp. 102–103 and find one fact abot which they can draw a conclusion.

Extend Thinking
Think Critically

Higher-order thinking skills

 Fact and Opinion • Analysis Reread page 101. What is one fact and one opinion about how the father supported the family? Possible responses: Fact: The father took any job he could find to support his family; Opinion: By working at any job he could find, he showed a strong sense of responsibility.

Text to World • Analysis On page 101, the narrator says that her father would go to the science museum to study rocks. If the story took place in today's world, what technological resource might the father use to learn more about rocks? Possible response: Today, the father might use a computer to visit Web sites that provide information about rocks.

Text to Self • Synthesis Why do you think the father keeps studying rocks even when he is having a hard time finding a job? What can you learn from his example? Possible responses: By studying rocks, he is continuing to learn about things that interest him, even though his job situation is stalled. His example shows me that keeping up with my hobby can help me get through hard times.

Differentiated Instruction

 Strategic Intervention

Have students make a T-chart with *Facts* in the left column and *Opinions* in the right column. Tell students to list facts and opinions as they read.

A **Advanced**

Ask students if they agree with the narrator's mother that rocks will never do the father "any good." Have them predict whether the father's unique interest in rocks will help him advance in life.

 Multidraft Reading

To assist struggling readers and to deepen reading for all, apply multidraft reading protocols. For each reading, have students set the purpose indicated.

- **First reading**—Literal comprehension: discuss Guide Comprehension questions to monitor and clarify understanding.

- **Second reading**—Application of skills: answer higher-order thinking skills questions to develop deeper understanding of text and make connections to the real world.

Objectives
- Review multiple-meaning words.
- Identify fact and opinion.

One afternoon he looked up to see a lady standing beside him. "I've seen you here before," she said.

"I come here a lot," he said. "I guess I've got rocks in my head."

"Tell me what you're looking for," she said.

"I'm looking for rocks that are better than mine," he said.

"How many did you find?" she asked.

"Ten," he said.

The lady looked around at the hundreds of rocks, in all those glass cases. "Only ten?"

"Maybe eleven," he said.

He smiled. She did, too.

"You *have* got rocks in your head," she said. "I'm Grace Johnson, the director of this museum. These rocks have come from all over the world."

"So have mine," said my father. He reached into his pocket. "Take a look at this one," he said.

"Did you study rocks at college?" she asked.

"Couldn't afford to go to college," he said.

"Let me see the rest of your rocks," she said.

Mrs. Johnson got out her big Packard touring car, and my father got in. They drove to our house.

"Where are the rocks?" she asked.

"Up here," said my father, leading the way to the attic. "Watch your step."

Two hours later Mrs. Johnson said, "I can't hire you as a mineralogist. The board won't allow it. But I need a night janitor at the museum. Will you take the job?"

"Will I be cleaning rocks?" he asked.

"Sometimes," she said.

So my father took the job as night janitor at the museum. Before he went home, he'd open some of the mineral cases and scrub some of the rocks with a toothbrush until they sparkled like diamonds.

102

103

Student Edition pp. 102–103

Guide Comprehension
Skills and Strategies

Review
Context clues

Multiple-Meaning Words Review the definitions of multiple-meaning words on p. 92. Remind students that when they encounter a multiple-meaning word they can use context clues to determine the correct meaning.

Guide practice

Point to the word *lot* on p. 102. Ask students to explain how context clues helped them determine the correct meaning of *lot*.

On their own

Use the *Let's Practice It! DVD* for additional practice with multiple-meaning words.

Let's Practice It!
TR DVD•278

Extend Thinking
Think Critically

Higher-order thinking skills

 Multiple-Meaning Words • Analysis What are two meanings for the word *rest* on page 103? Use context clues to determine the correct meaning in this sentence. **Possible response:** *Rest* can mean "to be still or quiet" or "what is left." The word *rocks* in the sentence tells me that the correct meaning here is "what is left."

 Fact and Opinion • Analysis Look at the first two sentences on page 103. Which sentence states a fact and which sentence states an opinion? How do you know? **Possible response:** The first sentence is an opinion, because it can't be proved. The second statement can be proved, so it is a fact.

Text to World • Synthesis The museum board wanted to hire someone who had studied rocks in college. What do you think people learn about rocks in college? **Possible response:** They might learn about all the different types of rocks and how they are formed.

Differentiated Instruction

SI **Strategic Intervention**

Multiple-meaning words Have students work in pairs to identify context clues for multiple-meaning words and determine the correct meaning.

A **Advanced**

Fact and opinion Point out that this biography provides many more facts than opinions about its subject, the narrator's father. Have students discuss whether including more opinions would or would not create a more accurate picture of the father.

Objectives
- Review fact and opinion.
- Review inferring.
- Review multiple-meaning words.
- Read aloud fluently with expression.

Name _____   Rocks in His Head

TEST PRACTICE

Possessive Pronouns

Directions Read the passage. Then read each question. Circle the letter of the correct answer.

Rock Collecting

(1) I have cool rocks in my collection. (2) Dad taught _____ family about rocks. (3) My dad gave me a rock from its collection. (4) The rock is odd, and its color is orange. (5) My sister Tara got down on her knees. (6) She found quartz on her first try. (7) Rock collecting is a good hobby, and it could be our.

1 Which word is the possessive pronoun in sentence 1?
- I
- rocks
- ● my
- in

2 Which pronoun correctly completes sentence 2?
- ● our
- mine
- hers
- its

3 What change, if any, should be made to sentence 3?
- Change *its* to he
- ● Change *its* to his
- Change *its* to mine
- Make no change

4 What change, if any, should be made to sentence 5?
- Change *our knees.* to **hers knees.**
- Change *our knees.* to **their knees.**
- Change *our knees.* to **my knees.**
- ● Make no change

5 What change, if any, should be made to sentence 7?
- ● Change *our.* to **yours.**
- Change *our.* to **him.**
- Change *our.* to **its.**
- Make no change

School+Home **Home Activity** Your child prepared for taking tests on possessive pronouns. Play a board game with your child. Have your child identify possessive pronouns used by any player as you play.

Conventions Possessive Pronouns **279**

Name _____   Gertrude Ederle

Suffixes *-er, -or, -ess, -ist*

Directions Add the suffix to each base word. Write the new word on the line.

1. edit + -or = **editor**
2. art + -ist = **artist**
3. conduct + -or = **conductor**
4. lion + -ess = **lioness**
5. sell + -er = **seller**

Directions Write the word from the box that best fits each definition.

dentist _____ 6. a doctor who cares for your teeth
shipper _____ 7. one who ships packages
director _____ 8. one who directs
chemist _____ 9. a scientist in the field of chemistry
hostess _____ 10. a woman who greets restaurant guests

chemist
dentist
hostess
shipper
director

Directions Add the suffix *-er, -or, -ess,* or *-ist* to the base word in ( ) to complete each sentence. Use the words in the box to help. Write the word on the line.

swimmer _____ 11. Gertrude Ederle was the first woman (swim) to swim across the English Channel.
instructor _____ 12. Many thought her coach was the greatest swimming (instruct) in the world.
actress _____ 13. After she became famous, Ederle was offered work as an (act), but she declined.
tourist _____ 14. Instead, she traveled as a (tour).
teacher _____ 15. Later, Ederle became a swimming (teach) for deaf children.

actress
instructor
swimmer
teacher
tourist

School+Home **Home Activity** Your child formed and wrote words with the suffixes *-er, -or, -ess,* and *-ist.* Together, think of additional job-related words that end with *-er, -or, -ess,* or *-ist* (such as *doctor, countess, biologist, police officer*). Help your child write a paragraph explaining which jobs sound most interesting to him or her and why.

280 **Phonics** Suffixes *-er, -or, -ess, -ist*

Let's Practice It! TR DVD • 279–280

Guide Comprehension
Skills and Strategies

Review Fact and opinion

Reread the first paragraph. Write a sentence that states a fact about Valentina Tereshkova's special interest. **Possible response: She liked to parachute; she started a parachute club.**

Tell students that a fact is a statement that can be proved to be true or false by looking in a reference book, or by using their own knowledge and experience. An opinion is a personal judgment about something.

Review Inferring

Use information from the text and what you know about people to make an inference about the character traits that helped Valentina Tereshkova become the first woman in space. **Possible response: Tereshkova made more than 100 parachute jumps during training, and even though she felt sick when she was in space, she took pictures and did her job. These details show that she was a courageous, hard-working, and responsible person.**

Review Multiple-meaning words

How do context clues help you determine the appropriate definition of the multiple-meaning word *capsule* in paragraph 5? **Possible answer: I know that a capsule is a kind of pill, but that meaning doesn't make sense here. Tereshkova blasts into space inside this capsule, so it must be a part of a space ship.**

Review with students that they can look for clues in surrounding text to distinguish among multiple-meaning words.

Review Fact and opinion

Reread the third paragraph. Underline the sentence that states Tereshkova's opinion about being accepted as a cosmonaut. **She thought she was the luckiest person in the world when she got the news.**

Have students identify the clue that indicates this is an opinion. (the word "thought")

Reread for Fluency

Model fluent reading

Have students listen as you read the first three paragraphs on p. 279 of "First Woman in Space" with appropriate expression. Explain that you will adjust your voice level to stress important words and phrases.

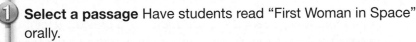

ROUTINE **Choral Reading**

① **Select a passage** Have students read "First Woman in Space" orally.

② **Model** Have students listen as you read with appropriate expression.

③ **Guide practice** Have students read along with you.

④ **On their own** For optimal fluency, students should reread three or four times with expression.

Routines Flip Chart

Objectives
- Read multisyllabic words with prefixes in context and independent of context.
- Spell words containing prefixes correctly.
- Use and understand possessive pronouns.
- Write about collections.

Word Analysis— Review
Prefixes

Review

Review the prefixes *pre-, mid-, over-, out-, bi-,* and *de-* using Sound-Spelling Cards 150, 151, 156, 159, 160, and 161.

Read words independent of context

Use the *Let's Practice It! DVD.* Point out that students know how to read these words. Then tell students they will all read the words in each row together. Allow several seconds previewing time for the first reading.

> **If...** students cannot read all the words in a row consecutively without an error,
> **then...** return to the first word in the row, and have students reread all the words in the row. Repeat until students can read the words fluently.

Read words in context

Use the passage on the *Let's Practice It! DVD.* Point out that there are many words in the passage that students already know how to read. Have students read the passage together.

> **If...** students have difficulty reading the prefixes *pre-, mid-, over-, out-, bi-,* and *de-,*
> **then...** guide them in using the word parts strategy. Have students read each sentence. Repeat until students can read the sentences fluently.

Spelling
Prefixes

Let's Practice It!
TR DVD•277

Review Prefixes

Write *midpoint, overgrown, outdoors,* and *preview.* Point out that these words have prefixes. Remind students that they have learned how to spell words with prefixes *pre-, mid-, over-, out-,* and *bi-.*

Spelling strategy

Tell students that adding a prefix to a base word does not change the spelling of the base word. Have them use the following spelling strategy.

> **Step 1: Draw a line between the base word and the prefix.**
>
> **Step 2: Study the word, one part at a time.**

On their own

Use p. 306 in the *Reader's and Writer's Notebook* for additional practice with prefixes.

Reader's and Writer's
Notebook p. 306

Conventions
Possessive Pronouns

Review
Possessive pronouns

- Some pronouns show who or what owns, or possesses, something. This kind of pronoun is a **possessive pronoun.**

- *My, mine, your, yours, her, hers, our, ours, his, their, theirs,* and *its* are possessive pronouns.

Guide practice

Read the following sentences. Have students identify the possessive pronoun(s) in each sentence.

> 1. **My** aunt has a collection of pet frogs.
>
> 2. **My** brother keeps **his** eyes open for additions to **our** collection.

On their own

For additional practice, use the *Reader's and Writer's Notebook* p. 307.

Reader's and Writer's Notebook p. 307

ROUTINE — Quick Write for Fluency — Team Talk

1. **Talk** Pairs discuss the objects that are collected in *Rocks in His Head* and "Marvelous Marble Mania."

2. **Write** Students write a paragraph about what they and their friends collect, using possessive pronouns correctly.

3. **Share** Partners read each other's paragraphs, checking for the correct use of possessive pronouns.

Routines Flip Chart

Wrap Up Your Day

✔ **Build Concepts** What was valuable about the interest that Carol Otis Hurst's father had in rocks?

✔ **Fact and Opinion** What are some statements of fact or opinion in *Rocks in His Head*?

✔ **Multiple-Meaning Words** How can you determine the meaning of a multiple-meaning word in a sentence?

Preview DAY 4

Tell students that tomorrow they will review *America's Champion Swimmer: Gertrude Ederle.*

Objectives
- Review the weekly concept.
- Connect the weekly selection to the Big Question.

Today at a Glance

Oral Vocabulary
ordinary, imagination, assemble, magnificent, organize, erect, suspend, accompany, provision, spectacle

⊙ **Comprehension**
Fact and opinion

⊙ **Vocabulary**
Multiple-meaning words

Fluency
Appropriate phrasing

Word Analysis
Suffixes (*-er, -or, -ess, -ist*)

Spelling
Suffixes (*-er, -or, -ess, -ist*)

Conventions
Contractions

Writing
Quick write for fluency

Concept Talk

 Question of the Week
What unique traits does it take to be the first to do something?

Revisit the concept

Today students will explore how the Unit 4 Big Question connects to *America's Champion Swimmer: Gertrude Ederle.* Remind students of the Question of the Week for *America's Champion Swimmer: Gertrude Ederle.*

> **ROUTINE** **Activate Prior Knowledge** **Team Talk**
>
> ① **Think** Have students think about the unique traits it takes to be the first to do something.
>
> ② **Pair** Have pairs of students discuss how the Question of the Week applies to Gertrude Ederle.
>
> ③ **Share** Call on a few students to share their ideas with the group. Guide the discussion and encourage students to make pertinent comments with prompts such as:
>
> - What unique traits did Gertrude Ederle have that enabled her to reach her goal? When did Trudy show these traits?
>
> - How and why did people celebrate Trudy's accomplishments?

Routines Flip Chart

Anchored Talk

Connect to the Big Question

Remind students of the Unit 4 Big Question, *What does it mean to be unique?* Use the prompts below to discuss how being unique can help you accomplish your goals. Remind students to ask and answer questions with appropriate detail.

- How can people use their imagination to set unique goals?

- How can a person's unique talents help him or her achieve a magnificent goal?

Oral Vocabulary
Amazing Words

Review Amazing Words

Display the Amazing Words. Remind students that the words are related to the week's concept, being one of a kind.

Amazing Words

ordinary	erect
imagination	suspend
assemble	accompany
magnificent	provision
organize	spectacle

Amazing Words — Oral Vocabulary Routine

1 Review Ask students for definitions of the words, starting at the top of the list. Listen for accurate definitions. Prompt students to connect the words to the unit concept of being One of a Kind whenever possible.

2 Demonstrate Have students use two or more Amazing Words in the same sentence. Guide the discussion by providing an example that shows the meaning of each word. *Many people suspend their daily activities to watch a magnificent spectacle.* Follow this pattern to the end of the list, covering as many of the ten words as possible.

3 Apply Assign the words in random order and have students come up with more sentences for them. *To show that you are becoming more comfortable using these Amazing Words, think up more new sentences for them.*

Routines Flip Chart

Apply Amazing Words

Have students use the Retelling Cards for *America's Champion Swimmer: Gertrude Ederle* to talk about the Amazing Words.

Connect to reading

Tell students that today they will be reading about another unique swimmer and rereading passages from *America's Champion Swimmer: Gertrude Ederle.* As they read, ask students to think about how having unique traits helps people accomplish goals.

Retelling Cards

ELL Build background Use ELL Poster 19 to review the week 4 lesson concept and to practice oral language. Point out and read the question: *What unique traits does it take to be the first to do something?*

Writing on Demand

Writing Fluency
Ask students to write as well as they can and as much as they can about being one of a kind.

ELL Poster 19

Objectives

- Review identifying facts and opinions.
- Make text connections.

From that summer on, it was hard to keep Trudy out of the water. She *loved* to swim. At the age of thirteen she became a member of the New York Women's Swimming Association and took lessons there.

At fifteen Trudy won her first big race.

The next year, she attempted to be the first woman to swim the more than seventeen miles from lower Manhattan to Sandy Hook, New Jersey. When Trudy slowed down, her sister Margaret yelled, "Get going, lazybones!" And Trudy did. She finished in just over seven hours. And she beat the men's record.

People were beginning to notice Gertrude Ederle. Newspapers described her as courageous, determined, modest, and poised. They called her the most perfect swimmer. Trudy's mother said she was "just a plain home girl."

In 1924 this "plain home girl" was good enough to make the U.S. Olympic team. Trudy won three medals at the games in Paris. Her team won more points than all the other countries' swimming teams combined.

By 1925 Trudy had set twenty-nine U.S. and world records. She was determined to take on the ultimate challenge: the English Channel. Many had tried to swim the more-than-twenty-mile-wide body of cold, rough water that separates England from France. But only five men—and no women—had ever made it all the way across.

128 / 129

Student Edition pp. 128–129

Guide Comprehension
Skills and Strategies

Review fact and opinion

🔊 **Fact and Opinion** Review the definitions of fact and opinion on p. 120. Remind students that a fact can be proved true or false by checking a reference source. A statement of fact can be correct or incorrect. An opinion is a statement of someone's belief. It cannot be proved true or false. You may or may not agree with an opinion.

Guide practice

Read aloud the first two sentences in the first paragraph on p. 128. Point out the word *loved* in the second sentence. Ask students if the word signifies a fact or an opinion. (opinion) Read aloud the third sentence. Ask students if the sentence can be proved true or false. (yes) Point out that the sentence is a fact.

On their own

Have students find a statement of fact on p. 129. Ask them to explain how they recognized it. Have students tell what conclusions they can draw from the fact they identified. Ask students to find evidence in the text that supports their conclusion.

Extend Thinking
Think Critically

Higher-order thinking skills

 Fact and Opinion • Analysis How was Trudy's mother's opinion of Trudy different from the public's opinion of Trudy? What conclusion can you draw from that? **Possible responses:** The public believed Trudy was courageous, determined, modest, and poised. They called her the most perfect swimmer. However, Trudy's mother said she was "just a plain home girl." Trudy's mother was realistic and down to earth.

Text to World • Analysis From a young age, Trudy began training seriously, winning her first big race at the age of fifteen. Think of athletes today, such as Olympic swimmers and gymnasts. How might their training compare to Trudy's? **Possible response:** Today's athletes may train even more intensely than Trudy. Many begin at an even younger age. They have professional coaches.

Text to Self • Synthesize Trudy received a lot of press for her accomplishments. At a young age, she experienced fame. How might you stay focused on your goals with so much attention? **Possible responses:** It would be difficult to remain focused with so much media attention. I would probably try not to listen to the news or read articles about myself. I would keep my focus on my goals.

 Differentiated Instruction

SI **Strategic Intervention**

Remind students that facts can be proved true or false. Have students select a fact from the selection. Guide them in using the Internet or other source to verify the fact.

A **Advanced**

Point out that a statement of opinion can be well supported or poorly supported. Have students revisit the selection and assess the support of different opinions.

 Multidraft Reading

To assist struggling readers and to deepen reading for all, apply multidraft reading protocols. For each reading, have students set the purpose indicated.

- **First reading**—Literal comprehension: discuss Guide Comprehension questions to monitor and clarify understanding.

- **Second reading**—Application of skills: answer higher-order thinking skills questions to develop deeper understanding of text and make connections to the real world.

Objectives

• Review using context to distinguish among multiple meaning words.

At about one-thirty in the afternoon, it started to rain. A strong wind stirred the water. For a while, Trudy would swim forward a few feet only to be pulled back twice as far.

By six o'clock the tide was stronger. The waves were twenty feet high. The rough water made the people aboard the *Alsace* and the news boat seasick.

Trudy's trainer was sure she couldn't finish the swim. He told her to give up.

"No, no," Trudy yelled over the sound of the waves. She kept swimming.

In the next few hours, the rain and wind became stronger and the sea rougher. At times the rough water pulled the boats away, out of Trudy's sight. She was scared. It was eerie being out there all alone.

Now Trudy began to have trouble kicking in the water. When the *Alsace* came close again, Trudy said her left leg had become stiff. Her trainer was frightened for her. He yelled, "You must come out."

"What for?" Trudy shouted, and kept swimming.

Trudy continued to fight the tide and the constant stinging spray of water in her face. She knew she would either swim the Channel or drown.

As Trudy neared Kingsdown, on the coast of England, she saw thousands of people gathered to greet her. They lit flares to guide her to shore.

At about nine-forty at night, after more than fourteen hours in the water, Trudy's feet touched land. Hundreds of people, fully dressed, waded into the water to greet her. When she reached the shore, her father hugged Trudy and wrapped her in a warm robe.

"I knew if it could be done, it had to be done, and I did it," Trudy said after she got ashore. "All the women of the world will celebrate."

Student Edition pp. 134–135

Guide Comprehension
Skills and Strategies

Review multiple-meaning words	**Multiple-Meaning Words** Review the definition of a multiple-meaning word on p. 122. Remind students that using context clues can help them determine the correct meaning of the word.
Guide practice	Point out the word *flares* in the third paragraph on p. 135. Guide students in using the three steps from p. 122 to determine the meaning of the word *flare*.
On their own	Use the *Let's Practice It! DVD* for additional practice with multiple-meaning words.

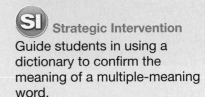
Extend Thinking
Think Critically

Higher-order thinking skills

 Multiple-Meaning Words • Analysis What meanings can you think of for the word *sting*? Use context clues to tell the meaning of *stinging* on page 135, paragraph 2. Possible responses: *Sting* can mean "to wound with a sharp-pointed part" or it can mean that "something hurts or is painful." When I look for context clues within the sentence, I see the word *fight*. This tells me that something was painful.

Fact and Opinion • Analysis What is the author's opinion of Trudy? What details from the selection support your understanding? Possible responses: He admires and respects Trudy. The author includes details about Trudy overcoming a prejudice against women and her lack of swimming skills. He describes the celebration held after she swam the English Channel. The author includes President Coolidge's quotation, "America's Best Girl," and agrees with it.

Text to Text • Analysis This biography is about a woman who overcame challenges to accomplish a goal. Can you think of another text, either fiction or nonfiction, in which someone overcomes a challenge to reach a goal? Possible response: a biography of Helen Keller.

Differentiated Instruction

SI **Strategic Intervention**
Guide students in using a dictionary to confirm the meaning of a multiple-meaning word.

A **Advanced**
Have students locate three multiple-meaning words within the text and write sentences to illustrate the different meanings of each.

Objectives
- Review fact and opinion.
- Review questioning.
- Review using context to distinguish among multiple meaning words.
- Read grade-level text with appropriate phrasing.

Name _____   Gertrude Ederle

Vocabulary

Check the Words You Know
- ___drowned   ___strokes
- ___medals   ___current
- ___continued   ___stirred
- ___celebrate

Directions Fill in the blank with a word from the box that fits the meaning of the sentence.

1. He ____continued____ to swim so that he could reach the shore.

2. The more she practiced, the stronger her swimming ____strokes____ became.

3. The swimmer won prizes and ____medals____ for every race she won.

4. The ocean ____current____ was strong, and he worked to swim against it.

5. The waves were high on the day she almost ____drowned____.

Directions Draw a line from the word to its meaning.

6. stirred   prizes or ribbons you win
7. celebrate   moved around
8. current   kept on going
9. medals   the movement of ocean water
10. continued   to have a party

Write a Newspaper Article

On a separate sheet of paper, write a newspaper article describing a swimming race. Use as many vocabulary words as possible.

Students' writing should use the lesson vocabulary in a description of a swimming race.

Home Activity Your child identified and used vocabulary words from *America's Champion Swimmer: Gertrude Ederle*. Read a sports article from a newspaper with your child. Encourage your child to discuss the article using this week's vocabulary words.

Vocabulary 283

Name _____   Gertrude Ederle
                                                         DEVELOP THE CONCEPT

Contractions

A **contraction** is a word made by putting two words together. When words are joined in a contraction, an apostrophe shows where a letter or letters have been left out.
- Some contractions combine a pronoun and a verb: *I + am = I'm; he + is = he's; we + are = we're; you + will = you'll; we + will = we'll; they + are = they're.*
- Some contractions combine a verb and *not: can + not = can't; is + not = isn't; do + not = don't; will + not = won't; are + not = aren't.*

Contractions   They're swimming in the lake, but I can't see them.

Directions Write the contraction in each sentence.

1. Watch the Olympics, and you'll see some great swimmers. ____you'll____

2. The Americans think they'll win many medals. ____they'll____

3. I won't miss their big race tonight. ____won't____

4. I can't believe she broke the world record. ____can't____

5. Maybe we'll swim in the Olympics someday. ____we'll____

Directions Write the contraction in each sentence. Then write the words that make up the contraction.

6. They're starting the race. ____They're; They are____

7. Jeremy is in this race, and he's in the first lane. ____he's; he is____

8. It's important to get a fast start. ____It's; It is____

9. Isn't a fast turn important also? ____Isn't; Is not____

10. The other swimmers can't beat Jeremy. ____can't; can not____

Home Activity Your child learned about contractions. With your child, read an article in a local newspaper. Have your child identify the contractions and the words that make up each contraction.

284 **Conventions** Contractions

Let's Practice It! TR DVD•283–284

Guide Comprehension
Skills and Strategies

Review Fact and opinion

Look back at the selection. Find one statement of fact and one statement of opinion about Karen Gaffney. Possible responses: Fact—Karen was born with Down syndrome. Opinion—Karen Gaffney is an inspiration to athletes everywhere.

Remind students that a fact can be proved true or false. An opinion is a statement of belief. To help students monitor their comprehension, have them tell what conclusions they can draw from the fact they identified.

Review Questioning

What question might you ask yourself after reading the fourth paragraph? Possible response: How does having Down syndrome affect Karen's ability to swim?

Review Multiple-meaning words

What meanings can the word *lap* have? to drink, body part formed when sitting, one length of a swimming pool What meaning does the word *laps* have in the first sentence? lengths of a swimming pool How does context help you determine the meaning? The sentence talks about swimming in a pool, so I know the author means lengths of a swimming pool.

Review Fact and opinion

What is your opinion about Karen Gaffney based on what you read in the selection? Possible responses: Karen is very brave. Karen is a really good athlete.

Have students support their opinion with information in the text. Remind them that others may or may not agree with their opinion. An opinion cannot be proved true or false.

Reread for Fluency

Model fluent reading

Remind students that when they read, it is important to read with appropriate phrasing in order to understand what they are reading. Model reading the first paragraph of "Karen Gaffney" with appropriate phrasing and have students track the print as you read.

Pair students and have them read "Karen Gaffney."

ROUTINE **Paired Reading**

1. **Reader 1 Begins** Students read the entire selection switching readers at the end of each page.

2. **Reader 2 Begins** Partners reread the selection. This time the other student begins.

3. **Reread** For optimal fluency, have partners continue to read three or four times.

4. **Provide Feedback** Listen to students read and provide corrective feedback regarding their appropriate phrasing.

Routines Flip Chart

Objectives
- Decode multisyllabic words with common suffixes.
- Spell words containing suffixes.
- Review contractions.
- Write about women athletes.

Word Analysis— Review
Suffixes

Review

Review the suffixes -er, -or, -ess, and -ist, using Sound-Spelling Cards 165, 166, 171, and 176.

Read words independent of context

Use the *Let's Practice It! DVD.* Point out that students know how to read these words. Then tell students they will all read the words in each row together. Allow several seconds previewing time for the first reading.

If... students cannot read all the words in a row consecutively without an error,

then... return to the first word in the row, and have students reread all the words in the row. Repeat until students can read the words fluently.

Read words in context

Use the passage on the *Let's Practice It! DVD.* Point out that there are many words in the passage that students already know how to read. Have students read the passage together.

If... students have difficulty reading the suffixes -er, -or, -ess, and -ist,

then... guide them in using the word parts strategy. Have students read each sentence. Repeat until students can read the sentences fluently.

Let's Practice It!
TR DVD•281

Spelling
Suffixes

Review Suffixes

Write *seller, actor, actress,* and *tourist.* Point out that these words have suffixes. Remind students that they have learned how to spell words with suffixes -er, -or, -ess, and -ist.

Spelling strategy

A good way to learn to spell words that include suffixes is to divide and conquer.

> **Step 1: Draw a line between the base word and the suffix.**
>
> **Step 2: Study the word, one part at a time.**

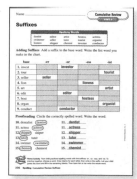

On their own

Use p. 308 in the *Reader's and Writer's Notebook* for additional practice with suffixes.

Reader's and Writer's
Notebook p. 308

Conventions
Contractions

Review Contractions

- A **contraction** is a word made by putting two words together.
- When words are joined in a contraction, an **apostrophe** shows where any letters have been left out.

Guide practice

Read the following sentences. Have students identify the contraction in each sentence.

1. I **didn't** know that swimming is an Olympic sport.
2. **I'd** like to be in the Olympics one day.
3. Unfortunately, I **don't** swim very well.

On their own

For additional practice, use the *Reader's and Writer's Notebook* p. 309.

Reader's and Writer's Notebook p. 309

ROUTINE **Quick Write for Fluency** **Team Talk**

1) **Talk** Pairs discuss what they've learned in the two selections this week about the accomplishments of female athletes.

2) **Write** Each student writes a few sentences summarizing the accomplishments of a particular female athlete, using contractions.

3) **Share** Students read their sentences to their partners, who then check for the correct use of contractions.

Routines Flip Chart

Wrap Up Your Day

Preview DAY 5

Tell students that tomorrow they will review *Fly, Eagle, Fly!: An African Tale.*

✔ **Build Concepts** What traits helped Ms. Ederle become the first woman to swim the English Channel?

✔ **Fact and Opinion** What are two statements of fact that you read about Gertrude Ederle from the selection?

✔ **Multiple-Meaning Words** How can parts of speech help you understand the meaning of a multiple-meaning word?

Objectives
• Review the weekly concept.
• Connect the weekly selection to the Big Question.

Today at a Glance

Oral Vocabulary
armor, agile, snout, protrude, extraordinary, scenery, pesky, unfurl, coil, intersection

Comprehension
◉ Cause and effect

Vocabulary
◉ Unknown words

Fluency
Rate

Phonics/Word Analysis
Syllables VCCCV

Spelling
Syllables VCCCV

Conventions
Prepositions

Writing
Quick write for fluency

Concept Talk

 Question of the Week
What behaviors are unique to different animals?

Revisit the concept

Today students will explore how the Unit 4 Big Question connects to *Fly, Eagle, Fly!* Remind students of the Question of the Week for *Fly, Eagle, Fly!*

ROUTINE **Activate Prior Knowledge** **Team Talk**

1. **Think** Have students think about the behaviors that are unique to different animals.
2. **Pair** Have pairs of students discuss how the Question of the Week applies to *Fly, Eagle, Fly!*
3. **Share** Call on a few students to share their ideas with the group. Guide the discussion and encourage students to make pertinent comments with prompts such as:
   • How does the eagle in the story behave?
   • Why does the farmer's friend want the eagle to fly?

Routines Flip Chart

Anchored Talk

Connect to the Big Question

Remind students of the Unit 4 Big Question, *What does it mean to be unique?* Use the prompts below to discuss what makes different animals unique. Remind students to ask and answer questions with appropriate detail, providing suggestions that build upon the ideas of others.

• How do the ways animals look, sound, or act make them unique?
• How do animals' extraordinary characteristics make them unique?

Oral Vocabulary
Amazing Words

Review Amazing Words

Display the Amazing Words. Remind students that the words are related to the week's concept, what it means to be unique.

Amazing Words

armor	scenery
agile	pesky
snout	unfurl
protrude	coil
extraordinary	intersection

Amazing Words Oral Vocabulary Routine

1. **Review** Ask students for definitions of the words, starting at the top of the list. Listen for accurate definitions. Prompt students to connect the words to the unit concept of uniqueness whenever possible.

2. **Demonstrate** Have students use two or more Amazing Words in the same sentence. Guide the discussion by providing an example that shows the meaning of each word. *The beautiful scenery in the valley made the view extraordinary.* Follow this pattern to the end of the list, covering as many of the ten words as possible.

3. **Apply** Assign the words in random order and have students come up with more new sentences for them. To show that you are becoming more comfortable using these Amazing Words, think up more new sentences for them.

Routines Flip Chart

Writing on Demand

Writing Fluency
Ask students to write as well as they can and as much as they can about what makes different animals unique.

Apply Amazing Words

Have students use the Retelling Cards for *Fly, Eagle, Fly!* to talk about the Amazing Words.

Connect to reading

Tell students that today they will be reading about birds of prey and rereading passages from *Fly, Eagle, Fly!* As they read, ask students to think about how animal behaviors are unique.

[Insert Retelling Card, 47684]

Retelling Card

ELL Build Background Use ELL Poster 20 to review the week 5 lesson concept and to practice oral language. Point out and read the question: *What behaviors are unique to different animals?*

ELL Poster 20

Objectives
- Review cause and effect relationships.
- Make text connections.

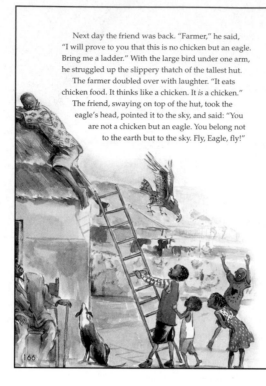

Next day the friend was back. "Farmer," he said, "I will prove to you that this is no chicken but an eagle. Bring me a ladder." With the large bird under one arm, he struggled up the slippery thatch of the tallest hut. The farmer doubled over with laughter. "It eats chicken food. It thinks like a chicken. It *is* a chicken." The friend, swaying on top of the hut, took the eagle's head, pointed it to the sky, and said: "You are not a chicken but an eagle. You belong not to the earth but to the sky. Fly, Eagle, fly!"

Again the great bird stretched out its wings. It trembled and the claws that clasped his hand opened. "Fly, Eagle, fly!" the man cried.

But the bird scrambled out of his hands, slid down the thatch, and sailed in among the chickens.

There was much laughter.

Very early next morning, on the third day, the farmer's dogs began to bark. A voice was calling outside in the darkness. The farmer ran to the door. It was his friend again. "Give me one more chance with the bird," he begged.

"Do you know the time? It's long before dawn. Are you crazy?"

"Come with me. Fetch the bird."

Reluctantly the farmer went into the kitchen, stepping over his sleeping children, and picked up the bird, which was fast asleep among the chickens. The two men set off, disappearing into the darkness.

166

167

Student Edition pp. 166–167

Guide Comprehension
Skills and Strategies

Review
Cause and effect

Cause and Effect Review the meanings of *cause* and *effect* on p. 154. Remind students that a cause is why something happens and an effect is what happens. Tell students that the words *because* and *so* are clues to cause-and-effect relationships. Sometimes an author uses these words, but many times the reader has to figure out the relationship based on the descriptions of events.

Guide practice

Point out the words of the farmer on p. 166, "It eats chicken food. It thinks like a chicken. It *is* a chicken." Explain that the effect is that the farmer believes the eagle is a chicken. Ask what causes the farmer to have this belief.

On their own

Have students write a sentence that tells the cause-and-effect relationship in the above example. Tell students to use the clue word *because* in their sentences.

Extend Thinking
Think Critically

Higher-order thinking skills

 Cause and Effect • Evaluation The farmer believes the eagle is a chicken because it thinks like a chicken and acts like a chicken. Are the reasons, or causes, for his belief valid? Why or why not? Possible response: No. Just because the eagle acts like a chicken doesn't mean it really is a chicken.

Text to Text • Synthesis In "Eagle Watching," the author describes how eagles act in the wild. What effect does the farmer have on the eagle when he takes it home? Possible response: He changes its behavior by teaching it to be a chicken.

Text to World • Evaluation The eagle is America's national bird, and represents freedom. How does the farmer try to change this representation of the eagle? Possible response: He tries to tame it and take away its true nature.

Differentiated Instruction

 Strategic Intervention

Text to text Prior to presenting this question to students, review the selection "Eagle Watching," pointing out the descriptions of the ways the birds behave in the wild.

 Advanced

Cause and effect Have students identify and explain the faulty reasoning behind the farmer's beliefs. Then ask them to come up with a cause-and-effect statement as to why the farmer might feel this way.

 Multidraft Reading

To assist struggling readers and to deepen reading for all, apply multidraft reading protocols. For each reading, have students set the purpose indicated.

- **First reading**—Literal comprehension: discuss Guide Comprehension questions to monitor and clarify understanding.

- **Second reading**—Application of skills: answer higher-order thinking skills questions to develop deeper understanding of text and make connections to the real world.

Objectives
• Review unknown words.
• Make text connections.

At last he said, "This will do." He looked down the cliff and saw the ground thousands of feet below. They were very near the top.

Carefully the friend carried the bird onto a ledge of rock. He set it down so that it looked toward the east, and began talking to it.

The farmer chuckled. "It talks only chickens' talk."

But the friend talked on, telling the bird about the sun, how it gives life to the world, how it reigns in the heavens, giving light to each new day.

"Look at the sun, Eagle. And when it rises, rise with it. You belong to the sky, not to the earth."

At that moment the sun's first rays shot out over the mountain, and suddenly the world was ablaze with light.

The golden sun rose majestically, dazzling them. The great bird stretched out its wings to greet the sun and feel the life-giving warmth on its feathers. The farmer was quiet. The friend said, "You belong not to the earth, but to the sky. Fly, Eagle, fly!"

He clambered back to the farmer.

All was silent. Nothing moved. The eagle's head stretched up; its wings stretched outwards; its legs leaned forward as its claws clutched the rock.

And then, without really moving, feeling the updraft of a wind more powerful than any man or bird, the great eagle leaned forward and was swept upward, higher and higher, lost to sight in the brightness of the rising sun, never again to live among the chickens.

170   171

Student Edition pp. 170–171

Guide Comprehension
Skills and Strategies

Review Unknown Words

Unknown Words Review the instruction for *unknown words* on p. 156. Remind students that they can use a dictionary or glossary to look up unknown words. They can then choose the meaning that makes the most sense in the context in which it is used.

Guide practice

Point out the word *reigns* in the fourth paragraph on p. 171. Help students use a dictionary to look up the word, check its pronunciation, and determine the intended meaning within this context.

On their own

Use the *Let's Practice It! DVD* for additional practice with unknown words.

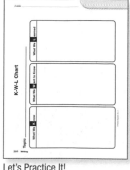

Let's Practice It!
TR DVD•286

Extend Thinking
Think Critically

Higher-order thinking skills

 Unknown Words • Analysis Use a dictionary to look up the meaning of the word *clambered* from paragraph 8 on page 171. What does it mean in this context? It means "climbed awkwardly."

 Cause and Effect • Evaluation Would the eagle have ever flown without the farmer's friend taking it to the mountain? Explain. Possible response: Probably not, because being on the mountaintop at the break of day made the eagle remember its true nature. When it was in the valley with the chickens, it could not realize its true nature.

Text to Self • Synthesis How can you apply the message of this folk tale to your own life? Possible response: I can make sure that I am true to myself no matter what the people in my life look like or act like.

Differentiated Instruction

SI Strategic Intervention

Unknown words Help students look up unknown words in the dictionary, reviewing how to use guide words and pronunciation keys. Then guide them in identifying the definition that fits the context. Suggest they replace the original word in the sentence with its definition. For example, *He climbed awkwardly back to the farmer.*

A Advanced

Text to self Have small groups of students discuss times when they have found it hard to be true to their beliefs or natures, such as when they experience peer pressure or disagree with the majority of people around them.

Objectives

- Review cause-and-effect relationships.
- Review monitoring and clarifying text.
- Review using a dictionary to find meanings of unknown words.
- Read aloud fluently at an appropriate rate.

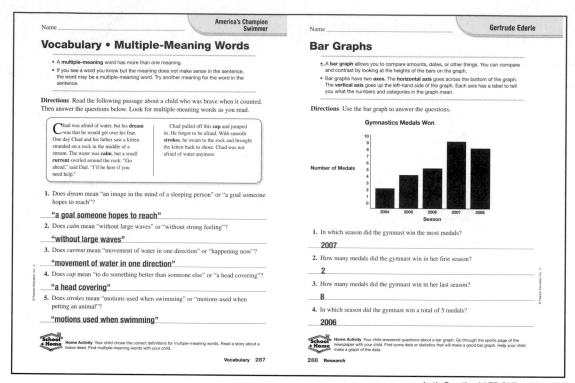

Let's Practice It! TR DVD • 287–288

Guide Comprehension
Skills and Strategies

Review
Cause and effect

What is the cause, or the reason, the baby mice grew fat and bold? Their mother took good care of them.

Remind students that an effect is something that happens and a cause is the reason that something happens. Review that cause and effect is often signaled by clue words. Read the following sentence from the text that contains a cause-and-effect relationship: "The baby mice grew fat and bold, thanks to their mother's good care." Point out that *thanks to* is a clue that means "because of."

Review
Monitor and clarify

The third paragraph begins, "Mother Mouse was horrified." Why is she horrified? Possible response: Her babies are outside in the daytime, which is not safe.

Tell students to reread and to read further to monitor and clarify their understanding of events in the story.

Review Unknown words

Read the first sentence of the last paragraph on page 287. Use a dictionary to determine the meaning of *venture.* It means "to go ahead in spite of danger."

Review with students how to use a dictionary to find the meanings of unknown words. If necessary, help students use guide words to find the term. Remind them that they need to use the context of the word to determine which meaning is intended. Have students find other unknown words and use a dictionary to find its meaning.

Review Cause and effect

Brother Mouse forgot to behave carefully, like a mouse. What effect do you think that had? Possible response: He may have become dinner for an owl.

Underline the last sentence of the folktale. Point out that Brother Mouse is not being careful as his mother warned. Then he hears an owl's wings overhead. Help students explain the two events by using a cause-and-effect relationship. Point out that not all cause-and-effect relationships have clue words. Sometimes readers have to infer the connection based on the events.

Reread for Fluency

Model fluent reading

Remind students that when they read, it is important to read with appropriate rate in order to understand what they are reading. Model reading the first paragraph of "The Foolish Mouse" on p. 287 with appropriate rate and have students track the print as you read.

ROUTINE **Paired Reading**

1. **Select a passage** For "First Snow," pair students and use the whole folktale.

2. **Reader 1** Students read the entire folking, switching readers at the end of each paragraph.

3. **Reader 2** Partners reread the passage. This time the other student begins.

4. **Reread** For optimal fluency, have partners continue to read three or four times.

5. **Corrective Feedback** Listen to students read. Provide corrective feedback regarding their rate.

Routines Flip Chart

Objectives

- Decode words with the syllabication pattern VCCCV.
- Spell words containing the syllable pattern VCCCV correctly.
- Use and understand prepositions.
- Write about unusual animals.

Word Analysis— Review
◉ Syllables VCCCV

Review

Review the syllable pattern VCCCV using Sound-Spelling Card 146.

Read words independent of context

Use the *Let's Practice It! DVD.* Point out that students know how to read these words. Then tell students they will all read the words in each row together. Allow several seconds previewing time for the first reading.

If... students cannot read all the words in a row consecutively without an error,

then... return to the first word in the row, and have students reread all the words in the row. Repeat until students can read the words fluently.

Read words in context

Use the passage on the *Let's Practice It! DVD.* Point out that there are many words in the passage that students already know how to read. Have students read the passage together.

If... students have difficulty reading the syllable pattern VCCCV,

then... guide them in using the word parts strategy. Have students read each sentence. Repeat until students can read the sentences fluently.

Spelling
Syllables VCCCV

Review Syllables VCCCV

Write *instant, partner,* and *address.* Point out that these words have the syllable pattern VCCCV. Remind students that they have learned how to spell words with syllable pattern VCCCV.

Spelling strategy

Use the following spelling strategy for words that are hard for you to spell.

> **Step 1: Say the word slowly and listen for the syllables.**
>
> **Step 2: Write the word and draw lines between the syllables.**
>
> **Step 3: Study the word syllable by syllable.**

On their own

Use p. 310 in the *Reader's and Writer's Notebook* for additional practice with syllable pattern VCCCV.

Let's Practice It!
TR DVD•285

Reader's and Writer's
Notebook p. 310

Conventions
Prepositions

Review Prepositions

- A **preposition** is the first word in a group of words called a prepositional phrase.
- A **prepositional phrase** ends with a noun or pronoun called the object of the preposition. A prepositional phrase tells more about other words in a sentence.

Guide practice

Read the following sentences. Have students identify the preposition in each sentence.

1. I read a folktale **about** an eagle.

2. The story was **in** my reading book.

On their own

For additional practice, use the *Reader's and Writer's Notebook* p. 311.

Reader's and Writer's Notebook p. 311

ROUTINE   **Quick Write for Fluency**   **Team Talk**

1. **Talk** Have pairs discuss the special features of the animals in *Fly, Eagle, Fly!* and "Purple Coyote."

2. **Write** Students write a few sentences describing one of these unusual animals, using prepositions correctly.

3. **Share** Partners read each other's sentences and check them for correct use of prepositions.

Routines Flip Chart

Wrap Up Your Day

✔ **Build Concepts** What behavior is unique to the eagle in *Fly, Eagle, Fly!: An African Tale?*

✔ **Cause and Effect** What effect did the friend's efforts have on the eagle in the folktale?

✔ **Unknown Words** How can you find the meaning of unknown words in the dictionary?

Unit Wrap-Up

The Big Question

What does it mean to be unique?

Understanding By Design

*Grant Wiggins, Ed. D.
Reading Street Author*

" Good questions elicit interesting and alternative views and suggest the need to focus on the reasoning we use in arriving at and defending an answer… They cause us to rethink what we thought we understood and to transfer an idea from one setting to others. "

WEEK 1

Question of the Week
 How do talents make someone unique?

Concept Knowledge

Students will understand that people:

- have many kinds of talents
- practice to develop their talents
- should be allowed to develop their talents

WEEK 2

Question of the Week
 What makes nature's record holders unique?

Concept Knowledge

Students will understand that nature has:

- unusual appearances
- extreme weather
- extreme events

Discuss the Big Question

Help students relate the Big Question for this unit to the selections and their own experiences. Write the question and prompt discussion with questions such as the following.

What is something that makes you unique? Possible responses:

- I have a state quarter collection that includes one from each state.
- I once scored three goals in a soccer game.

Question of the Week

 Why is it valuable to have unique interests?

Question of the Week

 What unique traits does it take to be the first to do something?

Question of the Week

 What behaviors are unique to different animals?

Concept Knowledge

Students will understand that interests:

- are valuable
- lead to learning and research
- lead to a job
- preserve information

Concept Knowledge

Students will understand that being first takes:

- bravery
- imagination
- willingness to work hard
- determination

Concept Knowledge

Students will understand that some animals:

- have lures on their heads
- blend in with their surroundings
- change colors

What is unique about the characters, animals, and places in the selections you read? Possible responses:

- *The Man Who Invented Basketball* James Naismith used his knowledge and skills to invent an indoor game.
- *Hottest, Coldest, Highest, Deepest* There are many places on the earth that have extreme characteristics.
- *Rocks in His Head* The author's father has a special rock collection that he is knowledgeable about.
- *America's Champion Swimmer: Gertrude Ederle* Gertrude has the record of being the first woman to swim across the English Channel.
- *Fly, Eagle, Fly* The eagle is trained to behave like a chicken.

Unit Assessment

Use Unit 4 *Benchmark Tests* to check:

✔ **Passage Comprehension**

✔ **Phonics**

✔ **Vocabulary Skills**

✔ **Writing Conventions**

✔ **Writing**

✔ **Fluency**

Benchmark Tests

Managing Assessment

Use *Assessment Handbook* for:

✔ **Weekly Assessment Blackline Masters for Monitoring Progress**

✔ **Observation Checklists**

✔ **Record-Keeping Forms**

✔ **Portfolio Assessment**

Assessment Handbook

Customize Your Writing

Weekly Writing Focus
Writing Forms and Patterns

- Instruction focuses on a different **product** each week
- Mini-lessons and models help children learn key features and **organizational patterns**.

Grade 3 Products fable, friendly letter, news article, autobiography, summary, realistic fiction, and so on

Grade 3 Organization Patterns poetic forms, compare and contrast, main idea and details, narrative, letter, and so on

Daily Writing Focus
Quick Writes for Fluency

- **Writing on Demand** Use the Quick Write routine for **writing on demand**.

- The Quick Write **prompt and routine** extend skills and strategies from daily writing lessons.

Unit Writing Focus
Writing Process ①②③④⑤

- Six **writing process** lessons provide structure to move children through the steps of the writing process.
- One week and two week pacing allows lessons to be used in **Writing Workshop**.

Steps of the Writing Process Plan and Prewrite, Draft, Revise, Edit, Publish and Present

Grade 3 Writing Process Products personal narrative, how-to report, cause-effect essay, problem-solution essay, persuasive essay, research report

Writing on Reading STREET

MINI-LESSON

- Daily 10-minute mini-lessons focus instruction on the **traits** and **craft** of good writing.

- Instruction focuses on one writing trait and one writer's craft skill every week.

Traits focus/ideas, organization, voice, word choice, sentences, conventions

Craft drafting strategies, revising strategies, editing strategies

Read Like a Writer

- Use **mentor text** every week as a model to exemplify the traits of good writing.

- **Interact with text** every week to learn the key features of good writing.

Mentor Text Examine literature in the Student Edition.

INTERACT with TEXT Underline, circle, and highlight model text in the *Reader's and Writer's Notebook*.

Write Guy
Jeff Anderson

Need Writing Advice?

Writing instruction is all about creating effective writers. We don't want to crush the inner writer in a child by over-correcting and over-editing. What makes effective writing instruction? Children need to write, write, write! But is that enough? Probably not. All kinds of instruction and guidance go into making an effective writer.

The Write Guy offers advice on teacher and peer conferencing, focusing on writing traits, revising strategies, editing strategies and much, much more.

Customize Your Writing

Sometimes you want to spend more time on writing—perhaps you do a **Writing Workshop**. This one or two week plan for the unit level writing projects can help.

1 Week Plan	Day 1	Day 2	Day 3	Day 4	Day 5
1 Plan and Prewrite	■	■			
2 Draft			■		
3 Revise				■	
4 Edit					■
5 Publish					■

2 Week Plan	Day 1	Day 2	Day 3	Day 4	Day 5	Day 6	Day 7	Day 8	Day 9	Day 10
1 Plan and Prewrite	■	■	■	■						
2 Draft					■	■	■			
3 Revise								■		
4 Edit									■	
5 Publish										■

Grade 3 Unit Writing Projects

Internet Guy
Don Leu

Unit Writing Project 1—21st Century Project

Unit 1 E-Pen Pals

Unit 2 Story Exchange

Unit 3 Photo Writing

Unit 4 Classroom Profile

Unit 5 E-Newsletter

Unit 6 Discussion Forum

Unit Writing Project 2

Unit 1 Personal Narrative

Unit 2 How-to Report

Unit 3 Cause-Effect Essay

Unit 4 Problem-Solution Essay

Unit 5 Persuasive Essay

Unit 6 Research Report

Problem-Solution Essay

Writing prompt

Write about a problem in your school or community and how that problem might be solved.

Purpose Identify a problem and offer a solution

Audience Peers, teachers or other interested adults

Introduce genre and prompt

In this writing process lesson, you will study a problem-solution essay and select an appropriate genre for writing a response to the prompt. In a problem-solution essay, a writer describes a problem, or something that he or she thinks needs to be fixed, and a solution for the problem, or a way the problem can be fixed, and offers reasons why the solution is a good one.

Introduce key features

Key Features of a Problem-Solution Essay

- identifies and explains a problem

- offers one or more solutions for the problem

- includes facts and details to support the solution and to convince readers to accept the solution

- uses descriptive details and persuasive words to convince readers to accept the solution

- has an introduction, body, and conclusion

Academic Vocabulary

Essay An essay is a composition or short piece of writing in which the author expresses an idea or opinion. Essays focus on one topic. They can be serious or funny.

English Language Learners

Introduce Genre Show a simple problem, for example, trying to reach something under your desk. Show a way to solve the problem, for example, using a ruler. Write *problem* and *solution* on the board. Explain that a problem is something that needs to be fixed, and a solution is a way of fixing it. Help students understand that a problem-solution essay describes both a problem and a solution. Discuss the key features of a problem-solution essay that appear on this page.

Objectives

- Understand and identify the features of a problem-solution essay.
- Use strategies such as brainstorming, research, interviewing, and graphic organizers to generate ideas for writing.
- Select a topic from a list.

 Plan and Prewrite

MINI-LESSON

Reading Like a Writer

■ **Examine Model Text** Let's look at an example of a student's problem-solution essay that identifies a problem at school and tells how it can be solved. This is an example of the type of essay you might write about a problem in your school or community. Display and read aloud to students "We Need a Longer Recess" on Writing Transparency WP22. Ask them to identify key features of a problem-solution essay in the student model.

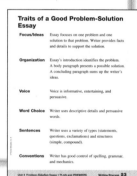

We Need a Longer Recess

Has this ever happened to you? The bell for recess rings. You put on your coat. You line up with everyone else and wait to go out to the playground. Finally, you're outside. You and your friends are deciding what game to play. What happens then? The bell rings, and it's time to go back inside! Our recess at Jefferson Elementary School is too short.

Here is a solution to this problem. Between 8:00 and 8:15 each morning, our principal reads daily messages, but these messages usually take only three or four minutes. For the rest of the time, the students sit at their desks, waiting and talking and fidgeting. It's a waste of time. If we added ten of those fifteen minutes to our morning lessons, recess could start ten minutes earlier, and then we would have time to get some real exercise.

Experts say that kids need regular exercise. It helps us think and learn as well as stay healthy. So spending a little more time on the playground would be good for us.

Writing Transparency WP22

■ **Evaluate Model Text** Display and read aloud "Traits of a Good Problem-Solution Essay" on Writing Transparency WP23. Discuss each trait as it is reflected in the model. For Focus/Ideas, ask students to identify the problem and the solution. For Organization, ask them to explain where the problem and the solution are presented in the essay and why they are in that order. Proceed in the same way for each of the remaining traits, defining it when necessary and helping students identify examples of the trait in the model.

Traits of a Good Problem-Solution Essay

Focus/Ideas	Essay focuses on one problem and one solution to that problem. Writer provides facts and details to support the solution.
Organization	Essay's introduction identifies the problem. A body paragraph presents a possible solution. A concluding paragraph sums up the writer's ideas.
Voice	Voice is informative, entertaining, and persuasive.
Word Choice	Writer uses descriptive details and persuasive words.
Sentences	Writer uses a variety of types (statements, questions, exclamations) and structures (simple, compound).
Conventions	Writer has good control of spelling, grammar, and mechanics.

Writing Transparency WP23

Generate ideas for writing

The writing prompt tells you the general topic of your writing: a problem in your school or community and how to solve it. Choose a genre in which to write. I'll show you how to write a problem-solution essay. Now you need to think of a specific topic: something at school or in your community that you think is a problem that you can think of a way to solve First, make a list of as many appropriate topics as you can.

Use range of strategies

Encourage students to try a range of strategies for thinking of topics, including these:

☑ With other students, brainstorm problems they know about in their school or community.

☑ Browse through local newspapers or Web sites to generate ideas about problems in the community.

☑ Interview family members or friends about school or local problems they think are a concern.

Narrow topic

Once you have a list of topics, you need to narrow your choices to one topic. Have students look more closely at their ideas for topics and decide which is the most suitable for the assignment. They might ask: *Do I know enough about this problem to explain it clearly? Can I think of a reasonable solution? Can I describe this problem and solution in two or three paragraphs?*

Topics	Evaluate
not enough rain in the area for healthy crops	too difficult; can't think of a reasonable solution
buses arriving late to school every day	too simple; not much to explain
messy and unused town park ★	an interesting community problem; can think of a reasonable solution

Corrective feedback

If... students have trouble deciding on a topic for their essay, **then...** suggest that they think about this question: *What is something I would like to change in my school or community?*

Write Guy
Jeff Anderson

Use Mentor Texts

Ask students to recall the problem James Naismith faced in the unit selection *The Man Who Invented Basketball* (traditional outdoor sports could not be played during the winter). Ask students how Naismith solved this problem (invented an indoor sport, basketball). Tell them that they will write an essay in which they describe a problem and its solution.

Differentiated Instruction

 Strategic Intervention

Alternative Writing Prompt
Help students brainstorm some simple problems, such as these.

• The car won't start.
• It's raining on the day of the barbecue.
• I lost my lunch money.

Write the list on the board. Have students write about one of the problems and describe a possible solution.

 Advanced

Alternative Writing Prompt
Have students identify a problem in the world beyond their school or community. Invite them to write an essay describing the problem and proposing a solution.

Objectives

- Categorize and organize ideas to prepare to write a first draft.
- Understand the criteria for an effective problem-solution essay.

1 PREWRITE Plan and Prewrite

MINI-LESSON

Planning a First Draft

■ **Use a Cause-and-Effect Chart** Display Writing Transparency WP24 and read it aloud to students.

Think Aloud This student plans to offer a solution to the problem of her town's messy, unused park. She has categorized her ideas by writing them on this graphic organizer along with a topic sentence that states the central idea or problem and a concluding statement. Now she can start writing a first draft by organizing her facts, details, and explanations into paragraphs.

Writing Transparency WP24

■ Have students use *Reader's and Writer's Notebook* page 311 to help them plan their first draft. Before you begin writing, use this graphic organizer to categorize and organize ideas about your problem and solution and to plan the paragraphs for your essay.

Reader's and Writer's Notebook, p. 311

 **Draft**

Display rubric Display the Scoring Rubric WP4 from the *Teacher Resource DVD*. Review with students the criteria for each trait under each score. Explain that students need to keep these criteria in mind as they develop drafts of their essays. Remind them that this is the rubric that will be used to evaluate their essays when they are finished.

Scoring Rubric: *Problem-Solution Essay*

	4	3	2	1
Focus/Ideas	Problem-solution essay well focused on one problem and solution	Problem-solution essay generally focused on one problem and solution	Problem-solution essay poorly focused; unclear problem and solution	Problem-solution essay lacking focus; no problem and/or solution
Organization	Well organized; clear topic sentence, body, concluding statement	Organized, with topic sentence, body, concluding statement	Lacking clear topic sentence, body, concluding statement	Not organized
Voice	Knowledgeable, confident voice	Generally knowledgeable and convincing	Uncertain voice	No clear voice
Word Choice	Uses descriptive and persuasive words effectively	Uses some descriptive and persuasive words	Few descriptive or persuasive words	No descriptive or persuasive words
Sentences	Clear, logical sentences	Reasonably clear, logical sentences	Choppy sentences with lapses in logic	Fragments or run-on sentences
Conventions	Few, if any, errors	Several minor errors	Frequent errors	Errors that hamper understanding

Prepare to draft Have students review the problem-solution charts they worked on earlier. Ask them to make sure that their charts are complete. Encourage them to include facts, details, and explanations relevant to their topic. You will be using your charts as you write the draft of your essay. Don't worry if your draft doesn't sound exactly the way you want your essay to sound. You will have a chance to revise your draft later.

Corrective feedback **If...** students do not grasp the connection between the Scoring Rubric and their problem-solution essays, **then...** have them help you use the Scoring Rubric to evaluate and score one or more traits of the model problem-solution essay on Writing Transparency WP22.

Differentiated Instruction

SI Strategic Intervention
Prepare to Draft Help students draft effective topic sentences and concluding statements by writing answers to the following questions: *What is the problem I am writing about?* and *Why would it be good to solve this problem?*

ELL
English Language Learners
Plan a First Draft Pair students with more fluent English speakers who can help them fill out their problem-solution chart. Encourage students to discuss their problem-solution essay topic with their partners.

② Draft

MINI-LESSON

Writing Trait: Organization

■ **Concluding Statements** Display and read aloud Writing Transparency WP25. Ask students what the sentences in each paragraph have in common. Help them think of sentences that sum up the ideas in each paragraph.

Think Aloud When I finish reading a piece of writing, I want to know that I've really reached the end. That's why the last sentence, or concluding statement, is so important. A good concluding statement sums up what the writer has been saying and brings the writing to a satisfying close for readers.

■ Have students use *Reader's and Writer's Notebook* page 312 to practice selecting and writing concluding statements.

Writing Transparency WP25

Reader's and Writer's Notebook, p. 312

Tips for Organizing Ideas into Paragraphs

✔ Introduce the problem in the opening paragraph. State your central idea in a clear topic sentence.

✔ Explain your solution to the problem in one or more paragraphs in the body.

✔ Consider beginning your conclusion with a transition word or phrase such as *finally* or *in the end* to let readers know this is the conclusion. End with a concluding statement that sums up your ideas.

Develop draft Remind students that the focus of drafting is to get their ideas down in an organized way. Display or photocopy the Tips for Organizing Ideas into Paragraphs for students. Direct them to use what they learned about concluding statements and organizing ideas into paragraphs as they write their drafts.

③ Revise

MINI-LESSON

Writer's Craft: Prepositional Phrases

■ One way to revise writing is to add specific details using prepositional phrases. A prepositional phrase is a group of words that begins with a preposition such as *at, for, in, of, on, to,* or *with.* It can be used to tell what kind, which one, where, when, or how. **Discuss this example with students.**

General   Trash attracts bugs.

More Specific   Trash on the picnic table attracts bugs.

The prepositional phrase *on the picnic table* tells which trash. Point out that adding specific details helps make writing clearer and more coherent, which in turn makes it easier for the audience to understand the writing.

■ Have students use prepositional phrases to add specific details on *Reader's and Writer's Notebook* page 313.

INTERACT with TEXT

Reader's and Writer's Notebook, p. 313

Revise Model | Display Writing Transparency WP26 and use it to model revising. Point out the revising marks, which students should use when they revise their work. This is part of the problem-solution essay about the messy town park. In the third sentence, the writer added a specific detail with the prepositional phrase *on summer evenings.* It tells when kids could play basketball. The writer also added a concluding statement to wrap up his ideas.

Ask student to point out and explain the other revisions the writer made. (Two prepositional phrases, *in the winter* and *for games and barbecues*, were added to explain when and why activities would take place. Both phrases add specific details to the essay.)

Writing Transparency WP26

Differentiated Instruction

(A) **Advanced**

Apply Revising Skills As they revise their work, have students consider ways to improve it.

• Look for places where details would make the writing clearer and more coherent.

• Add prepositional phrases answering the questions *where, when, how,* or *which one.*

• Try out two or more concluding sentences and choose the one that provides the most satisfying ending.

ELL

English Language Learners Prepositional Phrases Help students find examples of sentences with one or more prepositional phrases in their reading. Read each example aloud and ask students what detail each prepositional phrase adds to the sentence. Then read the sentence without the prepositional phrase(s) to show students how the sentence changes.

UNIT 4 Writing Process

Objectives

- Revise a draft of a problem-solution essay.
- Edit a revised draft of a problem-solution essay to correct errors in grammar, mechanics, and spelling.

③ Revise

Revise Draft

Earlier we wrote drafts of our problem-solution essays. Now we will revise our drafts. When we revise, we try to make our writing clearer and more interesting to our audience.

Peer conferencing

Peer Revision Write the Revising Checklist on the board and review the questions with students. Have pairs exchange drafts and follow the directions for peer and teacher conferencing on *Reader's and Writer's Notebook* page 314. Students' revision suggestions might include adding specific details in prepositional phrases to make the writing more coherent and easier for the audience to understand.

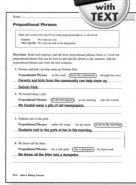

Reader's and Writer's Notebook, p. 314

Have students revise their problem-solution essays referring to their partner's suggestions and your comments as well as the Revising Checklist and the list of key features of a problem-solution essay (page CW11).

Revising Checklist

Focus/Ideas

☑ Is the problem-solution essay focused on one problem in the school or community?

☑ Does the writer offer a logical method of solving the problem?

Organization

☑ Are there a clear topic sentence and a concluding statement?

☑ Are details of the problem and solution organized in separate paragraphs?

Voice

☑ Does the writer care about and understand the problem?

Word Choice

☑ Are persuasive words used effectively in the solution?

Sentences

☑ Do prepositional phrases add details to the essay?

☑ Are sentences clear, varied, and logical?

 **Edit**

MINI-LESSON

Editing Strategy: Line by Line

■ Suggest that students use this editing strategy as they check their work: Read your writing line by line. As you read each line, check for correct spelling, capitalization, punctuation, and grammar.

■ Display Writing Transparency WP27 and use it to model the editing strategy. Point out the proofreading marks, which students should use when they edit their work. As I check line by line, I see that there are no errors in the first line. In the second line, the writer corrected the spelling of the word *assign.* In the third line, the writer corrected a run-on sentence by adding a period and capitalizing the letter *W.*

■ Ask students to point out and explain the other edits the writer made. (In the fifth line, the verb form *painting* doesn't sound right. The writer changed it to *paint.* In the seventh line, the writer joined the fragment *like lifeguards at a pool* to the preceding sentence, separated by a comma.)

You can create your own rubric using items from the rubric on p. CW15 and your own additions or changes, and have students use it to edit their own drafts. Have them check their drafts for spelling, grammar, and mechanics. Tell them to use proofreading marks to indicate needed corrections.

Writing Transparency WP27

Technology Tips

Students who write their problem-solution essays on computers should keep these tips in mind as they edit:

✔ Use the print preview or page layout feature to show how their work will appear on the page before it is printed.

✔ Go to the format or page layout menu to add special features such as borders and shading.

Write Guy
Jeff Anderson

Finding Fragments

If students have trouble distinguishing complete sentences from fragments while editing their drafts, have them ask these questions: "Who or what did something? What did they do?" If there is no answer to one of these questions, students know their words are a fragment. Help them make a complete sentence by adding a subject or a verb.

English Language Learners
Support Revising and Editing
Invite students to read their drafts aloud to you. Observe whether they note any spelling or grammatical errors by stumbling or self-correcting. Return to those errors and discuss how to correct them. Use the appropriate lessons in the *ELL Handbook* to explicitly teach the English conventions.

Objectives
- Write and present a final draft of a problem-solution essay.
- Evaluate one's own writing.

⑤ Publish

Present

Have students incorporate peer suggestions and their own revisions and proofreading edits into their problem-solution essays to create a final draft. Offer them two options for presenting their work:

Choose several essays and deliver or e-mail them to either the principal or the appropriate local authority, depending on the topics.	Illustrate their essay with "before" and "after pictures" showing the problem and the results of their solution.

MINI-LESSON

Evaluating Writing

- Display and read aloud Writing Transparency WP28. Model how to evaluate a problem-solution essay using the Scoring Rubric on page CW15.

Think Aloud I would give this problem-solution essay a 4. It focuses on the problem of the dirty park and a solution for improving it. The essay is organized into a problem paragraph, a solution paragraph, and a conclusion. The writer shows she is concerned about this situation. She uses descriptive details to help readers visualize both the problem and the solution. Sentences are clear, varied, and lively. Spelling, grammar, and mechanics are excellent.

- Have students use the Scoring Rubric to evaluate their problem-solution essays. Encourage them to use the evaluation process to help them identify areas for improvement in their future writing.

Let's Save DeSoto Park

No one uses Desoto Park because it is so messy and unsafe. Trash is everywhere. Papers blow across the soccer field. Old tires and furniture litter the brook. The playground fence is bent and rusty, and the slide and seesaw are broken. However, we can save the park.

Local families can get together to make the park fun again. First we would call a meeting to assign tasks. Then we would get to work. Teams of kids could clean up litter. We could throw trash and junk in a dumpster. Parents could help fix play areas and plant new grass. We could install litter bins and paint signs and fences. Each family would pay a few dollars and give a little time. Adult could take turns watching the playground, like lifeguards at a pool. Kids could pick up trash once a week. It would be worth the time and money.

A new DeSoto Park would improve our town. At last, kids would have somewhere safe and clean to play. We could play basketball on summer evenings. We could sled in the winter. Families could go to the park for games and barbecues. It just takes time and teamwork. Together we can make DeSoto Park a good place for everyone.

Unit 4 Problem-Solution Essay • PUBLISH and PRESENT   Writing Process **28**

Writing Transparency WP28

Customize Literacy in Your Classroom

Table of Contents
for Customize Literacy

Customize Literacy is organized into different sections, each one designed to help you organize and carry out an effective literacy program. Each section contains strategies and support for teaching comprehension skills and strategies. *Customize Literacy* also shows how to use weekly text sets of readers in your literacy program.

Weekly Text Sets
to Customize Literacy

The following readers can be used to enhance your literacy instruction.

	Decodable Readers	Concept Literacy Reader	Below-Level Reader	On-Level Reader	Advanced Reader	ELD Reader	ELL Reader
Unit 4 WEEK 4	Teller, Tailor, Seller, Sailor; Spring Show; A Princess or Not?	Women Who Were First!	Across the English Channel	Great Women in U.S. History	Changing Times: Women in the Early Twentieth Century	Helen Wills Moody: America's Tennis Champion	Helen Wills Moody: America's Tennis Champion
Unit 4 WEEK 5	Miss Mildred's Ostrich; Manfred's Monsters; Winston's Complex Costume	What Can Animals Do?	Swimming Like Buck	Buddy Ran Away	Toby the Smart Dog	Mealtime in Madagascar	Mealtime in Madagascar

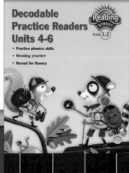

Customize Literacy in Your Classroom

Instruction in comprehension skills and strategies provides readers with avenues to understanding a text. Through teacher modeling and guided, collaborative, and independent practice, students become independent thinkers who employ a variety of skills and strategies to help them make meaning as they read.

Mini-Lessons for Comprehension Skills and Strategies

Envision It!
A Comprehension Handbook

Unit 1	Literary Elements, Sequence, Compare and Contrast, Author's Purpose, Background Knowledge, Summarize, Story Structure
Unit 2	Main Ideas and Details, Compare and Contrast, Draw Conclusions, Author's Purpose, Monitor and Clarify, Predict and Set Purpose
Unit 3	Draw Conclusions, Literary Elements, Graphic Sources, Generalize, Cause and Effect, Important Ideas, Text Structure
Unit 4	Generalize, Graphic Sources, Fact and Opinion, Cause and Effect, Inferring, Questioning
Unit 5	Compare and Contrast, Main Ideas and Details, Sequence, Draw Conclusions, Author's Purpose, Visualize, Summarize
Unit 6	Fact and Opinion, Cause and Effect, Graphic Sources, Literary Elements, Generalize, Questioning, Inferring

Anchor Chart Anchor charts are provided with each strategy lesson. These charts incorporate the language of strategic thinkers. They help students make their thinking visible and permanent and provide students with a means to clarify their thinking about how and when to use each strategy. As students gain more experience with a strategy, the chart may undergo revision.

See pages 107–134 in the *First Stop on Reading Street* Teacher's Edition for additional support as you customize literacy in your classroom.

Good Readers DRA2 users will find additional resources in the *First Stop on Reading Street* Teacher's Edition on pages 110–112.

47026

Contents

Pacing Guide

This chart shows the instructional sequence from *Scott Foresman Reading Street* for Grade 3. You can use this pacing guide as is to ensure you are following a comprehensive scope and sequence. Or, you can adjust the sequence to match your calendar, curriculum map, or testing schedule.

Grade 3

UNIT 1 — REVIEW WEEK — UNIT 2

READING	Week 1	Week 2	Week 3	Week 4	Week 5	Week 1	Week 2
Comprehension Skill	Character, Setting, and Theme	Sequence of Events	Sequence of Events	Compare and Contrast	Author's Purpose	Main Idea and Details	Compare and Contrast
Comprehension Strategy	Background Knowledge	Summarize	Visualize	Background Knowledge	Story Structure	Monitor and Clarify	Visualize
Vocabulary Strategy/Skill	Context Clues/ Homonyms	Word Structure/ Compound Words	Reference Sources/ Unfamiliar Words	Context Clues/ Multiple- Meaning Words	Word Structure/ Prefixes and Suffixes	Context Clues/ Synonyms	Context Clues/ Unfamiliar Words
Fluency	Accuracy	Rate	Express Characterization	Accuracy	Appropriate Phrasing	Accuracy	Expression
Phonics and Spelling	Short Vowels VCCV	Plurals -s, -es, -ies	Adding -ed, -ing, -er, -est	Long Vowel Digraphs	Vowel Sounds in *out* and *toy*	Syllable Patterns V/CV, VC/V	Words Ending in *le*

UNIT 4 — REVIEW WEEK — UNIT 5

	Week 1	Week 2	Week 3	Week 4	Week 5	Week 1	Week 2
Comprehension Skill	Generalize	Graphic Sources	Fact and Opinion	Fact and Opinion	Cause and Effect	Compare and Contrast	Main Idea and Details
Comprehension Strategy	Summarize	Important Ideas	Inferring	Questioning	Monitor and Clarify	Visualize	Inferring
Vocabulary Strategy/Skill	Context Clues/ Unfamiliar Words	Dictionary/ Glossary/ Unfamiliar Words	Context Clues/ Multiple- Meaning Words	Context Clues/ Multiple- Meaning Words	Dictionary/ Glossary/ Unfamiliar Words	Context Clues/ Synonyms	Context Clues/ Homophones
Fluency	Accuracy	Appropriate Phrasing and Punctuation	Expression	Appropriate Phrasing	Rate	Rate	Accuracy
Phonics and Spelling	Plurals	Vowels with *r*	Prefixes *pre-, mid-, over-, out-, by*	Suffixes *-er, -or, -ess, -ist*	Syllable Pattern VCCCV	Syllable Pattern CVVC	Homophones

Customize Literacy

 Are you the adventurous type? Want to use some of your own ideas and materials in your teaching? But you worry you might be leaving out some critical instruction kids need? **Customize Literacy** *can help.*

REVIEW WEEK

REVIEW WEEK

UNIT 3

Week 3	Week 4	Week 5	Week 1	Week 2	Week 3	Week 4	Week 5
Draw Conclusions	Author's Purpose	Main Idea and Details	Draw Conclusions	Character, Setting, Plot	Graphic Sources	Generalize	Cause and Effect
Questioning	Predict and Set Purpose	Text Structure	Important Ideas	Inferring	Text Structure	Story Structure	Predict and Set Purpose
Word Structure/ Compound Words	Context Clues/ Antonyms	Context Clues/ Unfamiliar Words	Context Clues/ Homophones	Dictionary/ Glossary/ Unfamiliar Words	Dictionary/ Unfamiliar Words	Context Clues/ Unfamiliar Words	Word Structure/ Prefixes and Suffixes
Rate	Appropriate Phrasing	Rate	Expression	Accuracy	Appropriate Phrasing	Rate	Expression
Compound Words	Words with *spl, thr, squ, str*	Digraphs *sh, th, ph, ch, tch*	Contractions	Prefixes *un-, re-, mis-, dis-, non*	Consonant Sounds /j/, /s/ and /k/	Suffixes *-ly, -ful, -ness, -less, -able, -ible*	Consonants with *wr, kn, mb, gn, st*

REVIEW WEEK

REVIEW WEEK

UNIT 6

Week 3	Week 4	Week 5	Week 1	Week 2	Week 3	Week 4	Week 5
Sequence	Draw Conclusions	Author's Purpose	Fact and Opinion	Cause and Effect	Graphic Sources	Plot and Theme	Generalize
Monitor and Clarify	Summarize	Background Knowledge	Questioning	Inferring	Important Ideas	Story Structure	Inferring
Word Structure/ Compound Words	Context Clues/ Unfamiliar Words	Context Clues/ Homonyms	Word Structure/ Prefixes	Context Clues/ Antonyms	Glossary/ Unfamiliar Words	Word Structure/ Prefixes and Suffixes	Context Clues/ Homographs
Expression and Punctuation	Accuracy	Appropriate Phrasing	Rate	Appropriate Phrasing	Accuracy	Rate	Expression
Vowel Sound in *ball*	Vowel patterns *ei, eigh*	Suffixes *-y, -ish, -hood, -ment*	Vowels in *tooth, cook*	Schwa	Words with *-tion, -sion, -ture*	Prefixes *im-, in-*	Related Words

Pacing Guide

LANGUAGE ARTS

UNIT 1 — REVIEW WEEK

	Week 1	Week 2	Week 3	Week 4	Week 5
Speaking and Listening	News Report	Description	Narrate a Story	Panel Discussion	Book Report
Grammar	Sentences	Subjects and Predicates	Statements and Questions	Commands and Exclamations	Compound Sentences
Weekly Writing	Narrative Poem	Fable	Friendly Letter	Description	Realistic Fiction
Trait of the Week	Word Choice	Conventions	Organization	Voice	Sentences
Writing	E-Pen Pals/Personal Narrative				

UNIT 2

	Week 1	Week 2
Speaking and Listening	Speech	Persuasive Speech
Grammar	Common and Proper Nouns	Singular and Plural Nouns
Weekly Writing	Poem	Fairy Tale
Trait of the Week	Word Choice	Word Choice

UNIT 4 — REVIEW WEEK

	Week 1	Week 2	Week 3	Week 4	Week 5
Speaking and Listening	Presentation	Weather Forecast	Interview	Sportscast	Book Review
Grammar	Singular and Plural Pronouns	Subject and Object Pronouns	Possessive Pronouns	Contractions	Prepositions
Weekly Writing	Persuasive Text	Story	Biography	Autobiography	Summary
Trait of the Week	Conventions	Conventions	Sentences	Organization/ Paragraphs	Word Choice
Writing	Classroom Profile/Problem-Solution Essay				

UNIT 5

	Week 1	Week 2
Speaking and Listening	Introductions	Readers' Theater
Grammar	Adjectives and Articles	Adjectives That Compare
Weekly Writing	Editorial	Personal Narrative
Trait of the Week	Organization	Conventions

REVIEW WEEK

Week 3	Week 4	Week 5
Presentation	Interview	Description
Irregular Plural Nouns	Singular Possessive Nouns	Plural Possessive Nouns
Persuasive Ad	Friendly Letter	Directions
Focus/Ideas	Conventions	Organization/Paragraphs

Story Exchange/How-to Report

UNIT 3

REVIEW WEEK

Week 1	Week 2	Week 3	Week 4	Week 5
Commercial	Dramatize	How-to Demonstration	Description	Oral Report
Action and Linking Verbs	Main and Helping Verbs	Subject-Verb Agreement	Present, Past, and Future Tense	Irregular Verbs
Fiction	Drama: Play	Formal Letter	News Story	Compare/Contrast Paragraph
Voice	Sentences	Conventions	Sentences	Word Choice

Photo Writing/Cause-and-Effect Essay

REVIEW WEEK

Week 3	Week 4	Week 5
Song or Poem	Radio Ad	Retelling
Adverbs	Adverbs That Compare	Conjunctions
Poem	Invitation	Story Review
Word Choice	Focus/Ideas	Conventions

E-Newsletter/Persuasive Essay

UNIT 6

REVIEW WEEK

Week 1	Week 2	Week 3	Week 4	Week 5
Announcement	Express an Opinion	Talk Show	Description	Song
Capital Letters	Abbreviations	Combining Sentences	Commas	Quotations and Parentheses
Taking Notes	Poem	Description	Comic Book	Historical Fiction
Focus/Ideas	Organization	Conventions	Organization	Word Choice

Discussion Forum/Research Report

Teaching Record Chart

This chart shows the critical comprehension skills and strategies you need to cover. Check off each one as you provide instruction.

Reading/Comprehension	DATES OF INSTRUCTION		
Use ideas (illustrations, titles, topic sentences, key words, and foreshadowing) to make and confirm predictions.			
Ask relevant questions, seek clarification, and locate facts and details about stories and other text and support answers with evidence from text.			
Establish purpose for reading selected texts and monitor comprehension, making corrections and adjustments when that understanding breaks down (e.g., identifying clues, using background knowledge, generating questions, re-reading a portion aloud).			
Paraphrase the themes and supporting details of fables, legends, myths, or stories.			
Compare and contrast the settings in myths and traditional folktales.			
Describe the characteristics of various forms of poetry and how they create imagery (e.g., narrative poetry, lyrical poetry, humorous poetry, free verse).			
Explain the elements of plot and character as presented through dialogue in scripts that are read, viewed, written, or performed.			
Sequence and summarize the plot's main events and explain their influence on future events.			
Describe the interactions of characters including their relationships and the changes they undergo.			
Identify whether the narrator or speaker of a story is first or third person.			

Customize Literacy

> "Tired of using slips of paper or stickies to make sure you teach everything you need to? Need an easier way to keep track of what you have taught, and what you still need to cover? **Customize Literacy** can help. "

Reading/Comprehension	DATES OF INSTRUCTION		
Explain the difference in point of view between a biography and an autobiography.			
Identify language that creates a graphic visual experience and appeals to the senses.			
Read independently for a sustained period of time and paraphrase what the reading was about, maintaining meaning (e.g., generate a reading log or journal; participate in book talks).			
Identify the topic and locate the author's stated purposes in writing the text.			
Identify the details or facts that support the main idea.			
Draw conclusions from the facts presented in text and support those assertions with textual evidence.			
Identify explicit cause and effect relationships among ideas in texts.			
Use text features (e.g., bold print, captions, key words, italics) to locate information and make and verify predictions about contents of text.			
Identify what the author is trying to persuade the reader to think or do.			
Follow and explain a set of written multi-step directions.			
Locate and use specific information in graphic features of text.			
Establish purposes for reading selected texts based upon own or others' desired outcome to enhance comprehension.			
Ask literal, interpretive, and evaluative questions of a text.			
Monitor and adjust comprehension using a variety of strategies.			
Make inferences about a text and use evidence from the text to support understanding.			
Summarize information in a text, maintaining meaning and logical order.			
Make connections between literary and informational texts with similar ideas and provide evidence from the text.			

Fact and Opinion

Student Edition p. EI•7

Objectives:
- Students define *fact* and *opinion*.
- Students use clue words to identify statements as fact or opinion.
- Students name ways to check statements of fact.

What is it? A statement of fact tells something that can be proved true or false. A statement of opinion tells a person's ideas or feelings and cannot be proved true or false. At Grade 3, students are identifying statements of fact and opinion and are naming ways to check statements of fact.

How Good Readers Use the Skill Students meet statements of facts and opinions throughout their day. We want to teach them how to distinguish the two and understand ways to check the veracity of factual statements and be able to judge statements of opinion thoughtfully. Evaluating statements of fact and statements of opinion boosts students' comprehension and helps them avoid being misled.

Texts for Teaching

Student Edition
- *Rocks in His Head*, 3.2, pages 94–104
- *America's Champion Swimmer: Gertrude Ederle*, 3.2, pages 124–139
- *The Story of the Statue of Liberty*, 3.2, pages 374–385

Leveled Readers
- See pages 22–27 for a list of Leveled Readers.

Mini-Lesson 1

Teach the Skill
Use the Envision It! lesson on page EI•7 to visually review facts and opinion.

Remind students that:
- a statement of **fact** tells something that can be proved true or false.
- a statement of **opinion** tells a person's ideas or feelings and cannot be proved true or false.

Practice
Write the following on the board and read them with students.
The Story of Ferdinand was written by Munro Leaf.
Everybody should read *The Story of Ferdinand*.
The Story of Ferdinand was first published in 1936.
Ask: Which statements are fact? How can you tell? Which is a statement of opinion?
Talk with students about how the facts (statements 1 and 3) could be proved to be true. (They could look at an actual book or they could check the internet or ask a librarian.) Point out the word *should* and explain that opinions often contain judgment words such as *should, I think,* and *best*.
If... students have difficulty distinguishing statements of fact,
then... ask: Could you check this information out? How?

Apply
As students read, have them be alert for statements of fact and opinions.

Writing
Students can write a sentence with a fact and one with an opinion.

Customize Literacy

Teach the Skill
Use the **Envision It!** lesson on page EI•7 to visually review fact and opinion.

Remind students that:
- a statement of **fact** tells something that can be proved true or false.
- a statement of **opinion** tells a person's ideas or feelings and cannot be proved true or false.
- **clue words** and phrases, such as *I think, I believe, cute, best,* and so on can signal an opinion.

Practice
Give students a familiar nonfiction selection and have partners read it together to identify statements of fact and opinion. Have them complete a chart, listing the statements they identify. Help students suggest how statements of fact can be checked.

Statement	Fact?	Opinion?
Mount Rushmore has the faces of 4 Presidents	Yes. We could look in an encyclopedia	

If... students have difficulty distinguishing opinions,
then... ask: Can you prove this is the [cutest] or is that just what someone thinks?

Apply
As students read, have them look for statements of fact and opinion.

Writing
Students can look at a photograph and write a statement of fact and a statement of an opinion.

Instruction

Teach the Skill
Use the **Envision It!** lesson on page EI•7 to visually review fact and opinion.

Remind students that:
- a statement of **fact** tells something that can be proved true or false.
- a statement of **opinion** tells a person's ideas or feelings and cannot be proved true or false.
- **clue words** and phrases, such as *best, in my opinion, I believe, I think,* and so on can signal an opinion.

Practice
Remind students that statements of opinion often have judgment words, such as *should, must,* or *best,* or phrases, such as *I think* and *in my opinion*. Let partners work together to write a paragraph that includes both statements of fact and opinion. Give pairs a topic or let them choose one of their own. Have students complete a chart like the one for Mini-Lesson 2 to show their facts and opinions. Then have students share their paragraphs.
If... students have difficulty writing statements of fact and opinion,
then... give them a topic and sentence starters to complete, such as *The weather today is... I think this kind of weather is...*

Apply
As students read, have them look for statements of fact and think about how they would check them out.

Writing
Students can write a few sentences that are statements of fact and then add a statement of opinion, underlining it.

Student Edition p. EI•3

Cause and Effect

What is it? A cause is why something happens. An effect is the result of the cause. Not all causal relationships are stated directly or signaled by clue words, such as *because, so,* and *since.* In these cases, students must infer either cause or effect, using information in the text and their prior knowledge. At Grade 3, readers use the terms *cause* and *effect* in their analysis of text.

How Good Readers Use the Skill Students experience cause-and-effect relationships every day. To be successful, they need to recognize these relationships in fiction as well as in all content areas. The ability to do so will help them increase their understanding when dealing with longer, more difficult texts. Readers begin their understanding of causal relationships by thinking about *What happened? Why did it happen?* Students then learn that a cause may have multiple effects and one effect can have many causes and that sometimes clue words signal causal relationships.

Texts for Teaching?

Student Edition
- *Around One Cactus,* 3.1, pages 510–527
- *Fly, Eagle, Fly!* 3.2, pages 158–171
- *Happy Birthday, Mr. Kane,* 3.2, pages 402–419

Leveled Readers
- See pages 22–27 for a list of Leveled Readers.

Objectives:
- Students define cause and effect.
- Students identify cause-and-effect relationships.
- Students understand that some, but not all, cause-and-effect relationships are signaled by clue words.

Teach the Skill

Use the **Envision It!** lesson on page EI•3 to visually review cause and effect.

Remind students that:
- an **effect** is *what* happens, and a **cause** is *why* it happens.
- **clue words** such as *because, so,* and *since* can help students figure out cause-and-effect relationships.

Practice
Write the following sentences. Have students identify the cause and effect within each sentence.

a. *The power went out at Joseph's house so he had to use a flashlight to see.* (Cause: The power went out. Effect: Joseph had to use a flashlight.)

b. *Because I played soccer on one of the hottest days of the year, I was very sweaty.* (Cause: I played soccer on a hot day. Effect: I was sweaty.)

Circle the clue word. Discuss how these words help determine the cause-effect relationship in each sentence.

If... students have difficulty identifying cause and effect,

then... provide additional example sentences and ask What happened? and Why did that happen?

Apply
As students read the assigned text, have them complete a cause-and-effect graphic organizer to help students identify cause-and-effect relationships.

Writing
Students can write a cause-and-effect relationship using clue words.

Mini-Lesson 2

Teach the Skill
Use the **Envision It!** lesson on page EI•3 to visually review cause and effect.

Remind students that:
- an **effect** is *what* happens, and a **cause** is *why* it happens.
- **clue words** such as *because, so,* and *since* can help students figure out cause-and-effect relationships.
- a passage can have multiple causes or multiple effects.

Practice
Have students listen for cause-effect relationships.

Last week we went on a field trip to a nature preserve. My friend Steve got lost because he ran ahead of the class. Our teacher, Ms. Olsen noticed he was missing when she took attendance at lunch. She ran back down the trail looking for Steve. She found him in the parking lot by the school bus. Ms. Olsen got really mad, so she made Steve stay by her side the rest of the trip

Ask: What event set off several other things? (Steve running ahead resulted in his getting lost, Ms. Olsen getting mad, and so on.) Students retell events using the words *cause* and *effect*.
If... students have difficulty identifying the cause and effects,
then... have students find clue words and use them to answer what happened and why.

Apply
Students read the assigned text and complete a cause-and-effect graphic organizer to chart cause-and-effect relationships.

Writing
Give students a topic, such as a football game, and have them write about it using cause-and-effect relationships.

Mini-Lesson 3

Teach the Skill
Use the **Envision It!** lesson on page EI•3 to visually review cause and effect.

Remind students that:
- an **effect** is *what* happens, and a **cause** is *why* it happens.
- **clue words** such as *because, so,* and *since* can help students figure out cause-and-effect relationships.
- a passage can have multiple causes or multiple effects.
- cause-and-effect relationships are not always explicitly stated within a text.

Practice
Have students identify the cause-and-effect relationships.

Allie is the star pitcher on our team. She broke her arm, so she could not play on Saturday. I was asked to pitch instead, so I practiced throwing all week. When Saturday came, the game was cancelled because it was thundering and lightening. Since I didn't have to pitch, I didn't find out if I was as good as Allie. Maybe I will next week

If... students have difficulty identifying the causal relationships,
then... have them read two sentences at a time and identify what happened and why it happened.

Apply
As students read the assigned text, have them complete the graphic organizer to help students find cause-and-effect relationships in the selection.

Writing
Students can write a passage with cause-and-effect relationship using clue words.

Instruction

Questioning

Mini-Lesson

Student Edition p. EI•23

Understand the Strategy

Questioning is asking good questions about important text information. Good readers ask and answer questions to preview, set purposes, construct meaning, clarify text, locate specific information, interpret text, and evaluate text.

Teach

Use the **Envision It!** lesson on page EI•23 to visually review questioning.

Remind students that we ask questions to help us get ready to read and to make sense of what we read. Show a picture and have students use question words (*who, what, when, where, why*) about it. Model using these question words as you preview unfamiliar text. Think aloud and write your questions on the board. Emphasize that questions should be ones that try to get at important information.

Asking Good Questions

Questions	Answers
Who are the people in the canoe?	
What kind of dog is that?	
Where are they all going?	
When did this trip take place?	
Why are some men wearing uniforms?	

After students read, help them look for answers. Help them understand that different kinds of questions require different actions on their part to answer.
• **In the Book:** The answers to these kinds of questions are right in the text, although they might be in two places. You might have to search.
• **In My Head:** These questions are answered by using information from the text along with your own ideas. Sometimes the author leaves clues in the text that can help answer these questions.

Practice

Provide a selection for students to read and practice the strategy with. Have students try to answer their questions after reading.
If... students have difficulty asking questions,
then... model asking questions using question words.

Apply

Always have students preview and then write a few questions to guide their reading.

Anchor Chart

Anchor charts help students make their thinking visible. With an anchor chart, the group can clarify their thinking about how to use a strategy. Display anchor charts so readers can use refer to them as they read. Here is a sample chart for questioning.

Questioning

1. Look over the story before reading.
Write down questions using:
Who? What? When? Where? Why? How?

2. Try to find answers to your questions as you read.
Write these down next to your questions. Do you
have other questions? Write these down too.

3. Keep asking questions to make sure you understand
what you are reading.
Do I get this? Does this make sense?
*Is this an important part? What can I do to
remember it?*
*Can I connect this to something else I have heard or
read about? How is it the same or different?*

4. Talk about the story and share your questions and
answers.

5. When you have questions to answer, remember the
answer question tips:

In the Book–find the answers in the text
In My Head–use information from the text, including
clues from the author, and your own ideas

Anchor Chart

Using Multiple Strategies

Good readers use multiple strategies as they read. You can encourage students to read strategically through good classroom questioning. Use questions such as these to help students apply strategies during reading.

Answer Questions

- Who or what is this question about?

- Where can you look to find the answer to this question?

Ask Questions

- What do you want to know about _____?

- What questions to do you have about the _____ in this selection? Use the words *who, what, when, where,* and *how* to ask your questions.

- Do you have any questions after reading?

Graphic Organizers

- What kind of graphic organizer could you use to help you keep track of the information in this selection?

Monitor and Fix Up

- Does the story or article make sense?

- What don't you understand about what you read?

- Do you need to reread, review, read on, or check a reference source?

- Do you need to read more slowly or more quickly?

- What is a _____? Where could you look to find out?

Predict/Confirm Predictions

- What do you think this story or article will be about? Why do you think as you do?

- What do you think you will learn from this selection?

- Do the text features help you predict what will happen?

- Based on what has happened so far, what do you think will happen next?

- Is this what you thought would happen?

- How does _____ change what you thought would happen?

Preview

- What do the photographs, illustrations, or graphic sources tell about the selection?

- What do you want to find out? What do you want to learn?

Prior Knowledge

- What do you already know about _____?

- Have you read stories or articles by this author before?

- How is this selection like others that you have read?

- What does this remind you of?

- How does your prior knowledge help you understand _____?

- Did the text match what you already knew? What new information did you learn?

Story Structure

- Who are the characters in this story? the setting?

- What is the problem in this story? How does the problem get solved?

- What is the point of this story?

Summarize

- What two or three important ideas have you read so far?

- How do the text features relate to the important ideas?

- Is there a graphic organizer that can help you organize the information before you summarize?

Text Structure

- How has the author organized the writing?

- What clues tell you that the text is structured _____?

Visualize

- When you read this, what do you picture in your mind?

- What do you hear, see, or smell?

- What do you think _____ looks like? Why do you think as you do?

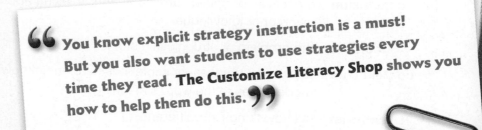

" You know explicit strategy instruction is a must! But you also want students to use strategies every time they read. **The Customize Literacy Shop** shows you how to help them do this. "

Glossary of Literacy Terms

This glossary lists academic language terms that are related to literacy.
They are provided for your information and professional use.

A

alliteration	the repetition of a consonant sound in a group of words, especially in poetry
allusion	a word or phrase that refers to something else the reader already knows from history, experience, or reading
animal fantasy	a story about animals that talk and act like people
answer questions	a reading strategy in which readers use the text and prior knowledge to answer questions about what they are reading
antonym	a word that means the opposite of another word
ask questions	a reading strategy in which readers ask themselves questions about the text to help make sense of what they read
author's point of view	the author's opinion on the subject he or she is writing about
author's purpose	the reason the author wrote the text
autobiography	the story of a real person's life written by that person

B

background knowledge	the information and experience that a reader brings to a text
biography	the story of a real person's life written by another person

C

cause	why something happens
character	a person, animal, or personalized object in a story
chronological order	events in a selection, presented in the order in which they occurred
classify and categorize	put things, such as pictures or words, into groups
climax	the point in a story at which conflict is confronted
compare	tell how things are the same
comprehension	understanding of text being read—the ultimate goal of reading
comprehension strategy	a conscious plan used by a reader to gain understanding of text. Comprehension strategies may be used before, during, or after reading.
conclusion	a decision or opinion arrived at after thinking about facts and details and using prior knowledge
conflict	the problem or struggle in a story
context clue	the words, phrases, or sentences near an unknown word that give the reader clues to the word's meaning
contrast	tell how things are different

details	small pieces of information
dialect	form of a language spoken in a certain region or by a certain group of people that differs from the standard form of that language
dialogue	written conversation
diary	a day-to-day record of one's activities and thoughts
draw conclusions	arrive at decisions or opinions after thinking about facts and details and using prior knowledge

D

effect	what happens as the result of a cause
etymology	an explanation of the origin and history of a word and its meaning
exaggeration	a statement that makes something seem larger or greater than it actually is
expository text	text that contains facts and information. Also called *informational text.*

E

fable	a story, usually with animal characters, that is written to teach a moral, or lesson
fact	piece of information that can be proved to be true
fairy tale	a folk story with magical characters and events
fantasy	a story that could not really happen
fiction	writing that tells about imaginary people, things, and events
figurative language	the use of language that gives words a meaning beyond their usual definitions in order to add beauty or force
flashback	an interruption in the sequence of events of a narrative to include an event that happened earlier
folk tale	a story that has been passed down by word of mouth
foreshadowing	the use of hints or clues about what will happen later in a story

F

generalize	make a broad statement or rule after examining particular facts
graphic organizer	a drawing, chart, or web that illustrates concepts or shows how ideas relate to each other. Readers use graphic organizers to help them keep track of and understand important information and ideas as they read. Story maps, word webs, Venn diagrams, and KWL charts are graphic organizers.
graphic source	a chart, diagram, or map within a text that adds to readers' understanding of the text

G

H

historical fiction	realistic fiction that takes place in the past. It is an imaginary story based on historical events and characters.
humor	writing or speech that has a funny or amusing quality
hyperbole	an exaggerated statement not meant to be taken literally, such as *I'm so hungry I could eat a horse.*

I

idiom	a phrase whose meaning differs from the ordinary meaning of the words. *A stone's throw* is an idiom meaning "a short distance."
imagery	the use of language to create beautiful or forceful pictures in the reader's mind
inference	conclusion reached on the basis of evidence and reasoning
inform	give knowledge, facts, or news to someone
informational text	writing that contains facts and information. Also called *expository text*.
interview	a face-to-face conversation in which someone responds to questions
irony	a way of speaking or writing in which the ordinary meaning of the words is the opposite of what the speaker or writer is thinking; a contrast between what is expected and what actually happens the story of a real person's life written by another person

J

jargon	the language of a special group or profession

L

legend	a story coming down from the past about the great deeds of a hero. Although a legend may be based on historical people and events, it is not regarded as historically true.
literary elements	the characters, setting, plot, and theme of a narrative text

M

main idea	the big idea that tells what a paragraph or a selection is mainly about; the most important idea of a text
metacognition	an awareness of one's own thinking processes and the ability to monitor and direct them to a desired goal. Good readers use metacognition to monitor their reading and adjust their reading strategies.
metaphor	a comparison that does not use *like* or *as*, such as *a heart of stone*
meter	the pattern of beats or accents in poetry

monitor and clarify a comprehension strategy by which readers actively think about understanding their reading and know when they understand and when they do not. Readers use appropriate strategies to make sense of difficult words, ideas, or passages.

mood the atmosphere or feeling of a written work

moral the lesson or teaching of a fable or story

motive the reason a character in a narrative does or says something

mystery a story about mysterious events that are not explained until the end, so as to keep the reader in suspense

myth a story that attempts to explain something in nature

M

narrative a story, made up or true, that someone tells or narrates

narrator the character is a selection who tells the story

nonfiction writing that tells about real things, real people, and real events

N

onomatopoeia the use of words that sound like their meanings, such as *buzz* and *hum*

opinion someone's judgment, belief, or way of thinking

oral vocabulary the words needed for speaking and listening

outcome the resolution of the conflict in a story

O

paraphrase retell the meaning of a passage in one's own words

personification a figure of speech in which human traits are given to animals or inanimate objects, as in *The sunbeam danced on the waves.*

persuade convince someone to do or to believe something

photo essay a collection of photographs on one theme, accompanied by text

play a story that is written to be acted out for an audience

plot a series of related events at the beginning, middle, and end of a story; the action of a story

poem an expressive, imaginative pieces of writing often arranged in lines having rhythm and rhyme. In a poem, the patterns made by the sounds of the words have special importance.

pourquoi tale a type of folk story that explains why things in nature came to be. *Pourquoi* is a French word meaning "why."

P

P

predict	tell what a selection might be about or what might happen in a text. Readers use text features and information to predict. They confirm or revise their predictions as they read.
preview	look over a text before reading it
prior knowledge	the information and experience that a reader brings to a text. Readers use prior knowledge to help them understand what they read.
prop	an item, such as an object, picture, or chart, used in a performance or presentation

R

reading vocabulary	the words we recognize or use in print
realistic fiction	a story of imaginary people and events that could happen in real life
repetition	the repeated use of some aspect of language
resolution	the point in a story where the conflict is resolved
rhyme	to end in the same sound(s)
rhythm	a pattern of strong beats in speech or writing, especially poetry
rising action	the buildup of conflicts and complications in a story

S

science fiction	a story based on science that tells what life in the future might be like
semantic map	a graphic organizer, often a web, used to display words or concepts that are meaningfully related
sensory language	the use of words that help the reader understand how things look, sound, smell, taste, or feel
sequence	the order of events in a selection or the order of the steps in which something is completed
sequence words	clue words such as *first*, *next*, *then*, and *finally* that signal the order of events in a selection
setting	where and when a story takes place
simile	a comparison that uses *like* or *as*, as in *as busy as a bee*
speech	a public talk to a group of people made for a specific purpose
stanza	a group of lines in a poem
steps in a process	the order of the steps in which something is completed
story map	a graphic organizer used to record the literary elements and the sequence of events in a narrative text

story structure structure how the characters, setting, and events of a story are organized into a plot

summarize give the most important ideas of what was read. Readers summarize important information in the selection to keep track of what they are reading.

supporting detail piece of information that tells about the main idea

symbolism the use of one thing to suggest something else; often the use of something concrete to stand for an abstract idea

S

tall tale a humorous story that uses exaggeration to describe impossible happenings

text structure the organization of a piece of writing. Text structures of informational text include cause/effect, chronological, compare/contrast, description, problem/solution, proposition/support, and ask/answer questions.

theme the big idea or author's message in a story

think aloud an instructional strategy in which a teacher verbalizes his or her thinking to model the process of comprehension or the application of a skill

tone author's attitude toward the subject or toward the reader

topic the subject of a discussion, conversation, or piece of text

T

visualize picture in one's mind what is happening in the text. Visualizing helps readers imagine the things they read about.

V

Instruction

Leveled Readers Skills Chart

Scott Foresman Reading Street provides more than six hundred leveled readers.
Each one is designed to:

- Practice critical skills and strategies
- Build vocabulary and concepts
- Build fluency
- Develop a lifelong love of reading

Grade 3

Title	Level*	DRA Level	Genre	Comprehension Strategy
The Opposite Cousins	F	10	Realistic Fiction	Background Knowledge
It's a Fair Swap!	F	10	Expository Nonfiction	Summarize
Life in the Arctic	F	10	Nonfiction	Visualize
Let's Surprise Mom	F	10	Realistic Fiction	Background Knowledge
E-mail Friends	F	10	Realistic Fiction	Story Structure
The Frozen Continent: Antarctica	F	10	Expository Nonfiction	Monitor and Clarify
Buddy Goes to School	G	12	Realistic Fiction	Visualize
The Metal Detective	G	12	Realistic Fiction	Questioning
Growing Vegetables	G	12	Narrative Nonfiction	Predict and Set Purpose
All About Birds	G	12	Nonfiction	Text Structure
Raisins	G	12	Nonfiction	Important Ideas
The Hunters and the Elk	G	12	Fiction	Inferring
Pictures in the Sky	H	14	Expository Nonfiction	Text Structure
Rescuing Whales	H	14	Expository Nonfiction	Story Structure
The Field Trip	H	14	Expository Nonfiction	Predict and Set Purpose
The Winning Point	H	14	Realistic Fiction	Summarize
How to Measure the Weather	H	14	Expository Nonfiction	Important Ideas
Grandpa's Rock Kit	H	14	Narrative Nonfiction	Inferring
Across the English Channel	H	14	Expository Nonfiction	Questioning
Swimming Like Buck	I	16	Animal Fantasy	Monitor and Clarify
A Tea Party with Obâchan	I	16	Realistic Fiction	Visualize
Independence Day/El Día de la Independencia	I	16	Nonfiction	Inferring
A Child's Life in Korea	I	16	Expository Nonfiction	Monitor and Clarify
The World of Bread!	I	16	Expository Nonfiction	Summarize
A Walk Around the City	I	16	Expository Nonfiction	Background Knowledge
The Statue of Liberty: A Gift From France	I	16	Expository Nonfiction	Questioning
Camping with Aunt Julie	J	18	Realistic Fiction	Background Knowledge
Let's Make a Trade!	J	18	Expository Nonfiction	Summarize
Ice Fishing in the Arctic	J	18	Nonfiction	Visualize
The Shopping Trip	J	18	Fiction	Background Knowledge

* Suggested Guided Reading Level. Use your knowledge of students' abilities to adjust levels as needed.

The chart here and on the next few pages lists titles of Leveled Readers appropriate for students in Grade 3. Use the chart to find titles that meet your students' interest and instructional needs. The books in this list were leveled using the criteria suggested in *Matching Books to Readers and Leveled Books for Readers, Grades 3–6* by Irene C. Fountas and Gay Su Pinnell. For more on leveling, see the *Reading Street Leveled Readers Leveling Guide*.

Target Comprehension Skill	Additional Comprehension Instruction	Vocabulary
Character, Setting, and Theme	Draw Conclusions	Context Clues/Homonyms
Sequence	Fact and Opinion	Word Structure/Compound Words
Sequence	Generalize	Dictionary/Glossary/Unfamiliar Words
Compare and Contrast	Main Idea	Context Clues/Multiple Meanings
Author's Purpose	Compare and Contrast	Word Structure/Prefixes and Suffixes
Main Idea and Details	Generalize	Context Clues/Synonyms
Compare and Contrast	Sequence	Context Clues/Unfamiliar Words
Draw Conclusions	Realism and Fantasy	Compound Words/Word Structure
Author's Purpose	Generalize	Context Clues/Antonyms
Main Idea and Details	Compare and Contrast	Context Clues/Unfamiliar Words
Draw Conclusions	Generalize	Homophones/Context Clues
Character, Setting, and Plot	Theme	Unknown Words/Dictionary/Glossary
Graphic Sources	Author's Purpose	Unknown Words/Dictionary/Glossary
Generalize	Sequence	Context Clues/Unfamiliar Words
Cause and Effect	Draw Conclusions	Prefixes/Suffixes/Word Structure
Generalize	Plot	Unfamiliar Words/Context Clues
Graphic Sources	Main Idea	Unknown Words/Dictionary/Glossary
Fact and Opinion	Fact and Opinion	Context Clues/Multiple Meanings
Fact and Opinion	Generalize	Context Clues/Multiple Meanings
Cause and Effect	Character	Unknown Words/Dictionary/Glossary
Compare and Contrast	Generalize	Context Clues/Synonyms
Main Idea and Details	Draw Conclusions	Context Clues/Antonyms
Sequence	Author's Purpose	Word Structure/Compound Words
Draw Conclusions	Main Idea	Context Clues/Unfamiliar Words
Author's Purpose	Generalize	Context Clues/Homonyms
Fact and Opinion	Fact and Opinion	Word Structure/Prefixes
Character and Setting	Theme	Context Clues/Homonyms
Sequence	Draw Conclusions	Word Structure/Compound Words
Sequence	Author's Purpose	Dictionary/Glossary/Unfamiliar Words
Compare and Contrast	Character	Context Clues/Multiple Meanings

Leveled Readers Skills Chart Continued

Grade 3

Title	Level*	DRA Level	Genre	Comprehension Strategy
New York's Chinatown	J	18	Expository Nonfiction	Inferring
One Forest, Different Trees	J	18	Realistic Fiction	Important Ideas
Swimming in a School	J	18	Animal Fantasy	Story Structure
Greek Myths	J	18	Nonfiction	Inferring
The Market Adventure	K	20	Realistic Fiction	Story Structure
These Birds Can't Fly!	K	20	Expository Nonfiction	Monitor and Clarify
Iguana Takes a Ride	K	20	Animal Fantasy	Visualize
The Last Minute	K	20	Realistic Fiction	Questioning
Our Garden	K	20	Realistic Fiction	Predict and Set Purpose
Bills and Beaks	L	24	Historical Fiction	Text Structure
In the Fields	L	24	Historical Fiction	Important Ideas
The Thunder and Lightning Men	L	24	Folktale	Inferring
Meet the Stars	L	24	Realistic Fiction	Text Structure
What a Day!	L	24	Realistic Fiction	Story Structure
Desert Life	L	24	Expository Nonfiction	Predict and Set Purpose
A Trip	M	28	Realistic Fiction	Summarize
Measuring the Earth	M	28	Expository Nonfiction	Important Ideas
Fun with Hobbies and Science!	M	28	Expository Nonfiction	Inferring
Great Women in U.S. History	M	28	Biography	Questioning
Buddy Ran Away	M	28	Realistic Fiction	Monitory and Clarify
Cowboy Slim's Dude Ranch	M	28	Realistic Fiction	Visualize
Celebrate Around the World	N	30	Nonfiction	Inferring
Joanie's House Becomes a Home	N	30	Realistic Fiction	Monitory and Clarify
Kapuapua's Magic Shell	N	30	Folktale	Summarize
Bobby's New Apartment	N	30	Realistic Fiction	Background Knowledge
Symbol, Signs, and Songs of America	N	30	Narrative Nonfiction	Text Structure
A Pet Bird	O	34	Expository Nonfiction	Inferring
Lily's Adventure Around the World	O	34	Realistic Fiction	Important Ideas
The Three Bears and Goldilocks	O	34	Animal Fantasy	Story Structure
Sweet Freedom!	O	34	Nonfiction	Inferring

* Suggested Guided Reading Level. Use your knowledge of students' abilities to adjust levels as needed.

You know the theory behind leveled books: they let you match books with the interest and instructional levels of your students. You can find the right reader for every student with this chart. 99

Target Comprehension Skill	Additional Comprehension Instruction	Vocabulary
Cause and Effect	Generalize	Context Clues/Antonyms
Graphic Sources	Generalize	Dictionary/Glossary/Unknown Words
Plot and Theme	Realism and Fantasy	Word Structure/Prefixes and Suffixes
Generalize	Compare and Contrast	Homographs/Context Clues
Author's Purpose	Generalize	Word Structure/Prefixes and Suffixes
Main Idea and Details	Compare and Contrast	Context Clues/Synonyms
Compare and Contrast	Draw Conclusions	Context Clues/Unfamiliar Words
Draw Conclusions	Sequence	Compound Words/Word Structure
Author's Purpose	Plot	Context Clues/Antonyms
Main Idea and Details	Setting	Context Clues/Unfamiliar Words
Draw Conclusions	Author's Purpose	Homophones/Context Clues
Character, Setting, and Plot	Main Idea	Unknown Words/Dictionary/Glossary
Graphic Sources	Plot	Unknown Words/Dictionary/Glossary
Generalize	Character	Context Clues/Unfamiliar Words
Cause and Effect	Generalize	Dictionary/Glossary/Unfamiliar Words
Generalize	Author's Purpose	Unfamiliar Words/Context Clues
Graphic Sources	Fact and Opinion	Unknown Words/Dictionary/Glossary
Fact and Opinion	Draw Conclusions	Context Clues/Multiple Meanings
Fact and Opinion	Main Idea and Details	Context Clues/Multiple Meanings
Cause and Effect	Sequence	Unknown Words/Dictionary/Glossary
Compare and Contrast	Main Idea	Context Clues/Synonyms
Main Idea and Details	Compare and Contrast	Homophones/Context Clues
Sequence of Events	Draw Conclusions	Word Structure/Compound Words
Draw Conclusions	Theme	Context Clues/Unfamiliar Words
Author's Purpose	Realism and Fantasy	Context Clues/Homonyms
Main Idea	Fact and Opinion	Word Structure/Prefixes
Cause and Effect	Main Idea	Context Clues/Antonyms
Graphic Sources	Compare and Contrast	Unknown Words/Dictionary/Glossary
Plot and Theme	Character	Word Structure/Prefixes and Suffixes
Generalize	Author's Purpose	Homographs/Context Clues

Matching Books & Readers

Leveled Readers Skills Chart Continued

Grade 3 Title	Level*	DRA Level	Genre	Comprehension Strategy
Mr. Post's Project	P	38	Realistic Fiction	Background Knowledge
What's Money All About?	P	38	Expository Nonfiction	Summarize
Journey Across the Arctic	P	38	Fiction	Visualize
The Road to New York	P	38	Realistic Fiction	Background Knowledge
With a Twist	P	38	Fantasy	Story Structure
All About Penguins	P	38	Expository Nonfiction	Monitor and Clarify
Puppy Problems	Q	40	Realistic Fiction	Visualize
A Family of Collectors	Q	40	Realistic Fiction	Important Ideas
The Magic of Coyote	Q	40	Realistic Fiction	Predict
Animals of the Concrete Jungle	Q	40	Expository Nonfiction	Text Structure
Grape Season	Q	40	Realistic Fiction	Important Ideas
Grandmother Spider Steals the Sun	Q	40	Folktale	Inferring
Animal Tracking: Learn More About Animals	Q	40	Expository Nonfiction	Text Structure
Whales and Other Amazing Animals	R	40	Expository Nonfiction	Story Structure
Coral Reefs	R	40	Expository Nonfiction	Predict and Set Purpose
Extraordinary Athletes	R	40	Biography	Summarize
Largest, Fastest, Lightest, Longest	R	40	Expository Nonfiction	Ask Questions
Gemstones Around the World	R	40	Expository Nonfiction	Inferring
Changing Times	R	40	Expository Nonfiction	Questioning
Toby the Smart Dog	R	40	Humorous Fiction	Monitor and Clarify
His Favorite Sweatshirt	S	40	Realistic Nonfiction	Visualize
Life Overseas	S	40	Expository Nonfiction	Inferring
It's a World of Time Zones	S	40	Expository Nonfiction	Monitor and Clarify
Mixing, Kneading, and Baking: The Baker's Art	S	40	Narrative Nonfiction	Summarize
Let's Go Have Fun!	S	40	Expository Nonfiction	Background Knowledge
The French Connection	S	40	Narrative Nonfiction	Questioning
China's Special Gifts to the World	T	50	Expository Nonfiction	Graphic Organizers
Thomas Hart Benton: Painter of Murals	T	50	Biography	Important Ideas
The Best Field Trip Ever!	T	50	Expository Fiction	Story Structure
Free in the Sea	T	50	Expository Nonfiction	Predict

* Suggested Guided Reading Level. Use your knowledge of students' abilities to adjust levels as needed.

You know the theory behind leveled books: they let you match books with the interest and instructional levels of your students. You can find the right reader for every student with this chart.

Target Comprehension Skill	Additional Comprehension Instruction	Vocabulary
Character and Setting	Theme	Context Clues/Homonyms
Sequence	Draw Conclusions	Word Structure/Compound Words
Sequence	Setting	Dictionary/Glossary/Unfamiliar Words
Compare and Contrast	Character	Context Clues/Multiple Meanings
Author's Purpose	Sequence	Word Structure/Prefixes and Suffixes
Main Idea and Details	Compare and Contrast	Context Clues/Synonyms
Compare and Contrast	Cause and Effect	Context Clues/Unfamiliar Words
Graphic Sources	Realism and Fantasy	Compound Words/Word Structure
Author's Purpose	Sequence	Context Clues/Antonyms
Main Idea and Details	Fact and Opinion	Context Clues/Unfamiliar Words
Draw Conclusions	Main Idea	Homophones/Context Clues
Character, Setting, and Plot	Fact and Opinion	Dictionary/Glossary/Unfamiliar Words
Graphic Sources	Compare and Contrast	Unknown Words/Dictionary/Glossary
Generalize	Author's Purpose	Context Clues/Unfamiliar Words
Cause and Effect	Draw Conclusions	Prefixes and Suffixes/Word Structure
Generalize	Draw Conclusions	Unfamiliar Words/Context Clues
Compare and Contrast	Author's Purpose	Word Structure/Compound Words
Fact and Opinion	Cause and Effect	Context Clues/Multiple Meanings
Fact and Opinion	Generalize	Context Clues/Multiple Meanings
Cause and Effect	Character and Setting	Unknown Words/Dictionary/Glossary
Compare and Contrast	Draw Conclusions	Context Clues/Synonyms
Main Idea and Details	Cause and Effect	Homophones/Context Clues
Sequence	Draw Conclusions	Word Structure/Compound Words
Draw Conclusions	Main Idea	Context Clues/Unfamiliar Words
Author's Purpose	Compare and Contrast	Context Clues/Homonyms
Fact and Opinion	Generalize	Word Structure/Prefixes
Cause and Effect	Generalize	Context Clues/Antonyms
Graphic Sources	Author's Purpose	Unknown Words/Dictionary/Glossary
Plot and Theme	Realism and Fantasy	Word Structure/Prefixes and Suffixes
Generalize	Compare and Contrast	Context Clues/Synonyms

Matching Books & Readers

What Good Readers Do

You can use the characteristics and behaviors of good readers to help all your students read better. But what are these characteristics and behaviors? And how can you use them to foster good reading behaviors for all your students? Here are some helpful tips.

Good Readers enjoy reading! They have favorite books, authors, and genres. Good readers often have a preference about where and when they read. They talk about books and recommend their favorites.

Develop this behavior by giving students opportunities to respond in different ways to what they read. Get them talking about what they read, and why they like or dislike it.

This behavior is important because book sharing alerts you to students who are somewhat passive about reading or have limited literacy experiences. Book sharing also helps you when you select books for the class.

Good Readers select books they can read.

Develop this behavior by providing a range of three or four texts appropriate for the student and then letting the student choose.

This behavior is important because students gain control over reading when they can choose from books they can read. This helps them become more independent in the classroom.

Good Readers read Independently for longer periods of time.

Develop this behavior by taking note of the level of support students need during guided reading. Use this information to gauge independent reading time accordingly.

This behavior is important because students become better readers when they spend time reading many texts at their independent level.

Good Readers use text features to help them preview and set purposes.

Develop this behavior by having students use the title and illustrations in fiction texts or the title, contents, headings, and other graphic features in nonfiction texts to make predictions about what they will be reading.

This behavior is important because previewing actually makes reading easier! Looking at features and sampling the text enables readers to predict and set expectations for reading.

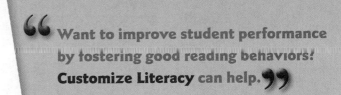

Want to improve student performance by fostering good reading behaviors? Customize Literacy can help.

Good Readers predict and ask questions before and while they read.

Develop this behavior by asking questions. After reading a passage, ask students what they think will happen next in a fiction text. Have them ask a question they think will be answered in a nonfiction text and read on to see if it is.

This behavior is important because when students predict and ask questions as they read, they are engaged. They have a purpose for reading and a basis for monitoring their comprehension.

Good Readers read meaningful phrases aloud with 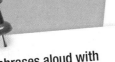 appropriate expression.

Develop this behavior by giving students lots of opportunities to read orally. As they read, note students' phrasing, intonation, and attention to punctuation and give help as needed.

This behavior is important because reading fluently in longer, meaningful phrases supports comprehension and ease in reading longer, more complex texts.

Good Readers read aloud at an appropriate reading rate with a high percent of accuracy.

Develop this behavior by timing students' oral reading to calculate their reading rates. You can also record students' miscues to determine a percent of accuracy. This will help identify problems.

This behavior is important because when students read fluently texts that are "just right," they find reading more enjoyable. A fluent reader is able to focus more on constructing meaning and is more likely to develop a positive attitude toward reading.

Matching Books & Readers

Good Readers use effective strategies and sources of information to figure out unknown words.

Develop this behavior by teaching specific strategies for figuring out unknown words, such as sounding out clusters of letters, using context, reading on, and using references.

This behavior is important because when readers have a variety of strategies to use, they are more able to decode and self-correct quickly. Readers who do these things view themselves as good readers.

Good Readers construct meaning as they read and then share or demonstrate their understanding.

Develop this behavior by having students retell what they read or write a summary of what they read in their own words.

This behavior is important because the ability to retell or write a summary is essential for success in reading. It shows how well a student has constructed meaning.

Good Readers locate and use what is explicitly stated in a text.

Develop this behavior by asking questions that require students to go back into the text to find explicitly stated information.

This behavior is important because the ability to recall, locate, and use specific information stated in a text enables readers to respond to literal questions, as well as support opinions and justify their responses.

Good Readers make connections.

Develop this behavior by asking questions to help students make connections: What does this remind you of? Have you ever read or experienced anything like this?

This behavior is important because making connections helps readers understand and appreciate a text. Making connections to self, the world, and other texts supports high-level thinking.

Good Readers interpret what they read by making inferences.

Develop this behavior by asking questions to help students tell or write about what they think was implied in the text: Why do you think that happened? What helped you come to that conclusion?

This behavior is important because the ability to go beyond the literal meaning of a text enables readers to gain a deeper understanding. When students make inferences, they use background knowledge, their personal knowledge, and the text to grasp the meaning of what is implied by the author.

Good Readers determine importance and evaluate what they read.

Develop this behavior by always having students identify what they think is the most important message, event, or information in a text.

This behavior is important because readers must be able to sort out important from interesting information. The ability to establish and/ or use criteria and providing support when making judgments is an important critical thinking skill.

Good Readers support their responses using information from a text and/or their own background knowledge.

Develop this behavior by always asking students to give the reason(s) they identified an event, message, or ideas as most important.

This behavior is important because the ability to justify one's response is important for all learners. It enables others to know the basis for a decision and provides an opening for further discussion.

CH-
QU-
ST-

Matching Books & Readers

Conversation Starters

Asking Good Questions When students read interesting and thought-provoking books, they want to share! You can encourage students to think critically about what they read. Use questions such as the following to assess comprehension as well as evoke good class/group discussions.

Author's Purpose

- Why did the author write this piece?
- How does figuring out the author's purpose help you decide how to read the text?

Cause and Effect

- Why did these events happen? How might they have been different if the causes had been different?
- Are there several causes that result in a single effect?
- Is there a single cause that has several effects?

Compare and Contrast

- What clues words show the author is comparing and/or contrasting in this article?
- How are the fictional characters and events in this story like and/or different from real people and events you know of?

Draw Conclusions

- Based on what you have read, seen, or experienced, what can you conclude about this event in the selection?
- This story seems to be a fantasy. Why might you conclude this?
- What words help you draw conclusions about the relationship between the characters?

Fact and Opinion

- What clue word or words signal that this is a statement of opinion?
- This seems to be a statement of opinion. Why is it really a statement of fact? (Alternately: This seems to be a statement of fact. Why is it really a statement of opinion?)
- Could this be a faulty opinion? How could you find out?

Generalize

- What generalization can you make about the story or the characters in it? What examples lead to that generalization?

- What details, facts, and logic does the author use to support this generalization?

- Is this a valid or a faulty generalization? Explain your ideas.

Graphic Sources

- How does the author use graphic sources (chart, maps, illustrations, time lines, and so on) to support ideas and opinions?

- This selection has many graphic sources. Which one or ones best help you understand the events or ideas in the selection? Why?

Literary Elements: Character, Setting, Plot, Theme

- Describe the main character at the beginning of the story and at the end of the story. How and why does this change take place?

- How is the setting important to the story? How might the story be different if its time or its place were different?

- What does the main character want at the beginning of the story? How does the main character go about trying to achieve this?

- A plot has a conflict, but the conflict isn't always between two characters. What is the conflict in this story? How is it resolved?

- In a few sentences, what is the plot of the story?

- What is the theme of the story? Use details from the story to support your statement.

Main Idea and Supporting Details

- What is the main idea of this paragraph or article? What are some supporting details?

- The author makes this particular statement in the article. What details does the author provide to support that statement?

Sequence

- How is the sequence of events important in the text?

- Is the order of events important in this story? Why or why not?

- Based on what has already happened, what will most likely happen next?

Connecting Science and Social Studies

Scott Foresman Reading Street Leveled Readers are perfect for covering, supporting, or enriching science and social studies content. Using these books ensures that all students can access important concepts.

Grade 3 Leveled Readers

Science

Earth and Space Science	Life Science	Life Science

Earth and Space Science

Nonfiction Books
- *The Frozen Continent: Antarctica*
- *Fun with Hobbies and Science!*
- *Gemstones Around the World*
- *Grandpa's Rock Kit*
- *How to Measure the Weather*
- *Measuring the Earth*
- *Meet the Stars*
- *Pictures in the Sky*

Fiction Books
- *What a Day!*
- *Journey Across the Arctic*

Life Science

Nonfiction Books
- *A Pet Bird*
- *All About Birds*
- *All About Penguins*
- *Animal Tracking: Learn More About It*
- *Animals of the Concrete Jungle*
- *Coral Reefs*
- *Desert Life*
- *The Field Trip*
- *Free in the Sea*
- *Growing Vegetables*
- *Ice Fishing in the Arctic*
- *Largest, Fastest, Lightest, Longest*
- *Life in the Arctic*
- *Raisins*
- *Rescuing Whales*
- *These Birds Can't Fly!*
- *Whales and Other Amazing Animals*

Life Science

Fiction Books
- *The Best Field Trip Ever!*
- *Bills and Beaks*
- *Buddy Ran Away*
- *Grape Season*
- *The Hunters and the Elk*
- *In the Fields*
- *Swimming in a School*
- *Swimming Like Buck*
- *Toby the Smart Dog*

Grade 3 Leveled Readers

Social Studies

Citizenship

Nonfiction Books
- *Sweet Freedom!*
- *Symbols, Signs, and Songs of America*

Fiction Books
- *Buddy Goes to School*
- *Camping with Aunt Julie*
- *The Opposite Cousins*
- *Our Garden*
- *Puppy Problems*

Culture

Nonfiction Books
- *A Child's Life in Korea*
- *A Walk Around the City*
- *Celebrate Around the World*
- *China's Special Gifts to the World*
- *His Favorite Sweatshirt*
- *Let's Go Have Fun!*
- *Life Overseas*
- *Mixing, Kneading, and Baking*
- *New York's Chinatown*
- *The French Connection*
- *The World of Bread!*

Fiction Books
- *A Tea Party with Obâchan*
- *Bobby's New Apartment*
- *Cowboy Slim's Dude Ranch*
- *E-mail Friends*

Culture

- *Grandmother Spider Steals the Sun*
- *Iguana Takes a Ride*
- *Kapuapua's Magic Shell*
- *The Last Minute*
- *Lily's Adventure Around the World*
- *The Magic of Coyote*
- *One Forest, Different Trees*
- *The Road to New York*
- *The Three Bears and Goldilocks*
- *The Thunder and Lightning Men*

Economics

Nonfiction Books
- *It's a Fair Swap!*
- *It's a World of Time Zones*
- *Let's Make a Trade*
- *What's Money All About?*

Fiction Books
- *A Family of Collectors*
- *Joanie's House Becomes a Home*
- *Let's Surprise Mom*
- *The Market Adventure*
- *The Metal Detective*
- *Mr. Post's Project*
- *The Shopping Trip*

History

Nonfiction Books
- *Across the English Channel*
- *Celebrate Independence Day/Celebra El Día de la Independencia*
- *Changing Times: Women in the Early Twentieth Century*
- *Greek Myths*
- *The Statue of Liberty: A Gift From France*

Fiction Books
- *A Trip*
- *The Winning Point*
- *With a Twist*

More Great Titles

Biography
- *Extraordinary Athletes*
- *Great Women in U. S. History*
- *Thomas Hart Benton: Painter of Murals*

Grade 2 Leveled Readers

Science

Earth and Space Science	Life Science	Physical Science

Earth and Space Science

Nonfiction Books

- *All About Astronauts*
- *An Astronaut Spacewalk*
- *Desert Animals*
- *Deserts*
- *Look at Our Galaxy*

Fiction Books

- *Blizzard!*
- *Maggie's New Sidekick*
- *Rainbow Crow Brings Fire to Earth*
- *A Slice of Mud Pie*

Life Science

Nonfiction Books

- *Arachnid or Insect?*
- *Compost: Recycled Waste*
- *Farming Families*
- *How a Seed Grows*
- *How Can Animals Help?*
- *How Do Plants Grow?*
- *How to Grow Tomatoes*
- *Plants Grow Everywhere*
- *A Vet for All Animals*

Fiction Books

- *Annie Makes a Big Change*
- *Camping at Crescent Lake*
- *Growing Up*
- *Too Many Rabbit Holes*
- *Where is Fish?*

Physical Science

Nonfiction Books

- *Many Types of Energy*
- *Sink or Float?*

Fiction Books

- *The Hummingbird*
- *Our School Science Fair*

Grade 2 Leveled Readers

Social Studies

Citizenship

Nonfiction Books

- *America's Birthday*
- *The Barn Raising*
- *Be Ready for an Emergency*
- *Everyone Can Make a Difference!*
- *Join an Adventure Club!*
- *Keeping Our Community Safe*
- *Protect the Earth*
- *Who Helps?*
- *Service Workers*
- *Special Animal Helpers*
- *Using a Net*
- *What Can You Do?*
- *Working Dogs*

Fiction Books

- *Andrew's Mistake*
- *Camping with Pup*
- *Freda the Signmaker*
- *Hubert and Frankie*
- *Let's Work Together!*
- *Marty's Summer Job*
- *Sally and the Wild Puppy*
- *Stripes and Silver*
- *Too Many Frogs!*
- *Training Peanut*

Culture

Nonfiction Books

- *Celebrations and Family Traditions*
- *Living in Seoul*
- *Showing Good Manners*
- *Special Chinese Birthdays*
- *A World of Birthdays*

Fiction Books

- *Ana Is Shy*
- *The Camping Trip*
- *Country Friends, City Friends*
- *Dotty's Art*
- *The First People to Fly*
- *Glooskap and the First Summer: An Algonquin Tale*
- *Happy New Year!*
- *The International Food Fair*
- *Just Like Grandpa*
- *Living on a Ranch*
- *The New Kid in Bali*
- *Voting Day*

Economics

Nonfiction Books

- *Services and Goods*

Fiction Books

- *Country Mouse and City Mouse*
- *A Quiet Place*
- *Snakeskin Canyon*

History

Nonfiction Books

- *A Few Nifty Inventions*
- *The Hoover Dam*
- *Living in a Democracy*
- *Making Travel Fun*
- *Saint Bernards and Other Working Dogs*
- *Starting a New Life*
- *Women Play Baseball*

Fiction Books

- *At Home in the Wilderness*
- *A Class Play*
- *A Cowboy's Life*
- *Down on the Ranch*
- *Hank's Tortilla Factory*

Government

Nonfiction Books

- *Communicating Then and Now*
- *Let's Send a Letter!*

More Great Titles

Biography

- *American Revolution Heroes*
- *Baseball Heroes Make History*
- *Thomas Adams: Chewing Gum Inventor*
- *Three Great Ballplayers*

Grade 4 Leveled Readers

Science

Earth and Space Science

Nonfiction Books

- Danger: The World Is Getting Hot!
- Darkness Into Light
- Day for Night
- Earth's Closest Neighbor
- Let's Explore Antarctica!
- Looking For Changes
- The Mysteries of Space
- One Giant Leap
- Orbiting the Sun
- Putting a Stop to Wildfires
- Severe Weather: Storms
- Storm Chasers
- Wondrously Wild Weather

Fiction Books

- Exploring the Moon
- Flash Flood
- Life on Mars: The Real Story
- Stuart's Moon Suit
- Surviving Hurricane Andrew
- To the Moon!

Life Science

Nonfiction Books

- Birds Take Flight
- Come Learn About Dolphins
- Dolphins: Mammals of the Sea
- Florida Everglades: Its Plants and Animals
- The Gray Whale
- How Does Echolocation Work?
- Migration Relocation
- Mini Microbes
- Mysterious Monsters
- Plants and Animals in Antarctica
- Saving Trees Using Science
- Sharing Our Planet
- What in the World Is That?

Life Science

Fiction Books

- The Missing Iguana Mystery
- Protecting Wild Animals
- The Salamander Stumper
- Top Hat Tompkins, the Detective

Grade 4 Leveled Readers

Social Studies

Citizenship

Nonfiction Books
- *Equality in American Schools*
- *Danger! Children at Work*
- *Animal Helpers*

Fiction Books
- *Mountain Rescue*
- *The Super Secret Surprise Society*

Culture

Nonfiction Books
- *The Black Ensemble Theater*
- *The Diné*
- *From Spain to America*
- *What It Takes to Stage a Play*

Fiction Books
- *A Book of Their Own*
- *A New Home*
- *Birthday Surprise*
- *Cheers for the Cheetahs*
- *The Grizzly Bear Hotshots*
- *Living with Grandpa Joseph*
- *The Show Must Go On!*
- *Something to Do*
- *To Be a Star*

Economics

Nonfiction Books
- *The Alaskan Pipeline*
- *Ranches in the Southwest*
- *Ranching in the Great American Desert*
- *Two Powerful Rivers*

Fiction Books
- *The Seahaven Squids Host a Pet Wash*

History

Nonfiction Books
- *Becoming a Melting Pot*
- *The Civil Rights Movement*
- *Code Breaking: Uncovering German Messages*
- *Let's Get to Know the Incas*
- *The Long Journey West*
- *Meet the Maya*
- *The Navajo Code Talkers*
- *Pompeii, the Lost City*
- *The Rosetta Stone: The Key to Ancient Writing*
- *The Sauk and Fox Native Americans*
- *Speaking in Code*
- *The Story of Libraries*
- *Thor Heyerdahl's Incredible Raft*
- *We Shall Overcome*
- *The Women's Movement*

History

Fiction Books
- *Bessie Coleman*
- *The Incredible Alexander Graham Bell*

Geography

Nonfiction Books
- *America's National Parks*
- *Maine, Now and Then*
- *A Trip to Capital Hill*
- *The Wonders of Western Geography*

Fiction Books
- *From Sea to Shining Sea*

Government

Nonfiction Books
- *The Power of the People*
- *The United States Government*

More Great Titles

Biography
- *Amazing Female Athletes*
- *Jim Thorpe*
- *John Muir*
- *The Legacy of César Chávez*
- *Lewis and Clark and the Corps of Discovery*

Planning Teacher Study Groups

Adventurous teachers often have good ideas for lessons. A Teacher Study Group is a great way to share ideas and get feedback on the best way to connect content and students. Working with other teachers can provide you with the support and motivation you need to implement new teaching strategies. A teacher study group offers many opportunities to collaborate, support each other's work, share insights, and get feedback.

Think About It

A weekly or monthly teacher study group can help support you in developing your expertise in the classroom. You and a group of like-minded teachers can form your own study group. What can this group accomplish?

- Read and discuss professional articles by researchers in the field of education.

- Meet to share teaching tips, collaborate on multi-grade lessons, and share resources.

- Develop lessons to try out new teaching strategies. Meet to share experiences and discuss how to further improve your teaching approach.

Let's Meet!

Forming a Study Group is easy. Just follow these four steps:

1. **Decide on the size of the group.** A small group has the advantage of making each member feel accountable, but make sure that all people can make the same commitment!

2. **Choose teachers to invite to join your group.** Think about who you want to invite. Should they all teach the same grade? Can you invite teachers from other schools? Remember that the more diverse the group, the more it benefits from new perspectives.

3. **Set goals for the group.** In order to succeed, know what you want the group to do. Meet to set goals. Rank goals in order of importance and refer often to the goals to keep the group on track.

4. **Make logistical decisions.** This is often the most difficult. Decide where and when you will meet. Consider an online meeting place where group members can post discussion questions and replies if people are not able to meet.

What Will We Study?

Use the goals to help determine what your group will study. Consider what materials are needed to reach your goals, and how long you think is necessary to prepare for each meeting.

How Will It Work?

Think about how you structure groups in your classroom. Then use some of the same strategies.

- **Assign a group facilitator.** This person is responsible for guiding the meeting. This person comes prepared with discussion questions and leads the meeting. This could be a rotating responsibility dependent on experience with various topics. This person might be responsible for providing the materials.

- **Assign a recorder.** Have someone take notes during the meeting and record group decisions.

- **Use the jigsaw method.** Not everyone has time to be a facilitator. In this case, divide the text and assign each portion to a different person. Each person is responsible for leading the discussion on that particular part.

Meet Again

Make a commitment to meet for a minimum number of times. After that, the group can reevaluate and decide whether or not to continue.

> " Have some great teaching tips to share? Want to exchange ideas with your colleagues? Build your own professional community of teachers. **The Customize Literacy Shop** gets you started. "

Trial Lessons

Use your colleagues experience to help as you think about new ways to connect content and students. Use the following plan to create a mini-lesson. It should last twenty minutes. Get the support of your colleagues as you try something new and reflect on what happened.

Be Creative!
As you develop a plan for a mini-lesson, use these four words to guide planning: *purpose, text, resources,* and *routine.*

- **Purpose:** Decide on a skill or strategy to teach. Define your purpose for teaching the lesson.

- **Text:** Develop a list of the texts you could use. Ask your colleagues for suggestions.

- **Resources:** Make a list of the available resources, and consider how to use those resources most effectively. Consider using the Leveled Readers listed on pages 22–27 and 34–39 of the Customize Literacy Shop.

- **Routine:** Choose an instructional routine to structure your mini-lesson. See the mini-lessons in the Customize Literacy Shop for suggestions.

Try It!
Try out your lesson! Consider audio- or videotaping the lesson for later review. You may wish to invite a colleague to sit in as you teach. Make notes on how the lesson went.

How Did It Go?
Use the Self-Evaluation Checklist on page 43 as you reflect on your trial lesson. This provides a framework for later discussion.

Discuss, Reflect, Repeat
Solicit feedback from your Teacher Study Group. Explain the lesson and share your reflections. Ask for suggestions on ways to improve the lesson. Take some time to reflect on the feedback. Modify your lesson to reflect what you have learned. Then try it again.

Checklist for Teacher Self-Evaluation

How Well Did I ...	Very Well	Satisfactory	Not Very Well
Plan the lesson?			
Select the appropriate level of text?			
Introduce the lesson and explain its objectives?			
Review previously taught skills?			
Directly explain the new skills being taught?			
Model the new skills?			
Break the material down into small steps?			
Integrate guided practice into the lesson?			
Monitor guided practice for student understanding?			
Provide feedback on independent practice?			
Maintain an appropriate pace?			
Assess student understanding of the material?			
Stress the importance of applying the skill as they read?			
Maintain students' interest?			
Ask questions?			
Handle student questions and responses?			
Respond to the range of abilities?			

Building Community

Books for Teachers

Kids aren't the only ones who need to read to grow. Here is a brief list of books that you may find useful to fill your reading basket and learn new things.

A Professional Bibliography

Afflerbach, P. "Teaching Reading Self-Assessment Strategies." *Comprehension Instruction: Research-Based Best Practices.* The Guilford Press, 2002.

Bear, D. R., M. Invernizzi, S. Templeton, and F. Johnston. *Words Their Way.* Merrill Prentice Hall, 2004.

Beck, I. L., M. G. McKeown. *Improving Comprehension with Questioning the Author: A Fresh and Expanded View of a Powerful Approach.* Scholastic, 2006.

Beck, I., M. G. McKeown, and L. Kucan. *Bringing Words to Life: Robust Vocabulary Instruction.* The Guilford Press, 2002.

Blachowicz, C. and P. Fisher. *"Vocabulary Instruction." Handbook of Reading Research,* vol. III. Lawrence Erlbaum Associates, 2000.

Blachowicz, C. and D. Ogle. *Reading Comprehension: Strategies for Independent Learners.* The Guilford Press, 2008.

Block, C. C. and M. Pressley "Best Practices in Comprehension Instruction." *Best Practices in Literacy Instruction.* The Guilford Press, 2003.

Daniels, H. *Literature Circles.* 2nd ed. Stenhouse Publishers, 2002.

Dickson, S. V., D. C. Simmons, and E. J. Kame'enui. "Text Organization: Instructional and Curricular Basics and Implications." *What Reading Research Tells Us About Children with Diverse Learning Needs: Bases and Basics.* Lawrence Erlbaum Associates, 1998.

Diller, D. *Making the Most of Small Groups: Differentiation for All.* Stenhouse Publishers, 2007.

Duke, N. and P.D. Pearson. "Effective Practices for Developing Reading Comprehension." *What Research Has to Say About Reading Instruction,* 3rd ed. Newark, DE: International Reading Association, 2002.

Fillmore, L. W. and C. E. Snow. "What Teachers Need to Know About Language." Office of Educational Research and Improvement, U.S. Department of Education, 2000.

Fountas, I. C. and G.S. Pinnell. *Guiding Readers and Writers Grades 3–6: Teaching Comprehension, Genre, and Content Literacy.* Heinemann, 2001.

Guthrie, J. and E. Anderson. "Engagement in Reading: Processes of Motivated Strategic, Knowledgeable, Social Readers." *Engaged Reading: Processes, Practices, and Policy Implications.* Teachers College Press, 1999.

Harvey, S. and A. Goudvis. *Strategies That Work: Teaching Comprehension to Enhance Understanding.* 2nd ed. Stenhouse Publishers, 2007.

Keene, E. O. and S. Zimmerman. *Mosaic of Thought.* 2nd ed. Heinemann, 2007.

Leu Jr., D. J. "The New Literacies: Research on Reading Instruction with the Internet and Other Digital Technologies." *What Research Has to Say About Reading Instruction,* 3rd ed. International Reading Association, 2002.

McKeown, M. G. and I. L. Beck. "Direct and Rich Vocabulary Instruction." *Vocabulary Instruction: Research to Practice.* The Guilford Press, 2004.

McTighe, J. and K. O'Conner. "Seven Practices for Effective Learning." *Educational Leadership,* vol. 63, no. 3 (November 2005).

Nagy, W. E. *Teaching Vocabulary to Improve Reading Comprehension.* International Reading Association, 1998.

National Reading Panel. *Teaching Children to Read.* National Institute of Child Health and Human Development, 1999.

Ogle, D. and C. Blachowicz. "Beyond Literature Circles: Helping Students Comprehend Information Texts." *Comprehension Instruction: Research-Based Practices.* The Guilford Press, 2001.

Pressley, M. *Reading Instruction That Works: The Case for Balanced Teaching,* 3rd ed. The Guilford Press, 2005.

Stahl, S. A. "What Do We Know About Fluency?" *The Voice of Evidence in Reading Research.* Paul H. Brookes, 2004.

Taylor, B. M., P. D. Pearson, D. S. Peterson, and M. C. Rodriguez. "The CIERA School Change Framework: An Evidence-Based Approach to Professional Development and School Reading Improvement." *Reading Research Quarterly,* vol. 40, no. 1 (January/February/March 2005).

Valencia, S. W. and M. Y. Lipson. "Thematic Instruction: A Quest for Challenging Ideas and Meaningful Learning." *Literature-Based Instruction: Reshaping the Curriculum.* Christopher-Gordon Publishers, 1998.

Building Community

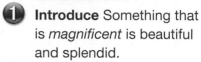
Gertrude Ederle

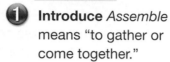 **Amazing Words** Oral Vocabulary Routine

DAY 1

ordinary

1. **Introduce** Something that is usual and not special in any way is *ordinary*.

2. **Demonstrate** We just live in an *ordinary* house. Most of our neighbors are *ordinary* people.

3. **Apply** Have students name a word that means the opposite of *ordinary*. Have them name a word that means almost the same as *ordinary*.

assemble

1. **Introduce** *Assemble* means "to gather or come together."

2. **Demonstrate** The whole school *assembled* on the playground to watch the game. Before they left on the hike, the club *assembled* in the park

3. **Apply** Have students tell when they think a group of people might *assemble*.

magnificent

1. **Introduce** Something that is *magnificent* is beautiful and splendid.

2. **Demonstrate** President Roosevelt said the Grand Canyon was *magnificent*. Mr. Simmons lives in an old house surrounded by *magnificent* oak trees.

3. **Apply** Have students describe something they think is *magnificent*.

DAY 2

erect

1. **Introduce** To *erect* something means "to build something, such as a house or other building."

2. **Demonstrate** They erected a new library after the old one burned. Our town *erected* a statue to remember the soldiers who fought in Vietnam.

3. **Apply** Have students tell why they think a town might *erect* a monument.

DAY 3

accompany

1. **Introduce** *Accompany* means "to go along with."

2. **Demonstrate** I *accompanied* my mom to the doctor. Bella *accompanied* her friend to school.

3. **Apply** Have students tell when they have *accompanied* a friend or relative somewhere.

DAY 4

spectacle

1. **Introduce** A *spectacle* is an impressive or unusual event.

2. **Demonstrate** The sunset last night was a wonderful *spectacle*. The fireworks made a fabulous *spectacle*.

3. **Apply** Have students name something they think would be a *spectacle*.

Fly, Eagle, Fly!

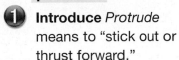 Oral Vocabulary Routine

DAY 1

agile

1 **Introduce** A person or animal that is *agile* can move quickly or gracefully.

2 **Demonstrate** A cat is an *agile* animal. The dancers were *agile.*

3 **Apply** Have students name a word that means almost the same as *agile.* Have them name a word that means the opposite of *agile.*

snout

1 **Introduce** A *snout* is the part of an animal's face that sticks forward and includes the nose, mouth, and jaws.

2 **Demonstrate** Pigs, dogs, and crocodiles have *snouts.* The dog stuck its *snout* in the hole sniffing out the animal that had been there.

3 **Apply** Have students make a list of other animals that have *snouts.*

protrude

1 **Introduce** *Protrude* means to "stick out or thrust forward."

2 **Demonstrate** The long loaf of French bread *protruded* from the grocery bag.

3 **Apply** Work with students to describe things that *protrude.* Students should use the word *protrude* in their descriptions.

DAY 2

scenery

1 **Introduce** *Scenery* means "the natural surroundings, especially when they are beautiful."

2 **Demonstrate** We enjoyed the *scenery* in the mountains. Harold enjoys painting the *scenery* near the coast.

3 **Apply** Have students describe the *scenery* from the classroom window.

DAY 3

pesky

1 **Introduce** Something that is annoying or bothers someone is *pesky.*

2 **Demonstrate** A *pesky* mosquito buzzed around my head. The *pesky* child pleaded with his dad to take him to the park.

3 **Apply** Have students discuss other situations where someone or something might be *pesky.*

DAY 4

intersection

1 **Introduce** The place where two streets or roads cross is in *intersection.*

2 **Demonstrate** This is a busy *intersection.* We are getting a traffic light at this *intersection.*

3 **Apply** Have students tell what they should do when they come to a busy *intersection.* Have them use the word *intersection* in their answers.

UNIT 4 Acknowledgments

Teacher's Edition

Text

KWL Strategy: The KWL Interactive Reading Strategy was developed and is used by permission of Donna Ogle, National-Louis University, Skokie, Illinois, co-author of *Reading Today and Tomorrow,* Holt, Rinehart & Winston Publishers, 1988. (See also the *Reading Teacher,* February 1986, pp. 564–570.)

Understanding by Design quotes: Wiggins, G. & McTighe, J. (2005). *Understanding by Design.* Alexandria, VA: Association for Supervision and Curriculum Development.

The *Texas Essential Knowledge and Skills for English Language Arts and Reading* reproduced by permission, Texas Education Agency, 1701 N. Congress Avenue, Austin TX 78701.

Illustrations

Cover Leo Timmers

Running Head Linda Bronson

Photographs

Every effort has been made to secure permission and provide appropriate credit for photographic material. The publisher deeply regrets any omission and pledges to correct errors called to its attention in subsequent editions.

Unless otherwise acknowledged, all photographs are the property of Pearson Education, Inc.

Student Edition

Acknowledgments

27 (C) ©Stephen Wilkes/The Image Bank/Getty Images
30 (TC) ©Shironina Lidiya Alexandrovna/Shutterstock
46 (CL) ©Bettmann/Corbis, (B) ©Stockxpert
47 (TR) ©Bettmann/Corbis, (BR) Jupiter Images
48 (CC) Corbis
49 (BR) ©William McKellar /Jupiter Images
50 (TL) ©AP Photo, (CR) ©DK Images
54 (CR) ©Frans Lanting/Minden Pictures, (B) ©Robert Harding Picture Library Ltd/Alamy Images
55 (CC) ©Bill Draker/Rolfnp/Alamy Images
60 (C) Alamy Images, (T) ©Greg Vaughn/Alamy Images, (B) ©Nik Keevil/Alamy
86 (B,) ©Ariel Skelley/Corbis
87 (CR) ©Don Smetzer/PhotoEdit
92 (B) ©Markos Dolopikos/Alamy, (C) ©Paul Doyle/Alamy Images, (T) ©SW Productions/Getty Images
110 (T, BC) ©ZZ/Alamy, (B) Jupiter Images
111 (BR) ©ZZ/Alamy
112 (CR) ©ZZ/Alamy
113 (TR, BR, BL) ©ZZ/Alamy
116 (B) ©Pete Saloutos/Corbis
117 (BR) ©Bequest of Mrs. Benjamin Ogle Taylor/Collection of The Corcoran Gallery of Art/Corbis, (TR) GRIN/NASA
122 (T) ©Annie Griffiths Belt/Getty Images, (C) ©David Madison/Jupiter Images, (B) ©Peter Adams/Corbis
144 (BC) ©George Silk/Time Life Pictures/Getty Images, (TR) ©Underwood & Underwood/Corbis
146 (CR) ©George Silk/Time Life Pictures/Getty Images
147 (CL) ©George Silk/Time Life Pictures/Getty Images, (CR) Bettmann/Corbis
150 (BL) ©David Shale/Nature Picture Library, (T) ©Joe McDonald/Corbis
151 (BR) ©Rick & Nora Bowers/Alamy Images
156 (C) ©Yann Arthus-Bertrand/Corbis, (B) ©Anne-Marie Weber/Getty Images, (T) ©Mireille Vautier/Alamy Images
188 (C) ©Jeremy Horner/Getty Images
190 (BC) ©Brian A. Vikander/Corbis, (B) ©Kayle M. Deioma/PhotoEdit
191 (BR) ©B&Y Photography/Alamy Images

196 (B) ©Goolia Photography/Alamy, (T) Philip Duff, (C) PhotoLibrary
216 (BC) ©Christie's Images/Peter Harholdt/Corbis, (BR) Art Resource, NY
217 (CR) ©Lynn Goldsmith/Corbis, (TR) Art Resource, NY
218 (TR) ©Historical Picture Archive/Corbis, (CR) ©Werner Forman/Corbis, (BR) Getty Images
219 (BR) ©Pavlovsky Jacques/Corbis, (TR) Corbis, (CR) Getty Images
222 (C) ©D. Hurst/Alamy Images, (BL) ©David-Young-Wolff/Alamy Images, (BC) ©Kevin Dodge/Corbis
228 (T) ©Demin Tony/PhotoLibrary Group, Ltd. (C) ©Richard Cooke/Alamy Images (T) ©Stefan Sollfors/Alamy Images
250 (TR) Getty Images, (BR) ©Morton Beebe/Corbis
251 (BR) ©Steve Vidler/SuperStock, (TR) Getty Images
254 (BL) ©Tibor Bognar/Corbis, (B) ©Vince Streano/Corbis
255 (BR) ©Robert W. Ginn/PhotoEdit
260 (C) Corbis, (T) ©Elmari Joubert/Alamy, (B) ©Stephen Oliver/Alamy Images
288 (BC, B) Jupiter Images
289 (BR) ©foodblio/Alamy Images
294 (B) Corbis, (T) ©Massimo Borchi/Corbis, (C) ©Vario Images GmbH & Co. KG/Alamy Images
314 (CR) George Ancona
315 (BC) George Ancona
316 (BR, B) George Ancona
317 (TR) George Ancona
320 (TL) ©George Doyle/Getty Images, (TL) ©Rhoda Sidney/PhotoEdit
321 (BR) Getty Images
326 (C) ©Randy Faris/Corbis, (B) ©travelstock44/Alamy
354 (BR) ©David Zimmerman/Corbis, (TR) ©Terry W. Eggers/Corbis
355 (BR) AP/Wide World Photos
356 (BR) ©Duomo/Corbis
357 (CR) ©David Thomas/PictureArts/Corbis, (BR) ©Royalty-Free/Corbis
364 (C) ©Kevin Dodge/Corbis
366 (C) ©Randy Faris/Corbis
372 (C) ©David Noble/Alamy Images, (B)

©Kai Wiechmann/Getty Images, (T) ©Taurus Taurus/PhotoLibrary Group, Ltd.
390 (CC) ©Jim Erickson/Erickson Productions, (TR) Corbis
391 (CR) ©Robert Holmes/Corbis
394 ©Canopy Photography/Veer, Inc.
400 (C) ©Foodcollection/Alamy, (T) Getty Images, (B) ©VStock/Alamy
424 (C) ©Joseph Sohm/ChromoSohm Inc./Corbis, (BC) Jupiter Images
425 (CR) ©Sandra Baker/Alamy Images
426 (BC) The Granger Collection, NY
427 (TR) ©Bill Howe/Alamy Images
430 ©David Young-Wolff/PhotoEdit, (BL) Getty Images
431 (B) ©David Young-Wolff/PhotoEdit, (BR) Jupiter Images
435 (TR) ©JM Labat/Photo Researchers, Inc.
436 (C) ©Don B. Stevenson/Alamy Images, (T) ©Ed Bock/Corbis, (BC) Getty Images, (B) ©Jim West/Alamy Images
438 (C) Meg Saligman
440 (CC) ©Ben Valenzuela
441 (B) ©Hector Ponce/Rich Puchalsky
442 (T) ©Hector Ponce/Rich Puchalsky
444 (C) *Reach High and You Will Go Far* ©2000 by Joshua Sarantitis. All Rights Reserved. Sponsored by the Philadelphia Mural Arts Program. Photograph ©2000 by Joshua Sarantitis. All rights reserved.
445 (CC) ©Paul Botello
447 (B) Getty Images
448 (B) ©Gianni Tortoli/Photo Researchers, Inc., (B) David Botello
449 (T) ©Gianni Tortoli/Photo Researchers, Inc., (BR) ©The British Museum/©DK Images, (BC) Courtesy of the U.S. Capitol Historical Society
450 (TL, B) Meg Saligman
460 (B) ©Purestock/Getty Images
461 (BR) ©Blend Images/Jupiter Images
466 (B) Alamy, (C) ©Matt Cardy/Alamy Images, (T) ©PhotosIndia LLC/Alamy
494 (B) ©David R. Frazier Photolibrary, Inc./Alamy Images
495 (TR) AP Images, (CC) Jupiter Images
499 (TR) ©Richard T. Nowitz/Corbis
500 (TR) ©Franz Waldhaeusl/Alamy, (B) ©American Images Inc/Getty Images, (C)

©Pictor/Alamy
524 (T) Jupiter Images
525 (BR) Jupiter Images
527 (T) Jupiter Images
528 (CR) ©Stockxpert
529 (CR) ©Matt Carr /Jupiter Images.

554

555

Teacher Notes

Teacher Notes

Teacher Notes

Teacher Notes

Teacher Resources

Looking for Teacher Resources and other important information?

In the **First Stop**
on Reading Street

Teacher Resources

Looking for Teacher Resources and other important information?

In the **First Stop** on Reading Street

- **Dear Third Grade Teacher**
- **Research into Practice on Reading Street**
- **Guide to Reading Street**
- **Assessment on Reading Street**
- **Customize Writing on Reading Street**
- **Differentiate Instruction on Reading Street**
- **ELL on Reading Street**
- **Customize Literacy on Reading Street**
- **Digital Products on Reading Street**
- **Teacher Resources for Grade 3**
- **Index**